MW00989906

City Songs and American Life, 1900–1950

City Songs

and American Life, 1900–1950

Michael Lasser

UNIVERSITY OF ROCHESTER PRESS

The University of Rochester Press gratefully acknowledges generous support from the John Daverio Endowment of the American Musicological Society, funded in part by the National Endowment for the Humanities and the Andrew W. Mellon Foundation.

First published 2019

University of Rochester Press
668 Mt. Hope Avenue, Rochester, NY 14620, USA
www.urpress.com
and Boydell & Brewer Limited
PO Box 9, Woodbridge, Suffolk IP12 3DF, UK
www.boydellandbrewer.com

ISBN-13: 978-1-58046-952-4

Library of Congress Cataloging-in-Publication Data

Names: Lasser, Michael L. author.
Title: City songs and American life, 1900–1950 / Michael Lasser.
Description: Rochester, NY : University of Rochester Press, 2019. | Includes bibliographical references.
Identifiers: LCCN 2019010526 | ISBN 9781580469524 (hardcover : alk. paper)
Subjects: LCSH: Popular music—United States—20th century—History and criticism. | Cities and towns—United States—Songs and music—20th century—History and criticism
Classification: LCC ML3477 .L38 2019 | DDC 782.421640973/091732—dc23 LC record available at https://lccn.loc.gov/2019010526

This publication is printed on acid-free paper.
Printed in the United States of America.

In remembrance of Steve Hinrichs, Maggie Schneider, John Hewey, and Bob Marshall, and for Alex DeSantis and Bill Dalton:

Together, we brought some of the world to others younger than we.

"For even daughters of the swan can share
Something of every paddler's heritage—"
William Butler Yeats, "Among School Children"

"'Men work together,' I told him from the heart,
'Whether they work together or apart.'"
Robert Frost, "The Tuft of Flowers"

"What will remain of us is cities and songs."

—Jane Jacobs to Adam Gopnik, September 26, 2016

CONTENTS

NOTES TO THE READER

I make no attempt to be encyclopedic in this book. I organize more or less chronologically, but I also reserve the right to move around. I start by talking about the city before moving on to some themes and images that help to define the songs and characterize the times that produced them. My chapter on Broadway isn't about the great musicals, from Jerome Kern, P. G. Wodehouse, and Guy Bolton's Princess musicals to Frank Loesser's *Guys and Dolls*, but rather about the ways songs portrayed the street, itself. When I write about Harlem, I'm less interested in black influences on American music—an essential story, but already told by many others—and more in how Harlem springs to life in American songs. That story is inseparable from the story of race in America and overlaps it, but it's not the same story. My chapters about aspects of the teens, twenties, thirties, and forties show how the songs from each decade express popular music's overarching city sensibility and then show what happens to that sensibility as times and songs change.

~ ~ ~

Mark Twain once wrote, "As to the Adjective: when in doubt, strike it out."[1] Twain was right, but this book is filled with adjectives. It relies on them because it has no other choice. How else can I come close to conveying the feel of the songs I write about? If I could, I would put all of them on a giant CD to hand you when you open the book, or, even better, I'd loosen the copyright laws so an author could quote more liberally from songs written after 1922. Neither is going to happen, so that takes me back to the need for adjectives, a lot of adjectives. Their task is to bring you closer to the songs.

Readers are bound to find that a fair number of the songs are unfamiliar to them. I'm not writing about the importance or *influence* of a song; I'm looking at the songs of the day as *reflections* of widespread attitudes, values, and behavior. It's not that songs influenced listeners but that listeners—the culture at large—influenced songs.

Much more troubling, especially in the chapter about Harlem, is the way minstrel songs and what were known as "coon songs" used racial epithets. There is, I regret to say, no way around their use. I apologize to those troubled by these offensive words, but I've chosen not to censor historical material.

Throughout, I had excellent libraries to work in and able librarians eager to help. My particular gratitude goes to Mary Fraser, Arts & Literature Division Librarian at the Central Branch of the Monroe County (NY) Public Library, and Rhonda Konig, librarian at the Grosvenor Room at the Buffalo and Erie County Public Library. Thanks also to the staff at the Sibley Music Library of the University of Rochester's Eastman School of Music and at the Richard and Ronay Menschel Library at the George Eastman Museum.

Special thanks to Sonia Kane, Julia Cook, and Ralph Locke of the University of Rochester Press for their informed enthusiasm and insight from beginning to end, Barbara Curialle for her copyediting prowess, Kim Kowalke for his practical wisdom, and Alex DeSantis for his always perceptive reading of several chapters. Steve Swayne, the Jacob H. Strauss 1922 Professor of Music at Dartmouth College (and an honorary member of my Dartmouth class of 1957), read the entire manuscript with a predictable mix of insight, high standards, and encouragement. I also received different kinds of help from Philip Furia, Gary Gilson, Jay Greene, Barbara Guhde, Sheldon Harnick, Dan Tompkins, Chris Wren, and especially my wife, Elaine Lasser, who read the manuscript more times than anybody should have to and whose proofreading acumen caught too many errors that I had missed. I must also express my particular appreciation to Sara Daugherty for her insight and friendship in the early stages of this book. I have missed both her grasp of history and her great good humor.

As for any errors you encounter, in the words of more than one lyricist, they "belong to me."

I'm also grateful to Robert Kimball, whom I once met for a cup of coffee. I'm sure he doesn't remember me, but he has given all of us the superb collections of the complete lyrics of Irving Berlin, Ira Gershwin, Cole Porter, Lorenz Hart, Frank Loesser, and Johnny Mercer, and then he and Robert Gottlieb iced the lyric writers' cake with *Reading Lyrics*, a masterful collection of over a thousand songs. The editors lay out the lyrics the way they're supposed to be, not so easy as it sounds but essential for getting the rhythms of the lines and the dazzle of the wordplay.

I had to listen to a lot of songs—songs I knew, unknown songs I stumbled on in my reading, and songs I could download, and then I read hundreds of lyrics in collections and online (even though such entries are notoriously prone to error). For songs before 1923, I used websites that let me hear a recording or read the original sheet music, especially the National Jukebox of the Library of Congress (www.loc.gov/jukebox), IN Harmony: Sheet Music from Indiana (http://webapp1.dlib.indiana.edu/inharmony/welcome.do), and the Lester Levy Sheet Music Collection in the Sheridan Libraries Special Collections at Johns Hopkins University (http://levysheetmusic.mse.jhu.edu).

A lot of songs I skimmed and set aside, but others stopped me in my tracks. Some were easy to find, but others made me regret that nobody bothered to make or keep a recording, no matter how tinny; I longed for a Ruth Etting or Mildred Bailey or Rosemary Clooney or Barbara Cook or a young Bing Crosby to appear from out of the blue to sing them for me. That would have been like having what the lyricist E. Y. Harburg called, with his particular combination of tough-minded language and tender sentiment, "a rainbow working for me."

Michael Lasser
Rochester, New York

INTRODUCTION

Encountering the City

This book is personal, even though it's about the songs rather than the author. I've been playing them on my public radio program, *Fascinatin' Rhythm: Songs from the Great American Songbook*, for nearly forty years. I spend a lot of time listening to them and thinking about them, and week in and week out I turn my ruminations into a script. More than anything, I think and write about the lyrics. Their language and inventiveness within a set of insistent conventions continue to engage me.

I was an English teacher who stumbled into broadcasting as an avocation in the late 1970s when I started to write and deliver a brief radio essay each week on WXXI-FM, the classical music station in

Figure I.1. Times Square north at night, New York City, ca. 1934. Library of Congress, Prints and Photographs Division.

Rochester, New York. I learned very quickly that the hardest task was finding a topic each week. During the early spring of 1978, I read a newspaper article about the thirty-fifth anniversary of the opening of *Oklahoma!* The following week, I spent three minutes talking about the show on the air. Listeners reacted favorably, so I began to talk about a different show, performer, or songwriter each week. Eventually, the station asked me to replace the weekly talk with an hour-long program devoted to the Great American Songbook—songs written between 1920 and 1950, when Tin Pan Alley, Harlem, and Broadway were paved with gold. It aired locally for nine years before going into national syndication, where it remains nearly thirty years later. It won a George Foster Peabody Award in 1994 for letting "our treasury of popular tunes speak (and sing) for itself with . . . sparkling commentary tracing the contributions of the composers and performers to American society."[1]

In a way, I do in this book what I do on the radio. A listener wrote in many years ago to say that my show wasn't a disc-jockey program at all. It was, she said, a "radio essay with songs used as illustrations." I've played at least twenty thousand songs since the show began in November 1980, written over twelve hundred scripts (along with two earlier books and hundreds of theater reviews), and given hundreds of talks at museums and colleges around the country. One of the conclusions I've drawn helps to explain what makes the Great American Songbook distinctive—and now we come to the heart of the matter.

I believe that the songs of the first half of the twentieth century are essentially urban. Many of their composers and lyricists were born and raised in New York City, and nearly all of them worked there or wrote for the movies after starting out there. Even when the words "New York" never appear in a lyric, these are city songs in imagery, attitude, and tone. Sometimes they're explicitly about the city, but it's more a matter of sensibility than subject matter, more outlook than location. The songwriters did their work when America was becoming—had become—an urban place. They knew a lot more about sidewalks than dusty lanes. The songs of the Great American Songbook are urban creatures. They breathe city air and make it their own. They sing the *city* electric.

Even though New York City was one of the most important subjects of popular music throughout the half century (and beyond), many lyricists set songs in other cities by adapting the urban sensibility to different places in different parts of the country. Songs about other cities—such as New Orleans and San Francisco—capture what's distinctive about their urban identities by relying on familiar themes of departure and returning. The answer to the question in the title "Do You Know What It Means to Miss New Orleans?" lies in Eddie De Lange's images of "moss covered vines" and "a creole tune" in the city "where you left your heart" long ago (Louis Alter and Eddie De Lange, "Do You Know What It Means to Miss New Orleans?" 1947). For a romantic view of a return to San Francisco, the lyricist Gus Kahn needed only a half dozen words set to Bronislau Kaper and Walter Jurmann's buoyant tune to encapsulate the wanderer's urge to return: "San Francisco, open your golden gate" (Bronislau Kaper, Walter Jurmann, and Gus Kahn, "San Francisco," *San Francisco*, 1936).

At the same time, other songs portray cities generically. Lyrics set in places from Pittsburgh to Kalamazoo are about leaving or returning, or about finding or losing a true love, but have no feel for the place. In "Pittsburgh, Pennsylvania," a young man falls for someone who is "peaches" and "honey," but "she cost me all my money" (Bob Merrill, "Pittsburgh, Pennsylvania," 1952). In "(I've Got a Gal in) Kalamazoo," another young man excitedly describes his impending return to the "freckle-faced kid" who's grown up to be "a real pipperoo" (Harry Warren and Mack Gordon, "[I've Got a Gal in] Kalamazoo," *Orchestra Wives*, 1942). Both songs lack any defining sense of urbanity.

To be fair, my point of view has another limitation. There are several places in the following chapters where I could have written about the Dust Bowl, Woody Guthrie, and the Almanac Singers. I also could have written about the Carter Family, Jimmy Rodgers, and the rise of what used to be called country and western music. Despite their importance, they lie beyond my scope. The urban sensibility found expression primarily in mainstream commercial popular music—the songs of Tin Pan Alley (the home of music publishing on New York's West Side from the 1890s into the 1930s), Broadway, and Hollywood. They spread from the largest cities to the smallest towns through vaudeville, road shows of Broadway musicals, recordings, radio, and talkies. Not every song is urban, but so many are that they reflect in significant ways how many Americans saw the world between 1900 and 1950.

I'm most interested in the urban sensibility in mainstream popular music because I'm convinced that it, more than anything, defines these songs: the bruised romanticism of New Yorkers, for instance, and a way of looking at the world that combined sentiment with wit, engagement with distance, deep feeling with edgy humor. It praised love, relished its beginning, bemoaned its loss, discovered it again, and, in the process, made room for much of what was on America's mind for fifty years. To delve into these songs and their sensibilities, I usually write about the lyrics.

As attitudes toward love changed, so did the songs. It's hard to tell what the songwriters believed because they weren't keeping diaries or writing polemics. Most of the time, they were trying to tease out a melody and shape a lyric that would become a hit because enough people liked what the resulting song had to say and how that song said it. That doesn't mean they didn't care about the work they did, but they rarely confused it with their own memories or beliefs. An old story says that whenever anybody asked lyricist Sammy Cahn which came first, the music or the words, he'd answer, "The phone call." For these men and women, songwriting was a craft and a business. Their songs were rarely personal or confessional.

~~~

Your taste and mine to the contrary notwithstanding, there are always good songwriters at work. But the Great American Songbook had an unequaled number of them working at the height of their powers, all at the same time. Preceded by ragtime, jazz, and the blues—the major formative influences—the Songbook flourished roughly from 1920 to 1950. Its practitioners included Harold Arlen, Irving Berlin, Hoagy Carmichael, Duke Ellington, George and Ira Gershwin, E. Y. Harburg, Oscar Hammerstein II, Lorenz Hart, Jerome Kern, Frank Loesser, Johnny Mercer, Cole Porter, Richard Rodgers, Thomas "Fats" Waller, Harry Warren, Kurt Weill, and many more. These are some of the very best, with dozens more only a half step behind: Eubie Blake, Johnny Burke, Sammy Cahn, Betty Comden and Adolph Green, Walter Donaldson, Al Dubin, Dorothy Fields, Mack Gordon, Gus Kahn, Jimmy McHugh, Andy Razaf, Jule Styne, Jimmy Van Heusen, and Vincent Youmans among them. What makes these men and women distinctive is not only the length of their careers and the number of good songs they wrote but also the many ways the composers combined romantic melodies, sophisticated harmonies, and smart rhythms, and then the lyricists added words derived from the distinctive music of American speech—what the poet Archibald MacLeish elsewhere called "the iron of English." And they usually did it within thirty-two bars of music and in only seventy-five or eighty words.

~~~

Ezra Jack Keats was a successful illustrator and author of books for very young children, including the classic *A Snowy Day.* He once tried to beg off from attending a writer's workshop at a midwestern university, but his hosts insisted; they wanted a children's author to speak and offer guidance to aspiring writers. "The money was good, and the food and whiskey promised to be plentiful," he once told me, sitting in a hotel bar in Midtown Manhattan, "so I went." On the final night, the writers gathered onstage to take questions. "How many words do you write each year?" somebody asked—as if it mattered. One novelist said twenty thousand, another said thirty thousand, and Jack Keats said sixty-five. When the audience stopped laughing, he waggled his finger at them and added, "But I choose each one very carefully."[2]

My particular passion is for a song's words, the few very well-chosen words of a professional lyricist, placed to merge with a melody as carefully as the words of a children's author sit amidst the illustrator's art. I savor a good lyric's dazzling economy, its evocative simplicity, its reanimation of clichés, its brilliant rhyming, and its spicing of romance with the taste of wit.

~ ~ ~

Frank Loesser's *Where's Charley?* starring Ray Bolger, was the first Broadway musical I saw. I was twelve years old, but in my mind's eye I can still see Bolger performing "Once in Love with Amy" in one (i.e., solo in front of a closed curtain), cavorting around the stage and half-climbing the closed curtain as he encouraged the audience to sing along.

Because I grew up in New Jersey in the shadow of Broadway, as a teenager I could walk from box office to box office in the West Forties, looking for tickets for that day. That's how I saw Alfred Drake in *Kismet,* Paul Muni in *Inherit the Wind,* Menasha Skulnik in Clifford Odets's *The Flowering Peach,* and Susan Strasberg and Joseph Schildkraut in *The Diary of Anne Frank.*

When I was still in college, some friends and I were strolling with our dates after seeing a play I've long since forgotten. We passed a sign in a window that read, "Matt Dennis, This Weekend Only." Two of us knew who he was so we dragged the others inside. That night, we heard Dennis sing his own songs in his foggy tenor: "Everything Happens to Me," "Angel Eyes," and "Violets for Your Furs."

Another time, my fiancée and I went to hear Marian McPartland at the Hickory House in the West Fifties, but she had the night off. Instead, we heard a new young piano player named Billy Taylor. In all great cities but especially in New York, I choose to believe, that serendipity is coin of the realm.

I'm well past the age of youthful discovery, but my enthusiasm for the songs and songwriters of the Great American Songbook remains as keen as ever. The jazz-tinged lilt of the music but especially the lyrics' rush of sentiment and wit continue to give me joy. Though I don't live there, songs make me feel close to New York City, a place I've always loved.

In *Private Lives,* Noel Coward gives his most touching throwaway line to Amanda. "Strange," she says, "how potent cheap music is."[3] The line is ironic, but she also means it. Even a hit song isn't supposed to survive; it has its moment and then it's gone. It's a throwaway, too. But some of these songs have survived and, many years later, still have the capacity to give us what my son as a little boy called a "song headache." How satisfying that we can listen to one of a thousand superbly crafted songs and say, in response to its lucid, limpid emotionalism, Yes, that's how it was; that's how it feels. I wrote this book to explore one essential reason for embracing these songs and remembering.

I invite you to join me as I write about the songs, especially the lyrics, and connect them to their times: through their subject matter, point of view, language, and—most important—their urban sensibility.

1

THE CITY'S CLANGOR

In a 1948 essay entitled "Here Is New York," E. B. White, the long-time writer for the *New Yorker*, wrote that "the island of Manhattan is without any doubt, the greatest human concentrate on earth, the poem whose meaning will always remain elusive."[1] But what if White got it wrong? What if Manhattan were a song instead of a poem, and a popular song at that? Nothing too artsy, mind you, but something jump-started and driven by Tin Pan Alley's grit, Harlem's sensual syncopation, and Broadway's gaudy pizzazz. Add to that an ear fine-tuned to the tough, funny way New Yorkers used to talk, plus the gift that good lyricists had for lifting that snappy talk through imagery and rhyme to woo and seduce in a million irresistible songs. This cultural inbreeding stands on the twin ironies of syncopation, which came initially from African American music, and the conversational lyric, devised mainly by Irish and Jewish songwriters. At the risk of oversimplification, you might even say that without the children of slaves and castoffs, America would have no sound of its own.

More often than not, the Great American Songbook is upbeat and optimistic. This is remarkable when you consider that the blues, ragtime, and jazz contributed to shaping the Songbook between 1900 and 1920—especially because all three were the musical release of oppressed peoples. Thomas Jefferson had promised Americans the right to pursue happiness, but Tin Pan Alley songwriters had only thirty-two bars to make the point. So Ted Koehler's lyric urges you to set your cares and troubles aside and be happy (Harold Arlen and Ted Koehler, "Get Happy," *The Nine-Fifteen Revue*, 1930). It's strange that we should pursue happiness in time to that jazzy syncopation, the sound of African Americans, people originally denied liberty's blessing. Then Jewish songwriters in Tin Pan Alley would borrow it to help define America's post–World War I identity.

If any songwriter embodies this serendipitous merging, it has to be Irving Berlin, whose songs "seem indivisible from the country's history and self-image."[2] Stephen Holden wrote that the best of Berlin's work "is a simple, exquisitely crafted street song whose diction feels so natural that one scarcely notices the craft. . . . For all of their innovation, [his greatest melodies] seem to flow straight out of the rhythms and inflections of everyday speech."[3] Berlin began by writing heavily syncopated ragtime songs but by the Twenties had moved on to ballads, rhythm tunes, and Broadway and Hollywood scores of every possible rhythm, tempo, and style. The most American of songwriters, this boyhood immigrant from Russia was also our greatest musical chameleon. In a letter to Alexander Woollcott, Berlin's first biographer, Jerome Kern wrote that Berlin "honestly absorbs the vibrations emanating from the people, manners, and life of his time, and in turn, gives these impressions back to the world—simplified, clarified, glorified. . . . Irving Berlin has no place in American music. HE *IS* AMERICAN MUSIC."[4] In 1988, as part of the celebration of Berlin's hundredth birthday, the violinist Isaac Stern added, "American music was born at his piano."

Berlin's first hit, "My Wife's Gone to the Country (Hurrah! Hurrah!)," was a comic number about a husband who feels liberated when his wife leaves town to escape the summer heat (George Whiting, Irving Berlin, and Ted Snyder, 1909). His earliest ballads were also city songs, including "Call Me Up Some Rainy Afternoon" (1910), an amusing "cuddling song" in which a young lady invites a beau to telephone her so she can "arrange for a quiet little spoon." Just over a decade later, Berlin's "Pack Up Your Sins" tapped into postwar electricity. Ragtime had worn out its welcome, but jazz was alive and kicking, and syncopation was everywhere. Duke Ellington had just moved to New York from Washington, DC; the bootlegger Owney Madden was thinking about opening his own place up in Harlem and calling it the Cotton Club; and Texas Guinan was already greeting the suckers at the 300 Club down on West 54th. In 1922, for his score to the second *Music Box Revue*, Berlin wrote a tune with a distinctively fractured rhythm. It's a contrapuntal duet with a unique staccato pulse that begins by adapting a line from a popular World War I song that had urged Britons and then Americans to pack up their troubles and smile. Berlin's lyric has a sharper tongue and an arched eyebrow, personified onstage by the comedienne Charlotte Greenwood—she of the long legs and high sideways kicks. Dressed head to toe in a red devil's costume, she sentenced jazz musicians to hell with the good news that, despite the "old reformers in heaven" who make you go "to bed at eleven," down below "you'll never have to go to bed at all." "H-E-double-L" is, without doubt, New York City, and who better than the lyric's "Mr. Devil" to lead an all-night jazz band in the heart of New York. The emotional landscape of Berlin's songs, like those of his contemporaries, consists of crowded streets jammed between tall buildings—the best kind of urban clutter (Irving Berlin, "Pack Up Your Sins," *Music Box Revue of 1922*, 1922).

"There is something fleeting about the American city," writes the architectural historian Witold Rybczynski, "as if it were a temporary venue for diversion, a place to find entertaining novelty, at least for a time, before settling down elsewhere. . . . For such a mobile people, street corners would be appealing."[5] In case you had come to doubt it during the Depression, in 1932, Irving Berlin had promised that just around the next one there would be a rainbow. (Irving Berlin, "Let's Have Another Cup of Coffee," *Face the Music*, 1932). Elsewhere during the same troubled decade, other songwriters transformed street corners into settings for love. Their songs might sing about "forever," but their popularity was likely to be shorter lived. Harry Revel and Mack Gordon described the search in "Looking Around Corners for You" (*Head over Heels*, 1937); Lewis E. Gensler and Leo Robin confirmed that it wouldn't be time wasted in "Love Is Just Around the Corner" (*Here Is My Heart*, 1934) But Cole Porter was more optimistic than any of them. For cooing, you replaced country lanes to affirm that "old West Fifty-Two / Is our favorite beat" (Cole Porter, "When Love Beckoned," *Du Barry Was a Lady*, 1939).

Even though many of its greatest songs are laments about loss, more often than not the Great American Songbook tossed away storm clouds to promise true love and great sex. But from the bubbly musical comedies of B. G. ("Buddy") DeSylva, Lew Brown, and Ray Henderson of the 1920s, continuing through the Rodgers and Hammerstein operettas of the 1950s, it quickly became city music for everyone, no matter where they lived. Just before the turn of the twentieth century, ragtime started in St. Louis and jazz in New Orleans, but when they spread to New York, largely through African American jazz musicians and Jewish songwriters, they became elemental parts of America's national music. Composers and lyricists in Tin Pan Alley and on Broadway were making something new from the jingle of ragtime and jazz, the jangle of slang, and the clang and clamor of the growing city. As George M. Cohan told his young protégé Irving Berlin, "The words must jingle, Irvy, the words must jingle."[6]

The nation was confident and expansive despite its burden of racism. Its growing cities were places of opportunity, excitement, and more social and sexual freedom than Americans had ever known. For the new arrivals, the city was *terra incognita*, the setting for the American

Figure 1.1. Young songwriter Irving Berlin (center), watched over by his flamboyant mentor, George M. Cohan (left). Courtesy of Photofest.

ideal of the self-made recast in a new urban place. The hottest city of all was New York, busily becoming the heart of America with each arriving train from the South or Midwest, and each docking steamship from Europe. The young and single, male and female alike, jammed the trains. When they dreamed of New York, they imagined that they saw the future and longed to be part of it. Elsewhere, the holds of the ships were piled high with what the novelist E. L. Doctorow later called the "rags." They came, he wrote, on a ship whose "decks were packed with people. Thousands of male heads in derbies. Thousands of female heads covered with shawls. It was a rag ship with a million dark eyes staring." When they first arrived, "They went into the streets and were somehow absorbed into the tenements. . . . But somehow piano lessons began to be heard. People stitched themselves to the flag. They carved paving stones for the streets."[7] And their children—some of them, anyway—pounded out songs in Tin Pan Alley or cavorted in vaudeville.

The new sounds of ragtime and jazz welcomed the newcomers when they arrived. Although a lot of songs were about New York, many more never mentioned it. But the idea and imagery of a city grounded them in their time and place. In 1900, 70 percent of New Yorkers had been born somewhere else.[8] The constantly changing city found its sound in the syncopated music of the day. It was the beat of American optimism, the sound of the modern. It got people moving in a new way, off the beat, with a flirtatious gleam and a suggestive step. There was something free about it, and sexual. This syncopation changed you (George Gershwin, Ira Gershwin, and Gus Kahn, "Harlem Serenade," *Show Girl*, 1929).

Rybczynski called the twentieth-century city "brash, pragmatic, and often vulgar. Bright lights, skylines, activity, excitement—there was little intellectual underpinning to the vertical city, whose appeal was visual and visceral. . . . Like jazz, the vertical city was marked by improvisation. . . . The builders of New York made it up as they went along."[9] The songwriters kept up with them, step for step. They were builders—makers—of another sort. Rybczynski is an architect, but one songwriter said much the same thing. In 1927, George Gershwin wrote, "If I were . . . suddenly set down by an aeroplane on this soil and listening with fresh ear to the American chorus of sounds, I should say that American life is nervous, hurried, syncopated, ever accelerando, and slightly vulgar." In other words, urban. In the middle of Manhattan, Gershwin heard the sound of America in the sounds of the city: "It is black and white. It is all colors and souls unified in the great melting pot of the world. Its dominant note is vibrant syncopation."[10]

~ ~ ~

Although love was their overriding subject, the songwriters also turned out large numbers of songs about New York City—its glamour and glitter, its blare and brass, but also its wise-guy cockiness and irreverent skepticism. In a way, there was nothing unusual about these songs. The songwriters used what they had—the attitudes and techniques of songs about love—to write about New York. They gave us one of the great subjects of American song when they recast New York as an object of romantic affection, not because they were fools, but because this was what they knew how to do. Somebody in a song fell in love *in* Manhattan and somebody else in a different song fell in love *with* Manhattan. Almost from the time a newspaperman named Monroe Rosenfeld gave Tin Pan Alley its name, song lyrics reveled in crowded streets all day, magically lit skyscrapers at night, and, a few years later, midnight jaunts to Harlem to listen to jazz. If love was the subject, then a city—especially New York City—provided outlook, style, or subtext. George Gershwin once told his longtime friend the playwright S. N. Behrman, that "he wanted to write for young girls sitting on fire-escapes on hot summer nights in New York and dreaming of love."[11] The sensibility of a song from those years was urban; there was always room for another lyric about the wonders of Manhattan.

The songwriters of the Great American Songbook had New York City in their DNA. Everybody's bio was different, but everybody's bio was also pretty much the same. Richard Rodgers was born at home in Harlem, and so were his two major collaborators, Lorenz Hart and Oscar Hammerstein II. Frank Loesser was a native New Yorker, and so was Dorothy Fields. Ira Gershwin and E. Y. Harburg were high-school friends on the Lower East Side. The lyricist Betty Comden was born in Brooklyn, her partner Adolph Green in the Bronx; they met in Manhattan. Their collaborator Jule Styne was born in London and worked in Hollywood before deciding that what he really wanted to do was write Broadway musicals. Cole Porter dropped out of Harvard Law School after a year to try his luck on Broadway, too. Harry Woods, born with no fingers on one hand, went to Harvard and then planned to live as a gentleman farmer on Cape Cod. When one of his first songs, "When the Red, Red Robin (Comes Bob, Bob Bobbin' Along)," became a hit, he gave up the pastoral life for Tin Pan Alley. Twelve-year-old Al Dubin, never short on *chutzpah,* used to cut school to take the train from Philadelphia to New York, where he'd spend the day trying to sell his songs before grabbing a train back home.

Like Dubin, songwriters unfortunate enough to have been born elsewhere got to New York City just as soon as they figured out how to get there. It was as if they were living out John Updike's observation, "The true New Yorker secretly believes that people living anywhere else have to be, in some sense, kidding."[12] They seemed to understand that New York was a company town, and, for them, anyway, the name of the company was Tin Pan Alley. Not many people knew where it was, but everybody knew they wanted to buy what it was selling. The Great American Songbook overflows with love songs that are also city songs. A lot of them are set in the city or are about the city, any city, but especially New York. The avenue might be Fifth, the Bridge the Brooklyn, but the sensibility is American urban, given sharper definition by New York's particularity and its singular role in American memory and myth. A reference to Central Park or the Empire State Building is enough to ground a song in a place rich in association. Yet with city songs, it's more a matter of sensibility than subject or setting. The songs have an outlook shaped by living in a city and then recounting that experience and expressing the emotion within a single song. The city

Figure 1.2. Al Hirschfeld, "Popular Song Composers." Clockwise: Richard Rodgers, Lorenz Hart, George Gershwin, Cole Porter, Harold Arlen, Dorothy Fields, Jerome Kern, Johnny Mercer, Ira Gershwin, Irving Berlin, Hoagy Carmichael, and Duke Ellington. Ink over pencil on illustration board. © Al Hirschfeld. Art reproduced by special arrangement with Hirschfeld's exclusive representative, the Margo Feiden Galleries, Ltd., New York. National Portrait Gallery, Smithsonian Institution.

sensibility appeared fully formed on Broadway by 1904, when George M. Cohan, playing a jockey stranded in London, sang about home. He couldn't have sung, "Give my regards to Belmont" because the legendary New York racetrack wouldn't open until the following spring. But he did sing, "Give my regards to Broadway, / Remember me to Herald Square." By the time he wrote the title song of *Forty-Five Minutes from Broadway* only two years later, Cohan demonstrated a full measure of what his great-grandchildren probably would have called attitude:

> Oh! What a fine bunch of reubens,
> Oh! What a jay atmosphere;
> They have whiskers like hay, and imagine Broadway
> Only forty-five minutes from here.
> (George M. Cohan, "Forty-Five Minutes from Broadway," *Forty-Five Minutes from Broadway*, 1906)

The tone and style of the urban sensibility keeps changing, but not the sensibility itself. Two decades after Cohan's song, an equally ebullient young man with other things on his mind announces a party and urges his friends to bring their dates, but not the "hullaba loo loo" of a girl named Lulu. This happy-go-lucky smart aleck has something up his sleeve. After observing that Lulu has a reputation for breaking up parties, he concludes, "I'll bring her myself" (Ray Henderson, Lew Brown, and Billy Rose, "Don't Bring Lulu," 1925). You come away, confident that he'll show up with her on his arm. By the middle of the Depression, in an entirely different mood, a bereft lover walks and walks, "always walking up and down," transforming a boulevard into a "street of sorrow" (Harry Warren, Al Dubin, "Boulevard of Broken Dreams," *Moulin Rouge*, 1934).

You couldn't hear Cole Porter's "Love for Sale" (*The New Yorkers*, 1930) on the radio because it was an invitation from a Depression-era streetwalker to "sample her supply." Beginning in 1934, the Motion Picture Production Code kept married couples on film in separate beds. To work around the code, the urbane screwball comedies of the thirties concocted a brew of double entendres worthy of Shakespeare. Audiences listened approvingly to such ostensibly innocent songs as "Do It Again, "You Took Advantage of Me," and "I'm in the Mood for Love." Their titles make their intentions clear, and the lyrics spell out those intentions in subtle but unmistakable ways. One lover may *tell* the other to stop but really means, "Do it again" (George Gershwin and B. G. DeSylva, "Do It Again," *The French Doll*, 1922). We don't learn until the seventh line of the refrain that all the singer wants is a kiss, but in the lead-up, such words as "ache," "take," and "waiting" give the lie to propriety and restraint: "My lips just ache / To have you take / The kiss that's waiting for you."

These songs knew how to talk about sex by talking about love, about passion by talking about romance. Each lyric has its own words and phrases that give the game away. What's youthfully sexy in "Do It Again" is irreverent in Rodgers and Hart's "You Took Advantage of Me." Initially sung in *Present Arms* by a divorced man and woman who still care for one another, the song lets them hide their deeper emotions beneath their flamboyantly happy accusations. They find themselves falling back in love, partly because the sex is terrific. Despite their mutual arousal, they still resist—at least for a little while longer (Richard Rodgers and Lorenz Hart, "You Took Advantage of Me," *Present Arms,* 1928). No matter how it turns out, the duet makes it clear that no one's to blame; the lyric's wisenheimer slang puts those who use it smack in the middle of a city.

"I'm in the Mood for Love" is the boldest of these three songs. As soon as the lover says that closeness puts her in the right mood for making love, she comments wryly on her own emotion even though she's willing to give in to it. Her intentions are clear but her feelings are complicated; she's both engaged and distant at the same time. That tension is very much an urbane way of looking at the word. This is someone who's been around. Later in the song, she sings euphemistically about putting their hearts together and asserts that they can temporarily escape their troubles. She tells him pointedly to forget them. The line is slangy and erotically charged, but just as earlier songs often nodded toward marriage, so Depression songs often portrayed love as an escape from troubled times, often with a kind of knowing skepticism that holds on to hope because there's no other choice (Jimmy McHugh and Dorothy Fields, *Every Night at Eight,* 1935).

Sometimes, though, the songs were unmistakably about life in the city, such as Richard Rodgers and Lorenz Hart's "Manhattan," Irving Berlin's "Easter Parade," and Will Jason and Val Burton's "Penthouse Serenade." The city skittered along just under the surface in the jangly rhythms of music and talk that mixed syncopation and slang. Lovers strolled down sidewalks rather than through meadows, and the "Forty-Second Street Moon" was made of neon[13] (Sigmund Romberg, Harold Atteridge, and Clifford Grey, "Forty-Second Street Moon," *Marjorie,* 1924).

The rhythmic drive of songs such as "I Got Rhythm," "Fascinating Rhythm," and "Crazy Rhythm" conjured up the way city people moved in a world where everything was on the go—staccato bursts of sound, volume, and motion. I can't think of anything that brings a song closer to the feel of a city than that unbridled rhythm. The music exploded around you and the lyrics seemed to tumble every which way. The subject in these "Rhythm" songs isn't love and it isn't even New York; it's rhythm itself, and that's enough. Ira Gershwin said that none of his lyrics was harder to write than "Fascinating Rhythm" until he figured out that the song was about itself, as driven and heedless as the people who heard it when it was still new. The rhythm has them on the move (George and Ira Gershwin, "Fascinating Rhythm," *Lady, Be Good!* 1924).

Every day, dozens of songwriters pounded out hundreds of songs. Most disappeared in an instant, but one or two survived for a couple of months and made somebody a bundle. Tin Pan Alley thrived on quantity, formula, and novelty, as long as the reliance on love never changed. Even George Gershwin, his brother Ira once wrote with tongue in cheek, "keeps pounding on tin." In 1935, after the mixed critical response to *Porgy and Bess*, the Gershwins decided to return to Hollywood to write for the movies. The allure of limitless sunshine and pots of money was hard to resist at least for a while, but nobody was eager to hire them. The studio moguls feared that George had gone longhair. When an agent on the West Coast wired, "They are afraid you will only do highbrow songs, so wire me on this score so I can reassure them," George shot back without a dash of ambiguity, "RUMORS ABOUT HIGHBROW MUSIC RIDICULOUS STOP AM OUT TO WRITE HITS."[14] It worked. Soon, he and Ira were writing songs at RKO Pictures for Fred Astaire to sing and for him and Ginger Rogers to dance to. All four of them—George, Ira, Fred, and Ginger—had first proved their worth in New York. Astaire would know what to do with the rhythmic imperative of "Slap That Bass" and the witty back-and-forth of "They Can't Take That Away from Me." He grew up on that kind of thing, first in vaudeville and then on Broadway.

~ ~ ~

Attitudes keep changing in these songs, but the urban sensibility persists. The emotional content isn't the point, but rather the sense that the characters who sing the lyrics have an outlook and a way of speaking that comes from living in a city. That urban sensibility recurs in song after song. It doesn't have to be New York, and often there's no mention of a particular city, except that New York was where the songwriters gathered and that was where they learned what a city is.

Just as syncopation thrusts songs forward regardless of tempo and provides a jaunty irregularity well suited to the rhythms of the new conversational lyric, so a city outlook defines America's way of singing about love (and everything else) through the twentieth century's first fifty years. The spirit of the age was urban and so was the Songbook, along with the jazz, ragtime, and blues that preceded and shaped it. From their imagined vantage point on the West Side of Manhattan, songwriters from Fred E. Ahlert (Fred E. Ahlert and Roy Turk, "Walkin' My Baby Back Home," 1930) to Vincent Youmans (Vincent Youmans and Irving Caesar, "Tea for Two," *No, No, Nanette,* 1925) reported on America to Americans.

The urban descendants of nineteenth-century minstrel songs, "coon songs"—written and performed mainly by whites—relied on degrading stereotypes to portray African Americans. Among the most successful: Fred Fisher, originally from Cologne, wrote "If the Man in the Moon Were a Coon" in 1905; Irving Berlin, who spent his earliest years in tsarist Russia, wrote "Alexander's Ragtime Band" in 1911;[15] and L. Wolfe Gilbert, born in Odessa, wrote "Waiting for the Robert E. Lee" with the composer Lewis F. Muir in 1912.[16] As Rachel Rubin writes, "What we now call Tin Pan Alley depended on a meeting of Jews and African Americans in the modern American city, where the two cultures interacted informally in neighborhoods, music halls, and businesses. The key figures of Tin Pan Alley—including Irving Berlin, George Gershwin, and Harold Arlen—were consummate modern New Yorkers. Their careers were intimately wound up with their relationships to actual African Americans and with the sights and sounds of blackness."[17] Todd Duncan, who played Porgy in the original 1935 Broadway production of *Porgy and Bess,* told the composer Ned Rorem, "I literally wept for what this Jew was able to express for the Negro."[18]

Does that mean there were no songs about small towns and country lanes? Of course not—but through the teens and into the twenties, most of them looked at rural America through newly citified eyes. Characters in Tin Pan Alley and Broadway songs, ostensibly speaking for the people who had forsaken rural life, used memory and the dream of return to conjure up what they had left behind: "Oh, gee, I wish again / That I was in Michigan, / Down on the farm" (Irving Berlin, "I Want to Go Back to Michigan," 1914). Decades later, Johnny Mercer from Savannah, Georgia, and Hoagy Carmichael from Bloomington, Indiana, wrote about small-town life even though they loved the urban rhythms of jazz. Both together and apart, they wrote such songs as "Watermelon Weather," "Casanova Cricket," and "Can't Get Indiana off My Mind." Other songwriters were writing rural songs throughout the half century, from "In the Good Old Summer Time" (1902) and "I'll Be with You in Apple Blossom Time" (1903), to "There's a Cabin in the Pines" (1933) and "Tree in the Meadow" (1948). Even so, most rural songs that became part of the Great American Songbook were about vacations or visits, or they were the nostalgic remembrances of someone now living in the city—or at the very least far from home. Late in the day, the setting sun and the chirping of the crickets makes a young man long for what he misses most: "My heart is ever yearning / Once more to be returning home" (Peter Van Steeden, Jeff Clarkson, and Harry Clarkson, "Home," 1931).

An urban sensibility required an awareness of the beat of the city and the sound of its talk. Songwriters walked along the streets at all times of the day or night, listening for a catchy turn of phrase to turn into a song. New Yorkers pretty much leave you alone but that doesn't mean they don't eavesdrop. To this day, a quick reading of "Metropolitan Diary" in each Monday's *New York Times* shows how much they still love to listen in. This well-known anecdote might be fictional; it might be true. Nobody's sure, but it makes the point. Late one night in 1927, the composer Jimmy McHugh and the lyricist Dorothy Fields, in need of a new song but stymied by their inability to write one, walked along Fifth Avenue to clear their heads. As they passed a couple staring into Tiffany's window, they heard him say to her, "Geez, I'd love to get you one of them rocks, honey, but for now I can't give you anything but love." The race was on back to the piano and the typewriter. (Jimmy McHugh and Dorothy Fields, "I Can't Give You Anything But Love," *Blackbirds of 1928*, 1928)

City people, and especially New Yorkers, like to view themselves as tough and cynical, but their imaginations make room for a belief in the permanence of love along with a healthy dose of skepticism about whether it will survive very long—at the same time. F. Scott Fitzgerald wrote in "The Crack-Up," "The test of a first-rate intelligence is the ability to hold two opposed ideas in the mind at the same time, and still retain the ability to function."[19] If he's right, most New Yorkers seem to have "a first-rate intelligence." The hyperbolic Walt Whitman, who used to cross from Brooklyn to Manhattan by ferry, uttered what must have seemed lofty and revolutionary when he said it, but maybe he was just being a New Yorker: "Do I contradict myself? / Very well then I contradict myself, / I am large, I contain multitudes."[20] The playwright George S. Kaufman, a notorious cynic when it came to romance, reacted to Irving Berlin's "Always," by suggesting that he change the familiar first line of the chorus to, "I'll be loving you, Thursday."[21] An urban sensibility feels at ease with ambiguity and skepticism, with juggling contradictory ideas and attitudes, and with feeling at home in a place that never stops changing. The songwriters of the time wrote songs devoted to the paradoxical propositions that nothing's better than being in love, it hurts like hell when it unravels, and it's worth risking again. The characters they created in their songs are the world's champion bruised romantics:

A city is as much an idea and a point of view as a place. Americans wanted songs that hummed to the dynamism of the metropolis because they reflected what most people had come to feel, believe, and value. By the early twentieth century, even in small towns, the city was on everybody's mind. Modernity was in the air, and attitudes toward romance, sex, and marriage were changing:

> Folks who stayed home all their lives
> Are dancing every night with other fellow's wives,
> You'd never know that old home town of mine.
> (Walter Donaldson and Howard Johnson, "You'd Never Know That Old Home Town of Mine," 1915)

Americans (and Americans-to-be) were on the move. The nation underwent three concurrent migrations: easterners and midwesterners continued to move west; millions of immigrants arrived from central, southern, and eastern Europe (and from China and Japan as well); and large numbers of native-born Americans left home for eastern and northern cities, especially New York. Cities were magnets for the native- and foreign-born alike. By the 1920s, a large number of African Americans had made the Great Migration from the Jim Crow South to settle in Chicago or, especially, Harlem.[22] These moves played an essential role in transforming America from a rural, agricultural nation to an urban, industrial one. Irish, Italian, and Jewish newcomers from abroad diversified the population. America was in motion, and its restlessness nourished popular music. Ambitious new songwriters took the train to New York; those same railroads carried vaudevillians with new songs in their suitcases to growing towns in the West. The rambunctious syncopation of ragtime and jazz set the pace of urban life and shaped the sound of our songs, and these new songs spread an urban beat across the nation.

The blues began in the Mississippi Delta and jazz began in New Orleans, but each became a national music only after it moved to New York. Black Swan, the first recording company owned by African Americans, started in Harlem in 1921.[23] Between 1900 and 1950, hundreds of songs celebrated cities from Chicago to Miami, Boston to Los Angeles, but more songs fell in love with New York City than all the others put together. They may never mention a sidewalk or a skyscraper, but their outlook is urban. They are, somehow, thirty-two-bar celebrations of romantic love that look out over the rest of America with that New York City point of view that skews everything but never quite loses hold of what the rest of the country believes, hopes for, or dreams. Places like Gary or Macon may be nothing more than dots in the distance but almost everybody there wanted to be here, especially in the years before 1950. You hear it in the songs, not because they're about this city or that, but because the syncopation, the jazziness, and the drive of the music, coupled with the staccato slang and the sense of possibility in the lyric have the taste of a city. The combination of optimism and toughness created a sense of possibility. In "Trusting My Luck," a speaker with a hunch about the future keeps her fingers crossed because she needs some good luck (Arthur Johnston and Maurice Sigler, "Trusting My Luck," *Sailing Along*, 1938).

Near the end of the nineteenth century, the city, already the center of American economic life, began to pulsate in the American imagination. Things happened in New York because New York itself was happening. By the time Tin Pan Alley moved from Union Square to resettle farther uptown, New York had become the nation's symbol of all that was in flux.[24] The big city could make or break the people who arrived seeking fortune and freedom, but they had come to take a chance. As the twentieth century turned, New York had become an industrial, commercial, and communications powerhouse. Its first subway opened in 1904, tying together four of the five recently consolidated boroughs. Its first skyscraper, the Flatiron Building, rose in 1902, followed by a host of competing high-risers that culminated in the Chrysler and Empire State buildings in the late 1920s and early

Figure 1.3. The Chrysler Building, masterpiece of "the honky-tonk sublime." Courtesy of Photofest.

1930s. When Rockefeller Center opened later in the 1930s, it housed the monumental art deco entertainment cathedral, Radio City Music Hall, as well as the NBC radio network.

You never quite get away from New York. Try to imagine the Chrysler Building anywhere else. Perhaps more than any other American building, it embodies its time and place. It was the world's tallest building only until the Empire State Building pushed past it a year later, but it was always in motion to its own jazzy tune. Next to it, the Empire State feels solid, almost stolid. I recently learned from Claudia Roth Pierpont's splendid essay about it that the auto magnate Walter Chrysler, who paid for the building, and the architect William Van Allen, who designed it, "were at each other's throats. But in their own brief flight toward the clouds, they managed to perfect, as much as F. Scott Fitzgerald or George Gershwin, the uniquely American style of the honky-tonk sublime."[25] How I wish I'd thought of that. In that single stunning, funny oxymoron, Pierpont has pinned it down and named it—that unrelenting whirl of vanity and variety, some of which shows up in the mix of sentiment and wit in our best songs: the songs written by all those Tin Pan Alley outsiders who wanted so desperately to be insiders.

In a photograph I came on some years back, Irving Berlin sits smack in the center of the frame, looking straight into the camera, surrounded by eight pretty young showgirls, eight sexy blondes, eight young American women, eight *shiksas.* He wears a dark suit and tie and a white shirt, his hair is well groomed, and his nails are manicured. One of the women has taken his arm as if they're together. She's the prettiest of the eight. It doesn't faze him. He was thirty-seven when the photograph was taken in 1925. He had already built his own theater to house the musical revues he wrote. He had already composed "Alexander's Ragtime Band," "All Alone," and "Always," and he had started a company to publish his own songs. Although he'd been raised in dire poverty on the Lower East Side, he now looked the part of a prosperous, confident man in his midthirties, entirely at his ease even though he's obviously posing. And then you notice his mouth. He appears to be just about to smile, with a trace of whimsy at the corners of his lips. It's as if he's saying, only half to himself, "How do you like the little Jewboy now?" Irving Berlin had nothing to prove to anyone, but he spent a lifetime acting as if he did.

In the half century before the Chrysler Building rose on Lexington Avenue, all those people who clambered off the ferry from Ellis

Island suddenly became Americans simply because they said they were. You couldn't go to France or Germany and become French or German, but you became American by arriving. It was the same with becoming a New Yorker. You left Indiana or one of the Carolinas to step off a train a few paces from Grand Central Terminal's vast concourse in the relentlessly vertical city. Soon you rented a room and landed a job, picked up the lingo and learned the ropes—along with the nearest subway stop—and before long you were another New Yorker. Even Hollywood backstagers from the early days of sound, like *42nd Street* and *Gold Diggers of 1933*, portrayed hungry kids in the chorus who wanted to star on Broadway rather than in the movies. That ironic conceit gave those movies their drive; they were stamping Broadway pizzazz on celluloid.

Hundreds of thousands also made the trip north and east so it had to be true enough, especially if you chose to believe in the lure of the city songs that traded in hopes and dreams. For a while, back in the first half of the twentieth century, it felt as if everybody wanted to turn into a New Yorker. Getting there required a train ride rather than a magic potion, and you woke up in Grand Central Terminal or Penn Station. The occasional star may have fallen on Alabama, but the city was, now and forever, a wondrous place. Only imagining could make it so, and in that way, New York City became America, at least for a while.

A few pages back, I quoted F. Scott Fitzgerald's observation about the ability "to hold two opposing ideas in mind at the same time" and still function. It pertains in yet another way. It wasn't quite what the songwriters did, but it came pretty close. A song's merging of sentiment and wit was an essential part of its urban sensibility. Consider "Love Is Here to Stay," George and Ira Gershwin's last song together (George and Ira Gershwin, *The Goldwyn Follies*, 1938). It's a love song for adults.

When I hear it, I imagine Ira in his midforties in the aftermath of George's recent death, sitting in an armchair, humming words that might very well have felt personal. The Gershwins had originally titled it "Our Love Is Here to Stay," but at the last minute Ira erased "Our," perhaps to make the song a bit less personal, an assertion of privacy, a distancing from any public display of grief over George's death. Ira was a much more private man than his brother. Or perhaps it's a different kind of distancing to add a note of skeptical restraint to the song's sentiment. Ira's lyric alludes to the political and diplomatic upheavals of the late 1930s ("The more I read the papers / The less I comprehend") before reaffirming the permanence of love. The removal of "our" adds a touch of the contrary to underscore the lyric's urban sensibility.

The speaker in the lyric reads the newspaper, pondering the confusions of "the world and all its capers." The ironic metaphor "capers" is the opening to the song's wit, through which the speaker professes the permanence of his love without losing his sense of humor. His playful but deeply felt hyperbole is a form of high capering. Wit and sentiment mingle as Ira's speaker contrasts the radio, the telephone, and the movies—perhaps nothing more than passing fancies—with his love, and then reaches for the comic hyperbole that makes his point more deeply. The passing fancy of even the Rockies and Gibraltar may consign them to crumbling and tumbling, but he reaffirms, as the lyric concludes with a restatement of the title, that "Our Love Is Here to Stay."

Everything in the song is accessible. You can hum it and understand it in the same breath; you may even grasp its emotional authority. Yet despite the simplicity of many fine songs, their ease of melody and lyric suggests a kind of deceptive urbanity in which emotions remain simple though intense, while wordplay and imagery are more complicated than most listeners notice. Simplicity is hard work, especially when sentiment and wit need to blend seamlessly. Lyricists accept the narrowness of their subject matter—romance, sex, and marriage—but they make things interesting for themselves (and us) by using the tricks of the poet's trade to make wit an essential part of the way songs express emotions clearly and briefly. It's how they wring out the endless permutations on their few available themes. Without wit, sentiment is in danger of floating out of orbit, losing its ties to what people feel and comprehend. The feeling becomes so abstract and amorphous that it drifts beyond what we can grasp. Then, suddenly, wit adds dazzle to language and ties dreams of forever to something solid and earthbound.

Here's another part of the problem: sentiment and wit aren't supposed to fit together well or easily, if at all. Sentiment brings you close and leads to engagement; it opens the heart to emotion. Wit, on the other hand, requires distance; it opens the mind to the truth. Wit tells you the emperor has no clothes on; sentiment, if it's deep enough, doesn't care. As the following saying, attributed to the lyricist

E. Y. Harburg, has it, "Words make you think a thought. Music makes you feel a feeling. A song makes you feel a thought." If Harburg was right, melody is the realm of sentiment, lyrics of wit—though it's not that simple. Music and words combine to express sentiment. Each longs to claim something from the other, and fighting through to a finished song is the goal. Another saying attributed to Harburg goes as follows:

> My heart wants roots
> My mind wants wings.
> I cannot bear
> Their bickerings.

A lyric joins romantic words to a romantic melody but weaves in wit through word choice and word sound. Not simply the meanings of a word, literal or suggestive, but its sound, its rhythm, the way it fits with other words, and its capacity for rhyme. Language, after all, has its own music and its own trickery. The best lyricists never lost track of it, especially when the music came first and they then wedded words to the composer's melody. The goal was to join words to music so the result was a new third thing, a song—and it needed to appear effortless. No matter how intense the emotion, in these city songs someone unseen was winking.

Song lyricists use alliteration often. It's not especially difficult to string together sounds that come close to twisting the tongue: among them, "Be My Little Baby Bumble Bee" (1911), with its buzzing "b" sounds; "Sister Susie's Sewing Shirts for Soldiers" (1914), a perfect tongue twister; and "No Love, No Nothin'" (1944), a sexy comic lament from World War II. Assonance, on the other hand, is more nuanced. It trades in implication because the sounds of words can shape a song almost as much as definitions do. Assonance is one of those song tropes that carries the wit, regardless of the song's emotion. Cole Porter wrote:

> Flying too high with some guy in the sky
> Is my idea of nothing to do.
> (Cole Porter, "I Get A Kick Out of You," *Anything Goes,* 1934)

The statement is clear enough, but what makes the lines work more deeply than melody and meaning alone is Porter's use of quick, long *i* sounds to tickle the ear with the feel of speed and uplift to carry you into the sky with someone you love. It's a subtler restatement of a line from the first hit song about airplanes, at a time when being up in the air was pretty bouncy:

> Come Josephine, in my flying machine,
> Going up, she goes! Up she goes!
> (Fred Fischer and Alfred Bryan, "Come Josephine in My Flying Machine," 1910)

Maybe Porter's lines fall just short of perfection because they feel made—not forced, but not quite natural either. Porter did himself one better with his use of assonance in "It's De-Lovely":

> Life seems so sweet that we decide
> It's in the bag to get unified.
> (Cole Porter, "It's De-Lovely," *Red, Hot and Blue,* 1936)

The first line's lilt relies on long *e* sounds that you barely notice unless you're listening for them. They suit the expression of a sentiment that's gentle and old fashioned. They also ease the line forward and underscore its meaning effortlessly and gracefully, but the second line picks up steam with the blunt slang of "in the bag" and the amusingly formal word "unified," which is also a naughty joke.

Like alliteration, rhyme is pretty easy, but songwriters liked to strut their stuff. They savored exact rhyming—not the sort of indulgence that lets somebody get away with "time" and "mine." They also loved internal rhyme as well as triple and quadruple rhymes. In the twenties, ballads had a strong rhythmic drive until they slowed down in the thirties and then got even slower in the forties. Rhythm ballads weren't necessarily fast, but they moved. The melodic line was short and often percussive, the lyrics were punchy, and three or four rhymes packed together in a line or two helped to whisk you through a syncopated chorus. The words in most lyrics may be very simple but their placement in the lines, the way they play with sound, and how they fit the music is anything but, especially when the rhymes sit in the middle and again at the end of the lines, even in something as straightforward and soft-shoe-y as this: "Day will break and I'll awake / And start to bake a sugar cake" (Vincent Youmans and Irving Caesar, "Tea for Two," *No, No, Nanette,* 1925).

Irving Berlin loved Lorenz Hart's use of internal rhyme. He called Hart "the first of the so-called sophisticated lyric writers. But he also wrote *words.* There is a very important distinction. 'Your looks are laughable, unphotographable.' That was a clever rhyme, but it tells a story about what he was trying to say about this girl. I'm not splitting hairs, and it's not semantics." Berlin then praises Hart for a lyric as simple as "With a Song in My Heart" (Richard Rodgers and Lorenz Hart, *Spring Is Here*, 1929). Although Hart had to marry his words to Richard Rodgers's music to create a song, Berlin suggests that Hart understood the need to shape the language—the words—to the emotional content, style, and mood of the music.[26] That kind of adaptability reconciles the contradictions and is, for a songwriter in the city, an elemental component of the urban sensibility.

Songs are among the most conservative of the arts. They can never get too far ahead of popular taste. They set out to please a broad public by reassuring rather than challenging. They don't promote upheaval. Rather, each song relies on a mix of the familiar and the fresh, much like the challenge of living in the city. You know your way around but each day brings the intrusion of something new, like it or not. The emotion is familiar. The surprise lies in the way you discern it or in what it does to you—a new image, a striking rhyme, a joke where you expect a tear, a momentary frisson. Surprise matters. As Irving Berlin explained, "Did you know that the public, when it hears a song, anticipates the next passage? Well, the writers who do not give them something they are expecting are those who are successful. . . . Every time the hearer begins to anticipate, fool him—give him something he isn't expecting."[27] In a triple rhyme, it's the third one that jolts you into an instant of recognition. You'd think it would call attention to itself, but it doesn't work that way unless it's forced or you're listening for it. The lines are short; the flow of music, combined with the swaying of the words, carries you through the rhymes. Wit enlarges and underscores sentiment. You may notice it, but the trick is never to stop to notice it. You smile approvingly, and you keep on singing. The city sensibility, like the city itself, rarely stops.

By the 1930s, the sense of the city was beginning to decline as songs became more reflective. The emotion was sufficient. The city remained, though not as frequently or insistently. One of the great standards, "As Time Goes By," is a slow ballad that offers hope and perhaps a touch of consolation to lovers who need to be reminded of "the simple facts of life," especially in the middle of the Great Depression or World War II (Herman Hupfeld, *Everybody's Welcome*, 1932; *Casablanca*, 1942). In the unusually long verse that precedes the classic line, "You must remember this," the songwriter Herman Hupfeld opposes the passing difficulties of the time with the persistence of love. The four rhymes become a summary of his contrasting point of view: "cause for apprehension," "new invention," "third dimension," and "relieve the tension." Removed from the song, they feel more than anything like urban self-awareness: a mix of anxiety and looking to the future as science imposes itself to rewrite the rules. Even so, some of the old rules remain. A kiss, after all, is still a kiss.

Irving Berlin called syncopation "the soul of every true American."[28] Wilfrid Sheed knew what he was talking about when he suggested that syncopation was at the heart of the popular ballads of the Great American Songbook.[29] Even when you can't find any syncopation in a particular melody, every song is surrounded by it, born out of it. Thanks to the music of African Americans, it became the American way of moving, the hesitation and quickstep we needed to keep our songs about love on the rhythmic up-and-up. It had nothing to do with speed or tempo, but that underlying grab and go that weds music and words to one another, and then back to the streets where syncopation strived and thrived. Regardless of the intent or effect of a lilting melody or a hot-paced lick, whether they lulled or lambasted, every song added to the cacophony that created the city's clangor we reveled in.

2

BROADWAY'S MELODY

One day in June 1928, about two-thirds of the way through Prohibition's fourteen-year-run, Nora Bayes asked Eddie Dowling to call on her. He managed New York City's legendary Palace Theater, and she had starred on Broadway and in vaudeville earlier in the century. Lately, though, she had been ill and was unable to work. Even though she had had a hand in writing "Shine on Harvest Moon" twenty years earlier and had performed all over the country for decades, her star had faded. During her six-year absence from Broadway, the ethnic and "coon songs" that she favored had lost their appeal. Dowling went to see her apprehensively; he knew how demanding she could be. She didn't ask for a spot on the bill, though. Instead, she sang him a few of her old songs and asked if he would find the large photographs of her in her prime and hang them in the lobby the following morning just as if she were starring at the Palace again. He could take them down before the matinee, but she wanted to know when she drove by that her pictures were on view. She had her driver take her past the Palace the next morning on her way to the hospital. She had surgery for cancer but died on the operating table.[1]

Fifteen months later, the stock market crashed. Radio and the talkies helped to kill off vaudeville, and within four years of Bayes's death, the Palace had replaced live acts with movies. If you could afford a night on the town in the 1930s, you might end up in Harlem after midnight, but first you made for Broadway. Those who couldn't afford either went to the movies or listened to the radio instead. Either way, vaudeville had become the oldest hat in town. The country was changing, and that meant Broadway was changing, too. In the 1940s, for the duration of the war, even the lights went out.

Figure 2.1 Imperious Nora Bayes was a great star of Broadway and vaudeville in the early years of the twentieth century. Library of Congress, George Grantham Bain Collection.

~ ~ ~

In 1918, the journalist John Reed described Broadway as "gashing the city like a lava-stream."[2] The radio and newspaper columnist Walter Winchell is said to have called it a "main artery of New York life—the hardened artery." For more than a century, Broadway has been as much an idea as a place, a subject for waxing poetic and profane. The oldest and longest thoroughfare in New York City, it runs north from Bowling Green at the southern tip of Manhattan Island until it crosses the Harlem River into the Bronx and then pushes up through Westchester County and the Hudson Valley all the way to Albany, if you count the highways it merges with. The Lenape people called it Wickquasgeck ("birch-bark country") Trail, but the Dutch renamed it *Brede weg*, literally "broad way," after they purchased Mannahata, "island of many hills."

It took another 250 years after the Dutch arrived for "Broadway" and "theater" to merge in the American imagination as the "Great White Way." Every city and town staged plays, but the American theater meant Broadway and Broadway alone. The rest of the country was "out of town" until the growth of regional theaters dispersed it in the 1970s. Over the first decades of the twentieth century, Broadway became not merely a place but a symbol of the city and its character:

> Just turn out the lights over on the Great White Way
> And the burgh is gone for fair.
> You all go to bed,
> New York town would be dead,
> If old Broadway wasn't there.
>
> (Kerry Mills, B. J. Costello, and Andrew B. Sterling, "What Would Become of New York Town [If Broadway Wasn't There]," 1910)

The most theatrical of streets, Broadway moved under flashing neon lights to an irresistible cacophony as crowds milled around and street musicians played for tenement kids and Park Avenue swells alike. A passerby's price of admission was a hot pretzel or a bag of chestnuts from the pushcart on the corner.

When the doughboys sailed for France in 1917, one of the songs that urged them on was "Good-Bye Broadway, Hello France." Soldiers say farewell to Broadway and hello to France—not goodbye to Broadway and hello to the Champs Élysées, or goodbye to New York and hello to Paris. It worked because Broadway had become a synonym for America, and no matter where the departing soldiers hailed from, everybody stateside understood: "Good-bye Broadway, Hello France, / We're ten million strong" (Billy Baskette, C. Francis Reisner, and Benny Davis, "Good-Bye Broadway, Hello France," 1917).

In literary circles, that's called *synecdoche*—using part of something to stand for all of it. Somebody sings "Broadway," and listeners understand that it means "New York"—that is, New York at its most exciting, an ever-humming electrical machine, its modernity heralded by the lights that illuminate the crowded streets around the clock. By 1927, the opening number for the musical comedy *Manhattan Mary* praised "a million lights to dim the stars" along a Broadway it called "the heart of the world" (Ray Henderson, Lew Brown, and B. G. DeSylva, "Broadway," 1927). Other, more insistent songs described Broadway's tight grip on what we imagined and how we behaved. Once it gets you, you can't escape (Nacio Herb Brown and Arthur Freed, "Broadway Rhythm," *Broadway Melody of 1936*, 1935, 1929). Broadway's rapid pace and bright lights defined its allure; they appear in song after song whose driving rhythms feel as if only exhaustion can slow them. Where does joy end and mania begin? The brightest stretch of Broadway was where American musicals (and American music) thrived.

By 1880, a half century earlier, arc lights had lit a mile of Broadway between Union Square and Thirty-Fourth Street, making it one of the first streets in the country to have electric lights. Just over a decade later, where the Flatiron Building still stands and Broadway crosses Madison Avenue at Twenty-Third Street, electric lights lit a theater marquee for the first time. John Kenrick writes that, in 1903,

> the first animated electric billboard appeared in Times Square . . . when Victor Herbert's musical *The Red Mill* installed a sign with carbon lights that imitated the revolving arms of a windmill. Soon every Broadway show had some kind of electrified signage. By 1905, the largest of these electric billboards . . . were actually stopping traffic around Times Square. . . . With the introduction of neon lighting in 1927, elongated shapes and bright colors became part of the eye-popping mix.[3]

The lights spread north so rapidly that by 1915, the lyricist Ben Deeley could write, "The lights are lit way up to Yonkers, turning night-time into day, / On the farm they chase the chicken, they do the same on our White Way" (W. L. Beardsley and Ben Deeley, "When the Sun Goes Down in Jersey, Life Begins on Old Broadway," 1915).

Despite the installation of streetlights, it took another twenty years and a *New York Morning Telegram* columnist named Shep Friedman to make permanent the connection between lights and Broadway. The expression "Great White Way" had first appeared in 1901 as the title of a novel about the South Pole, but on February 3, 1902, Friedman borrowed it for his newspaper column devoted to goings on in Midtown. Because the streets were covered with snow that day, he called his column "Found on the Great White Way."[4] In the same year, the novelist Stephen Crane wrote, "Broadway of late years has fallen heir to countless signs illuminated with red, blue, green and gold electric lamps, and the people certainly fly to these as moths go to a candle."[5] Before long, New Yorkers and tourists alike were calling the stretch of Broadway where brightly lit theaters drew large crowds the Great White Way. As the use of electricity expanded and the theaters moved farther uptown, the flashing bulbs of marquees and billboards soon defined the area, especially near the intersection of Broadway and Forty-Second Street, called Longacre Square until the newspaper magnate Adolph Ochs moved his newspaper there in 1913 and insisted that the city change the square's name to Times.[6] In popular understanding and in song lyrics, Broadway, Times Square, and Forty-Second Street were interchangeable and irresistible:

> When they do that Broadway rag,
> Millionaires with lots of brag
> Ev'ryone you're sure to meet
> From the Bow'ry up to Forty Second Street
> They all do that slide and shiver
> Then they shake and quiver
> When they do that Broadway rag.
> (Nat Osborne and Will H. Smith, "That Broadway Rag," 1918)

During the twenties, a now-forgotten slang term referred to the lights of the Theater District as the "42nd Street Moon." This expression soon became the title of a song by Sigmund Romberg, Clifford Grey, and Harold Atteridge. The lyric asserts that the combination of "Doc Edison" and the moon—the theater lights—are the best cure for a melancholy mood: "When you're blue and you need medicine . . . / Turn on that Forty-Second Street moon" (Sigmund Romberg, Clifford Grey, Harold Atteridge, "Forty-Second Street Moon," *Marjorie*, 1924).

In 1907, late enough for song lyrics to refer to Broadway routinely as the Great White Way, Ludwig Englander, Sydney Rosenfeld, and James Clarence Harvey wrote "Great White Way" as the opening number for the musical revue *The Gay White Way*, portraying it hyperbolically as a place everybody knew about even if they had never been there. In 1924, Henry I. Marshall began his song "The Great White Way," "Bright nights, bright lights, on the street of world renown" (Henry I. Marshall, "The Great White Way," 1924).

Despite many cautionary tales, Broadway remained a place to dream about. Its grime seemed to disappear in the bright lights at night, dispelling everything but the illusion of glamour. Its raffish vulgarity took on a patina of charm. Songs praised its aura as well as its transforming effect on the new arrivals who sought it out. Forsaking the typical imagery of Pollyanna songs, where bluebirds and blue skies effortlessly replace blackbirds and dark clouds, a 1937 lyric by Arthur Freed begins with an admonition to newcomers to leave their worries behind and bring a happy-go-lucky mood to Broadway (Nacio Herb Brown and Arthur Freed, "Broadway Melody," *Broadway Melody of 1936*, 1935). The speaker in the song has learned that Broadway's bright lights and vitality can bring a smile that drives away the gloom. In another song written a couple of years later, love blossoms when a lover forgets the crowded streets, noisy traffic, and bright lights (Ralph Rainger and Leo Robin, "Blossoms on Broadway," *Blossoms on Broadway*, 1937). Other celebratory songs reveal themselves in their titles: "The Bright Lights of Broadway," "I Miss You, Dear Old Broadway," "Broadway Reverie," and "There's a Little Street in Heaven That They Call Broadway."[7]

The Theater District first grew up downtown, in Union Square, near Broadway and Fourteenth Street, in the decades after the Civil War. It housed thirty-three theaters, with more soon to come. By the 1890s, the district had moved up to Madison Square, where, James Traub writes, "men of wealth and standing could gather with their own kind, and eat, drink and spend with abandon."[8] Fittingly, it settled only a few blocks from Tin Pan Alley, on West Twenty-Eighth Street, where publishers and songwriters flourished as well, even though they rarely wrote about the *nouveau riche* of the Gilded Age. By the early years of the twentieth century, the Theater District had continued to spread uptown until it found its best-known home in and around Times Square. New theaters rose and, by the 1927–28 season, more than seventy houses presented more than 250 shows.[9]

Broadway's greatest year for musicals was 1927, made so by the openings of the *Ziegfeld Follies of 1927* (with Irving Berlin's "Shakin' the Blues Away"); Harry Tierney and Joseph McCarthy's *Rio Rita* (the title song); Vincent Youmans, Clifford Grey, and Leo Robin's *Hit the Deck* ("Sometimes I'm Happy," "Hallelujah!"); Ray Henderson, Lew Brown, and B. G. DeSylva's *Good News* (the title song and "The Best Things in Life Are Free"); Sigmund Romberg and Dorothy Donnelly's *My Maryland* ("Your Land and My Land"); Harry Ruby and Bert Kalmar's *The Five O'Clock Girl* ("Thinking of You"); George and Ira Gershwin's *Funny Face* ("'S Wonderful," "He Loves and She Loves") and *Strike Up the Band* ("Soon" and the title song); Richard Rodgers and Lorenz Hart's *Connecticut Yankee* ("My Heart Stood Still," "Thou Swell"); and Jerome Kern and Oscar Hammerstein II's *Show Boat* ("Only Make Believe," "Ol' Man River").

The Broadway Theater District ran, roughly, from Thirty-Ninth to Fifty-Third Streets. Its borders were fluid enough to include Tin Pan Alley down on Twenty-Eighth Street and, decades later, the Carnegie Deli up on Seventh Avenue near Fifty-Fifth. Its attitudes were broad minded enough to make room for the old Metropolitan Opera House between Thirty-Ninth and Fortieth Streets, as well as Hubert's Flea Circus on West Forty-Second. The meal you ate and the play you saw were rarely as important as the lights that never dimmed and the excitement that never flagged, and the exhilarating and sometimes dangerous mix of high rollers and lowlifes who populated the place. Before 1930, this list included Evelyn Nesbit and Harry Thaw, Texas Guinan and Jimmy Walker, Mae West and Damon Runyon, Sophie Tucker and Babe Ruth, Helen Morgan and Florenz Ziegfeld, and Fred and Adele Astaire. It doesn't stop there. With the electric lights came other things as well. Jerome Charyn writes that during the twenties, Broadway "becomes the capital of night," defined by "appetite and excess."[10] The historian Donald Meyer called it the capital of "dangerous love."[11]

Broadway characters, larger than life, came alive at night—a night scrubbed away by a million flickering bulbs. In myth, the line between fact and fiction fades. Over in Murray Hill, Irving Berlin, the insomniac songwriter, wrote after midnight and slept half the daytime away. The fictional characters in Damon Runyon's stories spent their afternoons at the track and frequented the sidewalks and saloons of Times Square and its environs at night. The show business *tummlers* hung out at Lindy's after midnight. Scribblers such as Walter Winchell and Ed Sullivan worked the tables at El Morocco and the Stork Club before they hid away in the wee hours to write the gossip that sold a version of Broadway's story to "Mr. and Mrs. America and all the ships at sea." No one ever slept; neither did the town they inhabited. As with Runyon's Nathan Detroit and Sky Masterson, Broadway and its talk were largely a matter of imagined style. Winchell, who seemed to coin more expressions than anyone else, called New York "the slang capital of the world."[12]

Broadway in the light of day was nothing more than a street where theaters, restaurants, clip joints, and nightspots clustered within a few cluttered blocks. Then at night it became the place "where the underworld can meet the elite" (Harry Warren and Al Dubin, "42nd Street," *42nd Street,* 1933) in joints as varied as the 21 Club and Chez Morgan, a speakeasy where Helen Morgan fronted for mobsters and sat on a piano every night to pour out her heart in a tiny, timeless soprano. Broadway types in fiction and fact played fast and loose with the rules of grammar and etiquette, and put them to bed for good.[13] Society dames and hookers mingled on the same few blocks. During the bad years of the 1930s, both had their own melancholy songs, courtesy of Cole Porter, in "Down in the Depths (on the Ninetieth Floor)" and "Love for Sale."

No matter when the songs appeared, no matter what else was happening in the world, the portrayal of Broadway, good and bad, rarely changed. For half a century, it held the imagination despite the appearance and disappearance of fads and fancies, rising and falling economies, even war and peace. Songs emphasized the link between its irresistible allure and sometimes shattering results.

In one of the darkest of these songs, a young woman wanders with the Broadway throng "where she doesn't belong." Broadway may have become her home, but she makes no connections. She hangs around until "the lights go out on old Broadway" (Al Selden, Max Friedman, and Sam H. Stept, "When the Lights Go Out on Broadway," 1917). The lyric never mentions the traditional values the woman has left behind, but they appear more overtly in a number of songs that describe young women who evade or escape Broadway's temptations, including one who remains innocent and modest even though she lives "Just 'Round the Corner from Broadway." Instead of spending her time there, she's the breadwinner for her family. (Gus Edwards and Blanche Merrill, "Just 'Round the Corner from Broadway," 1914) Another pretty girl, perhaps as innocent but certainly smarter than most, may never have been hugged or kissed, but "she knows some things you don't learn at school." Yet she resists the allure of the gold digger's life:

I could be living on Fifth Avenue,
But I'm not that kind of a girl.
And then by using some powder and paint,
I could make myself look just what I ain't. . . .
I could get married to some millionaire,
Who's picked out his grave and has one foot in there,
I could take his millions and give him the air,
But I'm not that kind of a girl.
(Albert Von Tilzer and Lew Brown, "I'm Not That Kind of a Girl," 1919)

The idea of Broadway was a magnet for the rest of the country. It was a place to be thrilled by and a little afraid of. To its inhabitants it was a land of plenty—plenty of dolls, plenty of guys on the make, plenty of booze, plenty of money and fame—but it was all a bubble, and the snow turned grimy in a couple of hours. Part of its magnetism lay in its danger. In Harry Von Tilzer and George Whiting's "I'm a Little Bit Afraid of You, Broadway" (1913) a young woman, still new to the city, speaks directly to Broadway to admit, "Your white lights are like goblins, when they gleam." Although she lacks the daring "to tango in the mornings" or take a peek into Shanley's Cabaret because she fears that "You'd swallow me right up," she never considers leaving.

The novelist Theodore Dreiser wrote in 1900 that along Broadway the "gleam of a thousand lights is often as effective as the persuasive light in a wooing and fascinating eye."[14] Jerome Charyn characterized the first decades of the twentieth century as "an age of glitter and six foot headdresses, of chorus girls who pranced with marvelous precision, of gangsters as rich as Kublai Kahn, where the only substance was excitement itself."[15] Broadway trembled with a dissolute magnetism that bordered on the erotic, its appeal inseparable from the lights that flickered and flashed but never dimmed. Just as many immigrants found themselves drawn to a country across the sea whose streets, they had been promised, were paved with gold, so young men and women from small towns in the Midwest and South followed the allure of Broadway's promise of adventure, freedom, wealth, and fame. They soon learned the grittier truths. Fred Fisher and Howard Johnson wrote one of the most famous of the melancholy ballads about Broadway in 1915, the story of a foolish dreamer who longs to remain where the lights glow and everyone seems happy. The reality, though, is different: "There's a broken heart for every light on Broadway, / A million tears for every gleam, they say" (Fred Fisher and Howard Johnson, "There's a Broken Heart for Every Light on Broadway," 1915).

The sheet music historian Nancy Groce writes, "For every glamorous, celebratory song [about Broadway], . . . there is another one about the loneliness, poverty, and disillusionment."[16] For every innocent young woman who becomes a star or finds true love in a popular song about Broadway, many more fail. Women, much more than men, were the subjects of Broadway's—and popular music's—tales of heartbreak. These songs were more than cautionary tales or latter-day sentimental ballads. They reflected the anxiety that accompanied urbanization; many of them were at least implicitly sexual. Everybody understood; nobody needed to say that these were Fallen Women. The old values of steadfast virginal love, self-sacrifice, religious devotion, and the enjoyment of simple rural pleasures gave way to a tempting world characterized by freedom of choice, sexual assertiveness, and constant change. It was thrilling but also risky. Songs about the single women who fled small towns for a future on Broadway reflected these seductive changes.[17] Some told stories, others made personal statements. Both were confessions of a sort, but both offered testimony in a changing world. Attractive young Mabel who has come to New York loves the bright lights so much that she rejects good advice to "take care" because, as she says, "I'm too young to be careful, / I'm too sweet to be good." The lyric does not go beyond that decisive moment, but Mabel's future sounds worrisome (George W. Mayer, "I'm Too Young to Be Careful [And Too Sweet to Be Good]," 1919).

Broadway's oft-told stories of wise counsel disregarded, and fame and fortune achieved and lost, teach the lesson that young women often throw good sense aside in their eagerness to become stars. Like the early talkies, songs told and retold the story of aspiring canaries and hoofers who yearned to see their names in lights on the marquee of the Winter Garden or the New Amsterdam. Your name in neon was proof of stardom, evidence of at least momentary immortality. Andrew Sterling's comic lyric from 1906 joshed all those dreamers in "I'm the Only Star That Twinkles on Broadway." A young amateur performer from Kankakee, short on talent but long on herself, takes her short-sighted friends' advice, "Maybe you ought to be down on Broadway." Soon after she arrives, she turns down an offer from the famed producer Charles Frohman, so she says, and compares herself favorably to the actress Sarah Bernhardt. Finally, the theater impresario Oscar Hammerstein I makes her a star. She is soon boasting witlessly about an audience's reaction to her performance as Juliet: "Someone shouted this is more than I can stand, / Then another yelled, 'Strike up the band'" (Harry Von Tilzer and Andrew Sterling, "I'm the Only Star That Twinkles on Broadway," 1905).

Ironically, the same songwriters who extolled the virtues of Broadway's freewheeling ways also told the stories of virtue compromised, reputations sullied, and fame lost. In 1919, Richard A. Whiting and Herbert Spencer wrote that while young innocent "girls from ev'rywhere / Come hurrying down" to "answer Broadway's call," within a year they have changed into "Broadway Belles," who exert their allure by weaving "such spells / Men all bow to / They kowtow to" (Richard A. Whiting and Herbert Spencer, "Broadway Belles," 1919). The lyric never spells out how the young women become seducers; it doesn't need to. Everyone knew that Broadway had the power to shatter the innocence of those who fell under its spell. A similar anecdote, told from a different point of view, concerns Billy McCoy, "a city-bred boy," who finds out too late that the "demure little maid" who longs to see "what they call the white way," is really a con artist. Later on the subway, he groans, "Gee, I'm the rube, / Who'd have thought I'd have fallen for that" (Frances Seamans, "Kindly Direct Me to Broadway," 1914).

"Broadway Belles" takes a generalized look at the making of a seductress, but Harry Von Tilzer and Andrew B. Sterling's "Take a Look at Me Now" creates an individual who comes to New York with "just one home-made gown." After an appearance in a single show, she wears diamond earrings and a five-hundred-dollar gown. She boasts to the cousin who first taught her the ropes, "Remember when I first came to this town, / Take a look at me now." She anticipates "diamonds by the quart" because "I know just where they grow" (Harry Von Tilzer and Andrew Sterling, "Take a Look at Me Now," 1911). In only a few months, she has changed from a small-town girl to a shrewd, self-aware gold digger who describes the change with cynical humor. She knew what she wanted, and she learned how to get it.

Not all tales of fame and fortune end so contentedly. Stories about the price paid for stardom are hardly new. A young woman who had flowered "amidst the throng, gay life and song" of Broadway, has now become "a faded little rose, / Beneath the white light's glare." Despite her "fancy clothes" and "silken hose," she is "alone, as they all pass you by." She manages to hide her cares beneath a smile as an observer offers encouragement: "Still at heart you're a gem, / though the whole world condemn / no one knows of your woes, Broadway Rose" (Otis Spencer, Martin Fried, and Eugene West, "Broadway Rose," 1920). Although the song is from 1920, its melodramatic emotions, its hidden tears behind obligatory smiles, and its moral lesson resemble a sentimental ballad from thirty years earlier.

The women in song lyrics who succeed on Broadway pay a price for the changes they undergo. Songs find them irresistible but capricious; the values of permanence and conviction prove weaker than the delights of novelty and titillating personal satisfaction. The speaker in "Flutter On My Broadway Butterfly" is charmed by a showgirl but realizes she will never be true to him. He understands that "you've always been a rover" and have given "your honey sips / To O so many lips" (Sigmund Romberg, Jean Schwartz, and Harold Atteridge, "Flutter On By My Broadway Butterfly," *Monte Christo Jr.*, 1919). Those who succeed become tough, independent women. As one "real live bang-up showgirl" says, "I ain't bowing down to no girl, / For I've had a shot at most all kinds of parts." When she takes a job in burlesque because it pays better than a Broadway chorus, she offers a comic cry of independence as she heads out of town: "I know I can do without old Broadway / But can old Broadway do without me?" (W. Raymond Walker and Ballard MacDonald, "Can Old Broadway Do without Me?" 1911).

When the girls who try to make their way in show business are not from small southern or midwestern towns, they are immigrants who leave behind the alleys of the city's tenement neighborhoods. Both groups give short shrift to romantic love, although they often resort to seduction to get what they want. At other times, neither love nor sex plays a role, though they take advantage of their flirtatious good looks to get ahead. Many of them are Irish working girls named Sally, who are looking for something they think of as better—a job in a Broadway show. In "I Wonder What's Become of Sally," the lyricist Jack Yellen writes that "The sunshine's missing from our alley / Ever since the day Sally went away" (Milt Ager and Jack Yellen, "I Wonder What's Become of Sally," 1924). Her absence has impoverished those who remain, from the street-corner quartet that no longer harmonizes to the neighborhood butcher, baker, and grocer who miss her smile. They plead with her to return because they miss the bright manner and warm laughter that propelled her to stardom, but there is no sense that she will respond. If anything, the lyric implies their unrequited affection. Without her, an essential spark is missing from their lives.

Though the lyric does not spell it out, the alley is a dismal place, less hopeful than before, because Sally's spirit gave them their only happiness (Dave Stamper and Gene Buck, "Sally Won't You Come Back," 1921). In a similar song, "She Lives Down in Our Alley," those who remain behind are less sanguine. They recognize the difference between Sally's new life and their own, but they also know that she has turned her back on whatever they once meant to her. The change occurs with amazing speed, so recently that she has not had a chance to move away. Only a month ago, this Sally was wearing working-class calico, but then she joined a Broadway show. When she refuses to acknowledge her old friends on the street, everybody has something to say about it:

> They call her "La Belle Marie,"
> But her right name's "McNally,"
> Big high heels and silken hose,
> Paris hats and Paris clothes,
> But why should she turn up her nose?
> She lives down in our Alley.

Their resentment becomes more explicit in the second chorus: "Her French ways are all a bluff, / She's as French as 'Paddy Duff'" (Charles McCarron and Charles Bayha, "She Lives Down in Our Alley," 1915).

~ ~ ~

Tin Pan Alley has always turned out songs about New York City and Broadway, but similar songs were also important in scores for Broadway musicals. By the 1920s, a newly invigorated American theater cast off the banal melodramas and tepid adaptations of London musicals that had been the theatrical fare of choice for many years.[18] Over the next decade, Broadway became equally the home of a serious dramatist (Eugene O'Neill), a comic writer (George S. Kaufman), and musical collaborators (Richard Rodgers and Lorenz Hart). But before the twenties, the teens provided important signs of what was to come. For musicals, two showmen who emerged in the first decade of the new century remained indispensable to the myth of Broadway. They embodied its assertive confidence, flashy sentimentality, and devotion to commerce. George M. Cohan and Florenz Ziegfeld were essential to making Broadway a place of universal appeal through their shows, styles, and larger-than-life personalities. Cohan opened his first successful musical comedy on Broadway in 1904, and Ziegfeld his first *Follies* three years later. Cohan's audiences consisted largely of shopgirls and salesmen; Ziegfeld played to the carriage trade and had the highest ticket prices in town.

Although he started as a vaudevillian, Cohan became a complete man of the theater—playwright, composer, lyricist, producer, director, singer, dancer, and actor. He may have been born in Providence, Rhode Island, to Irish vaudevillians, but he became a New Yorker, "born," he liked to say, "on the Fourth of July," even though his real birth date was July 3, 1878. The dramatic license served him well; he was a nostalgic innovator and a shameless flag-waver who considered himself a cock-of-the-walk New Yorker. As John Bush Jones writes, regardless of subject, Cohan's songs "fused an Irish lilt with an American flair."[19] Between 1901 and 1938, he wrote, produced, and starred in more than two dozen musicals, emerging as the "embodiment of American aggression, brashness, vigor, and naivete."[20] Because he told stories about ordinary people rather than affluent sophisticates, "characters like Johnny Jones and Nellie Kelly appealed to a whole new audience. He wrote for every American, instead of highbrow Americans."[21] His shows and songs were democratic and populist. They embraced America's fondest assumptions about itself and expressed them in brassy tunes and slangy lyrics that audiences still recognize. Usually his own leading man, Cohan was the character he played. He knew how to sing his songs because he wrote them for himself about himself. He tailored even his love songs to the antics of an old-fashioned song-and-dance man with a hard edge and a sentimental bent.[22]

Nothing erotic simmered in Cohan's love lyrics and barely anything romantic. He wrote a showman's songs with little depth or reflection. They thumped along in a toe-tapping way and expressed their clear, simple emotions in familiar, effortless chatter. He composed an occasional "lesson song" like "Life's a Funny Proposition, After All," but he preferred to write and perform rollicking numbers in which a character could pledge his love to a sweet colleen for her innocence ("Mary's a Grand Old Name") or her irresistible sparkle and charm:

> The boys are all mad about Nellie,
> Daughter of Officer Kelly,
> And it's all day long they bring
> Flowers all dripping with dew,
> And they join in the chorus of Nellie Kelly,
> I love you!
>
> (George M. Cohan, "Nellie Kelly, I Love You," *Little Nellie Kelly*, 1922)

Cohan was most enthusiastic, though, when he wrote about America ("You're a Grand Old Flag") or New York. *Little Johnny Jones*, his first successful musical, strands the title character in London to await the clearing of his name in a horse-racing scandal. Watching an ocean liner set sail for America, the innocent Jones performs a song that lists what he misses most about his home town. It is Cohan's most important love song to New York. "Give my regards to Broadway," he sang, "Remember me to Herald Square" (George M. Cohan, "Give My Regards to Broadway," *Little Johnny Jones*, 1904).

Unlike Cohan, Florenz Ziegfeld did all his work backstage. He produced each annual edition of the *Ziegfeld Follies*, from its beginning in 1907 until his death in 1932. A perfectionist who supervised every aspect of a production, he chose costumes and sets, directed performers, and continued to add, cut, and generally tinker with songs and scenes throughout the run. His costs were so high that he was always low on money. Once, shortly before opening night, he insisted on adding expensive Irish linen petticoats to the showgirls' costumes for a single number. "Why?" somebody protested. "You can't see them." "I know," Ziegfeld replied, "but Irish linen does something to their walk."[23] He also risked self-parody more than once. In 1909, the showgirls appeared in taxicab costumes with hidden battery packs. At just the right moment, the stage darkened and the girls turned on their headlights.[24] No matter what else he did, in every *Follies* there was that "staircase down which stepped his glorified showgirls in perfect step."[25] He asked very little of them—except perfection. They did not have to sing or dance or even speak as long as they could wear scanty but elaborate costumes and walk and sit as he instructed. Although she was never a *Follies* girl, the movie star Paulette Goddard appeared in the chorus in the 1928 operetta *Rio Rita*, produced by Ziegfeld. All she had to do was sit on a moon made of cardboard and smile. She wrote, "I could tap [dance] but I was never given the chance. Ziegfeld used to say I was a great sitter. I sat and I walked."[26]

More than any of his contemporaries, Ziegfeld shaped America's perception of female beauty. His greatest creations were not the revues or even the performers he elevated to stardom but rather the showgirls, glamorous but distant, erotic but unapproachable. Although he hired the best songwriters, the most talented singers, and the funniest comedians year in and year out, he lavished his fondest attentions on the girls who did nothing but walk. He dressed them in the most beautiful fabrics, celebrated them in song, and built his annual *Follies* around their beauty. Most of these young women had little education, but Ziegfeld's fascination with them extended beyond the stage.

Once he had taught them to walk and dress and instructed them in the social graces, some of them were smart enough to stow away a fortune by becoming very approachable to hovering sugar daddies. Ultimately, though, the showgirl was a creature of fantasy: "Ziegfeld was a master of illusion, a gambler, and an exhibitionist. . . . He was a calculating romantic . . . who truly adored women but who also used them without hesitation to embody whatever dream of the moment was playing out in his restless imagination."[27]

Some excellent songwriters worked for Ziegfeld, most notably Irving Berlin, but also Victor Herbert, Gus Edwards, Gene Buck, and Fred Fisher, among many others. Few of them wrote their best songs for him, although "Shine on Harvest Moon" from the 1908 *Follies,* "By the Light of the Silvery Moon" from 1909, and "Peg o' My Heart" from 1913 became standards. But such long-lasting songs were few and far between. The shows had no consistent view of love and romance, partly because their topicality pegged them to the fads and fancies of the day; they turned current events into entertainment. Six years after the Wright Brothers' flight, for example, the beautiful Lillian Lorraine flew in circles over the audience's heads in a large model airplane hung from the ceiling as she sang "Up, Up, Up in My Airship." In 1918, the score included Irving Berlin's cheery World War I love song "I'm Gonna Pin My Medal on the Girl I Left Behind."

Fittingly, a song for the showgirls was the most important number to come from the *Ziegfeld Follies.* Shortly before opening night in 1919, Ziegfeld begged Irving Berlin for an additional song. He showed the songwriter a series of drawings for still-unused costumes. "I have to have a song," he pleaded, "my bookkeeper will kill me." Berlin's "A Pretty Girl Is Like a Melody" immediately became the girls' signature song. What Berlin wrote was one of the *Follies*' most old-fashioned numbers, a lyrical celebration of beauty and grace, but he also laid out the melody so the girls could parade in their costumes to its sweeping but measured rhythms.[28] No matter how romantic a song might be, if it was for the showgirls, they had to be able to walk to it.[29]

Within ten years of Cohan's and Ziegfeld's arrivals on Broadway, musical comedies and their songs took their first recognizably modern form in the Princess musicals of Jerome Kern, P. G. Wodehouse, and Guy Bolton. Only a year after Kern composed the defining modern show tune, "They Didn't Believe Me," these shows at the tiny

Princess Theater on West Thirty-Ninth Street discarded the fairyland kingdoms of operetta to tell up-to-date New York stories of optimistic, urban young men and women whose manner, attire, and speech reflected their audience's. Their characters, like their stories, were simplified and exaggerated but still recognizable, especially in Kern's tripping melodies and Wodehouse's chatty but elegant lyrics. Kern and Wodehouse (and sometimes Bolton as well) set the songs on the city's streets and in its apartment houses, and nearly all of them possessed a New York sensibility whether or not they called the city by name. If not urban, then always urbane. A century later, their rhythms still glide, their pace remains quick, and their talk has a kind of staccato lyricism that suits the city. The songs are not the elevated romantic arias that Kern would write later in his career; his music still felt young.

Wodehouse's lyrics were not specifically about New York, but their approach to love combined innocence and sophistication. They seem to anticipate the arrival of Fred Astaire a decade later, when his romantic readiness intermingled with his jaunty grace, the unique combination that defined his particular American urbanity for forty years. An early, pre-Astaire form of it appears in a 1917 Kern-Wodehouse song like "You Never Knew About Me" from *Oh, Boy.* George Budd and Lou Ellen Carter have eloped and now return to George's apartment to spend their wedding night, but first they express regret that they hadn't known one another through all the years of childhood. The song is sweet, with an undertone of mock regret, as Wodehouse combines love and the approach of passion with wit and a last vestige of innocence. Their singing to one another is both funny and sweetly regretful:

> I was often kissed 'neath the mistletoe
> By small boys excited with tea.
> If I'd known that you existed,
> I'd have scratched them and resisted, dear!
> But I never knew about you,
> (Oh! the pain of it.)
> And you never knew about me.
>
> (Jerome Kern and P. G. Wodehouse, "You Never Knew About Me," *Oh, Boy*, 1917)

The songs of the Princess Musicals were more innocent than audiences came to expect in the lyrics that Dorothy Fields (with Kern), Irving Berlin, and Ira Gershwin wrote for Astaire and Ginger Rogers in the 1930s, but Wodehouse had begun what they would continue: the unlikely but satisfying merging of romance and wit. He observed the human comedy with a cocked eyebrow and a sympathetic heart; his songs with Kern never failed to see the irony in every love affair but they also never gave up on romance. Wodehouse knew exactly how to express love's contradictory complications. Even though he was British and would eventually return home to invent Bertie Wooster's addled shenanigans and Jeeves's in-the-nick-of-time solutions, his songs with Kern, in their youthfully poetic approximation of everyday speech and their wry sense of romance, can only be described as urban; they breathe the air of Manhattan:

At the opera I like to be with Freddie,
To a musical show, I go with Joe.
I like to dance with Ted, and golf with Dick or Ned,
And at the races and other lively places,
Sam and Eddie are fun.
But I'm pining till there comes in my direction, one combining,
Every masculine perfection,
Who'll be Eddie,
And Joe, and Dick and Sam and Freddie,
And Neddie and Teddie rolled in one.
(Jerome Kern, P. G. Wodehouse, "Rolled into One," *Oh Boy*, 1917)

All the lyricists who possessed the gift for merging romance and wit were Wodehouse's natural successors, but whereas most of them wrote at least a few songs about New York, only some wrote specifically about Broadway, Times Square, or Forty-Second Street. Cole Porter was one of them. Porter, who became a New Yorker by choice, was like no other songwriter of his time. Wealthy, Protestant, and midwestern, with a Yale education and a determination to flaunt his sophistication, he lived a lavish, indulgent life.

Porter wrote for Broadway and Hollywood. He was eager to have his songs recorded by popular singers he admired because he wanted a broad public to accept his music, but he was also unconcerned about the values of the day. He lived on his own terms, and wrote that way as well. Unlike other songwriters, who prided themselves on being able to write every kind of song, Porter settled contentedly for doing only what he did best; his most characteristic work consisted of either witty catalogue songs or pulsating erotic love ballads. He wrote a few anomalies—"Don't Fence Me In" and "True Love," among them—but mainly he stuck to what worked for him.

After nearly a decade of failure in New York and the high life in France, he eventually established himself with three Broadway hits in a row—*Paris* (1928), *Fifty Million Frenchmen* (1929), and *The New Yorkers* (1930)—each a tribute to his urban sensibility. Their scores included his first important hit songs, including "(Let's Do It) Let's Fall in Love," "You Do Something to Me," and "Love for Sale." For *The New Yorkers*, he also wrote the tolling anthem "I Happen to Like New York." It's the way "happen" jumps out at you. Its insouciance makes the song distinctively Porter's, but it's also the most emphatic word in the line. His songs relish New York for its grit and glamour, its dirty streets and bright lights; they take it as it is.

Porter dramatized the antithetical qualities of the glamorous and the tawdry that were so important in songs about the city, but he could combine both points of view in individual songs. He first managed the feat twice in the space of a few months. In 1930, to amuse friends who had traveled to Philadelphia for the out-of-town opening of *The New Yorkers*, Porter wrote a song about someone who knows exactly what New York is, good and bad, but can't bear to be away: "Take me back to Manhattan," he wrote, "That dear old dirty town" (Porter, "Take Me Back to Manhattan," *The New Yorkers*, 1930). After the show opened to rave reviews, Porter sailed off to Monte Carlo for a vacation but two days later wired a new song to the show's producer, E. Ray Goetz, to add to the score. "I Happen to Like New York" expanded on the oxymoronic sentiment of "Take Me Back to Manhattan" by setting its understated conversational title to a throbbing anthem. Like its predecessor, it affirms permanent but cleareyed affection for the city. Porter recognizes—even relishes—New York's dark side, but his affection never diminishes: "I like the sight and the sound and even the stink of it. / I happen to like New York" (Porter, "I Happen to Like New York," *The New Yorkers*, 1931).

Porter's songs sizzle even when they're funny. His sexiest songs feel as if they're right here, right now, with a kind of assertive urban drive that says New York. Their sensibility ranges from the pulsating to the comic, the impassioned to the casual, to putting on a tux for an evening on the town to the playful business of getting in shape for love, at least until the martinis arrive. They come as close as Porter ever did to writing for flappers in a song that's an invitation to be outrageous: "There's something wild about you, child, / That's so contagious," (Porter, "Let's Misbehave," cut from *Paris*, 1928).

Unlike Porter, George and Ira Gershwin rarely wrote a song whose overt subject was New York City. "Sweet and Low Down," in which a speaker urges the listener to hail a cab for a night of dancing to music that is both sweet and low, is one of the exceptions (*Tip-Toes*, 1925). Yet George's music consistently caught the sound and feel of New York. Ira's lyrics were their verbal counterpart during the fourteen years they worked together—especially in the 1920s, when George's music was more percussive than lyrical, with a short, almost pugnacious melodic line. The songs he and Ira wrote sitting side by side at the piano embodied New York City when New York City embodied America. What they brought to popular music was a double sensibility, both sweet and low down: George intense and Ira laid back, their songs rooted in the expansive, witty discipline of jazz and light verse. They could combine syncopated melody with syncopated sentiment and wit in the same song.

The Gershwins' first show together, *Lady Be Good*, from 1924, begins with a brother and sister who have just been evicted from the apartment they share. Rather than despairing, they demonstrate the resilience that New Yorkers admire above nearly everything else: they set up housekeeping on the sidewalk as Dick Trevor (Fred Astaire) cheers up his sister Susie (Adele Astaire) in the show's first number. Although "Hang on to Me" is perilously close to being a Pollyanna song, its syncopated exuberance demonstrated that the musical theater had a new voice, quirky and fragmented in rhythm, assertive and urbane in attitude, and youthful and optimistic in sentiment. After Berlin and Wodehouse, it was the next step forward (George Gershwin and Ira Gershwin, "Hang on to Me," *Lady, Be Good*, 1924). The Gershwins' songs were the anthems of a jubilant New York City coming into the fullness of its magnetism and power; they were writing for Broadway and for New Yorkers. It didn't matter what the songs were about or where they were set in the brothers' fourteen Broadway musicals between 1924 and 1935. In the inventive rhythms of their melodies and their words—in the guise of love songs—they were New York.[30]

3

HARLEM'S RENAISSANCE

For nearly two decades, the Harlem Renaissance burned with the immediacy of hot jazz. You can't pin a starting date on something as elusive as a renaissance, but a century later, you can still detect its beginnings. African American soldiers returning home from World War I assumed that things would be better now that they had proved their patriotism and bravery in France. Quite the contrary. Sarah and Elizabeth Delany described what it was like for their brother, Manross: "All the colored veterans came back just as proud as they could be, strutting around Harlem in their uniforms. Manross and his buddies thought they had proved themselves. They thought they would surely come home and be treated like citizens. . . . Manross said, 'What more do I have to do to prove I'm American, too?'"[1] Black leaders soon concluded that their efforts to improve conditions through education, economics, and politics had failed. In a conscious effort to change white attitudes, they turned to culture instead. At the urging of such figures as the sociologist and editor of the National Urban League's *Opportunity* magazine Charles S. Johnson; the historian, sociologist, and civil rights activist W. E. B. Du Bois; the poet, songwriter, activist, and attorney James Weldon Johnson; the NAACP's Walter White; and the Howard University philosopher Alain Locke, the Harlem Renaissance arose from the premise that arts and letters could transform a society. It was, first and foremost, a literary movement, made possible in part by financial support from Madam C. J. Walker, the first self-made female African American millionaire.

Such notable writers as Langston Hughes, Zora Neale Hurston, Jean Toomer, and Countee Cullen were coming into their own. A newly educated black middle class was growing in size and influence, and sophisticated white readers were ready to take black writers seriously—or so the argument went. After the war, Harlem became the "Mecca of the New Negro,"[2] as a new intelligentsia of writers and artists affirmed racial identity, personal dignity, and equality in a larger white world.[3] Alain Locke observed in 1925 that "the mind of the Negro seems suddenly . . . to be shaking off the psychology of imitation and implied inferiority."[4] This was the uplifting side of the Harlem Renaissance, propelled by a strong sense of social justice and personal morality, and driven by the need of a new generation of black writers to find readers and establish reputations. The Harlem Renaissance embraced a noble but ultimately futile attempt to change America's heart through literature. It didn't stop with poems and novels but soon broadened to include painting and sculpture, photography, theater, modern dance, and classical composition and performance as well. But at its center lay something more raffish—the expression of this new spirit by the songwriters and performers who drew thousands of whites to Harlem after dark. Many more people discovered Fats Waller and Cab Calloway than Hurston and Hughes. Their music was earthier and more irreverent, with a freer, looser spirit than anything whites had heard before.

White society was pretty tame by comparison. The biggest hit from a Broadway show in the years right after World War I was "Alice Blue Gown," performed by a character who is demure despite a tendency to flirt:

> In my sweet little Alice Blue Gown,
> When I first wandered down into town,
> I was both proud and shy,
> As I felt ev'ry eye,
> But in ev'ry shop window
> I'd primp, passing by.
>
> (Harry Tierney and Joseph McCarthy, "Alice Blue Gown," *Irene,* 1919)

That's a long way from songs written in the same year by African American writers, such as Eubie Blake and Noble Sissle's "Gee, I Wish I Had Some One to Rock Me (In the Cradle of Love)" and, in a different frame of mind, Spencer Williams and Clarence Williams's "Ain't Gonna Give You None of My Jelly Roll." Anita Loos, who was publishing short stories and writing film scripts out in Hollywood, said, "How could any epoch boast of passion with its hit song bearing the title, 'When You Wore a Tulip, a Big Yellow Tulip, and I Wore a Big Red Rose'?"[5]

For decades, African Americans referred to Harlem as "Uptown." Something different was going on up there. Harlem after dark was the place for bootleg hooch, casual sex, and cocaine,[6] along with music you couldn't shake. Even during the Thirties, David Grafton wrote, "Harlem was regarded as the next-best thing to an anything-goes madcap heaven in Depression-bound America."[7] Songwriters Milton Ager

Figure 3.1. "Genuine jazz for the Yankee wounded. In the courtyard of a Paris hospital for the American wounded, an American negro military band, led by Lt. James R. Europe, entertains the patients with real American jazz," 1918. Library of Congress, Prints and Photographs Division.

and Jack Yellen captured this decadent side of the Harlem Renaissance in a song they wrote for an early talkie. They recognized Uptown's irresistible electricity ("With your blues! joys! jazz! noise!") and hypnotic allure ("Dark brown Darktown! I hear you cooin' to me"). It drives you "Harlem Mad" (Milton Ager, Jack Yellen, "Harlem Madness," *They Learned About Women,* 1929). However you viewed it, though, the Harlem Renaissance could claim at least three *symbolic* harbingers, all of them inseparable from the musical sound of the city.

For the first of them, David Levering Lewis makes the strong case that people in Harlem heard the first clarion call on the day James Reese Europe and his 369th Regiment (the "Harlem Hellfighters") Army Band returned from France. Before the War, Europe had been Vernon and Irene Castle's musical director and had written their signature "Castle Walk." Daniel Friedman writes that the conductor was also one of George Gershwin's earliest musical influences: "There is a story that in 1905, Gershwin was roller-skating in the streets of Harlem when he heard Europe playing at the Baron Wilkins Club, and this began Gershwin's fascination with African American music."[8] Now, though, as General John Pershing led the triumphant doughboys through the Washington Square Arch and up Fifth Avenue, Europe and his band played and marched with them, past Governor Al Smith in the reviewing stand at Sixtieth Street. People knew about their music and also knew from newspaper reports that these black musicians and their leader had spent 191 consecutive days in the trenches.

Although the parade soon ended, Europe and the band continued to march—up to 100th Street, then west to Lenox Avenue. The sidewalks were thick with people watching, clapping, and moving with the music. It felt as if everybody in Harlem was there. Europe was one of their own. When the band passed an unofficial reviewing stand at 130th Street, in what Lewis calls "the heart of Harlem," the marchers broke into a different kind of song—jubilant and jazzy, celebratory and sexy. There was no mistaking what was on everybody's mind. Major Arthur Little described the scene: "Ranks opened, gait loosened . . . and every fourth soldier of the ranks had a girl upon his arm—and we marched through Harlem singing and laughing."[9]

> Here comes my daddy now (oh pop, oh pop, oh pop.)
> Here comes my daddy now,
> I'll get what I've waited for,
> Get what I'm longing for,
> Here comes my daddy now.
> (Lewis F. Muir, L. Wolfe Gilbert, "Here Comes My Daddy Now (Oh Pop! Oh Pop! Oh Pop!)," 1912)

Although the composer Eubie Blake and the lyricist Noble Sissle were linked more closely to vaudeville and Broadway than the Harlem Renaissance, their most important collaboration sounded the second harbinger. As songwriters and performers, they moved easily between white vaudeville and Broadway musicals and only occasional forays farther uptown. Even so, their major work was *Shuffle Along*, a show that was conventional and even stereotypical on one hand but revolutionary on the other. By 1921, Blake and Sissle came as close to being headliners as black vaudeville performers could be on bills where all the other acts were white. Determined to avoid any hint of stereotyping, they dressed in tuxedoes with starched dickeys to perform the songs they wrote. But also by 1921, the Broadway stage had systematically excluded African Americans for more than a decade. Jim Crow was not limited to the South. Earlier, such black songwriters as Will Marion Cook, Bob Cole, Paul Laurence Dunbar, James Weldon Johnson, J. Rosamond Johnson, Bert Williams, and George Walker had contributed songs and scores to such Broadway musicals as *Clorindy, or The Origin of the Cake Walk* (1898), *Sally in Our Alley* (1902), *In Dahomey* (1903), *Abyssinia* (1906), and *Bandanna Land* (1908). By 1910, though, Williams was the only African American working on Broadway. He was the exception because he was so popular with white audiences and because he appeared in the *Ziegfeld Follies.* Only a producer as powerful as Florenz Ziegfeld could have gotten away with making a black man into a star.

When Blake and Sissle met the comedians Fluornoy E. Miller and Aubrey Lyles backstage at a 1920 NAACP benefit, they agreed to challenge the exclusion of blacks from Broadway by collaborating on a new musical. Miller and Lyles slapped together a plot from reworked versions of their routines, and Blake and Sissle wove a batch of old and new songs into a score. Although the show opened without publicity on May 23, 1921, in a dilapidated auditorium nearly a mile north of Broadway's action, word of mouth soon had audiences seeking out Daly's 63rd Street Theatre. In the middle of Manhattan, Miller and Lyles' ramshackle plot played out in Jimtown, a small town in the rural South, inhabited entirely by blacks. The show lasted for 464 performances, a long run for the time. More important, Broadway producers never again systematically excluded African Americans from the theater, although black songwriters and performers would face different forms of discrimination through the twenties and beyond.[10]

Shuffle Along's success at returning African Americans to Broadway was enough to make it revolutionary. Yet Blake and Sissle's appealing score combined the old-fashioned with the modern. The company took to calling it "a musical melange."[11] The titles of such songs as "Bandana Days," "Sing Me to Sleep, Mammy Dear," and "In Honeysuckle Time (When Emmaline Said She'd Be Mine)" are enough to call up memories of the minstrel songs that had demeaned African Americans during the nineteenth century. But Sissle and Blake also wrote some modern songs that combined jazz, dancing, and sex ("Just because I like to do a wiggle / In a regular Salome style"; Eubie Blake and Noble Sissle, "I'm Just Simply Full of Jazz," *Shuffle Along*, 1921), and up-to-date urban blues ("It's not because I'm broke with all my clothes in pawn"; Eubie Blake and Noble Sissle, "Lowdown Blues," *Shuffle Along*, 1921), along with some lively vaudeville tunes, most notably "I'm Just Wild About Harry." In a plot about a small town's mayoral campaign, "Harry" is the campaign song for the one honest candidate. He wins both the election and the girl by the final curtain.

Of equal importance, Blake and Sissle's score includes two romantic love ballads, "Everything Reminds Me of You" and "Love Will Find a Way":

> When in the blues of the skies,
> I see the blue of your eyes,
> In the trilling song of a bird,
> Your voice is heard,
> It thrills me, stills me,
> With love anguish fills me.
> (Eubie Blake and Noble Sissle, "Everything Reminds Me of You," *Shuffle Along*, 1921)

> Dry each tear-dimmed eye,
> Clouds will soon roll by,
> Though fate may lead us astray,
> My dearie, mark what I say,
> Love will find a way.
> (Eubie Blake and Noble Sissle, "Love Will Find a Way," *Shuffle Along*, 1921)

James Weldon Johnson wrote shortly before his death in 1938: "The years have not been many since Negro players have dared to interpolate a love duet in a musical show to be witnessed by white people. The representation of romantic lovemaking by Negroes struck the white audience as somewhat ridiculous; Negroes were supposed to mate in a more primeval manner."[12] Sissle's lyrics changed all that. Despite their stiffness and conventionality, they shattered another stereotype and deepened the ways in which the common humanity of blacks could find expression. In more practical terms, black performers and eventually black songwriters began to move back and forth between Harlem and the Great White Way by the end of the twenties.

The Harlem Renaissance's third harbinger belongs, with more than a trace of irony, to Irving Berlin. He was white and worked on Broadway, where black songwriters would try to make their way over the next two decades. He was also one of the many thousands who occasionally grabbed a cab uptown to see the show at the Cotton Club. His instinct for America's changing attitudes and his ear for its newest sounds rarely failed him. He somehow grasped where his audience would go before it did. So here he was, in 1922, a year after Blake and Sissle revived the syncopated sound of the cakewalk in *Shuffle Along*, helping to set the Harlem of the coming Renaissance to the city's own music.

Berlin's "Pack Up Your Sins and Go to the Devil" sizzles with a combination of mockery and frenetic pleasure. The lyric offers guidance from "a departed man I used to know" to those pursuing a night of pleasure uptown. Berlin sets the lesson in Hades, where fellow revelers are likely to meet; they are, ironically, "the finest of gentlemen and the finest of ladies." The song never mentions Harlem, but I think the setting is unmistakable once Mr. Devil rouses the band to "put a trick in it, / A jazzy kick in it," in a place where "you never have to go to bed at all." The music's frenzied rhythms match the lyric's equally frenzied partying as everyone—"Joneses and Browns, / O'Hoolihans, Cohens, and Bradys"—heads uptown (Irving Berlin, "Pack Up Your Sins and Go to the Devil," *Music Box Revue*, 1922).

African Americans have lived in New York City almost from the start, but it took more than two centuries to turn an area in northern Manhattan into the largest African American neighborhood in the United States. At first, African Americans were scattered all over the city—Astor Place down by Washington Square; then down to Five Points, where the Irish displaced them; then on to Greenwich Village and the Tenderloin in the middle of the nineteenth century; and up near where Lincoln Center stands today as the new century arrived. In those days, people called that last neighborhood either San Juan Hill or the Jungles.[13] Then the push to Harlem began as large numbers of southern and West Indian blacks arrived just before World War I.[14]

Formerly called Uptown by locals, Harlem is generally considered as stretching across Manhattan Island from the East and Harlem Rivers to the Hudson, and from 110th Street (west of Central Park) and Ninety-Sixth Street (east of Central Park) to 155th Street on the north. During the 1920s, important African Americans such as W. E. B. Du Bois, Walter F. White, and Duke Ellington lived in Sugar Hill at Harlem's north end, more than three centuries after three absentee Dutch landlords established farms there that became the area's first permanent settlements. Before that, several Lenape tribes had done some farming nearby, although they were generally nomadic. In 1660, the despotic, one-legged Peter Stuyvesant, the last Dutch director general of New Netherland, formally incorporated the settlement as Nieuw Haarlem, after the city in the Netherlands.

When the British took control of New Netherland in 1664, they tried to change Haarlem's name to Lancaster, but it never caught on. Instead, the area adopted the English spelling "Harlem" and, by the middle of the eighteenth century, had become a country resort for wealthy New Yorkers. Because the British burned it during the Revolution and because it was so far out of the way, it grew more slowly than the rest of Manhattan in the first decades of the new republic. An economic boom after the Civil War and the eventual opening of subway lines drew more and more people, among them African American laborers who had joined the Great Migration (ca. 1915–70) to escape Jim Crow in the South and find better-paying jobs for themselves and a better education for their children. The final decades of slavery, followed by Emancipation and the struggle for acceptance and equality, led eventually to the "New Negro" and the Harlem Renaissance of the 1920s and 1930s. Harlem became the mecca of the "New Negro," as a new intelligentsia of writers and artists affirmed racial identity, personal dignity, and equality in a larger white world.[15]

When property values plummeted during the Panic of 1873, New York City annexed Harlem. The annexation and the recovery from the panic led to another real estate boom. Developers couldn't build row houses fast enough for a surging population—until they very quickly reached a saturation point. Down went real estate values once again. This time the resulting drop in rentals drew Italians and European Jews. In 1860, Harlem had twelve Jewish residents. By 1915, it had two hundred thousand. By the 1920s, one hundred thousand Italians also lived there, three times as many as in Lower Manhattan's Little Italy.[16]

Jonathan Gill writes, "Starting with the arrival of eleven Africans in chains in New Amsterdam in 1626, the search for freedom by Manhattan's blacks was inextricably linked to real estate."[17] A few blacks had lived in the area from the very beginning, but mass migration from the South began in the first years of the twentieth century after yet another real estate crash. Landlords could not find enough white renters willing to move so far uptown, but newly arrived blacks from the South were desperate to find decent places to live despite the high rents.[18] In 1910, Central Harlem was 10 percent black. A year or two after the crash of 1929, it was 70 percent black, but 25 percent of its labor force was out of work. On the side streets off Seventh Avenue, people lived in poverty. They couldn't have afforded a night at the Cotton Club even if its mobster owner had been willing to let them in.

Despite the poverty, Harlem had seductive glamour in the twenties, a time of widespread prosperity and growth, but they were soon followed by the thirties, a time of struggle and deepening poverty. Through both decades, the Harlem Renaissance found its voice, first in a time of flowering and then in the fight to survive that eventually doomed it in the thirties.

Both the neighborhood and its urban black sensibility helped to define Harlem's most distinctive songs. During the century between the minstrel shows that lasted from the 1830s to the turn of the twentieth century, and the rise of African American songwriters and performers during the Harlem Renaissance, stands the socially and culturally degrading "coon song." Written mainly but not exclusively by white songwriters, it was popular from about 1890 to 1920, roughly overlapping the beginning of the Great Migration. The same three decades also saw the beginnings of distinctive voices shaped in part by African American poetry and fiction, but also by African American music. Such composers as Tom Turpin, Charles "Luckey" Roberts, Scott Joplin, and W. C. Handy, and such songwriters as Will Marion Cook, Bob Cole, James Weldon Johnson, J. Rosamond Johnson, and the poet-turned-lyricist Paul Laurence Dunbar strove to portray black experience in popular songs and Broadway musicals in an attempt to counter the caricatures and stereotypes of the minstrel show.

What they began flowered in the songs of Duke Ellington, James P. Johnson, Thomas "Fats" Waller, and Andy Razaf, among others, all denizens of New York City and especially Harlem. Their music was urban, most at home amid the sensual insinuations and broad laughter of Harlem joints, but then fed into the great publishing maw of Tin Pan Alley and, lastly, onto the bright stages of Broadway. From rags to the urban blues and on to jazz, to an urban shaping of American song and sensibility, songs by African American songwriters and performers played an essential role. Alain Locke expressed pleasure at what he observed in Harlem: "not merely the largest Negro community in the world, but the first concentration in history of so many diverse elements of Negro life. . . . In Harlem, Negro life is seizing upon its first chances for group expression and self-determination."[19] It reflected, Jonathan Gill says, "a joyful reinvestment in an ancient African inheritance that suddenly seemed both totally modern and absolutely American."[20]

It sounds like a stretch, but minstrel songs and the blues anticipated the coming of songs that celebrated life in Harlem during the twenties and thirties. In one form or another, they began in the rural South but changed when they moved north. Like the "New Negro," "coon songs" and the urban blues found their footing in cities. As African Americans adapted to northern city life, so did the songs that portrayed them—by black and white songwriters alike. At the same time, the songs of the Harlem Renaissance rejected coon songs but embraced the urban blues.

The implied setting of minstrel songs was the plantation during slavery. They describe full moons shining on lazy rivers while "darkies" strum banjos contentedly after a day of picking cotton. Despite their differences, minstrel songs and coon songs had much in common. Coon songs derived from minstrel songs; both feast on stereotypes of African Americans. They portray blacks as lazy, dishonest, and dim witted: they steal chickens, would rather eat watermelon than work, and ape their betters. In minstrel shows, they appear as mischievous children rather than chattel. In coon songs, though, they are pretentious and foolish. Descended from Zip Coon, a minstrel caricature of a dandy who moved North only to become "uppity," male and female characters in coon songs bedeck themselves in garish jewelry and strut down the street on a Saturday night. Coon songs condescendingly treat their attempts at good manners and respectability as a joke. Even their clergymen are fools, thieves, and seducers in such songs as "De

Congregation Will Please Keep Their Seats (Kase Dis Bird Am Mine)" (1900) and "It Takes a Long Tall Brown-Skin Girl to Make a Preacher Lay His Bible Down" (1917). The minstrel show's Mr. Interlocutor, descended in spirit from a kindly slave owner, keeps such rambunctious children as Mr. Bones and Mr. Tambo under control, but in post-Emancipation coon songs, these characters are left to their own devices, and thus become figures of endless mockery in songs whose comic titles and lyrics undermine personal dignity and the capacity for romantic love: "You Ain't de Kind of Coon I'se Looking Fo'" (1898), "You're Gwine to Get Somethin' What You Don't Expect" (1910), and "I Want a Coon to Match My Own Complexion" (1898).

When the Great Migration carried African Americans north, popular songs followed. Blacks brought their music from the South, but Tin Pan Alley was also ready to make room for them, though more as characters within songs than as a market—at least for now. The minstrel show's rambunctious but ultimately submissive "black boys"—named Tambo and Bones, evocative of slave names but given the ironic title of "Mister"—changed in New York. To the familiar stereotypes of minstrel songs, mostly white songwriters added the image of the razor to spin new coon-song tales of drinking, hustling, gambling, and fighting. The audience for these offensive songs was entirely white. In "Brother Low Down," a preacher ironically named "Low Down," preaches on street corners to "satin blacks," "choc'late browns," "old pool sharks," "card players," and "bootleggers." When they refuse to ante up for his collection, what started as a comic portrait turns ominous. "'Cause you know I totes a razor," Low Down reminds them, "and I wields a wicked blade" (Al Bernard, Larry Briers, "Brother Low Down," 1921). "I'm Gwine to Kill a Coon" anticipates a fight between a woman's lover and "a race horse nigger" he's jealous of: "If he trifles with ma baby as sure my name is Brown, / I'se gwine to carve enough meat from that darky's head for to feed all the dogs in town" (Dave Barton, "I'm Gwine to Kill a Coon," 1898). Anger, resentment, and threat replaced the gentler sentiments of the sentimental ballads that white audiences had become accustomed to in the nineteenth century.

Minstrel and coon songs alike rely on stereotypes of appearance, behavior, and language. They spew such racial epithets as "darky," "pickaninny," and the loathsome "nigger" without a trace of self-consciousness in such songs as "If the Man in the Moon Were a Coon" (1907), "De Darkie's Jubilee" (1897), "Pickaninny, It's Time You Was in Bed" (1906), and "Did You Ever Hear a Nigger Say 'Wow?'" (1890). Their lyrics use an exaggerated version of rural southern black dialect: the language of subservience suited to life on a plantation during slavery. Even in a restrained minstrel song like "Carry Me Back to Old Virginny" (1878), James A. Bland, a free-born African American, relied on standard English except for such words as "Virginny" and "Massa," and such black grammatical constructions as "this old darkey's heart am longed to go." But the song is also troubling. The lyric portrays an aged black man who longs to return to the plantation to live out his days and then be buried with "Massa and Missis": "There we'll be happy and free from all sorrow, / There's where we'll meet and we'll never part no more." As in a number of earlier minstrel songs (including Stephen Foster's 1851 "Old Folks at Home"), the view of a former slave is sympathetic but also affirms the domestic virtues of slavery.[21]

Although whites wrote most coon songs for white audiences, some important coon songs had black composers and lyricists. Regardless of who wrote them, the music was syncopated, the lyrics were slangy and conversational, and respectable middle-class families deemed many of them acceptable for the piano in the parlor.[22] In this coon song by black writers, though, the language's surface condescension disguises a different sort of attitude. Like many of the other songs that invite black people to step out for a joyful evening of dancing—among them Shelton Brooks's "Darktown Strutters' Ball" (1917)—Will Marion Cook and Paul Laurence Dunbar's "Darktown Is Out Tonight" captures the rich mix of the urban African American experience before white revelers began to crowd Harlem in the 1920s. The potential for violence darkens the otherwise celebratory atmosphere:

> Warm coons a-prancin',
> Swell coons a-dancin',
> Tough coons who'll want to fight;
> So bring 'long yo blazahs,
> Fetch out yo razahs,
> Darktown is out tonight!

But Cook and Dunbar's point supersedes the danger. This is a night to "Jine dis promenade! / Tek mah ahm, / What's de harm? / Needn't be afraid!" because "White fo'ks yo' got no sho'; / Dis heh's Darktown's night" (Will Marion Cook and Paul Laurence Dunbar, "Darktown Is Out Tonight" *Clorindy; or, The Origin of the Cakewalk*, 1898).

Writers routinely used similar language in such coon songs as "Hol' Me Down, I'se Gwine to Fly" (1891), "How I Lubs Dat Gal Ob Mine" (1899), and "I Ain't Gwine Ter Work No Mo'" (1900). But songs about "mammies" and infant "pickaninnies" persisted with the same kind of touching sentimentality that a white audience of the time might have assumed exists between a white mother and her infant. "Mammies" and their children played an important role in the most sympathetic coon songs: "Mammy's Pickaninny Boy" (1896). "You'se Honey to Yo' Mammy Just de Same" (1899), and "Mammy's Lt'l Choc'late Cullud Chile" (1919). Audiences found it easier to accept songs that portrayed African American maternal love than romantic love between an African American man and woman, especially since the stereotype of the mammy and her affectionate rearing of white children had played an important role in the South's myth of itself deep into the years before the Civil War.

In addition to writing coon songs and Broadway scores, African American songwriters began to write in a new way at the turn of the twentieth century. As in coon songs, the settings and attitudes were urban, and the lyrics relied on familiar stereotypes, including the now-common razor. Everybody in the all-white audiences got the jokes, but the way that black songwriters used stereotypes made it possible to depict black people and their lives with a deceptive honesty and disguised realism that anticipated the songs of the Harlem Renaissance. In the first two decades of the twentieth century, no one was more important to that task than the songwriter-performer Bert Williams. By the time he wrote and performed "The Darktown Poker Club" in 1914, he had replaced the grotesquely overstated performing style of the minstrel show with his own subtle, understated way of presenting his material.[23] In "The Darktown Poker Club," he tells the story of Bill Jackson, who loses money steadily until he realizes that someone is cheating. He doesn't name the person but he does announce to the men around the table, "Well, you see this nice new razor, / I had it sharpened just today" (Bert Williams, Will H. Vodery, and Jean Havez, "The Darktown Poker Club," 1914).

Williams never threatened white audiences, but he was never a clown or buffoon despite his clown-like costume. In the complex character he played, he achieved what the poet Marianne Moore called "spiritual poise."[24] He appeared in the *Ziegfeld Follies* and several early all-black musicals as a city dweller and a mocker of fashion in his ragged frock coat and well-worn top hat and shoes.[25] He called the

Figure 3.2. Bert Williams in costume ca. 1910, when he was starring in the *Ziegfeld Follies.* Courtesy of the Charles L. Blockson Afro-American Collection, Temple University Libraries, Philadelphia, PA.

character he portrayed a "Jonah Man," a metaphor modeled on Jonah, a minor biblical prophet. The Jonah Man is the unluckiest man in the world, someone largely resigned to his fate. The white songwriter J. Russel Robinson and the white entertainer Ted Lewis collaborated on a song that began, "Not since those bygone days of old Jonah, / Has a person had such luck as mine" (Ted Lewis and J. Russel Robinson, "Unlucky Blues," 1920). A Jonah Man often appears to be deferential but Williams's subtext of self-awareness and defiance undermines any trace of submissiveness or self-pity. Yet an awareness of suffering lies even deeper. Williams once said of a Jonah Man that if it rained soup, he'd be holding a fork. In her biography of Williams, Camille Forbes explains the depth of his treatment of this stereotype: "Not merely miserable or unlucky, the unfortunate Jonah Man was contemplative. He communicated the experience of the wretched."[26] Williams first adopted this character that he would play for the rest of his career in "I Am a Jonah Man,"[27] the first of many musical tales of woe (Alex Rogers, "I Am a Jonah Man," *In Dahomey*, 1903), but it received its fullest expression two years later in "Nobody" (Bert Williams and Alex Rogers, "Nobody," *Abyssinia*, 1905).

God commands the biblical Jonah to travel to Nineveh to warn its people to repent. Stubborn and defiant, Jonah flees by ship. God sets out to teach him a lesson. Jonah ends up in the belly of a giant fish, then agrees to go to Nineveh. He convinces the city to repent, then sits by a wall outside Nineveh, fearing its destruction. Williams doesn't blame his plight on divine intervention, but "I'm a Jonah Man" does begin, "My hard luck started when I was born." The character doesn't explain why, but he knows it to be true. When a friend gives him a six-month meal ticket, he runs to the restaurant, only to find that it has just burned down.

Bad luck can happen to anyone, but the image of the Jonah Man applies especially to African Americans, released from bondage only to face the dangers and degradations of Jim Crow. Whites laughed at the stereotype, but the sly irony of Williams's performance allowed him to transcend race to reach a level of sympathetic common humanity: "Why am I dis Jonah I sho' can't understand, / But I'm a good substantial full fledged real first class Jonah man."

"Nobody" was an even more powerful song and became Williams' signature. He sang it so often that he came to detest it. "Before I got through with 'Nobody,'" he said, "I could have wished that both the author of the words and the assembler of the tune had been strangled or drowned."[28] In part, he was talking about himself, "the assembler of the tune." It was the kind of comment one might expect from someone familiar with the Jonah Man. Williams's manner onstage was conversational but diffident. He half talked, half sang in a quietly doleful voice that suggested he bore a burden both personal and historical.

He often sounded like a detached observer as he searched his pockets for a notebook. He would start to sing as he turned the pages almost in slow motion until he found what he wanted: "Who soothes my thumpin', bumpin' brain? . . . / Nobody." Williams would draw out the long "o" in "nobody" to draw a laugh but also to suggest the weight of his burden. And then the anger would surface just as quietly, hidden by the tone of his singing and by the lyricist Alex Rogers' wordplay: "And until I get somethin' from somebody, sometime, / I don't intend to do nothin' for nobody no time"[29] (Bert A. Williams and Alex Rogers, "Nobody," *Abyssinia,* 1905).

As the frustrations and failures mount, Williams's Jonah Man meets all of them with the same understated wit. The troubles take many forms, but nothing weighs as heavily as poverty. As one Jonah Man concludes, "It's all goin' out an' nothin' comin' in" (Bert Williams, George Walker, "When It's All Goin' Out and Nothin' Comin' In," 1902). Another Jonah bemoans his lot, because "the good things all run out before they get to me." If something good does come his way, it usually passes him by. He's learned to be content:

> "Gimme de leavins" when you get through,
> Jes' gimme de leavins'
> And dat will do
> Man wants but little bit here below,
> Smaller my little bit seems to grow,
> I got so now I don't look for no mo'
> Dan de leavins'
> Gimme de leavins.
> (Bob Cole and James Weldon Johnson, "Gimme De Leavins," 1904)

That same understated resentment also takes form as a comment on whites. Even as popular a black man as Williams needed to handle this kind of dig carefully—with humor, self-effacement, and wry thoughtfulness. It had to be less an attack than a rueful observation. Williams and his fellow songwriters found a range of targets, all of them treated with humor. This lyric reminds Americans who wish they had a royal title that "Ham was a king in ancient days" and all blacks are (legendarily) the sons of Ham. That explains, he says ironically, why whites treat their black servants so well: "Fu' dat coon may be a king" (John H. Cook, E. P. Moran, and Paul Laurence Dunbar, "Evah Dahkey Is a King" *In Dahomey,* 1902). Elsewhere, another Jonah who struggles with poverty—the most common theme in these songs—tries his best to get ahead, but "my money is just like de sand 'cause it sho' gets away from me." No matter what he tries—from buying an ice-cream parlor to becoming an inventor—"when I think of money, / Oh, I wonder where and how / De white folks get so much of it! / Oh, Oh, I got de headache now!" (Bert Williams and George Walker, "I Got De Headache Now: A Darkey Lamentation," 1900).

The most overt of these songs is also the most unusual. The Jonah doesn't speak. The lyric consists of observations from other African Americans, and this time Jonah is a woman. The tone is disapproving, even mocking, but because an African American performed it for a white audience, it's also confusing and deferential—or so one might be tempted to believe. Nobody ever said that race in America lacked irony and ambiguity. By mocking the Jonah woman for becoming "uppity," the observers also mock whites. Since staying at the big hotel as a white woman's maid, Miss Sally Horn has been putting on airs. She prefers to dine on "humming birds hearts" rather than chicken "boiled or fried"; she no longer sings "the Swanee river" but "warbles 'Il Trovatore"; and, most telling of all, she uses irons to straighten her hair and "kalsomine to help to make her fair." The observers draw their conclusion from this devastating portrait that leaves no one unscathed: "She's getting mo' like the white folks ev'ry day" (Bert Williams and George Walker, "She's Getting Mo' Like the White Folks Every Day," 1901).

~ ~ ~

Hudson "Huddie" Ledbetter, known as Leadbelly, begins his recording of "Good Morning, Blues" with as good a description of the blues as I know: "Ya' can't sleep, what's the matter; the blues has gotcha. Ya' get up you sit on the side of the bed in the mornin'. May have a sister a mother a brother 'n' a father around, but you don't want no talk out of 'em. What's the matter; the blues has gotcha'. When you go in put your feet under the table look down at ya' plate got everything you wanna eat, but ya' shake ya' head you get up you say, 'Lord I can't eat I can't sleep what's the matter?' The blues gotcha."[30] And then he begins to sing, because rather than reporting on despair or wallowing in it, the blues exorcises it.[31] It doesn't become a mere Pollyanna music, but it does provide an oppressed people with an outlet for survival with spirit intact. This was never clearer than in the urban, or city, blues of the 1920s. A traditional blues lays out its tale in three-line stanzas: the first line, the first line closely repeated, and then the third line that advances the story or point of view:

> I couldn't sleep last night, I was turning from side to side.
> Oh Lord, I was turning from side to side.
> I wasn't sad, I was just dissatisfied.
> (Alan Lomax, Leadbelly, Good Morning, Blues," 1941)

The blues changed when it moved to the city. Originally an indigenous black music whose most important theme was the loss or betrayal of love, it now cast off its traditional structure and broadened its subject matter. At the same time, it also became a national music by becoming a performance music. No one played a more important role in that transformation than the musician, orchestra leader, and composer W. C. (William Christopher) Handy. Although his father was a preacher who believed that musical instruments were the tools of the devil, young William sang in the church choir and wrote later that he found inspiration in natural sounds: "As I grew older, I added the saxophonic wailing of the moo-cows and the clarinets of the moody whippoorwills. All built up within my consciousness a natural symphony. This was the primitive prelude to the mature melodies now recognized as the blues. Nature was my kindergarten."[32] Yet even though he spent his formative years in small cities and towns mainly in the South, the most compelling images in his most important blues are urban—"Memphis Blues," "Yellow Dog Blues," and, of course, "St. Louis Blues."

Handy learned to play the cornet as he grew up and joined a traveling band that played at the Chicago World's Fair in 1893. He was a trained musician, but a decade later he would learn that "the blues did not come from books. Suffering and hard luck were the midwives that birthed these songs. The blues were conceived in breaking hearts."[33] In 1903, he traveled through Mississippi, conducting a small touring band. One night, in Cleveland, Mississippi, someone asked if he would mind if some local musicians played some of "our native music." Handy found what they played repetitive and monotonous but also haunting. When they finished, "A rain of silver dollars began to fall around the outlandish, stomping feet. . . . Then I saw the beauty of primitive music. . . . Their music wanted polishing, but it contained the essence. Folks would pay money for it. . . . That night a composer was born, an *American* composer."[34] Handy borrowed from traditional blues—this "primitive music"—when he began to compose. Among his borrowings were the repetition of the first line in a chorus—"I hate to see de ev'nin' sun go down, / Hate to see de ev'nin' sun go down" (W. C. Handy, "St. Louis Blues," 1914)—as well as conventional rural imagery—"Oh, that melody, sure appealed to me, / Just like a mountain stream rippling on it seemed" (W. C. Handy, "Memphis Blues," 1912). Despite the elements of traditional, rural blues that often appeared in his work, he set most of his best-known compositions in places like Memphis and St. Louis, and his strongest imagery had an urban bent. His rural imagery felt more like a useful borrowing and less like a direct response to experience. His city references, on the other hand, have the taste of believable emotion, especially for an urban African American audience.

> St. Louis woman, wid her diamon' rings
> Pulls dat man roun' by her apron strings.
> (W. C. Handy, "St. Louis Blues, 1914)

> Love is like a hydrant, it turns off and on,
> Like some friendships when your money's gone,
> Love stands in with the loan sharks when your heart's in tongs.
> (W. C. Handy, "Loveless Love," 1921)

When Handy was traveling through Mississippi in 1903, Gertrude "Ma" Rainey, known as the "Mother of the Blues," became one of the first to perform the blues onstage for money. She also broadened the blues' subject matter and point of view. Before long, a generation of extraordinary female singers was touring the country to sing the blues—Bessie Smith ("Empress of the Blues"), Trixie Smith, Mamie Smith, Ida Cox, Victoria Spivey, Sippie Wallace, young and skinny Ethel Waters (who billed herself as "Sweet Mama Stringbean" when she first broke into show business in 1913), and Alberta Hunter, among others. They worked mainly in a circuit of black-owned vaudeville theaters known as the Theatre Owners Booking Association; the underpaid African American performers reviled TOBA and preferred to call it "Tough On Black Asses." In theaters from the East Coast as far west as Oklahoma, their bawdy irreverence, blunt sexuality, overheated emotionalism, and defiant independence were outspokenly urban in spirit. The loss of love will always play a major role in the blues, and the rural South will always provide a setting, but these singers turned the women they sang about into women to be reckoned with. Soon, the attitudes of the urban blues found their way to Tin Pan Alley, where songwriters absorbed the blues singers' way of looking at the world. "Fifty-Fifty" isn't a blues, urban or otherwise, but its attitude derives from what the earliest urban blues had begun to say with conviction and humor. In a song by two African Americans, a woman lays it out for her man:

> I'm gettin' even, it's even-steven,
> I'm wise to your lies 'cause you opened up my eyes.
> It you want to get along and be a friend of mine,
> It's gotta be fifty-fifty all of the time.
> (Chris Smith and Jim Burris, "Fifty-Fifty," 1914)

The women of the urban blues embrace worldliness emphatically. A later example from the Harlem Renaissance, called "Gimme a Pigfoot (and a Bottle of Beer)," tells the tale of Miss Hannah Brown, who joins the rest of Harlem at a Saturday-night rent party where they fill up on corn liquor and strut their stuff. After dancing all night, Hannah has lost none of her moxie. She demands a pigfoot, a bottle of beer, a reefer, and a drink of gin, and warns everyone to hide their razors and guns because the police will be there any minute (Wesley Wilson and Coot Grant, "Gimme a Pigfoot [and a Bottle of Beer]," 1933). With its provocative tone, raucous humor, and references to drugs and razors, the song is obviously urban. The place and the people sound dangerous as they demonstrate the link between the urban blues and the coon songs that had originally staked out an urban setting that distinguished them from the earlier minstrel songs. But unlike the white composers and lyricists who wrote most coon songs, black songwriters wrote the urban blues about black life for black audiences. Blacks found coon songs repugnant, but the urban blues confirmed its distinctiveness in the way it spoke to black people and found its voice in the new assertiveness of women that accompanied bohemianism in Greenwich Village, suffrage, and the Harlem Renaissance.

James Weldon Johnson knew what a night in Harlem was like before the Great Depression broke the spirit of the Harlem Renaissance. In addition to winning recognition as an author, teacher, and activist, Johnson had worked as a professional lyricist. He embraced the highest aspirations of the Harlem Renaissance, but he had also made a living on Broadway and in Tin Pan Alley. He was eager to see writers like Hurston and Hughes succeed, but he also believed that Harlem in the twenties was the apotheosis of city life, a place where people from everywhere danced "to such jazz music as can be heard nowhere else; and they get an exhilaration impossible to duplicate. . . . [G]ay crowds skipping from one place of amusement to another, lines of taxicabs and limousines standing under the sparkling lights of the entrances to the famous nightclubs, the subway kiosks swallowing and disgorging crowds all night long—gives the impression that Harlem never sleeps and that the inhabitants thereof jazz through existence."[35] Some of the people Johnson was writing about were white; they had no idea that jazz—or "jass"—was black slang for sex. An anecdote, perhaps true, has floated around for years. Asked if he played jazz, Louis Armstrong supposedly answered with a mocking question of his own, "Are you asking me do I jass?" Jazz in the twenties was hot. Its heat rose from the music's insistent syncopation, where something hot in another way, something implicitly sexual, also lurked. Instead of Tin Pan Alley's clever wink, Harlem gave its visitors an eyes-wide-open, earthy growl. It was the low-down alternative to the claim to dignity and equality by the "New Negro."

When Prohibition went into effect on January 16, 1920, black jazz musicians raced to Manhattan. Bars were closing all over the country, but the saloons and nightclubs stayed open in Harlem, and new ones were opening every day. Where clubs, music, and dancing went, jazz followed—to clubs where black customers were excluded, others where the races mingled,[36] and still a few others where blacks had the music to themselves. As southern blacks filled Harlem's apartments, Alain Locke, in "The New Negro," distinguished them from the writers and thinkers he relied on to lift his race, but also counted on their embrace of jazz to spread "Negro" culture throughout America. Jazz, he explained, was three quarters American Negro but an essential one-quarter American. "In Harlem," he wrote, "Negro life is seizing upon its first chances for group expression and self-determination."[37] Despite his approval of the way that "Negroes" had begun to embrace the arts, Locke omitted the importance of African American songwriters who, ironically, set out to appeal to broad audiences, and performers and jazz musicians who worked in clubs that kept blacks out.

The well-heeled whites flocking to Harlem night after night were searching for the "authenticity" of being black in America. Many whites believed that blacks were freer and that their true selves lurked just beneath a recently acquired veneer of civilization. It must have felt thrilling to squirm to Duke Ellington's "jungle music" or sway along with Cab Calloway's liquid moves, but it was also danger on the safe side, a fantasy of black experience and sexuality.[38] The Cotton Club and the nearby Plantation Club decorated their stages so they looked like the Old South, with cotton plants, slave cabins, and—at the Plantation—real live mammies.[39] But most of the decor emphasized a combination of the primitive and the upscale. Downtown whites also had a taste for "jungle decor," so the Cotton Club obliged with artificial palm trees along with its expensive fixtures and table settings.[40]

Harlem was roughly four miles north of Times Square, but in the 1920s, it was as exciting as Broadway, an up-to-date urban Jimtown reimagined for the city. Young Americans found it electrifying to dance and drink (despite Prohibition), and watch the "bronze beauties" in the Cotton Club chorus strut their stuff, to sit amid all those exotic dark-skinned performers, packed in so tightly you could hear the singers breathe and see the dancers sweat. Lena Horne said, "The shows had a primitive naked quality that was supposed to make a civilized audience lose its inhibitions."[41] A Cotton Club dancer named "Stretch" Johnson acknowledged the sophistication of the revues but also understood that "they were cloaked in primitive and exotic garb. . . . They were top-flight performances designed to appease the appetite for a certain type of black performance. . . . And while it wasn't stated as such, certainly the light color of the flesh gave it a kind of exoticism and forbidden-fruit quality."[42]

In "Harlem Sweeties," the poet Langston Hughes praises the many skin tones of African American women, from "caramel" and "honey-gold" to "Ginger, wine-gold, / Persimmon, blackberry," as he strolls down "luscious, / Delicious, *fine* Sugar Hill."[43] Such a range of browns, even though the Cotton Club's dancers, known as the "Copper-Colored Gals," couldn't be darker than a brown paper bag.[44] Black women's skin color, long a standard of beauty among African Americans, played an important part in the wooing of white audiences as well. The most obvious distinctions at the Cotton Club kept blacks outside, in the kitchen, or onstage. Whites made up the audience. On the inside, though, distinctions were subtler. Male dancers could be any shade of brown, but all the chorus girls had light skin (known as "high yaller"), which was considered sexier and more appealing to whites. The title of Duke Ellington's "Black and Tan Fantasy" refers to this double standard.[45] As the anthropologist Michele Wallace wrote, a black woman was considered beautiful only "if her hair was straight, her skin light, and her features European."[46] References to skin color in lyrics were most common in coon songs but also persisted through the Harlem Renaissance in such songs as "Copper-Colored Gal of Mine," (1936) "She's Tall, She's Tan, She's Terrific," (1937) and "Tan Manhattan" (1941).

The twenties were also the decade when Sigmund Freud and his science of psychoanalysis first intrigued the popular imagination, mainly of urban whites who came to see blacks as creatures of the id. The stereotypes of the nineteenth century—the buffoon blessed with natural rhythm, the loyal mammy, the promiscuous Jezebel, the child-like savage[47]—didn't disappear, but they did reorient themselves. The shenanigans were suggestive rather than confrontational. The lyricist Noble Sissle wrote with a bawdy wink, "If you've never been vamped by a brown skin, / You've never been vamped at all" (Eubie Blake and Noble Sissle, "If You Haven't Been Vamped by a Brown Skin," *Shuffle Along*, 1921). The crude stereotype of the black sexual predator became partly subsumed in entertainment and performance: in the defiant sexuality of women in the urban blues, the exuberance of tap dancing, and the humor of double-entendre songs. Whites wrote many of the songs about Harlem, but black composers and lyricists began to force their way in by imitating Tin Pan Alley in such songs as "Sweet Georgia Brown" (Maceo Pinkard, Ben Bernie, and Ken Casey, 1925) and "S'posin'" (Paul Denniker and Andy Razaf, 1929). Or they wrote songs the Alley couldn't match—angry, loving, or mocking, but always close to the ways blacks looked at their lives. Their titles often smack of recklessness and defiance: Porter Grainger and Everett Robbins's "'Tain't Nobody's Biz-ness If I Do" (1922) and Thomas "Fats" Waller and Andy Razaf's "Doin' What I Please" (1932).

Fats Waller may have spent much of his adult life doing "just what I please," but he ultimately outsmarted only himself. A heavy drinker, he was born in New York City and died on a train on his way back to New York from Los Angeles. He never made it to forty. He often sold his songs to white songwriters for just enough to keep himself in gin; in the early days, he would walk into a music publisher's office and announce, "I'll write you a song for $2.50."[48] But his gifts were as prodigious as his appetites. He once had to provide a song for an all-black Broadway chorus to dance to. The jazz pianist Mary Lou Williams overheard what happened when someone asked him:

> "Have you anything written for this number, Fats? And Fats would reply, "Yeah, go on ahead with the dance, man." Then he composed his number while the girls were dancing.[49]

Unfortunately, he hated the discipline of sustained effort; fortunately, he turned out songs without it, floating effortlessly atop his great talent.

His most important collaborator, Andy Razaf, was an elegant young man when they first met and decided to try writing together. They could not have been more different. Waller's biographer and occasional lyricist, Ed Kirkeby, wrote about them: "Each was the perfect complement to the other in temperament as well as ability. Waller's aims were confined to the needs of the moment—tomorrow would take care of itself. Andy, on the contrary, . . . always kept one eye on the horizon. . . . Certainly Fats needed a serious and careful partner, a check-rein applied lightly to his rollicking didoes. Andy, on the other hand, was immensely inspired by the carefree personality and endless melodic resources of his collaborator."[50]

Waller and Razaf had great success together from the late twenties until Waller's death in 1943, though they wrote their three greatest songs in a single year, 1929: "Ain't Misbehavin,'" "(What Did I Do to Be So) Black and Blue," and "Honeysuckle Rose."[51] That year, the Immerman brothers, a couple of former butchers who owned Connie's Inn, the Cotton Club's main competition, hired Waller and Razaf to write the score for a lavish new revue to be called *Connie's Hot Chocolates.* It was so successful that, a few weeks after its Harlem opening, it moved to Broadway. Renamed *Hot Chocolates,* it played at the Hudson Theater on Broadway at 8:40 and then again, as *Connie's Hot Chocolates,* at Connie's Inn after midnight.

Originally conceived as the show's theme song, "Ain't Misbehavin'" is an unusually evocative song and an exemplar of the kinds of songs that emerged from Harlem as the twenties wound down. Its lyric portrays someone who swears fidelity to an absent lover. The relatively slow to moderate tempo underscores the sadness of separation, but the typical bounce that Waller gave his melodies suggests that other emotions are at play. The person is lonely but also sexually eager. Every use of the title in the lyric emphasizes her desire to do just the opposite. She says she is happy and contented to spend the night listening to the radio, but her pledge along with her contentment as she waits at home alone aren't the whole story. The tone of the song suggests something sad and hot at the same time. She can't wait to get her hands on him.

"(What Did I Do to Be So) Black and Blue" is an unusually provocative song because of the way it exemplifies the sense of pride that Alain Locke attributed to the New Negro. Although it is the Broadway musical's first significant protest song, irony played an important role in its composition. During rehearsals for *Connie's Hot Chocolates*, the mobster Dutch Schultz, who had put up the money for the show, told Razaf that it would be funny to have a scene with a dark-skinned woman lying on a bed in an all-white room. He told Razaf to write a comic song about being too black and losing men to lighter-skinned women. When Razaf told Schultz that he couldn't write that kind of song, the Dutchman held a gun to his head: "You'll write it or you'll never write anything again."

The terrified Razaf told Waller that despite the threat he intended to set a comment on racism to Waller's mournful melody. The result was a spare, elliptical lyric set to music that evoked torch ballads, spirituals, and the blues, but also felt immediate and spontaneous. On opening night, standing at the back of the theater, Razaf was suddenly aware that Schultz was standing next to him. At first, the audience—and Schultz—laughed as actress Edith Wilson sang, "Gentlemen prefer them light," but then she sang, "Cold empty bed, springs hard as lead." Dutch stopped smiling. When the song ended, the audience sat absolutely still for a moment and then leaped to its feet to cheer. Schultz clapped Razaf on the back and walked away.[52]

Hot Chocolates was so successful that the Immermans hired Waller and Razaf for a second revue, *Load of Coal*. To get Waller to settle down to work, Razaf enticed him to his aunt's house in Asbury Park, New Jersey with promises of good food and plenty of it. Moving between the piano and the kitchen, Waller turned out two songs and was halfway through a third designed for a soft-shoe routine. Suddenly, he announced, "I gotta go back to New York. I just remembered I got a heavy date." Nothing Razaf did could dissuade him, even though he had set a partial lyric to Waller's unfinished music. Waller was gone but Razaf continued to work. He finished the lyric and began calling New York to find Waller. Once he had Waller on the phone, he sang what he had written until he reached the bridge. "Give me a tune," he said, "I don't remember that middle eight you wrote for it." Waller hummed; Razaf told him to hold on while he tried it on the piano.

Words and notes fitted. Razaf raced back to the phone to announce, "Got it, Fats, see you tomorrow." There was no reply. Waller had hung up.[53]

The finished song, "Honeysuckle Rose," does have the light touch of a soft-shoe, along with the imagery of flowers and honeybees rescued from triteness by the lyric's use of bawdy if understated wit. It borrows the common imagery of double-entendre songs but softens it. Its wit also buoys up the conversational lyric to make the song sweet, sassy, and stylish. No mean feat, but it's the sass that connects it in spirit to Harlem (Thomas "Fats" Waller and Andy Razaf, "Honeysuckle Rose," *Load of Coal*, 1929).

Harlem's major crossroads remained the intersection of Lenox Avenue and 125th Street. The Cotton Club was farther up Lenox at 142nd Street, and Connie's Inn was over on Seventh Avenue at 131st Street. Downtown types gathered nightly to listen to Ellington, Calloway, Armstrong, Waters, and Adelaide Hall, and to watch Bill Robinson and the Nicholas Brothers, all at the Cotton Club. Connie's Inn featured Armstrong, Waller, the Fletcher Henderson Orchestra, and the one-legged tap dancer Peg Leg Bates. Deborah Grace Winer observed "a peculiar amalgam of racial segregation and a genuine opportunity for black performers to shine and be appreciated by white New York audiences."[54] Like the audiences, the songwriters were also white—Jimmy McHugh and Dorothy Fields at the Cotton Club in the twenties, followed by Harold Arlen and Ted Koehler in the early thirties. They learned fast. Nothing happened faster than syncopating the overheated exoticism of Harlem and its people. The up-tempo songs were buoyant, the romantic songs bluesy and suggestive, as the writers attuned themselves to black singers who, in turn, attuned themselves to white audiences: McHugh and Fields in such songs as "Diga-Diga-Doo" (1928) and "I'm Doin' That Thing" (1930), and Arlen and Koehler in "I Got a Right to Sing the Blues" (1932), "Ill Wind" (1934), "Kickin' the Gong Around" (1931), and "Shakin' the African" (1931), where shifting the accent to the final syllable makes a small risqué joke.

In 1923, Owen "Owney" Madden, a bootlegger with mob ties, had taken over the former heavyweight champ Jack Johnson's failing Club De Luxe and reopened it for whites. He called it the Cotton Club—an unsubtle evocation of the Plantation South—and it became one of the most important nightclubs in the history of American entertainment. In 1935, when the Cotton Club was about to close, a journalist wrote that those who had gone to Harlem were "a combination of high-society aristocrats, nouveau riche entrepreneurs, and celebrities looking for the peculiar exhilaration the rich find in excitement tinged with danger."[55] Thrill-seekers got their excitement without a lot of risk (though not without high prices) because places such as the Cotton Club and Connie's Inn made sure the clientele was almost exclusively white.[56] Most whites came to Harlem to watch blacks, not mix with them. Jimmy Durante said, "It isn't necessary to mix with colored people if you don't feel like it. You have your own party and keep to yourself. But it's worth seeing. How they step!"[57] Meanwhile, Owney Madden's toughs barred the door to interracial couples who tried to talk their way in, as well as the neighborhood folks who hung around to watch the arriving celebrities, among them George Gershwin, Mayor Jimmy Walker (before they arrested him for corruption), the actor George Raft (who had his own mob connections), the bandleader Eddie Duchin, and the heiress Emily Vanderbilt. The Rolls-Royces and Duesenbergs lined up around the block. One night, the muscle turned away the great blues composer W. C. Handy.[58] Jack Johnson, an African American, could not have gotten a table in the club he used to own.

When Lena Horne joined the chorus at sixteen, her grandmother accompanied her each night on the subway, and then waited in the dressing room for the teenager to finish working. She and the other chorus girls couldn't use the bathrooms because they were reserved for the white patrons.[59] Not every club was as elegant or restrictive as Madden's. The Sugar Cane Club, at 135th and Fifth, was dim and damp, and down a flight of stairs. Two dozen tables pushed up against a tiny dance floor, and couples had just enough room to press together and shuffle their feet. People started calling it "dancing on a dime."[60] William Safire defined it as grinding "bodies together in clothed but sexual contact."[61] By 1940, out in Hollywood, the composer Burton Lane and the lyricist Frank Loesser had turned the expression into a romantic ballad describing a couple who dance indiscreetly; there's not even an inch between them (Burton Lane and Frank Loesser, "Dancing on a Dime," *Dancing on a Dime*, 1940). Loesser's lyric calls the close dancing sublime, but there was nothing sublime about the Sugar Cane Club. When whites showed up there and in other unfashionable Harlem bars as well, they called it "slumming."

Langston Hughes wrote about the few joints that catered to customers of both races: "Nor did ordinary Negroes like the growing influx of whites toward Harlem after sundown, flooding the little cabarets and bars where formerly only colored people laughed and sang, and where now the strangers were given the best ringside tables to sit and stare at the Negro customers—like amusing animals in a zoo."[62] Those who populated these clubs found a different kind of experience. A contemporary observer named Stephen Graham wrote, "Tall elegant negresses with carven faces, held by bellicose fighting bulls, sun bonneted mammas with crazy rustic boys, mightily hipped hostesses keeping time by contortioning their buttocks in unison with the males who gripped their waists. . . .[W]hite men dancing with coloured girls, and negroes dancing with white women."[63] It was a long way from the stately Anglo-Saxon beauties of the *Ziegfeld Follies* or even the extravagant stage shows at the Cotton Club. It was more in the spirit of Harlem's bawdiest lyrics (more on that in a moment).

Once upon a time in the late 1920s or early 1930s, a young woman from a small town in the Midwest convinced her parents to let her move to New York City to live and work. I don't remember who told me this story many years ago, and maybe it sounds a little too good to be true, but it serves a purpose. The young woman's parents agreed to finance her for a year as long as she agreed to live at the respectable Barbizon Plaza Hotel for Women and stayed close to one aunt who had chosen a career in the city rather than a more conventional life back home. The aunt met her when she arrived at Grand Central Station. She said, "Dear, we'll check in at the Barbizon and then tonight we can go to Carnegie Hall or the Metropolitan Opera. Which would you like?" Her niece had her answer ready. "I want to go to the Cotton Club," she said.

How did this innocent from the hinterlands know about the Cotton Club? Perhaps because by the midtwenties, David Sarnoff, the first president of RCA, was stringing together several radio stations in temporary networks that soon became permanent. Some of these earliest network broadcasts originated at the Cotton Club, and, according to the jazz musician Jim Cullum, it became "the best venue in the country to introduce a new song."[64] Duke Ellington, whose orchestra began its tenure at the Cotton Club on December 4, 1927, credited these broadcasts with his sudden rise to fame in the late twenties and early thirties.[65] He had started out in Washington, DC, playing sweet music for white society types to dance to, but once he left for New York, he hired the trumpeter James "Bubber" Miley and the trombonist Joe "Tricky Sam" Nanton, who could play what Ellington called a more "jungleistic"—a jazzier—sound.[66] What Ellington himself named "jungle music" grew from Miley's growling trumpet and Nanton's use of a plunger mute. It was insinuatingly hot but with a sense of humor, gravelly and without the polish whites were used to. That's what made it so exciting. On a transcription of a live 1929 broadcast from the Cotton Club, a white radio announcer introduces Ellington as the "greatest living master of jungle music, that rip-roaring harmony hound, none other than Duke Ellington." He ends with the racial condescension typical of the time, "Take your bow, Dukey." The band then plays Ellington's "East St. Louis Toodle-Ooo," an important example of "jungle music." During these same years, Ellington also wrote such instrumentals as "Jungle Nights in Harlem" (1930) and "Echoes of the Jungle" (1931).

Linking African Americans and jazz to something called "jungle music" gets tricky, especially when the term appears only a few years after the rash of "jungle" and "monkey" songs that were so popular between 1907 and 1915. Jazz historians tend to focus on Miley's and Nanton's performing styles and Ellington's composing before he moved on to the impressionistic mood pieces of the early thirties, most notably "Mood Indigo." John Fordham emphasizes Ellington's "then audacious use of multiple themes, key changes, and richly colored textural effects and harmonies."[67] These writers often overlook the long racist history of Tin Pan Alley songs, dating back to the coon songs of the ragtime era, including songs about African natives and amorous monkeys and chimpanzees. Without ever saying so directly, these songs—Bob Cole, James Weldon Johnson, and J. Rosamond Johnson's "Under the Bamboo Tree" (*Sally in Our Alley*, 1902) and Arthur Fields and Walter Donovan's "Aba Daba Honeymoon" (1914) among the best known—are condescending comic portrayals of African Americans despite the appeal of their jaunty melodies and clever lyrics. "Under the Bamboo Tree" deprives blacks of civilization, "Aba Daba Honeymoon" of humanity. The first is a stereotypical love song about a couple of savages who speak "dusky" royalty's version of broken English. They are no threat to anyone. Nor are the monkey and chimpanzee who sing to one another until the "big baboon" marries them and sends them off on their "aba daba honeymoon."

Other "jungle songs" feature animals that form bands to play music that mocks the music of black jazz musicians:

Listen to the Chimpanzee,
On the key, off the key,
Monkey tootsie wootsies,
Dancing hootchie kootchies,
Listen to that Jungle band.
(James Kendis and Alfred Bryan, "Listen to That Jungle Band," 1910)

These relatives of coon songs have titles like "Down in Jungle Town," (Theodore Morse and Edward Madden, 1908) with its suggestive links to Jimtown and Darktown; "Monkey Jubilee" (James White, 1915), with its use of "Honkey, honkey, honkey, tonkey, tonkey, tonkey, won't you be my blushing bride?"—nonsense syllables to approximate the supposed similarities between a black native's language and a chimpanzee's jabber; and "Cannibal Love," (Harry I. Robinson and Will J. Harris, 1909) with its story of a cannibal who "was spooning with his lady love" in Zululand. Although they tell similar stories of courtships, weddings, and honeymoons, they usually don't use the racist language or distorted dialogue of most coon songs. But they do act on the underlying racist assumption that black people resemble monkeys, chimpanzees, and baboons, both physically and intellectually, and underscore the point in the illustrations on the sheet music covers.

Other songs describe the demure wooing between two Zulus, a warrior and a princess. Her name is usually Lulu because it rhymes with Zulu, and he often wins her by winning a battle first. Typically, she ("a pretty little dark brown maid") and he ("of the tribe of a dark brown shade") sit together making love until he wins her heart and she becomes "a little Zulu bride" (Chas. Kohlman and M. J. Fitzpatrick, "My Zulu Lu," 1903). In some of these songs, the newlyweds set up housekeeping in "a bamboo hut" until Zulu babies come along. The tone is tender, mildly amusing, and slightly condescending, as if the whole episode is a gentle game in which children play at being adults—even though they, like the monkeys in other songs, are old enough to court and marry:

She kept a-shouting from the tree
For his nutty melody
Till the crazy little monkey looked up and said,
"I want to spoon 'neath the monkey honey moon
To the nutty wedding tune, soon."
(Irving Berlin, "That Monkey Tune," 1911)

~ ~ ~

As we've seen, songs typically portray Broadway as both alluring and dangerous. A lot of them describe single women who want to become stars. They are young and innocent—and white. Songs set in Harlem, on the other hand, usually prefer to portray only its allure. The place is usually inviting without being frightening, with few prices to pay beyond a hangover. Harlem in the hands of white songwriters was a place to visit, observe, and describe, perhaps even to feel your way into, but never quite to be part of. Some white songwriters observed it with great skill; others moved extraordinarily close. No black songwriters wrote for the Cotton Club, and no white songwriters came closer than Harold Arlen and Ted Koehler to grasping black sensibilities.

When Arlen and Koehler signed on to write for the Cotton Club in 1930, Arlen had published exactly one significant professional song, his and Koehler's "Get Happy." Yet they felt ready to tackle the job of writing songs for black performers to sing in Harlem to white audiences. Despite his inexperience, Arlen felt closer than any of his songwriting contemporaries to the spirit of Harlem and its people. After the songwriter Roger Edens had the chance to watch Arlen rehearse with the Club's black performers, he wrote, "He was really one of them. He had absorbed so much from them—their idiom, their tonalities, their phrasings, their rhythms—he was able to establish a winning rapport with them."[68] Koehler, a fine carpenter, used to help build the sets while Arlen learned the latest dance steps from the cast and picked up their speech and singing styles.[69] Like Arlen, Koehler also developed a closeness to Harlem and its people; you feel it in his lyrics. From growing up in Newark, New Jersey, and living in New York City, he had an ear for the clipped, almost brusque way city people actually spoke, especially if they were New Yorkers. Almost everything in this song is stated in sharp, syncopated monosyllables, as a stylish gent tells everyone he's broke but happy (Harold Arlen and Ted Koehler, "Happy As the Day Is Long," *Cotton Club Parade of 1934*, 1934).Paul Woodbury observed that Koehler's writing was especially well suited to Arlen's jazz-influenced music: "For Koehler, Arlen's wide-ranging music evoked images of the city streets and the working people with whom he grew up."[70]

Arlen had been drawn to jazz and the blues in his native Buffalo, New York, but in Manhattan he learned some things about how poor African Americans got by: how, for instance, they paid the rent by coming up with the ingenious solution of the rent party. It started a few years before the Harlem Renaissance but was part of the improvisational spirit of the time. You charged anything from a dime to a dollar to get in; then you piled fried chicken, pig's feet, and greens in the kitchen; floated bottles of bootleg hooch in the bathtub; and hired a stride piano player—maybe, if you were lucky, James P. Johnson, Thomas "Fats" Waller, or Willie "the Lion" Smith—to pound an upright for all-night dancing. Smith remembered, "They would crowd a hundred people or more into a seven-room railroad flat and the walls would bulge. . . . When there wasn't a crap game, or poker, going on in the back bedroom, they'd use it for a place to rest up, or sleep it off, or make love. The rent party was the place to go to pick up on all the latest jokes, jive, and uptown news."[71] The music and dancing were fast and loose until dawn when the dancers started doing something close and bent over called the "Monkey Hunch."[72] Frankie Manning said that when the music slowed, "We'd put the lights down low, grab a girl, and just lay her up against a wall."[73] You never knew who'd show up—by reputation, race, even age: "It was only years later that the host of one party realized that the wide-eyed youth from the neighborhood sitting cross-legged by the piano had been a local named George Gershwin."[74] Regardless of who came, odds were that by morning, you had your rent.

In 1932, as the Depression deepened, the number of rent parties increased. The hand-lettered announcements appeared in shops and restaurants, so it didn't take long for Arlen and Koehler to notice them. They already knew that the Cotton Club's patrons responded to songs that, in Jim Haskins's words, "seemed to give them an 'inside look' at that world."[75] The two songwriters soon turned rent parties and the need to pay the rent into a song for the *Cotton Club Parade of 1933*. Their score included a couple of happy-go-lucky Pollyanna songs—"Get Yourself a New Broom (And Sweep the Blues Away)" and "Happy as the Day Is Long"—along with "Stormy Weather," the greatest of all Cotton Club songs. "Raisin' the Rent" managed to swing and be blues-like at the same time. The person in the song is burdened with worries and woes, but Arlen's strong rhythms propel the melody through its taut, sad melodic line. They suit the character's struggle, portrayed in Koehler's equally taut lyric through a mix of self-awareness, worry, and the saving grace of irony. That doesn't mean it's easy. The character is dead broke with no solution in sight. She feels alone because the landlord will be around tomorrow to collect. Finally, she decides to leave. It doesn't make her happy but it's something she can live with. The song is a brooding jazz-tinged look at one aspect of life in Depression Harlem (Harold Arlen and Ted Koehler, "Raisin' the Rent," *Cotton Club Parade of 1933*, 1933).

The differences between two songs about rent parties—"Raisin' the Rent," and Thomas "Fats" Waller, J. C. Johnson, and Andy Razaf's "The Joint is Jumpin'" (1937)—lie in the choices between an exploration of character and mood, and a celebration of survival after an all-night binge. In Arlen and Koehler's song, a sympathetic understanding of the singer's melancholy makes no mention of the all-night party, but the black songwriters who lived and worked in Harlem express the joy and danger of the party itself, as real as it is necessary, as buoyant as it is desperate. To Waller's sassy, strident tune for "The Joint Is Jumpin'," Johnson and Razaf's lyric explodes in bursts of talk that sound as if they come between swigs from a jug. Its drive is the essence of songs about Harlem, especially when the songwriters were African American. No matter what, its speed never flags when they write about their fellow Harlemites—the reminder to pay your way through the door, the admonition to leave your razors outside, and the urge to grab the first pretty girl and start to dance. Even when the police arrive toward dawn, the party keeps moving as the title line recurs through the lyric. The all night frenzy is an escape from poverty and the desperate need to pay each month's rent.

Anyone writing a Cotton Club revue, as Arlen and Koehler did for four years, had to crank out a number of formulaic songs to fit predetermined slots—production numbers, dance numbers, double-entendre songs, smoky ballads, and songs to conjure up the Harlem their white audiences thought they were visiting, with such titles as "A La Lenox Avenue" and "Harlem's Hot as Hades." They also wrote songs that had nothing to do with Harlem but rose to a level of skill and polish that made them some of the best songs of their time—"Stormy Weather," "I've Got the World on a String," "As Long As I Live," and "Between the Devil and the Deep Blue Sea," among others. They then handed them over to African Americans to perform. Maybe it happened because the audience was white and affluent, and was used to hearing songs like these on Broadway. Regardless of the reasons, blacks were now performing them, and that was something new. A decade earlier, when African American performers returned to Broadway after *Shuffle Along,* it would have been almost impossible for white audiences to accept them at that level of sophistication.

Levels of irony abound. Through the years of the Harlem Renaissance, the black songwriters Eubie Blake and Noble Sissle supported themselves by continuing to write songs for Broadway that curried white approval by harking back to the style and feel of the minstrel show, such songs as "Gee, I'm Glad That I'm from Dixie." "Dear Old Southland," and "Bandana Days": "In those dear old Bandana Days, / Cane and cotton ne'er forgotten, Bandana Days." Arlen and Koehler, however, wrote songs that expressed something genuine about Harlem in the present: a place that can drag people down but also lifts them up to offer a respite from the Depression blues. The titles make the point, from the downcast "Wail of the Reefer Man" (Harold Arlen and Ted Koehler, "Wail of the Reefer Man," *Cotton Club Parade of 1932,* 1932) to the pleasures of getting high during bad times in "Harlem Holiday" (Harold Arlen and Ted Koehler, "Harlem Holiday," *Cotton Club Parade of 1932,* 1932).

Songs set in Harlem often tackled the Depression's emotional effect on the people who lived there. These songs written for African American performers interweave hard times, imagined better times, and life in the neighborhood. They may not always name Harlem but they explore the range of its experiences, attitudes, and temptations: a melancholy that spreads from loss and deprivation, but also an urban drive to suggest that the momentary escape is worth grabbing and that better days may be possible, both points of view set somewhere near Lenox Avenue. Those that cut closest to Harlem life in the 1930s are also the darkest songs Arlen and Koehler wrote together. Like many of Arlen's blues-like ballads, as in "I Got a Right to Sing the Blues," they bemoan the bleakness of lost love (Harold Arlen and Ted Koehler, "I Got a Right to Sing the Blues," *Earl Carroll's Vanities,* 1932). Although they wrote the song for a Broadway revue, they applied what they had learned uptown. The lyric's references to the river and sea are generalized images rather than places away from the city; the loss of love creates a pervasive weariness and despair.

Cab Calloway was a black bandleader attired in white tie and tails or an exaggerated zoot suit. His signature song was "Minnie the Moocher," about Minnie who loved a man despite his use of cocaine (Clarence Gaskill, Cab Calloway, and Irving Mills, 1931). Calloway turned this song about drug use into an improbable hit through the use of scatting and audience response—"Hi de hi de hi de ho"—that had nothing to do with the content of the song. His stylistic exaggerations and flamboyant storytelling bleached anything ominous from his performance.

Arlen and Koehler also wrote several songs about drug use for Cotton Club revues. The most important of them—"Minnie the Moocher's Wedding Day," and "Kickin' the Gong Around"—are modeled on "Minnie the Moocher." Arlen and Koehler wrote these songs for Calloway to perform in his outrageously jivey style.

These and other songs about drug use date mainly from the Great Depression. In such an atmosphere, they create a seductive but corrupting netherworld. No radio station could air these songs, although Waller, Calloway, and others wrote and recorded them, and they became widely known in Harlem. Typically, the lyrics to these songs associate getting high with the pleasures of drinking and sex, a temporary escape from cares, and defiance of authority. They make no place for the horrors of heroin or even the low after a high; their enjoyments are everywhere, from the sophisticated ladies ("My, oh my, when they get high / There's danger in their eyes," Chick Webb and Nat Reed, "Holiday in Harlem," 1937) to the dream of "a reefer five feet long" because she's "got to be high before I can swing" (Thomas "Fats" Waller, "You're a Viper," 1927). With their use of drug slang and references to "cokies," "hoppies . . . pickin' poppies," and "kickin' the gong," the songs hint breezily at the dark secret that whites might discover behind Harlem's closed doors (Alexander Hill and Irving Mills, "'Long About Midnight," 1934).

Although such black songwriters as Waller, Razaf, James P. Johnson, and J. Russel Robinson often geared their work toward broad audiences—as did any other Tin Pan Alley songwriters—they also wrote songs that belonged to Harlem. Razaf, the most important African American lyricist of his time, wrote at least three classic Harlem numbers—"The Joint Is Jumpin,'" Keepin' Out of Mischief Now," and "Stomping at the Savoy"—but he also wrote the lyrics for such mainstream standards as "Memories of You" (Eubie Blake, 1930), "Concentratin' on You" (Fats Waller, 1931), and "In the Mood" (Joe Garland, 1938). Although Robinson was nowhere near as well known as Razaf, he was also a highly professional songwriter. In addition to writing "Reefer Man" for Calloway in 1932, he had collaborated with Con Conrad on "Margie," and with Conrad, Sam M. Lewis, and Joe Young on "Singing' the Blues," both in 1920.

Even in their mainstream love songs, these African American writers occasionally included a line or two to suggest that a song's outlook and sensibility originated in Harlem. In "A Porter's Love Song to a Chambermaid," an amusing but surprisingly gentle song by James P. Johnson and Andy Razaf, the porter lists a series of metaphorical connections, including dust pan and broom, clothes pin and "pulley line," and window and window shade. Although the imagery reflects where they stand in the world's scheme of things, the most telling lines are the first: "Though my position is of low degree, / And all the others, they look down on me" (James P. Johnson, Andy Razaf, "A Porter's Love Song to a Chambermaid," 1934). In a much blunter lyric, a man comes home after work, looks in the pot cooking on the stove, and reacts to the mess he sees. Beneath the sound of real people bickering, the song is a sustained double entendre used to describe a large woman with small breasts: "I'm really steamin' / All that meat and no potatoes" (Fats Waller and Ed Kirkeby, "All That Meat and No Potatoes," 1941).[76] Lines that evoke the feel of Harlem are sometimes drug related, always insinuating and high energy.

A shape-shifting irony plays an essential part in America's persistent conversation about race: White songwriters on Broadway or in Hollywood wrote some of the best and most provocative songs about Harlem. By the 1930s, Harlem had insinuated itself into America's imagination, and songwriters knew how to manipulate common assumptions and attitudes to create a point of view. Sometimes those songs were insightful and engaged; sometimes they were nothing more than exercises by professionals doing their job. The white songwriters who had little direct connection to Harlem but wrote about it anyway included Cole Porter ("Happy Heaven of Harlem," *Fifty Million Frenchmen*, 1929), Ray Henderson and Lew Brown ("Home to Harlem," *Strike Me Pink*, 1933), and Jerome Kern and Oscar Hammerstein ("High Up in Harlem," *Very Warm for May*, 1939). Actually, Porter did have an unlikely though limited connection. He and his pal Monty Woolley often sought out gay sex in Harlem (though you'd never know it from Porter's song). Porter's biographer William McNeil observed that Porter could be patronizing toward blacks but he also associated them as many whites of the time did with spontaneity and vigor, qualities he admired.[77]

One of the most significant of these songs by outsiders is Irving Berlin's "Harlem on My Mind." Berlin had a gift for empathy in his songs that he did not always demonstrate in his dealings with other people. He wrote this song expressly for Ethel Waters to introduce in one of the most important Broadway revues of the thirties, his and Moss Hart's *As Thousands Cheer* (1933). Berlin also wrote two more songs for Waters to introduce in the show: the anti-lynching lament "Supper Time" and the bawdy comic number, "Heat Wave." But the story actually begins with Arlen and Koehler's "Stormy Weather," also introduced by Waters at the Cotton Club.

"Stormy Weather" was, without question, Arlen and Koehler's most important song together. The bleak lyric lacks a strong sense of urbanity, but like some other blues-influenced ballads by the same writers, it replaces a sense of place with an image of persistent rain to correspond to the character's despair. Misery, we're told, is everywhere. To deepen the connection, Koehler's lyric alludes to spirituals to hint at the woman's desperation.

Irving Berlin rarely painted the town red. He went to nightclubs only infrequently, and he almost never started to write before midnight. However, he made a point of visiting the Cotton Club to hear Ethel Waters sing "Stormy Weather." As soon as she finished, he went backstage to hire her for *As Thousands Cheer*. Berlin and Hart's revue used a different newspaper headline to precede each scene or number. For example, the headline on the curtain read, "Heat Wave Strikes New York." The curtain opened and Waters sang "Heat Wave," complete with swaying hips. The show's most deeply felt scene portrayed a young mother who cooks dinner in a southern cabin while her children sit at the table awaiting their father's return. The mother, played by Waters, learns that a mob has lynched her husband. In her sorrow, she sings "Supper Time." It may be a rural lament set amid scrubby pines in the Deep South, but Berlin, living and working in New York City, wrote an artful and socially charged song that addressed lynching in the 1930s.

Another song from *As Thousands Cheer*, "Harlem on My Mind" was more typical of its time and is among the most important standards about Harlem. Like so many songs from earlier in the twentieth century, it's about returning. In this case, though, its focus is on longing and melancholy. Most songs about returning want to leave the city for the idyllic life of a small town, but here the singer—a specific singer—wants to return to New York. As a result, the song is both topical and bluesy because the character is Josephine Baker, the star of the

Folies Bergère and the toast of Paris between the wars, and because the return is to Harlem. The result is a witty lament. Its bluesy quality frames the wit, while the wit gives comic bite to the despair. Despite her appeal to Parisian elites and her public ebullience, her heart is blue because, no matter how elegant and refined she's become, she never escapes the simple truth expressed in the song's title: "Harlem on My Mind."

When Berlin hired her, Waters had already appeared in three all-black Broadway revues dating back to 1927, but this was the first time an African American performer received equal billing with whites. When the other featured members of the cast told Berlin just before opening night that they would not take bows with her, he replied that he understood. He would never force them to do anything they didn't feel they could. So, he added, there would no bows at all. That took care of that.

Berlin's stand succeeded because he was Irving Berlin, and because Waters's singing appealed so strongly to white audiences. It could be sassy but it wasn't the kind of "low-down" singing that whites associated with blacks. Her light soprano could caress a ballad but also express the emotion in a powerful lyric like "Supper Time" and, a decade later, in Arlen and E. Y. Harburg's "Happiness Is Just a Thing Called Joe" (*Cabin in the Sky*, 1943). Friends had previously urged her to add mainstream songs to the blues she usually sang. "White people would love you for the rest of your life," the performer Earl Dancer told her. "You don't have to sing as you do for colored people." White audiences responded so favorably that a white theater owner once raised her initial salary of $40 per week to $350 for the rest of a booking. From then on, she typically performed a more varied program—popular and theater songs as well as the blues.[78] The African American struggle for acceptance that began in the aftermath of Emancipation made some of its most visible strides through popular music, first with ragtime, and then with jazz, the blues, and mainstream popular music during the Harlem Renaissance. It was infuriatingly slow and selective, but it moved. It wouldn't have happened—at least not as it did—without Harlem.

⁓ ⁓ ⁓

Harlem came alive at night, in fact and in the imagination. At the end of the day, the people who worked in the city take commuter trains back to the suburbs. The city they leave behind awakens and stays awake all night long. The stylish people in the streets and the honking saxophones in the dimly lit clubs make people ache to be Uptown (Harold Arlen and Ted Koehler, "Rockin' in Rhythm," *Earl Carroll's Vanities,* 1932). As people hopped on the subway or hailed a cab, the ride uptown gave lyricist Nick Kenny a chance to interweave several familiar themes: Harlem's allure and sexual heat coupled with a rejection of the South and the merging of Harlem with someone you love: the one who waits for you makes Harlem feel like heaven (Duke Ellington and Nick Kenny, "Drop Me Off in Harlem," 1933).

First, though, you have to get there. This song began with a chance remark. The newspaper columnist and occasional song lyricist Nick Kenny ("Love Letters in the Sand," "Gone Fishin'") offered to share a cab with Duke Ellington. The composer said, "Drop me off in Harlem." The line stuck in Kenny's mind and, a few days later, he sought out Ellington at the Cotton Club to show him a finished lyric. The song makes getting there sound as exciting as being there, for blacks who feel they belong and for whites who cast off restraints each time they're uptown. On a similar theme, one of the greatest Harlem songs reflects the feelings of African Americans about their home turf, despite the nightly incursions of upscale whites. You get there by taking the Eighth Avenue A train up Manhattan's West Side. The result is a song of anticipation set on a subway platform as the train arrives heading uptown (Billy Strayhorn, "Take the 'A' Train," 1941). In another song about getting to Harlem, the African American songwriters Earl Bostic and Redd Evans affirm that whites are as keen to get uptown as blacks. The song offers jivey guidance for negotiating your way to Harlem and discovering its "uptown rhythm." If you're looking for a night of pleasure, its title provides the solution: "Let Me Off Uptown" (Earl Bostic and Redd Evans, "Let Me Off Uptown," 1941).

Because so many blacks had moved to New York and settled in Harlem in the previous few decades, the South figures prominently in songs about Harlem life: in the rejection of Jim Crow Dixie coupled with an open-hearted embrace of Harlem by the newcomer and, on the other side, in a desire to return to the South. Although the songs about returning differ dramatically from each other, each one is ambiguous, even contradictory. The black person who speaks in "Cabin in the Cotton" (Frank Perkins and Mitchell Parish, 1932) evokes minstrel songs several decades after they disappeared. The speaker embraces warm memories of a childhood in Virginia before adding in a more general way that growing up involved accepting what was both good and bad in Southern life. The attempt at compensation falls far short of a believable memory of the Jim Crow South.

Also in 1932, the same year as Irving Berlin's "Supper Time" and "Harlem on My Mind," Harry Revel and Mack Gordon wrote "Underneath the Harlem Moon" for a movie entitled *Rufus Jones for President.* It sounds conventional enough but, as Yuval Taylor and Jake Austen point out, Gordon's lyric trades in the most obvious racial and sexual stereotypes about black women.[79] Yet the song also emphasizes the opportunities available for African Americans in the North. Unlike those who lived in rural cabins in the South, "their cabin is a penthouse up on Lenox Avenue" and "every sheik is dressed up like a Georgia gigolo" (Harry Revel, Mack Gordon, "Underneath the Harlem Moon," *Rufus Jones for President,* 1932). The heavy-handed stereotypes never disappear, but the song also expresses a broader understanding. James Bush Jones correctly calls it "a heartbreaking realistic lament" about a black man eager to return south because he's "out of place here in Harlem."[80]

As sympathetic an observer of Harlem life as Ted Koehler must have understood the implications for a black man who admits that he would "gladly pick all the cotton . . . / Among my kind of folks once more" (Rube Bloom and Ted Koehler, "Cotton," *Cotton Club Revue of 1935,* 1935). He looks forward to returning home despite the backbreaking labor in store for him. He is honest with himself, but his outlook remains ambiguous.[81] Finally, some off-kilter rhyming by the twenty-five-year-old Johnny Mercer distinguishes someone who wants to head back South. His playful use of language makes it clear that he knows how to solve his problem, as he rhymes "fix it" with "Mason-Dix it": (Bernie Hanighen and Johnny Mercer, "Fare-Thee-Well to Harlem," 1934). The irreverent lyric lacks the other songs' ambiguity but beneath the wordplay lies a sure sense of the feelings of southern blacks displaced by moving north and yearning to return.[82]

Whites wrote most of these songs about returning to the South for white audiences; blacks knew enough not to believe them. They preferred songs that idealized the familiar, much as Tin Pan Alley had done for years. For them, though, that meant the sights, the people, and the sounds of Harlem, where music was everywhere: "Happiness is in the air, / Not a soul has got a care" (Chick Webb, Nat Reed, "Holiday in Harlem," 1937). More than anything in these songs, the joy in

Harlem finds expression in dancing—often in its sheer physical vitality combined with an uninhibited spontaneity found in the freedom to approach strangers, the arousal from closeness set to insinuating rhythms, and the ever-present eroticism. Andy Razaf's lyric to "Hotcha Razz-Ma-Tazz" urges someone to grab a girl and learn the latest hot dance. The vitality appears in the imperative to get loose and follow the music (Will Hudson, Irving Mills, and Andy Razaf, "Hotcha Razz-Ma-Tazz," 1934).It's the kind of looseness that makes dancing unrestrained and jazz possible, and that lends heat to the music and dancing. A song like "Runnin' Wild" abandons all restraint for the sensual pleasure of the moment: "Runnin' wild, lost control, / Runnin' wild, mighty bold" (A. Harrington Gibbs, Joe Grey, and Leo Wood, "Runnin' Wild," 1922).

Ted Koehler, who spent so much time in Harlem, was able to report approvingly that the newest dances drew even more people uptown. As soon as folks from downtown see a new dance step, it spreads everywhere, he wrote, because Park Avenue types are doing it (Rube Bloom and Ted Koehler, "Truckin'," *Cotton Club Parade*, 26th Edition, 1935). In another song, also with a lyric by Koehler, music, rhythm, and especially dancing pulsate at the heart of Harlem, but the idea is to do it in public, where you can be seen. The music and dancing are contagious, in part because of the song's self-confidence; the people are fearless. The music they dance to draws in everyone regardless of circumstance. Harlem becomes the universal democratic magnet (Jimmy McHugh and Ted Koehler, "Spreadin' Rhythm Around," 1935).

No dance was more popular, at least within song lyrics, than the low down—even though it was entirely fictional. There was no such dance. During the 1920s, though, calling something "low-down" suggested something about black styles deriving from the blues, something earthy and erotic, syncopated and sexual. Like a style of gravelly singing also rooted in the blues, it resembled a song like Alberta Hunter's "Rough and Ready Man" ("I want a two-fisted, double-jointed, rough and ready man") or Eddie Green's "A Good Man Is Hard to Find" ("You look and find him foolin' round some old gal"). It ranges from the tap dancer Bill Robinson's jaunty performance for white audiences in *Blackbirds of 1928* (Jimmy McHugh and Dorothy Fields, "Doin' the New Low-Down," 1928) to the syncopated movements of the genuine article (Irving Berlin, "When the Folks High Up Do That Mean Low-Down," *Reaching for the Moon*, 1930). The syncopation and the off-kilter rhythms seem to encourage some idiosyncratic rhyming, repetition, and assonance that contribute to the anything-goes atmosphere. Like most Harlem dancing portrayed in songs, the low down quickly spreads downtown to draw whites uptown. There seems to be no limit to its appeal: "Screen celebs and stage satellites, / Social debs and high hat-ellites," everybody does the uptown low down (Harry Revel and Mack Gordon, "Doin' the Uptown Low Down," *Broadway Through a Keyhole*, 1933).

But Harlem was an evanescent place. When such songwriters as Waller and Razaf wrote conventional love ballads, Harlem largely disappeared from their writing. Some songs are as corny as Eubie Blake and Noble Sissle's saccharine "So why should we fear when we're guarded, my dear, / By a million little angels in the sky?" (Eubie Blake and Noble Sissle, "There's a Million Little Cupids in the Sky," *In Bamville*, 1924). Some also have a lilt or rhythm to make them distinctive, including Blake and Razaf's "You're Lucky to Me"; J. C. Johnson, Razaf, and Bob Schafer's "My Special Friend (Is Back in Town)"; and Waller and Razaf's unusually romantic "My Fate Is in Your Hands." But the best of these love songs add humor to Harlem's heat to invest them with a dose of playful sexuality: "She knows a million ways to please / With her this and that and these. My! My! My!" (J. Russel Robinson and Jo Trent, "My! My! My!" 1929). An element of boisterous humor also runs through these songs, apparently based on the premise that sex is good dirty fun. The sexual allusions are indirect but unmistakable, thanks to the insinuating blues-like melodies that carry the words. Often a title like Waller and Razaf's "This Is So Nice It Must Be Illegal" and Don Redman and Razaf's "Gee, Baby, Ain't I Good to You?" along with a suggestively indirect lyric, is sufficient to make the point.

It's a short step from these suggestive love songs to a kind of song that became a Harlem staple and was an essential part of every Cotton Club revue—the double-entendre song. Andy Razaf wrote one whenever he needed to make a fast buck, and even the fastidious Harold Arlen wrote them with Ted Koehler for Cotton Club revues. Arlen agreed to do so only if he received no credit for them. Double-entendre songs derived from the urban blues. Although they were little more than catalogue songs constructed from bawdy puns and performed with delight, mainly by female singers, they came from that part of the blues that crowed about drinking, sex, infidelity, and gambling. These subjects have long been part of the blues, but they were central to the urban blues. One number associated with Bessie Smith begins with a familiar complaint about weariness and loneliness, but it doesn't prepare you for an immediate shift to a series of bawdy puns that make it clear she misses not companionship but sex. (Clarence Williams, Dally Small, and J. Tim Brymn, "I Need a Little Sugar in My Bowl," 1931). The double-entendre songs of the time make no attempt to express any emotion except lust, often described with raucous humor. Unlike torch songs, which also drew on the blues, they had no great burden of melancholy to endure.

Double entendre songs weave a list of clever bawdy associations derived from a title like "Kitchen Man" or "My Handy Man." They borrow joyful illicit sex from the urban blues but make it even more delectable by suggesting that a married white woman is misbehaving with her black male servant when her husband is out of the house. They turn domesticity on its ear. In "Kitchen Man," the verse that precedes the ribald choruses devoted to jelly rolls, open clams, and doughnuts, gives the song a different dimension. A wealthy Madame Buffs, presumably white but waited on by innumerable black servants, cries out in despair when her kitchen man suddenly gives notice. She begs him not to leave, as the chorus switches from the third-person perspective to let Madame Buffs speak for herself about the pleasure she takes from interracial sex. Razaf recasts the deep cultural fear of sex between black men and white women as a boisterous joke (Alex Belledna and Andy Razaf, "Kitchen Man," 1931).

Other songs in the same hyperbolic spirit and with deep roots in Harlem tell different kinds of truths. Still comic but less blunt than double-entendre songs, the comic "Your Feet's Too Big" satirizes love lyrics by turning them upside down. Instead of loving her, he can't stand her, and he especially hates her big feet. His mix of compliment and insult are the source of the comedy. Ironically, a successful white composer (and German immigrant) named Fred Fisher and his unknown lyricist, Ada Benson, wrote the song (Fred Fisher and Ada Benson, "Your Feet's Too Big," 1936).

Equally boisterous, "Find Out What They Like" is an unpredictable proffering of good advice. It is anything but a Pollyanna song, though it does promise great loving and equally great lovemaking, if you'll only do what you're told. The singer's love affairs used to go bad, but once she figures out what her man wants, she adapts with great speed and skill (Fats Waller and Andy Razaf, "Find Out What They Like," 1929).

Few songs equal the comic vulgarity of "Fat and Greasy," a song in which black songwriters audaciously mock appearances. The subject of the mockery is a man with "chunks of fat hanging over his chair." The lyric delivers the insults with irresistible enthusiasm and good-humored revulsion at someone who's "fat and greasy as a grizzly bear" (Charlie Johnston and Porter Grainger, "Fat and Greasy," 1936).

A song like "Fat and Greasy" may be an unlikely way to end a chapter, but its drive and down-to-earth honesty suggest how much it belongs to Harlem. Songs that illuminated Harlem's great appeal were more typical: the music, the dancing, the sex, and the freedom. They play and replay an idealized view of Harlem whose delights are available as soon as the sun goes down. It's almost as if the songs replace one set of stereotypes with another. And then suddenly, something real appears. A place like the Cotton Club may have softened Harlem's edges for visitors, but Harlem songs by the Harlem songwriters came a lot closer to the truth.

4

RECORDINGS, RADIO, AND TALKIES

I grew up with one foot in the world of radio and the other in the world of early television—of an age to listen to *Lux Radio Theatre* on my Arvin portable hidden under the blankets after bedtime and also to watch Milton Berle rehabilitate burlesque comedy on the *Texaco Star Theatre.* Before I started my homework on late winter afternoons, I pulled my chair close to the tiny screen of our first TV set to watch old Hoot Gibson westerns aired by a primitive station in Newark, New Jersey. Soon, on Saturday mornings, I would start listening to Martin Block's *Make Believe Ballroom* on WNEW in New York so I could write down which recordings had made that week's top ten. By the time I left for college, my musical tastes were formed and deepened by WNEW's disc jockeys: Block, Al "Jazzbo" Collins, Art Ford, and especially William B. Williams.

A decade and a half earlier, the lyricist and jazz writer Gene Lees "grew up, ear to the radio, on the sounds of the big bands of the 1930s." Network radio, he wrote, "was an irresistible cultural force, presenting—live, not on records—music of immense cultural diversity, almost every kind of music that America produced, and making it popular"[1]—from Duke Ellington to Arturo Toscanini. Dance bands performing live in hotel ballrooms or crammed into tiny studios were an essential part of early radio, but by the midthirties, the first disc jockeys were playing recordings by the bands and singers that defined the popular music of the day.

Lees listening to live music and I to recordings, but both of us shaped by the songs of the Great American Songbook made immediate and accessible through records and radio. I'm not writing a history of recorded sound, though; this isn't about physics or engineering, but rather about how recordings and the radio complemented America's rise as an urban country and culture and how those changes found expression in our music. I write about songs eventually but it's also about how they reached us and how we responded. Recordings first outsold sheet music, radio first became a national phenomenon, and the first talkies sang and danced as Americans watched, enraptured—all in the same decade, the 1920s.

During those years of great change, songwriters in Manhattan turned the music of African Americans into a commercial form embraced by a national white audience. Although African Americans had little influence over the sheet music and recording businesses, their music was central to this distinctively American music that recordings spread everywhere. You didn't even need electricity; you could turn a crank on a phonograph to tighten a spring that unwound slowly enough to let you play three or four songs before you had to wind it up again.

Ragtime faded by the early twenties, but jazz spread across the continent—in urban nightclubs during Prohibition, but also on recordings and, before long, on radio. Jazz began in New Orleans but moved up the Mississippi when trumpeter Joe "King" Oliver left for Chicago in 1918 and Louis Armstrong followed in 1922. It became a national music soon after Armstrong moved to New York in 1924. The result was a merging of technology, culture, and the city. Phonographs became more available, and recordings improved in quality. Before long, radio stations, loosely organized into temporary networks, transmitted live performances by jazz musicians and jazz-influenced singers in Manhattan to listeners far beyond Manhattan. These innovations arrived when the Harlem Renaissance was in full flower, the musical comedy with scores by such writers as Rodgers and Hart and the Gershwins flourished on Broadway, and black songwriters found greater opportunities with music publishers and eventually in Broadway musicals. The musical taste of the "college boys, socialites, and flappers" in New York and other cities soon became America's taste.[2] It wasn't jazz, but it was a popular music influenced by jazz—in its syncopation, its essential rhythms, its feel of spontaneity, its witty inventiveness, its ear for everyday speech, and its underlying hint of eroticism. It was hot, jazzy, and urban.

As jazz did later, the blues accompanied the Great Migration to northern cities after World War I. By then, such female blues singers as Gertrude "Ma" Rainey and Bessie Smith were turning it into a performance music in all-black vaudeville houses in the South and clubs in the North. Meanwhile, another blues singer named Mamie Smith had been singing Perry Bradford's "Harlem Blues" in an all-black show called *Maid of Harlem.* In August 1920, Bradford made a few changes in the lyric and convinced Okeh Records to let Smith record it as "Crazy

Blues." The results stunned the music business. Smith's recording sold one hundred thousand copies almost overnight and led to the signing of other black female blues singers to appeal mainly to African Americans. Smith was the first black performer to record the blues and also the first black star created by recordings. People at the time said you could hear the song coming from open windows in nearly every African American neighborhood in America.[3] The New Orleans jazz musician Danny Barker said, "There was a great appeal amongst black people and whites who loved this blues business to buy records and buy phonographs. Every family had a phonograph in their house, specifically behind Mamie Smith's first record."[4]

By the midtwenties, Americans were buying 130 million records per year, more than four times the number they bought in 1914.[5] Assailed by recordings and eventually radio, vaudeville declined, and the record player replaced the piano as the main source of music in the home. David Ewen wrote, "Beginning in 1920, and increasingly so from then on, a hit song began to be measured more by the number of records sold than by copies of sheet music."[6]

It had taken more than forty years to reach this point. On December 15, 1877, Thomas Edison filed a patent application for a machine to record and reproduce sound on a wax cylinder. He called it a phonograph. Although he intended it as an aid to dictation in offices, he came to see that beautiful music, currently the preserve of the rich, "available to only a few lucky city dwellers, was to become a mass-produced . . . sound recording—which would be cheap enough to be available to all."[7] It grew far beyond anything Edison envisioned. By 1977, before the advent of downloaded music or even compact discs (first available in 1982), Americans had bought $3 billion worth of recordings to play on more than 75 million record players.[8]

A decade after Edison's patent, Emile Berliner developed a flat disc that sat on a revolving turntable. It was more durable, easier to handle, and cheaper to make. Berliner soon established the Berliner Gramophone Company to compete with Edison's company. Columbia Records was founded in 1887 and the Victor Talking Machine Company in 1901. The record business had begun.[9]

Figure 4.1 A large billboard in NYC's Herald Square advertises the Edison Phonograph in 1909 or 1910. Courtesy of Photofest.

As recordings grew in appeal during the new century, singers and orchestras recorded every kind of popular music, including patriotic marches; coon songs; comic songs that lampooned immigrants, especially the Irish, Italians, and Jews; elevated ballads from operetta and more down-to-earth love songs from vaudeville; and remembrances of a rural past set mainly in an idealized South still nurturing memories of life before the Civil War. More often than not, the people buying these 78-rpm records lived in or near cities. That's where much of the new technology was developed and where it was first available.

At the same time, people living in the South and much of the Midwest embraced such early country performers as the Carter Family, who made their first recordings in 1927 and, a decade later, broadcast live from a powerful "border blaster" just across the Rio Grande in Mexico. Yet records and radio also carried songs from Tin Pan Alley and Broadway from coast to coast. People who bought the recordings of Jimmie Rodgers and Vernon Dalhart also embraced the dance bands of Paul Whiteman and Fred Waring and the crooning of Gene Austin and Nick Lukas. Late at night, they tuned in to "remotes," broadcasts of big bands, not from studios but from hotel ballrooms, often aired on fifty-thousand-watt "clear channel" radio stations whose signals, unimpeded by interference from other stations, spread for hundreds, even thousands, of miles. Regional differences notwithstanding, the Great American Songbook shaped by an urban sensibility became the nation's music.

Before 1920, publishers of sheet music and the first recording companies eyed one another suspiciously until it became clear that records could promote both songs and performers. Perhaps people heard a new song for the first time in a vaudeville house or a Broadway theater, or they bought the sheet music to play on the piano in the parlor after a piano player demonstrated it in a music store. Hearing and playing the song often led people to buy a recording.

Al Jolson was among the most important entertainers to achieve nationwide fame during the twentieth century's first two decades; recordings played an important part in his initial success. He opened in his second Broadway show, *Vera Violetta*, in late November 1911. A month later, he recorded songs from the score. One of them, "That Haunting Melody" by George M. Cohan, became Jolson's first number-one hit. By the end of the decade, eight more of his recordings rose to first place.[10]

On February 26, 1917, in New York City, the Original Dixieland Jass Band recorded "Dixie Jass Band One Step" and "Livery Stable Blues," considered the first jazz recording. A year later, they recorded "Tiger Rag," the first jazz hit. Despite the black origins of the music, the five musicians of the ODJB were white. Rather than playing authentic jazz, they adapted the music to white tastes, but they were important because they popularized jazz on records.[11] Through the 1920s, important white jazz musicians emerged, most notably Bix Beiderbecke and Jack Teagarden. White dance bands promoted themselves as jazz bands even when they were anything but. Fans of the real thing found it laughable that the bandleader Paul Whiteman insisted on billing himself as the "King of Jazz."[12]

In 1919, Ben Selvin and his orchestra's recording of "Dardanella" became the first popular dance record to sell at least a million copies. Its success set off a craze for recorded instrumentals by dance bands. The next year, Whiteman's "Whispering" and "Japanese Sandman" on the two sides of a single disc also sold a million copies. People could dance in their living rooms to a fox trot's quick tempos provided by bands led by Selvin, Whiteman, Isham Jones, George Olsen, Ted Lewis, and Fred Waring, among others.[13] Soon after the Hotel Pennsylvania (located across Eighth Avenue from Penn Station) hired Vincent Lopez and his orchestra in 1921, he became the first bandleader to perform on a live radio remote. The music played by these bands was syncopated but also tightly arranged. It was bouncy. People called it jazz, but it was no such thing.[14] Dance bands appearing live in nightclubs and, increasingly, on the radio, also wanted their audiences to know that they made records. Some bandleaders renamed their outfits to create an aura of modernity for themselves, as in Horace Heidt and His Victor Recording Californians, Ace Brigade and His Celebrated Recording Orchestra, and Perley Stevens and His Velvet Tone Recording Orchestra. At the same time, songwriters took advantage of the fad. People could buy sheet music and recordings of songs about staying home to dance to one-steps, fox-trots, tangos, and waltzes played by dance bands on the radio:

> You hold your sweetheart fondly and tight,
> And whisper we don't have to go out tonight,
> You can hug and kiss her there's no one in sight
> When you dance to that radio waltz.
> (Ralph Murray and Arthur Grace, "When You Dance to That Radio Waltz," 1922)

Interests change and fads fade. As recordings grew in availability and appeal, sheet music sales declined, but dance-band recordings also lost much of their appeal by the midtwenties. Singers were the beneficiaries. The shift occurred just as the electrical condenser microphone replaced the acoustic era's wide conical horn, which collected and focused sound waves for a recording. Sound quality improved, and singers used the microphone to sing in the new, more personal style called crooning. The crooner Gene Austin became the first singer to achieve national fame through recordings. By the midtwenties he was turning out such hits as "When My Sugar Walks Down the Street" (1925), "Bye Bye Blackbird" (1926), and "My Blue Heaven" (1928). By the end of his career, he had sold an estimated 86 million recordings.[15]

Recordings and radio interwove through my boyhood and adolescence, but their mix of technology and culture had begun decades earlier. Through the 1920s, increasing numbers of Americans had records and record players in their homes, and by the end of the decade, commercial radio had spread across the country. We were changing from music makers to music consumers. A hesitant Irving Berlin observed, "We have become a nation of listeners, rather than singers. Our songs don't live anymore. They fail to become part of us. Radio has mechanized them all." A singer touring in vaudeville before 1920 could sing the same few songs for years. People played the recordings over and over until they wore out or broke. As Berlin put it, "The radio runs them ragged for a couple of weeks—then they're dead."[16] The concern was genuine, but Berlin and his friends and associates who wrote and published songs need not have worried. In the fast-paced years after World War I, Americans wanted the music at their fingertips. Newly enfranchised, women followed the siren songs of the dance bands and crooners to move freely into the world. People no longer sang the songs of the day standing around a piano in the living room. Recordings and the radio gave young urban men and women an American popular music as "wild, happy, disenchanted, and unfettered as it had become fashionable for them to think they had become."[17] One of the biggest sellers of 1921, Gus Van and Joe Schenck's recording of "Ain't We Got Fun," helped to set the frivolous, starry-eyed style that lasted until the 1929 stock market crash almost instantly dispatched it:

Ev'ry morning,
Ev'ry evening,

Ain't we got fun?
Not much money,
Oh, but honey,
Ain't We Got Fun?
(Richard A. Whiting, Gus Kahn, and Raymond Egan, "Ain't We Got Fun," 1920)

The history of recordings is inseparable from American cities and especially New York; it is one of the essential subtexts in the story of recorded sound. Some of the earliest recording companies were first based in Washington, DC. Nevertheless, through the decades from Edison's invention of the phonograph in 1877 in Menlo Park, New Jersey (only forty-five minutes from Manhattan) to the rise of a national audience for recordings, New York City stood at the heart of American entertainment. It was home to the writing, publishing, performing, recording, and disseminating of popular music. It was also home to pre-Hollywood silent movies (many shot on Long Island), Broadway and Harlem, ASCAP (discussed below), and the major radio networks soon to appear. The NBC radio network started in 1926, the CBS network a year later. The great city welcomed whatever was new and profitable, everything from silly fads to life-changing innovations.

And then everything changed. The Great Depression devastated the sale of recordings. Free music on the radio and the arrival of talkies made things even tougher as the record industry struggled to survive. But it was lucky. For the only time in its history, jazz didn't merely influence popular music; in the midthirties, it merged with it to form something called swing. Swing-era groups mainly were big bands of a dozen or more pieces, in which soloists improvised over tight arrangements. Often, the emphasis was on setting down strong rhythms for dancing. Once again, instrumentals became more important than vocals. People bought recordings by Benny Goodman's and Duke Ellington's jazz bands, and by Guy Lombardo's and Kay Kyser's sweet bands. The purest jazz bands recorded ballads for the foxtrot. The most saccharine sweet bands turned their hands to up-tempo numbers for the lindy hop (later renamed the jitterbug to separate it from Charles Lindbergh, who had praised Adolf Hitler in public speeches and received a medal from the Führer).

Most of the time, people listened to recordings in their homes, but thanks to jukeboxes, they soon began hearing them in ice-cream parlors, bars, and restaurants as well. One nickel equaled one song play. People also got a mechanical show for their five cents: a window through which they could watch the tone arm (which held the needle) lift out of the way, a flat plate slide their selected disc onto the turntable, and the tone arm return to play the song. And all the while the neon lights on the box kept flashing. Coin-operated machines had been around in one form or another since around 1890, but the jukebox didn't make its gaudy appearance until the late 1930s. By 1939, 225 thousand were in operation and were said to be responsible for sales of 13 million records a year.[18]

Adults dressed up to go dancing on Saturday nights at the Trianon in Chicago, the Rendezvous in southern California, and dozens of other large dance halls and local roadhouses within driving distance of nearby cities.[19] At the same time, from the Depression through World War II, their teenage offspring plied jukeboxes with nickels at their favorite malt shops as they drank "sodapop rickeys" and danced "to swingeroo quickies, / Jukebox Saturday night" (Paul McGrane and Al Stillman, "Jukebox Saturday Night," *Stars On Ice*, 1942).

~ ~ ~

The growth of radio happened fast. During 1920, the *Detroit News*'s station, WWJ, broadcast a few commercial programs. KDKA in Pittsburgh followed on November 2 of the same year by airing the returns of the presidential race between Warren G. Harding and James M. Cox. Closer to New York, Westinghouse opened WJZ in Newark, New Jersey. In 1921, twenty-eight stations were on air; by the middle of the decade the number had reached five hundred and was still growing. In 1926, NBC started the first true network by broadcasting a star-studded gala to celebrate the opening of its new Manhattan studios. For the first time in history, millions of people could hear the same performance at the same time.[20] By 1929, sales of what had begun as a "crystal set toy for amateurs"[21] reached $800 million, and over one third of American families had radios to provide "entertainment in the parlor."[22] In that same year, Edison's recording company quietly folded. RCA, originally founded by General Electric to manufacture radios, bought the Victor Recording Company, the nation's largest maker of recordings.[23]

Music publishers had feared that recordings would put them out of business until it became clear that records could promote both songs and performers and earn profits for everyone. Similarly, a few years later, those in the recording business believed that free music available night and day on the radio would doom them. At first, it looked as if they were right. Record sales plummeted from 100 million a year in the late twenties to 6 million in the early thirties. Something both free and entertaining was bound to flourish, especially during the Depression, but there had also been signs along the way that recordings and radio could be mutually beneficial. The tenor John McCormack had introduced Irving Berlin's "All Alone" live on New Year's Day 1925 on a network of eight radio stations. Sales of the recording took off; it became the second-biggest record hit of the year, proof that radio sold records. Through the thirties, more and more people first heard a song performed live in the studio (and heard the commercials as well) and then bought the recording. Record sales began to rise again in the middle of the decade; by the late thirties, they had risen to 140 million discs per year.

Right from the start, radio stations had struggled to fill the airwaves with sound. Announcers read everything from farm reports to the Sunday comics to keep the audience's attention, but "music was the mainstay of commercial radio during its early days."[24] A recording gave a listener a performance of a hit song by a popular singer or band, but radio also gave large numbers of listeners a wide range of live studio performances. Audiences liked the diversity in a single day or week. As one station put it, "Music you want when you want it."

If you could carry a tune or play an instrument, and if you worked cheap, you could get a job in early radio—especially on the stations that proliferated in big towns and small cities from New Hampshire to New Mexico. Just as Harlem had provided employment for African American jazz musicians during Prohibition, so radio proved a godsend for singers and musicians during the Depression.

Even when radio presented much more polished programming in the late thirties and through the forties, musicians were eager to get on the air, regardless of the money involved. The clarinetist and bandleader Woody Herman said, "If we had to lose two thousand or three thousand dollars a week, it didn't matter because we were getting the right kind of air time." Leonard Maltin explained that bands "made their name on the airwaves, and then made their money on the road."[25]

Once the craze for dance-band recordings had faded, singers became more important on both recordings and radio. The electrical condenser microphone that transformed recording also changed singing on the radio. Crooning rather than belting was the new order of the day. Actually, singers didn't have much choice. The singing styles of vaudeville, on Broadway, and in opera were too loud for the equipment. A female singer named Vaughn De Leath was the first to figure out the need for a new approach. It's fair to call her the first crooner, but such male crooners as "Whispering" Jack Smith and Rudy Vallee soon dominated the airwaves.

Smith's popularity faded after a few years, but Vallee's success soared. Soon, he and his band, the Yale Collegians, were appearing in such places as New York's posh Heigh Ho Club (from which Vallee picked up his on-air greeting, "Heigh-ho, everybody"), but the club's manager disliked the rougher clientele that Vallee's radio remotes drew to the club. He fired Vallee, who reorganized his band, changed its name to the Connecticut Yankees, and went looking for radio dates. He shrewdly recognized the potential in the new medium. When one radio station offered his photograph to listeners, it received fifty thousand requests, mostly from women, in the first week.[26] He made recordings, performed those same songs on the radio to help push record sales, touring the country to perform for standing-room audiences. By 1929, he was in Hollywood to make movies even though his acting is most kindly described as stiff. Despite his thin, nasal voice, he was clean-cut and youthful, and women in the audience took to him. A woman who had never seen him perform won a letter-writing contest to Vallee in 1930 when she gushed, "Always breathing romance, singing the praises of love, enrapturing his phantom sweetheart with his ardent whisperings, and at the same time yearning for his own dream girl—he makes the women believe that each one is the only one."[27] With a lot of help from screaming flappers, Vallee became America's first mass-media singing star. In 1931, he had a hit recording that included a passing reference to a successful crooner:

> There's a guy in the show, the girls love to kiss
> Gets thousands a week just for crooning like this.
> (Ray Henderson and Lew Brown, "Life Is Just a Bowl of Cherries," *George White's Scandals of 1931*, 1931)

Aside from technological improvements and financial growth, radio made new stars but also punished those performers who couldn't make the adjustment to the new medium. Comedian George Burns, who starred in vaudeville, then on radio and television, and then in the movies, said he knew vaudeville was finished when radio arrived: "Theaters began advertising that their shows would be halted for fifteen minutes so that the audience could listen to 'Amos & Andy.' And when the 'Amos and Andy' program came on, the vaudeville would stop, they would bring a radio onstage, and the audience would sit there watching radio."[28]

Entertainers who made the switch successfully soon found themselves in a show-business world in which everything fed everything else. At its heart was the lure of the city and its population's growing desire for entertainment. Establishing a pattern that would continue into the present, musical performers moved back and forth between vaudeville, recordings, radio, live theater, and sound movies.

The career of Cliff Edwards, who performed as Ukulele Ike, is a good example. Born in Hannibal, Missouri (population twelve thousand) in 1895, he taught himself the ukulele to attract customers when he worked as a newsboy. He toured in vaudeville and first appeared on Broadway in 1921 for the short run of a show called *The Mimic World.* Before his career declined rapidly in the thirties, he thrived in New York. He headlined at the Palace and appeared in George and Ira Gershwin's *Lady, Be Good,* where he introduced the songs "Fascinating Rhythm" and "Little Jazz Bird." He also made recordings in New York during these years. His version of Isham Jones and Gus Kahn's "It Had to Be You" was the first of his records to make the charts. Late in the decade, he signed to appear in talkies as well, including one of the first movie musicals, MGM's *Hollywood Revue of 1929,* in which he introduced Nacio Herb Brown and Arthur Freed's "Singin' in the Rain," dressed in a poncho as the rain came down in buckets. He emerged from obscurity briefly in 1940 to provide the voice of Jiminy Cricket, singing Leigh Harline and Ned Washington's "When You Wish Upon a Star" in Walt Disney's animated version of *Pinocchio.*[29]

The bandleader Les Brown described how the relationship between radio and recordings had changed by the late thirties: "Record companies weren't interested in you at all unless you were on the air and you could plug your records." In 1941, soon after he had signed with Columbia Records, the Blackhawk Hotel in Chicago hired Brown and His Band of Renown for four weeks but kept them on for four months. The radio station WGN featured them on remotes from the hotel during the full length of their run. "[W]e had 50,000 watts," Brown said. "and we got to be known after that, and our records started selling."[30] An appearance in a hotel led to a radio remote, led in turn to a recording session, led to playing a newly recorded song as part of a radio remote from the hotel. Radio turned show business into a great circle, airing live remotes and recordings in every city and town large enough to have a station.

Radio had prided itself on live entertainment, but during the 1930s, disc jockeys—a term coined by the New York gossip columnist Walter Winchell in 1935—and the recordings they played took up more and more airtime. It wasn't entirely the finances, but saving money mattered, especially during the Depression. Only the DJs were live; the music was on records. Small stations relied on them because they couldn't afford to hire live performers, and larger stations often used them to fill the hours after midnight. In 1932, Al Jarvis, a radio announcer on KFWB in Los Angeles, had an idea about playing records on the air. He'd skim *Billboard* and *Variety* to find a little information he could use to introduce each song, but his laid-back speaking style—the spoken equivalent of crooning—gave his time on the air a distinctive quality. The show, titled "The World's Largest Make Believe Ballroom," became popular in Los Angeles, but LA was a minor market in those days, and nobody paid much attention.

Martin Block was also working at KFWB. When he moved east soon after, he took the concept with him and used almost the identical format to become one of the nation's dominant radio personalities for the next twenty-five years. From its first broadcast on New York City's WNEW on February 3, 1935, Block's "Make Believe Ballroom" was a sensation. Within four months, he had a daily audience of 4 million listeners, and stations everywhere were copying his format.

As in many stories, timing and luck played important roles. WNEW had been covering the trial of Richard Bruno Hauptmann for kidnapping and murdering Charles Lindbergh's baby son. During a break in court, Block decided to launch his new idea, but the station did not own a single recording. He supposedly raced around the corner to the Liberty Music Shop, where he bought five recordings by Clyde

McCoy. He played them back-to-back to make the broadcast sound live and ad-libbed introductions that sounded as if he were talking to the bandleader in the studio. After the Hauptmann trial ended, the program settled into a two-and-a-half-hour slot and soon acquired the first of its two theme songs, an invitation to dance (Paul Denniker and Andy Razaf, "Let's Dance at the Make Believe Ballroom," 1937).

Three years later, Block joined in the writing of a new theme (or else cut himself in for a share of the royalties from a song played on the air five days every week, year in and year out). Glenn Miller was so taken by the song that he and his band recorded it. Miller paid for the recording session himself and hired the Modernaires to sing the lyrics that announce: "It's Make-Believe Ballroom Time" when "the bands are here to bring good cheer your way" (Harold Green, Mickey Stoner, and Martin Block, "It's Make-Believe Ballroom Time," 1940).[31]

Your Hit Parade first aired on NBC in New York in the same year that Martin Block began the *Make Believe Ballroom.* It presented the top ten songs in the country for the preceding week. In other words, it was a live radio performance of songs that had gained their popularity primarily through recordings. Perhaps after listeners heard Frank Sinatra, Dick Haymes, Doris Day, Dinah Shore, Martha Tilton, or any of the other fifty singers who appeared on the program during its twenty-eight years, they might buy one of the records and then tune in again next week to hear the songs and the singers.

The show based its findings on a closely guarded secret combination of record and jukebox plays, record and sheet-music sales, and dance-band performances. It even kept the names of the top three songs from the performers who'd sing them until the last possible minute. The gimmickry built suspense, as did the fanfare before "the number-one song in the nation." Surprisingly, it all worked, even when the top three songs were pretty obvious, especially to regular listeners. When Frank Sinatra, then the program's lead singer, attended a White House reception in 1944, President Roosevelt tried to get him to whisper the name of the top tune on the next broadcast. Sinatra couldn't tell the president because he didn't know.

A dismal pall settled over many of America's city streets and neighborhoods during the Great Depression, but radio offered people everywhere a lift. Not only could they listen to their favorite performers but crooning also created an air of intimacy, whether live or on a recording spun by a favorite DJ. Because crooning on the radio or a recording "had the effect of the singer singing to only one listener," Timothy D. Taylor writes, "it offered a greater sense of intimacy than live singing."[32]

Radio was public, but it was also personal. It redefined the idea of privacy. Before radio, the only way to see a performer was literally to see a performer. Now, though, you could hear the singing and music without getting out of your chair. Taylor adds, "People didn't have to leave their homes to be entertained. The performers came into their house."[33] Often families sat near the consoles in their living rooms, two or three generations tuned in to the same program. Yet with crooning, the performance felt intimate, as if the crooner were singing to one person only. Millions of listeners to a successful network show had similar reactions to what they heard at exactly the same time, but they were sitting in thousands of houses in hundreds of cities and towns. The combination of crooning and an emotionally receptive audience created an illusion of intimacy as radio made the relationship between singer and listener both public and private simultaneously. As Taylor writes, "Even as radio was brought into the realm of social life . . . it was reconfiguring the nature of the private, of intimate space—it was being integrated into individual lives, into individual private fantasies."[34] A boy and girl would turn down the lights in the parlor to listen to the radio because "Each station throughout the nation will have a song coming through" as "the networks will do your wooing for you" (Richard A. Whiting and Johnny Mercer, "Love Is on the Air Tonight," *Varsity Show*, 1937).

A theatrical performance is a public event, even though everyone sits in the dark facing the stage. During the heyday of radio, a program was public in a different way. Even though a popular program reached millions of people, they consisted of small groups of family members, friends, and individuals sitting alone. Radio didn't do much for conversation, but as a program proceeded, people might chat with one another for a moment, somebody else might go to the kitchen for a snack, and somebody else might be half listening and half reading the

Figure 4.2. A still from the 1932 First National Pictures movie, *They Call It Sin.* Even though Prohibition was still in effect, Loretta Young and George Brent have found a way to combine a radio console with a complete home cocktail lounge. Courtesy of Warner Bros. and Photofest.

newspaper. The degrees of engagement changed constantly, person by person, minute by minute. Yet a woman during World War II, her lover gone to serve, often listened alone with a different kind of intensity to the crooners who rendered songs designed to encapsulate her experiences and emotions. Radio changed the way Americans listened to music, but it also helped to change the nature of the songs they listened to.

Perhaps the best way to illustrate the change is to contrast two typical love songs, one from World War I and the other from World War II. They were written twenty-five years apart, but central to both are the themes that define the love ballads of both wars—parting, separation, loneliness, and the hope of return. The song from World War I occurs in the world. It affirms love by telling the story of two lovers who tie their feelings to behavior and place. They meet in the strophic World War I song, "K-K-K-Katy": "Like an act of fate, Kate was standing at the gate / Watching all the boys on dress parade." Among the marchers is Jimmy, "a soldier brave and bold," who tells Kate that evening that he loves her. He is about to sail for France but has bought a wedding ring that he will keep with him until he returns. The repeated chorus is Jimmy's stuttering love song to Kate as he prepares to depart: "K-K-K-Katy, beautiful Katy / You're the only g-g-g-girl that I adore" (Geoffrey O'Hara, "K-K-K-Katy," 1918). The affirmation of love is genuine, but it lacks the passion that would find full expression in the ballads crooned on recordings and over the air in the 1940s.

The song from World War II is introspective and lyrical; it resides in the heart and mind of the lover, who probably heard it first on the radio. Its embrace of deeply held emotions defines every part of it. In this case, its lyric consists of a one-sided conversation as the woman imagines herself speaking to her lover. The pretense is her only consolation: "I'm making believe that you're in my arms / Though I know you're so far away" (James V. Monaco and Mack Gordon, "I'm Making Believe," *Sweet and Low-Down*, 1944).

Technology stood out as a subject for songs in the first decades of the twentieth century, but Tin Pan Alley turned out fewer songs about radio and recordings than about telephones, trains, automobiles, airplanes, and movies (both silent and sound). They devoted fewer songs to electric lights or to anything as utilitarian as indoor plumbing. You wanted to turn off the lights in the name of romance, but plumbing hardly conjured up images of cuddling.

Did a lot of the songwriters find the changes in sound technology and the music business too threatening to write about? Change often rattled many of the publishers and songwriters in what was basically a conservative business dependent on the whims of a broad public. If recordings and, later, the radio and talking pictures were going to affect sheet-music sales, the independence of publishers would decline, as would their royalty payments to the many songwriters they had under contract. The royalties paid out depended on how many copies of a song a publisher sold. Many of these publishers had reputations for keeping the royalty amounts very low. As a result, composers and lyricists banded together in 1914 to form ASCAP (American Society of Composers, Authors and Publishers) to guarantee what they saw as their fair share of royalties for performances of their works and to protect their copyrights. Among the founders were such major figures as Victor Herbert, Irving Berlin, Jerome Kern, John Philip Sousa, and James Weldon Johnson. With ASCAP to protect them through licensing agreements with those who provided live, recorded, or broadcast performances, they took advantage of the new sound technology and protected their claims to the income it produced.[35]

But contracts and fees don't necessarily turn into songs. I found fewer than I had anticipated, but by the midteens, ASCAP songwriters had begun to write songs that personalized the effect of recordings on listeners. A decade later, they were receiving royalties from radio play of their songs and also writing the same kinds of songs as they had about recordings. Many of these songs fall into two broad categories. Most are about people who are close but find even greater intimacy; others, more dramatically, depict lonely people who try desperately to find one another.

Usually the lyrics tell stories about two people whose listening to records and the radio plays an important part in their lives. The same kind of emotional attachments had also been true through the telephone, the automobile, and silent movies when they were new in such songs as "Call Me Up Some Rainy Afternoon," "In My Merry Oldsmobile," and "Take Your Girlie to the Movies (If You Can't Make Love at Home)." Some songs went so far as to promote specific makes of phonographs—Sonoma, Pathé Pathephone, Victrola—by linking them to courtship and love.

One of the most appealing of these songs tells the comic tale of a young married couple who dressed up and went to all the parties. He feels jealous when the men crowd around his wife, so he buys a phonograph. That way, they can stay home, and he can have her all to himself for dancing and more:

That's why he bought the Victrola, the little Victrola
They never go out any more
And after dancing she's all out of breath
He loves to take her and hug her to death!
Then they start the Victrola, the little Victrola
And go dancing around the floor!
(Maurice Abrahams and Grant Clarke, "They Start the Victrola (And Go Dancing Around the Floor," 1914)

That this affluent couple goes to parties night after night but can easily afford a phonograph as early as 1914 suggests that they are city dwellers. Their social lives change: less partying, more suggestions of sex. The next song does something similar though without the first couple's patina of sophistication. Staying home to listen to the phonograph soon links recordings to domesticity and eventually to intimacy. That may explain why the men and women in these songs are married, whether the fashionable couple in "They Start the Victrola" or the working-class folk in "In a Cozy Kitchenette Apartment":

In a cozy kitchenette apartment for two
I'll be setting the table
While you're cooking a stew for me and you.
I'll be there to help you put the dishes away;
Then together we'll listen to the phonograph play
The tuneful "Humoresque"—
And oh, what bliss
When it's time to kiss
In a cozy kitchenette apartment for two!
(Irving Berlin, "In a Cozy Kitchenette Apartment," *Music Box Revue*, 1921)

The evolution in song lyrics about the relationships between the sexes reflects changing social and sexual attitudes. The earliest song I could find about dancing at home, from 1902, is more about friendship and social life than anything remotely sexual. Nell Mooney is fun-loving and charming; to add to her popularity, she's bought a phonograph. During the years when women were becoming more visible and more active in the world, songs about recordings underscored the pleasures of dancing at home with your friends and, later, your lover:

> The neighbors and the girls and boys on Sunday after tea,
> All call around to Nellie's home, the sight is great to see . . .
> There is no grand piano or Sousa with his staff,
> But we dance to the latest music by Nell Mooney's phonograph.
> (John H. Flynn, "Nell Mooney's Phonograph," 1902)

By the midteens, playing a record often leads to dancing but increasingly to intimacy—even to a situation in which the woman takes the initiative. A "bashful boy" never makes any advances at a "winning miss" until she gets tired of waiting. When she turns on the Victrola, he suddenly leaps up from his chair and speaks: "Let's suppose that I'm a big Victrola, dear, and you're a little talking machine, / I'd make a play for you." As the lyric explains, "The Victrola was the cause of their bliss" (James Duffy, "If I Were a Big Victrola and You a Little Talking Machine," 1915).

The ability to dance at home promoted the kind of cuddling that was so important in such early twentieth-century songs as "Cuddle Up a Little Closer, Lovey Mine" and "Put Your Arms Around Me, Honey (I Never Knew Any Girl Like You)." In one musical tale of a courting couple, Billy and Flo go right from putting on a record to turning "the lights down low." The more explicit this kind of cuddling song became, the more humorous it was. The only time Billy stopped squeezing and kissing was "when he had to rewind the machine." Eventually, Flo's father yelled down that it was time for Billy to leave, but:

> When their lips were in position,
> There'd be an intermission,
> And he'd put another record on.
> (Elmer L. Greensfelder, Edward B. Claypoole, and Leonard Weinberg, "Then He'd Put Another Record On," 1914)

Songs about the radio also present it as a cure for loneliness. The radio becomes a way to reach one's far-off beloved or to get through the time until they're together again. A fellow who imagines that his girl is as lonely as he thinks that he can reach her on the radio. He believes that if he can broadcast that he loves her, she'll hear him. Among the millions who listen, he chooses to believe, "I may find you, dear, / List'ning on some radio" (Louis A. Hirsch, Dave Stamper, and Gene Buck, "List'ning on Some Radio," *Ziegfeld Follies of 1922*, 1922). Another young man calls his favorite station, call letters LOVE, to ask a singer to send a message to someone he loves and to "say it with music, how lonesome I've been" (Grant Clarke, Edgar Leslie, and Lew Cobey, "Tell Her I Love Her on the Radio," 1924). "Ain't Misbehavin'," the most important of these songs, has only a passing reference to the radio but it's telling. What in 1929 would have sounded more like a woman than a man says she doesn't stay out late because she's alone, waiting for the return of her lover. She's home by eight o'clock and spends the evening listening to her radio (Fats Waller, Harry Brooks, and Andy Razaf, "Ain't Misbehavin'," *Connie's Hot Chocolates*, 1929). The title affirms the lover's fidelity but also suggests an underlying restlessness. It appears in the difference between behaving and not misbehaving. She uses the radio to fill the hours of waiting.

As radio combined live and recorded music, the differences came to matter less. More important is how quickly recordings and then radio became a conduit for the depiction of emotion, a metaphor for loneliness and intimacy and the expression of private feelings. They helped us party our way through the 1920s and survive the Great Depression.

Talking pictures didn't begin with Al Jolson's performance in the 1927 movie *The Jazz Singer*, but they might as well have. In the middle of a performance in a restaurant, Jolson's character, Jack Robin, suddenly ad-libs a few words to his audience—those at the tables and, implicitly, those watching the screen as well. "Wait a minute, wait a minute," Robin cries out, "I tell ya', You ain't heard nothin' yet." And then he launches into "Toot, Toot, Tootsie (Goo' Bye)," complete with the full Jolson treatment (Gus Kahn, Ernie Erdman, and Dan Russo, "Toot, Toot, Tootsie ([Goo' Bye]," 1922). Hands clapping, eyes rolling, and hips swaying, he turns the song into a high-powered seduction of his audience. Beyond his hammy but undeniable authority, Jolson's ecstatic performance announces the arrival of talkies and the eventual death of silent movies.

The scene reverses itself twenty-five years later but makes the same point. Halfway through the MGM musical, *Singin' in the Rain*, sound pictures suddenly arrive. The studio head, R. F. Simpson (Millard Mitchell), tells the movie stars Don Lockwood (Gene Kelly) and Lina Lamont (Jean Hagen) that they will have to reshoot their newest picture as a musical. Lina, a great silent star but an obtuse virago off-screen, has a speaking voice best compared to the shattering of glass. When the audience at the movie's premiere calls out for Lina to sing as she had onscreen, the studio brass force the featured player and Lockwood's love interest, Kathy Selden (Debbie Reynolds), to dub the singing behind a curtain while Lina lip-syncs the words. In the middle of the ruse, Kelly, along with his sidekick, Donald O'Connor, and Millard Mitchell, takes great pleasure in opening the curtain to reveal the truth. The audience's mockery ends Lina's career, and Kathy becomes a great new star—in talking pictures.

In the fate of Lina Lamont, fiction comes perilously close to historical reality. According to the film historian Scott Eyman, "As [*The Jazz Singer*] ended and applause grew with the houselights, Sam Goldwyn's wife Frances looked around at the celebrities in the crowd. She saw 'terror in all their faces,' she said, as if they knew 'the game they had been playing for years was finally over.'"[36] The next year, a trio of songwriters made the same point in a more public way. The best-known stars are out of a job and panicking because "Ev'ryone must talk out loud or kiss the town good-bye." Their departures open the door to stardom to every "bathroom singer" and "guy with leather lungs" (Walter O'Keefe, Robert Emmett Dolan, and James Cavenaugh, "Ever Since the Movies Learned to Talk," 1928).

~ ~ ~

The idea of a talking motion picture is almost as old as sound recordings, but it took a long time to develop something that worked. Only three months after Thomas Edison filed his patent for a phonograph, he and the photographer and motion-picture pioneer Eadweard Muybridge met to discuss the possibility of developing a sound picture that would combine Edison's new phonograph with Muybridge's zoopraxiscope.[37] Muybridge's invention featured a disc with a series of painted images around the outside. Spin the disc within a projector, and the images appear to move on a screen or wall. Other inventors and engineers in Europe and the United States were soon at work developing their own systems and looking for ways to exhibit what they'd achieved. Clément-Maurice (Clément Maurice Gratioulet) and Henri Lioret were the first to show sound films publicly—at the Paris Exposition in 1900.[38]

From the beginning, no problem proved more vexing than the synchronization of image and sound, especially since they had to be recorded and played back on separate machines. Even after improved projectors made it possible to show talkies in large theaters, the volume was still too low, the sound quality too poor, and the machines too large and clumsy. In 1919, Lee De Forest received a patent for a system that would lead to the first sound-on-film technology and, with it, the eventual solution to the problem. From that point on, movie studios tried different approaches to implement De Forest's system, even though Hollywood in general remained suspicious of the new technology. James Quirk, the editor of *Photoplay* magazine, wrote in March 1924, "Talking pictures are perfected. *So* is castor oil."[39] As early as 1921, though, a silent movie called *Dream Street* was rereleased with a live-recorded song added to it. Yet there were no more experiments with recorded singing for another six years.[40]

In 1925, Warner Bros. was a small but ambitious studio. Sam Warner, one of the three Warner brothers, saw a demonstration of Western Electric's sound-on-disc system and convinced his brothers that it was worth experimenting with.[41] First, they released *Don Juan*, the first feature-length movie to use a synchronized sound system for its musical score and sound effects. It had no recorded dialogue, but it was the first true sound film exhibited by a Hollywood studio. In May 1927, Warner released a short titled *They're Coming to Get Me*, the first fiction film with synchronized dialogue.[42]

And then came *The Jazz Singer*, not the first sound picture but the one that changed the movie business for good. It's the one that got everyone's attention—in the movie business and around the country. It earned $2.6 million, even though it wasn't quite a talkie. It was largely a silent film that shifted to sound recorded on the set when Jolson performed. Its success rested on its casting of one of America's most popular stars plus a limited use of synchronized sound. Most important from my perspective, the sound consisted mainly of songs. The movie is set in New York City neighborhoods, beginning on the Lower East Side, moving on to Broadway, and embracing both at the end. Its Tin Pan Alley songs, such as Kahn, Erdman, and Russo's "Toot, Toot Tootsie" and Irving Berlin's half melancholy "Blue Skies," come laced with jazz-tinged syncopation and a toe-tapping beat.

Jack Robin, born Jakie Rabinowitz, is a cantor's son (just as Jolson was born Asa Yoelson, also the son of a cantor) whose success in show business convinces him that he has a place in America. For him, anyway, America is noisy, bright, and alluring. Its magnetic poles are Broadway and Tin Pan Alley, but it's a lot bigger world than the Lower East Side. He and many of his contemporaries, singers and songwriters alike, were immigrants or the children of immigrants. In the struggle between the synagogue and the street, the *shul* never had a chance. For Jewish youngsters, the vaudeville houses and nickelodeons (and eventually the radio and the talkies) offered a magical if bruising escape into self-expression, sexuality, prosperity, and freedom.

After *The Jazz Singer*, every studio began to develop and release talking pictures. Soon the problem lay not with the studios but with the twenty-two thousand movie theaters around the country. In 1929, only eight hundred of them could project sound pictures. The changeover happened rapidly, though, because Hollywood was turning out musicals. That same year, *Broadway Melody*, the Oscar winner for best picture, was one of the first of a batch of backstage stories, following *On with the Show* (1929) and *Gold Diggers of Broadway* (1929). Many of those not set in show business also covered New York, from seedy boxing clubs to Park Avenue penthouses.

Movie studios released more than one hundred musicals in 1929, but only fourteen in 1931. Audiences grew so sick of them that studios cut songs from movies about to be released. *Fifty Million Frenchmen*, one of Cole Porter's early Broadway hits, had its songs unceremoniously snipped before Warner released it. The dip in interest in musicals lasted only until 1933. The team of the composer Harry Warren, the lyricist Al Dubin, and the dance director Busby Berkeley transformed the backstage tales of tough-minded chorines and aspiring innocents into throbbing Depression-era musicals that combined sentiment and surrealism in a phantasmagoric backstage world that was larger than life but never let go of the daily grind. These gritty "Gold Digger" movies from Warner Bros. played opposite Ginger Rogers and Fred Astaire's elegant but no less urban escapism at RKO (see chap. 6).[43]

~ ~ ~

Songwriters worked under contract for the studios, much as they had for the music publishers earlier in the century. Increasingly in 1930s movie musicals, such stars as Bing Crosby and Fred Astaire introduced the songs that they or other singers would then record and sing on the radio. Musicals became part of the entertainment loop. As we've seen, at each step in the technological history of the twentieth century, songwriters referred to the inventions that were closest to the hearts of the American people. The songwriters had feared recordings and radio, but they'd survived them. More than that, they'd come to see how profitable recorded sound and broadcasting could be. By the time talkies arrived, they knew they had nothing to fear. Not only did movies introduce and promote their songs but the studios also hired them to write more songs. Yet they wrote surprisingly few songs about sound pictures and the ways they affected people's attitudes and behavior.

In 1919, when movies were still silent, Pete Wendling, Burt Kalmar, and Edgar Leslie described Beatrice Fairfax's advice to a lovelorn lad who can't find a way to be alone with his girl: "Take your girlie to the movies, If you can't make love at home" because "you can say an awful lot in seven reels." It's where you "take your lessons" so you can have "love scenes of your own" (Pete Wendling, Burt Kalmar, and Edgar Leslie, "Take Your Girlie to the Movies [If You Can't Make Love at Home]," 1919). Through the decades of talkies, few songs put lovers in the balcony to smooch until, in 1957, John D. Loudermilk (writing as Johnny Dee) wrote pretty much the same song but set it to the persistent beat of early rock and roll: "I'll hold your hand and I'll kiss you too, / The feature's over but we're not through." The major difference seems to be that the latter-day lothario doesn't need Ms. Fairfax to guide him (Johnny Dee, "Sittin' in the Balcony," 1957).

With the coming of talkies, the studios were desperate for material. They were likely to take an option on anything that showed the remotest chance of being adaptable into a movie, everything from classic novels to *Saturday Evening Post* short stories to unproduced plays. With the arrival of movie musicals, they adapted successful Broadway shows, but mainly they wanted songwriters from New York, and plenty of them. They offered sunshine and money along with coast-to-coast audiences to watch movie stars perform their songs. Almost nobody resisted. Some, such as Irving Berlin, Richard Rodgers, and Cole Porter, turned out the songs and got back to New York as fast as they could.

Others, such as Harry Warren, stayed but never really liked the life in California. And others, such as Ira Gershwin and Harold Arlen, settled in and made it their home.

The movement west from Broadway and Tin Pan Alley matched what was happening in a lot of other places. The movies, themselves; the movie magazines that specialized in idealized, sanitized versions of movie stars' lives; and the still enlarging idea of celebrity persuaded a lot of young adults to head for Hollywood to crash the movies. Nearly everybody knew the story of how sixteen-year-old Judy Turner played hooky one day from Hollywood High School to get a Coke at Schwab's Drug Store. The director Mervyn LeRoy happened to see her there, was taken by her beauty (if not her tight sweater), and offered her a screen test on the spot. Once the studio changed her first name, she became the movie star Lana Turner. Soon girls from all over the country were hanging out in Schwab's in the hope of being discovered—except that young Judy had actually sipped her Coke at the Top Hat Café, a block from Hollywood High, and the man who saw her was Billy Wilkinson, who published a movie trade paper.[44] The story wasn't entirely true, but it was true enough. The hopefuls kept arriving "to get their names up in lights" (Richard A. Whiting and Johnny Mercer, "Hooray for Hollywood," *Hollywood Hotel*, 1938).

For a lot of young Americans during the Depression, Hollywood was the pot of gold. A lot of the songs were about Hollywood itself, rather than talkies. In the 1933 movie *Going Hollywood*, Bing Crosby plays a rising crooner who's leaving for California to make his first movie. As he boards the train, he looks forward to the sunshine and gaiety he assumes he'll find, but he's also capable of a touch of irony. As the train leaves the station, nothing is more important than finding his beret (Nacio Herb Brown and Arthur Freed, "Going Hollywood," *Going Hollywood*, 1933). It's an easy life to satirize, especially with all those no-talent stars who rely on being beautiful or handsome. It's a place that lives on hyperbole, a place "where you're terrific if you're even good" (Whiting and Mercer, "Hooray for Hollywood").

Most common, though, are the love songs—as you'd expect: songs of praise and songs where love rescues the lover from loneliness. The most ebullient of these songs expresses enthusiastic delight. Your beauty, your voice, and the way you kiss would make anybody your fan because, as the title insists, "You Oughta Be in Pictures" (Dana Suesse and Edward Heyman, 1934). Less clever but more directly emotional, songs about loneliness treat the movies as the rescue, not because they're a distraction but because they make an emotional connection. Someone who sits "in the gloom of my lonely little room" wishes that the picture of the loved one could talk. That way, he could "applaud each time you whispered, 'I love you, love you'" (Ray Henderson, Lew Brown, and B. G. DeSylva, "If I Had a Talking Picture of You," *Sunny Side Up*, 1929).

Perhaps so few songs sang about the talkies when they were new because so many talkies were singing to us. It wouldn't be long before great stars and small, big-budget and B movie musicals alike, would spread across the country. From Judy Garland, Gene Kelly, and Fred Astaire at the very top to the hoofer Donald O'Connor, the leading man John Payne, and the long forgotten Jane Frazee, we delighted in their performances, hummed the songs they introduced or revived, and soon found recordings that let us recreate our moment of discovery as often as we wished.

5

STARTING THE CENTURY

In 1885, soon after publishing his first song, Charles K. Harris opened his music publishing company in a storefront on Grand Avenue in Milwaukee. The sign he hung in the window read, "Charles K. Harris, Banjoist and Songwriter. Songs Written to Order." It seemed as if he proclaimed that songwriting had suddenly turned pro, although talented professionals had been around for decades. You can't listen to "Oh, Susannah," "Beautiful Dreamer," "My Grandfather's Clock," or the great songs of the Civil War without conjuring up the names of Stephen Foster, Henry Clay Work, and George Frederick Root. Their writing was polished and engaging, but songwriting didn't earn much in those days. Foster died penniless and alone in a New York hotel room in 1864, aged thirty-seven. Although art and commerce mixed together from the start, music publishing was much more haphazard then. It would change before the end of the century.

In 1892, Harris wrote and published "After the Ball," a long, melodramatic tearjerker that weaves a tale of love lost and lives wasted. The public adored it. When it became the first song to sell a million copies of sheet music within a single year, Harris (and others) were convinced that the music business could earn publishers and songwriters a lot of money. A few years later, he moved his business to New York; other songwriters soon followed. Why not? Book publishing was there, Broadway and vaudeville were there, radio and recordings would soon be there, and now Tin Pan Alley was there as well. Only motion pictures left New York later on, and that was to chase the warmth and sunlight in California. It must have felt as if they were making movies at the end of the world.

Meanwhile, back east, Harris became one of the first publishers to set up shop on West Twenty-Eighth Street in what became known as Tin Pan Alley. Similar businesses often clumped together in Manhattan. Cutters worked from patterns in the Garment District, diamond merchants sold their wares (and still do) on West Forty-Seventh Street, Macy's and Gimbel's competed face to face in Herald Square, and

Figure 5.1. Songwriter Charles K. Harris wrote the enormously successful "After the Ball" in 1892, and moved to New York City to write and publish songs a few years later. He was one of the founding members of Tin Pan Alley. Library of Congress, New York World-Telegram and the Sun Newspaper Photograph Collection.

songwriters did their piano thumping for the publishers who employed them in Tin Pan Alley. The songwriters had come from everywhere to make it in Manhattan and in the process, killed off the sentimental ballad. At the start, it was a young man's game. Harris wrote that in 1898, over at the publisher M. Witmark & Sons, "the head of the firm was about twenty years of age, his brother Julius was about eighteen and Jay about fifteen."[1] Talk about hustlers.

Although they hit Manhattan with the goal of writing hits, songwriters were no different from the many others who chose towns over farms, cities over villages, and big cities over everything else. In the years after the Civil War, large numbers of people moved to whatever city the railroad would take them to.[2] These children and grandchildren of the pioneers reversed the move west and, in the process, accelerated America's change from rural to urban. By the late nineteenth century, a second industrial revolution had begun to transform the everyday lives of ordinary Americans—with the Model A, indoor plumbing, and electric lights, for starters. Of more direct interest to Leo Feist, Jerome Renwick, and the other big shots in the music publishing business, color printing for sheet-music covers had dropped in price, the new tabloid newspapers made publicity easier, and railroads took singing vaudevillians to every corner of the country to introduce the new songs, followed closely by bales of sheet music. Who knew what technological miracle was next for the lucky ones who lived in cities:

> Tis the era of inventions and the age of the machine,
> Most wonderful contrivances America has seen.
> When everyone was thrilled about Ben Franklin and his key
> They did not have an inkling of the wonders that would be.
> Electric fans, electric combs to galvanize the hair,
> Electrical photography to make the public stare,
> Kinetoscope and vitascope and cinematograph,
> What electricity can do, we do not know by half:
> Electricity! Electricity!
> It's bound to revolutionize the race . . .
> (Karl Hoschna and Harry B. Smith, "Electricity," 1905)

~ ~ ~

George M. Cohan was among the first to master the new conversational lyric. His lilting waltzes and brassy marches came at you straight on, and then he'd pepper his language with slang as hard elbowed as the man himself. He jam-packed his lyrics with up-to-date jabber that audiences loved to sing. In 1904, when he was twenty-six, his song "Yankee Doodle Boy" created "the kid who's all the candy," who made his "name and fame and boodle / Just like Mister Doodle did, by riding on a pony" (George M. Cohan, "The Yankee Doodle Boy," *Little Johnny Jones,* 1904). Everybody in Tin Pan Alley and along Broadway was writing songs that ranged from the bawdy to the ethereal, the gritty to the worshipful. When the songs arrived, they were ready made for dancing, stealing a kiss and more, and eventually popping the question.

Tin Pan Alley wanted to sell copies rather than make waves. Whenever the world changed, publishers and songwriters eventually hiked up their trousers and forged ahead. They usually made their first moves with humor, even mockery, until they knew for sure that the new terrain was safe. As a result, songs from the early years of the twentieth century had a different sound—the first signs of modernity, somewhere between the sentimental ballad of the nineteenth century and the jazz-infused syncopated ballad of the 1920s. As early as 1911, a song entitled, "If You Talk in Your Sleep Don't Mention My Name," took a funny, nonjudgmental look at adultery. The joke mattered more than any moral stance. Set in an urban restaurant with private dining rooms, the song allows a married woman to meet a married man without being properly introduced. They soon have what the lyric calls "luncheon" behind closed doors, and decide to meet every day for more of the same. When the man notices the woman's wedding ring, he offers her the practical advice that is the song's title and punch line (Nat D. Ayer and A. Seymour Brown, "If You Talk in Your Sleep Don't Mention My Name," 1911).

As America turned into an urban country with a city point of view, and as more and more people embraced new ways of looking at the world, the Alley followed along but hedged its bets. Skirt hems rose and laces loosened but, despite the growing restlessness of young women, the Victorian habit of elevating them persisted a while longer. Many songs remained melodic and romantic, though the waltz now had competition from ragtime. Many new songs relied on syncopation's urban twitch along with conversational lyrics that sounded more and more like the language of the streets. City life was more innovative and daring than small-town life, less bound by convention, but love ballads still spoke obliquely about sex. They could suggest something sexual in the rhythms of the music and the wordplay in the lyrics. For instance, songs about Hawaii first became popular in 1916, but at first they cared less about tropical romance than sexual innuendo. This song's setting might be a tropical paradise, but the last line in the chorus points to the aroused and irreverent city slicker who tells the story:

> Beneath her banyan parasol
> She couldn't talk my talk at all,
> But, oh, how she could Yacki, Hacki, Wicki, Wacki Woo.
> (Albert Von Tilzer, Stanley Murphy, and Chas. McCarron, "Oh! How She Could Yacki Hacki Wicki Wacki Woo [That's Love in Honolulu]," 1916)

The large, skittish market for sheet music rarely strayed very far from what silent movies and stage shows, magazine illustrations, and successful songwriters were already saying about women. It's not that songs lied; rather they told the truth of dreams, where you get to imagine the world you want. But as the social role of women changed in the first decades of the twentieth century, their image in love songs changed, too. What began as a simple combination of a pretty face and a few passive virtues grew into a complex personality endowed with an active body and a will of its own. Named the "New Woman" by the writer Sarah Grand in the *North American Review* in March 1894, she was increasingly independent and self-supporting.[3] She was also a lot smarter than anyone gave her credit for. Songs, still sometimes made of gossamer, were beginning to spin something truthful after all. Through a haze of romance, they built a brief dream on an underpinning of changing assumptions, attitudes, and values that those hearing the songs would recognize.

Before 1900, middle-class audiences largely believed in the convergence of romantic love with female virtue. Comic songs might hint at infidelity, but the girl in a sentimental love song was virtuous. Love songs in the early years of the new century were more modern in outlook and language than their nineteenth-century forebears, but they also serenaded in the shadow of the previous century's sentimental ballad.

The purest examples of the sentimental ballad, such as "After the Ball," were tearjerkers. While they reaffirmed tender feelings about romance and marriage, more often they told stories of lost love, loneliness, and death, especially the death of a child or an innocent young woman about to marry. They usually set ideal romance in the country rather than the city, and the ideal woman was a simple rural maid. The last generation of sentimental ballads still looked back to find romantic love in a long-ago-and-far-away bucolic setting, in a past whose alleged purity was giving way to the crasser ethics of urban society. For the next two decades, as young men and women poured into America's cities, songwriters enticed them with nostalgic visions of the homes and people they had left behind. Songs about this forsaken world varied in tone from deep melancholy ("On the Banks of the Wabash") to eager anticipation. ("When the Midnight Choo-Choo Leaves for Alabam'"). It wasn't by accident.

When music publishers realized that these young, largely single newcomers to the city were a potentially huge new audience for their sheet music, they instructed the songwriters they had under contract to turn out songs specifically for this audience. The key, they realized, was not the future but the past.

As the twentieth century neared its second decade, some love songs continued to describe its good girls in ardent, sentimental terms that Stephen Foster would have recognized. At the same time, love songs were also becoming more realistic, more connected to everyday life. Lyricists were developing a more conversational style that gave their lyrics a new expressiveness and immediacy. Although they appeared within a year of one another, the old-fashioned endearment "You're the flower of my heart" (Harry Armstrong and Richard H. Gerard, "Sweet Adeline," 1903) is a far cry from "I'll be your tootsie-wootsie" (Kerry Mills and Andrew B. Sterling, "Meet Me in St. Louis," 1904). The vernacular style also went well with ragtime, that new music whose brisk melodies and choppy urban rhythms clashed with elevated romanticism.

As love songs after 1900 began to sound like everyday talk, the musical conversation became more and more about sex. Tin Pan Alley disdained sophisticated women, but its lyricists had nothing at all against a girl taking one-on-one lessons in spooning. In the "cuddling songs" of the day, a young man would urge his sweetheart to cuddle, nestle, spoon, kiss, and squeeze. It was acceptable for her to lay her head on his shoulder as she got lovey-dovey in a cozy kind of way. Some women in songs urged prudish young men to be more romantic, but usually the man had to overcome a woman's reluctance. She was the one with the reputation to protect. In "Cuddle Up a Little Closer," the most popular "cuddling song" of the day, the man did the talking:

Cuddle up a little closer, lovey mine
Cuddle up and be my little clinging vine
Like to feel your cheeks so rosy
Like to make you comfy cozy
'Cause I love from head to toesy,
Lovey mine.
(Karl Hoschna and Otto Harbach, "Cuddle Up a Little Closer," *The Three Twins,* 1908)

Although these lyrics were suggestive, the caresses they described stayed within the limits of what a "nice girl" would do. Even so, the forces of commercialized libido stretched the limits, song by song. In "Give Me the Moonlight," the speaker demands that the light be turned out (and the heat turned up) for what looks like a prolonged session of billing and cooing:

Give me a bench for two, where we can bill and coo, and mine she's bound to be.
If there's anyone in doubt, and they'd like to try me out,
Give me the moonlight,
Give me the girl and leave the rest to me.
(Albert Von Tilzer and Lew Brown, "Give Me the Moonlight, Give Me the Girl [And Leave the Rest to Me]," 1917)

This lyric typifies the ways that popular love songs contributed to the breakdown of Victorian restraints on women's behavior. Although Tin Pan Alley's conservatism limited songs to changes that society had just begun to accept, popular love lyrics with their insistence on cuddling and spooning went a long way toward sanctioning lovers' enjoyment of sex. Just as the movies taught many adolescents how to pucker up and kiss, popular songs described all sorts of things two lovers might do while managing to stay just within the bounds of acceptable behavior. The love songs from these years convinced young women that love needed physical contact. Paradoxically, the breakdown of traditional standards usually occurred first and more rapidly in cities, but a fair number of songs about spooning were set in the country though maybe only for a day as lovers went off by themselves.

Nothing was more important for lovers than to be alone together at night; that was the oxymoronic goal. It also helps to explain why the moon was an especially important image in the easygoing love songs of the time. They lack the ardor of the sentimental ballads that preceded them and the introspection of songs that came later, but they were very likable. Men knew that the moon would make women feel spoonier because its "silv'ry beams" fostered "love dreams" that led to cuddling. In "By the Light of the Silvery Moon," the moon sanctifies the "sound of kisses floating on the breeze," and ensures that lovers will "be cuddling soon" (Gus Edwards and Edward Madden, 1909). By the same token, in "Shine on, Harvest Moon," the moon's absence frustrates a young fellow who pleads with it to reappear:

> Oh, shine on, shine on harvest moon up in the sky.
> I ain't had no lovin'
> Since April, January June or July,
> Snow time ain't no time to stay outdoors and spoon,
> So, shine on, shine on, harvest moon,
> For me and my gal.
> (Jack Norworth and Nora Bayes, *Follies of 1908*, 1908)

Again and again, the moon unites lovers and blesses their trysts. Songwriters plied the variations until audiences grew weary of them less than a decade before such literate lyricists as Lorenz Hart, Ira Gershwin, and Cole Porter transformed popular songs, beginning in the 1920s.

With all this emphasis on sneaking off to secluded spots and spooning under the moon, the line between female virtue and vice blurred. In "There's a Little Bit of Bad in Every Good Little Girl," the lyricist Grant Clarke observed that the "good girls" were doing things that only bad girls used to do (Fred Fischer and Grant Clarke, 1916). The longing to be alone explains why there were so many songs about taking walks and paddling canoes, although technology soon accelerated the assault on female chastity.

After 1900, flowery bowers, moonlit parks, and canoes gave way to the automobile as the favorite spot for spooning. The days of chaperones following a few paces behind courting lovers were gone. Songwriters quickly grasped what the public already knew: the horseless carriage was a godsend for lovers. The lines "You can go as far as you like with me / In my merry Oldsmobile" refer archly to the ease with which an auto could whisk a pair of lovers beyond supervision. What gives the song a veneer of respectability is its proposal of marriage: "Down the road of life we'll fly, / Automobubbling you and I" (Gus Edwards and Vincent Bryan, "In My Merry Oldsmobile," 1905). In 1912, Irving Berlin issued a warning about a particular peril for girls who went "automobiling":

Keep away from the fellow who owns an automobile;
He'll take you far in his motor-car;
Too darn far from your Ma and Pa. . . .
There's no chance to talk, squawk or balk
You must kiss him or get out and walk.
(Irving Berlin, "Keep Away from the Fellow Who Owns an Automobile," 1912)

By the time of the sexually assertive flapper a decade later, the shoe was on the other foot. On one couple's way home after a joyride in the country, "Back from Yonkers / I'm the one that had to walk" (Joseph Meyer and B. G. DeSylva, "If You Knew Susie," 1925).

During these first decades of the century, women began to earn a place for themselves in business, education, the professions, and the arts. Their new freedom was inseparable from marching suffragists, bohemians in Greenwich Village, and the independent New Woman embodied in the Gibson Girl and those who came after her. Named for her creator, the magazine artist Charles Dana Gibson, the Gibson Girl had a powerful effect on fashion and behavior from the 1880s until shortly before World War I. Although the artist initially named her Penelope Peachblow, an enchanted public soon gave her Gibson's name and transformed her from an individual into a representative social type. She was chic, cool, and graceful; tall and straight; beautifully dressed and alluring. She was freer and more daring than her mother but never truly wicked. A modern woman in many ways, she also remained very much a woman of her own time. She was decorous and virginal, with a full bosom and wasp waist, but she was also less massive and more natural in appearance, attire, and behavior than the Victorian young ladies who preceded her. She was also confident, healthy, and active. With her starched white blouse, bloomers, and pert straw hat, she might be out riding her bike, returning an undemanding forehand from a tennis-playing beau, or daring a brief dip in the sea.[4]

In Florenz Ziegfeld's first *Follies* in 1907, a stunning actress named Annabelle Whitford appeared onstage in a contemporary bathing costume. Ziegfeld probably chose her because of her striking resemblance to Gibson's original drawings. Fully covered except for her arms and a bit of neck, she sang a long-forgotten number called "The Gibson Bathing Girl," a mock plea to Gibson for his understanding. A young woman sufficiently daring and emancipated to appear publicly in a bathing suit, she pleads coyly with the paternalistic Gibson.

Though she is aware of her appeal and her sexuality, she sings a chorus of dependency:

> One day we arose
> In revolt at long clothes
> And presented this tearful petition:
> Mister Gibson, Mister Gibson,
> Why can't we take a swim?
> Paint us, please, with dimpled knees
> And plenty of rounded limb.
> Mister Gibson, Mister Gibson,
> Just give your brush a whirl,
> And they'll say on the beach
> There's a peach, a peach
> Of a Gibson bathing girl.
> (Paul West and Alfred Solman, "The Gibson Bathing Girl," *Follies of 1907*, 1907)

Despite her flirtatious dependence and her interest in appearances, the Gibson Girl reflected an early stirring of feminism. The novelist Margaret Deland wrote in the respectable *Atlantic Monthly* only three years later: "Restlessness! Restlessness! A prevailing discontent among women—a restlessness infinitely removed from the [contentment] of a generation ago."[5] These were the years after the impresario Tony Pastor had turned vaudeville into a suitable entertainment for respectable women, who sat in the audience each night as the brassy, defiant Eva Tanguay brayed her theme song across the footlights:

> I don't care,
> I don't care,
> What they may think of me.
> I'm happy go lucky,
> Men say I am plucky,
> So jolly and care free.
> (Harry O. Sutton and Jean Lenox, "I Don't Care," 1905)

Given Tanguay's flamboyant behavior and numerous love affairs, the meaning of her theme song is obvious. She once appeared in a costume made of dollar bills sewn together. Reveling in her vulgarity, she became the most popular vaudeville performer of her time.

Vaudeville was the most popular and widespread form of American entertainment after the decline of minstrel shows. It consisted of a string of live performances by a wide variety of "acts," anything and everything from trained seals to an opera singer performing arias.

Robert W. Snyder writes that it flourished as Victorian society unraveled. The attitudes it expressed onstage in sketches and routines, and offstage in its stars' sensational lives, provided people with "new ways of thinking, feeling, and behaving. . . . Middle-class women experimented with alternatives to the chafing restraints of Victorianism when they watched the singing and dancing of [such stars as] Eva Tanguay."[6] The same was true of silent movies. The lives, both onscreen and off, of such silent-screen stars as the innocent Mary Pickford, the hoydenesque Clara Bow, the mysterious Greta Garbo, and the sensual Joan Crawford fascinated American women. The new female stars exerted influence through their flaunting of convention, their exercise of power, and their attitudes toward sex.

It's hard to overstate the effect of these celebrities on young women all over the country. They learned what they thought celebrity taught; it was part of the urbanizing of America. The goal was to be free and independent, and the best way to reach it was a career in show business. The ordinary women who declare their independence within the songs of the time are often outsiders or newcomers, either star-struck working girls originally from the small towns of the South and Midwest, or immigrants from eastern and southern Europe. Despite the huge differences among them, ultimately it didn't matter if they came from Alabama or Galicia, Indiana or Umbria. Once they reached New York, they had the freedom to remake themselves in the Land of Opportunity.

The way for a woman to reinvent herself was almost always sexual, at least in story and song. For a man, sexuality was one of many choices: witness Rudolph Valentino's sleek athleticism. For a woman though, sex was pretty much the only choice. Mabel Brown, the young woman in Irving Berlin's "How Do You Do It, Mabel?" probably grew up learning the Protestant work ethic. Perhaps her grandparents settled Ohio or Indiana as part of a generation of pioneers, but now she returns to the East of her family's origins because she sees her future in New York. Mabel may have arrived in the city dressed in gingham, but she soon finds a job in a Broadway chorus and soon after that acquires a sugar daddy—although he never makes an appearance in the lyric. She then writes back to her boyfriend to tell him she is earning, "so to speak," twenty dollars a week. Motivated by curiosity but without suspicion or guile, he pays her a surprise visit:

> The minute that he saw her flat
> He whisper'd in her ear:

"How do you do it, Mabel,
On twenty dollars a week?
Tell us how you are able,
On twenty dollars a week.
A fancy flat and a diamond bar,
Twenty hats and a motorcar;
Go right to it,
But how do you do it,
On twenty dollars a week?"
(Irving Berlin and Edgar Leslie, "How Do You Do It Mabel, on Twenty Dollars a Week?" 1911)

Similarly, Sadie Cohen leaves a "happy home" to become an actress in the theater, but instead lands a spot in burlesque where she appears as Salome in Dance of the Seven Veils. The two young songwriters, Irving Berlin and Edgar Leslie, were trying to capitalize on the scandalous dance of the same name from Richard Strauss' 1907 opera *Salome* by writing a funny song that was also about the successful workings of the melting pot. They weren't setting out to write a chapter of social history, but because they were responsive to the world at the time, that was the result. *Salome* had popularized the character of the infamous Salome and her titillating dance, and led to a large number of voluptuous Salomes appearing in vaudeville theaters all over the country. The problem arises in the song when Sadie's sweetheart arrives to see her dance. She has assimilated more rapidly than he, and when she begins to shake and shimmy, he cries out in a Yiddish accent:

Don't do that dance, I tell you, Sadie,
That's not a business for a lady!
'Most everybody knows
That I'm your lovin' Mose,
Oy, oy, oy, oy,
Where is your clothes?
(Irving Berlin and Edgar Leslie, "Sadie Salome [Go Home]," 1909)

Though Mabel and Sadie have significant differences, their arrival in New York gives them a chance to become rich and famous in show business. Mabel has a sugar daddy whose affections enable her to live in high style in return for sexual favors, whereas Sadie's story focuses on her show-stopping appearance in an abbreviated costume. Visits from their boyfriends lead to the similar jokes on which both songs rest. One young man remains a rube, the other a greenhorn. The women are more daring, independent, and modern than the men. They shed the sexual repression of the Protestant small town and the Jewish shtetl. As the new century gains momentum, Mabel and Sadie are, in a word, New Women living in New York City. The songs make fun of them but take their side. They are on their way to becoming up-to-date Americans.

People who moved to the city in the late nineteenth and early twentieth centuries felt freer to behave in ways they would not have dared back home, partly because they had movie stars to guide them and, eventually, subways and taxis to take them where they wanted to go. If they had come from Palermo or Odessa, rather than Michigan or Tennessee, they soon latched on to opportunities they could not have imagined beforehand. America changed them just as their ways of looking at the world changed America. It wasn't easy or gentle, but it happened. Perhaps the move to the city had to happen first; at least that's the way it was in America. One by one, men and women, many of them young and single, found work, opportunity, and independence in the city. It was an exciting, frightening time, and some who came failed. Rayhane Sanders wrote recently but could have written a century ago: "There is something unique about New York, some quality, some matchless, pertinent combination of promise and despair, wizardry and counterfeit, abundance and depletion."[7] That same combination characterizes other American cities as well, yet together the men and women who arrived from elsewhere made a new America, first in New York City. The songwriters were part of that world, and their songs reflected what America was up to. Thirty-two bars at a time, they sang to Americans about America.

The early twentieth century was a time of innovative tension between city and country. Americans understood, at least intuitively, that the nation's future lay in such places as Chicago and New York. They had begun to move to large cities in ever-growing numbers, but through most of the nineteenth century, songs continued to portray the small town as America idealized, an Eden-like symbol of the people's virtues and verities. Although a city sensibility was taking hold in songs, with such songs as "Sidewalks of New York" and the Mulligan Guard musicals of David Braham and Ned Harrigan becoming popular in the 1880s and 1890s, the rural ideal hung on. Not many years before the flapper showed us how much things had changed, we were still singing a gentle lyric about building "a sweet little nest / Somewhere in the West" (Ernest R. Ball and J. Keirn Brennan, "Let the Rest of the World Go By," 1919). Tin Pan Alley's city songs had an entrenched tradition to overcome and replace.

A century earlier, as Americans first moved west to Kentucky and Indiana, they discovered the richness of the land and a continent that seemed never to run out of room. They dreamed a new myth of the garden. Like many things characteristically American, it combined the solid and suggestive, the practical and symbolic. The myth was about the migration west, agriculture, and the capacity of the land to feed a growing, increasingly urban nation. Under the influence of America's expansionist view of itself, it soon merged with Manifest Destiny, in which the practical matter of settling the continent and building towns came wrapped in a spiritual cloak. That sense of the land and its meaning helped to shape American attitudes for more than a century, even in something as small and frivolous as a popular song.[8]

A lot of Tin Pan Alley songwriters probably had never heard of the myth of the garden, Manifest Destiny, or Frederick Jackson Turner's frontier thesis. Although they were often better educated than Tin Pan Alley mythology has it, few of them had intellectual aspirations. They wrote songs to make a living. When they and the music publishers they worked for recognized the new city dwellers as a market, they turned to the kinds of emotion that popular songs are perfect for. Oh, a few paeans of praise for the honking horns and busy night life, but mostly songs that portrayed young men longing to return to a small town, a mother, and a sweetheart down the lane. The dream was romantic as well as nostalgic; once the boy returned, he and his beloved would wed to enjoy the same kind of idyllic marriage as their parents. Songs about returning reflected some recognizable attitudes toward life in the city: the complexities and dissatisfactions of urban living.

A few of these songs, such as Irving Berlin's "This Is the Life" from 1914, celebrated life in the city. After a weeklong visit that includes seven nights of carousing, the country bumpkin concludes, "I love the cows and chickens, / But this is the life!" Someone who probably rose at dawn now looks forward to raising the dickens at night, "While I'm cabareting / Where the band is playing" (Irving Berlin, "This Is the Life," 1914). He gladly replaces a life attuned to nature's rhythms with one that promises the unpredictable pleasure and excitement that come with freedom and affluence in the big city. But most of the songs anticipated a return to the small town for a wedding and a life of married bliss. In "Settle Down in a One-Horse Town," also from 1914, Berlin composes a young man's letter to the one he loves. "Come, let's settle down," he writes, "in some small country town." Unlike the farmer who moves to the city, he is "getting tired of the glare and light" and wants to be "far, far away from cabarets." He plans to return home for good: "So if you're strong for a shower of rice, / We could make a paradise / Out of a one-horse town" (Irving Berlin, "Settle Down in a One-Horse Town," *Watch Your Step*, 1914). Which did Berlin himself believe? It doesn't matter; the songs aren't about him. They're contradictory, not only because he manipulated America's beliefs for his own profit, but also because he turned his observations into songs. Americans believed both, and, honest emotional broker that every songwriter must ultimately be, Berlin gave each point of view its say.

Although the return home in songs is not overtly religious, it does evoke a vision of a return to Eden, a turning away from the temptations of the city for the purity of the small town and farm, where idealized love defines the rest of the sojourner's life. The return is not to the biblical Eden but to an American Eden, not a place of religious certainty or nationalistic feeling, though it may reflect both. Although the term probably never appeared in a single Tin Pan Alley tune, the American Eden, imagined in popular songs for three quarters of a century, was a place where romantic love, confirmed in return and marriage, was permanent and unchanging, a cornucopia of romantic delights.

The music publishers' goal was to appeal to former southerners and midwesterners, now perhaps living in fourth-floor cold-water flats, but the publishers soon learned to their satisfaction that those who remained behind in such places as Georgia and Ohio were also buying the songs. The new city dwellers bought the sheet music enthusiastically, but what made the publishers' innovation even more profitable was the enthusiasm of the people who stayed back home. They bought the songs because they liked the portraits of the idyllic small towns where they preferred to live. Everyone embraced the songs' idealized view of rural life. In such songs as "Peoria," "Down by the Ohio," "Carolina in the Morning," "Georgia on My Mind," "Indiana," and hundreds more, the return was not only to a cherished place but to a way of life embodied in a singular young woman. Returning soon became a central theme in American popular songs:

There's a preacher preaches down in Georgia,
Always ready to say:
"Will you love and obey?"
I bet you'll pick yourself a peach of a wife,
Settle down to a peach of a life,
Ev'ry thing is peaches down in Georgia.
(Milton Ager, Geo. W Meyer, and Grant Clarke, "Everything Is Peaches Down In Georgia," 1918)

The decision by New York music publishers to traffic in nostalgia produced a crop of songs that viewed rural America as the embodiment of the American Eden. Songwriters in the early twentieth century grafted a portion of America's myth of itself onto a body of work intended to describe nothing more than the promptings of romantic love. At the same time, though, different, apparently contradictory, things were happening. Americans may have been moving to the city, but in their imaginations they were leaving it. They were both thrilled by city living and suspicious, even frightened, of it. Although more of the city's new arrivals were male, a surprisingly large number were single and female, and cautionary lyrics spun stories about the perils they would face. One of the most melodramatic of these songs grew from the same dark sense of city life as Theodore Dreiser's *Sister Carrie.* A young woman, drawn to the "sights and the bright city lights," finds herself ignored and then misled by strangers:

So the poor little girlie just drifted along.
Nobody cared if she lived or died
Nobody cared if she laughed or cried.
She's just a lost sister
And nobody missed her,
She's there in the city
Where there's no pity
In the city that has no heart.
(Thos. S. Allen and Joseph M. Daly, "In the Heart of the City That Has No Heart," 1913)

Songs also derived from the city's widely recognized traps and temptations, especially with so many young women living on their own. During the teens, as the ragged rhythms of the dance craze and the formalized eroticism of the tango became increasingly insistent, songs expressed their allure and their dangers for a relative newcomer who remains eager but still tentative. Broadway fascinates her, as does "its latest decadent fad—daytime dancing at tango teas."[9] The lyric gains immediacy by addressing Broadway directly:

> How I long once to turkey trot at Healey's,
> Or just to peek at Shanley's Cabaret,
> But you're so big and I'm so small,
> You'd swallow me right up, that's all,
> So I'm just a little bit afraid of you, Broadway.
> (Harry Von Tilzer and George Whiting, "I'm a Little Bit Afraid of You, Broadway," 1913)

From the time song publishers first aimed their wares at the potential new market of recent arrivals, many songs set out purposely to express the homesickness these newcomers must have felt despite their brave embrace of the future. The songs of Tin Pan Alley, beginning as early as the 1890s and continuing into the 1920s, offered them a reminder of what they longed to rediscover and regain.[10] The return was to something familiar yet implicitly new. R. W. B. Lewis wrote, "The American myth saw life and history as just beginning. It described the world as starting up again under fresh initiative, in a divinely granted second chance for the human race, after the first chance had been so disastrously fumbled in the darkening old world."[11] In a much smaller way, popular songs embraced this paradoxical mix of the fresh and the familiar. Young men in the city imagined returning home to live according to old ways and traditional values, but it would not be too long before they were driving automobiles and listening to crystal sets. In the busy, rambunctious American Eden, returning had become a new beginning. We would not merely inhabit it; we would build it:

> And sometime,
> I'm goin' to build a little home for two,
> For three or four, or more;
> In Loveland,
> For me and my gal.
> (George W. Mayer, Edgar Leslie, and E. Ray Goetz, "For Me and My Gal," 1917)

The urge to return also harked back to the urban parlor songs of the late nineteenth century. As the middle class rose in wealth, influence, and authority, it embraced the values of domesticity, propriety, and decorum. In families shaped by the division of labor, women were responsible for the household and all that came with it, including the raising of children and the family's cultural life. The mother, not the youngsters, chose the sheet music that sat on the piano in the parlor, and she chose lyrics that told tales of true love and fulfillment in a serene domestic setting.[12] Such up-to-date songs from the Twenties as "Blue Room" (1926) and "My Blue Heaven" (1927) looked back to this gentler time.

Songs were about longing to return, anticipating the trip back, remembering what you would be returning to, and leaping up and heading for the train station—or, on the other side, the inability or failure to return in songs of heartbreak and despair. In other words, the young people in these songs inhabited the city, and its intrusions defined their emotional state. In Irving Berlin's "When the Midnight Choo-Choo Leaves for Alabam'," a young man is so excited by his imminent departure that he bolts from his apartment and eventually grabs the conductor "by the collar" to cry out, "Alabam'! Alabam'!" (Irving Berlin, "When the Midnight Choo-Choo Leaves for Alabam'," 1912)

These songs usually emphasize hope rather than despair by focusing on the possibility of return rather than the melancholy of separation. When a boy in the city falls in love with a girl back home, the girl and the town have a way of merging, as do his memories with his dream of the future. Many songs could barely sing about one without singing about the other. They set their sights on idealized love by setting it somewhere particular and essential. In a jaunty song of returning to the Midwest or South—it's impossible to know for sure—a young man describes his plans for an imminent trip back to the "shack where the Black-eyed Susans grow." Rather than dwelling on homesickness, he emphasizes his delight in returning. As in many songs, the lyric is a dramatic monologue in which the traveler speaks to his absent beloved as if she's with him or, as here, to a friend. He imagines strolling down a country lane to find her and offering "a ring for the finger of my sweet." Then, once he's married, he looks ahead to a life about which he gently teases his urban friend:

> Maybe I'll introduce you
> To my corn-fed bride,
> When I come back from the shack
> Where the Black-eyed Susans grow.
>
> (Richard A. Whiting and Dave Radford, "Where the Black-Eyed Susans Grow," 1917)

Elsewhere in the song, the boy describes the girl's parents as "plain old" farmers but also praises them for raising "some pretty daisy / When they raised my little Sue." What's striking about this otherwise formulaic song is the way it interweaves the place and the girl; both have the same name. By making the black-eyed Susan the most desirable of all the flowers, the young man implicitly makes Susan the most desirable of all young women. He praises her by praising it, as flower and girl become interwoven and inseparable in his imagination. This pattern recurs throughout the songs of the time; it was an essential part of popular music's expression of the romantic ideal before songs became increasingly introspective in the 1930s. Love was the ever-present theme, but changing attitudes and the need for novelty challenged songwriters to re-imagine the beloved. Placing the love affair far away gave both the song and the girl an extra dimension of character that could be refreshed in as many ways as there were places to put her.

As Tin Pan Alley's songwriters developed the knack of using place to suggest something about the person inside a song, they first merged setting with beloved. When love for a girl is part of what a young fellow remembers and envisions, she and the place often become inseparable in his imagination for as long as they're apart. It was an effective way to intensify a song's emotionalism. One of the many songs that performs such tricks of association and transformation is "Carolina in the Morning," Walter Donaldson and Gus Kahn's standard about returning. It's also one of several songs in which the name of a state doubles as the name of a girl. In "Carolina," the place and the girl who lives there are inseparable. Kahn's lyrics create the feel of a new beginning as the young man returns so early in the morning that the dew is still "pearly." He immediately links being there with "strolling" with his "girlie," also "in the morning." He associates his return with "morning glories," "butterflies" that "flutter up," and "each little buttercup" that the two of them encounter as they stroll along "at dawning" (Walter Donaldson and Gus Kahn, "Carolina in the Morning," 1922). The song celebrates reunion through the imagery of a new beginning.

In the aftermath of Black Thursday (October 24, 1929), songs' outlook and style changed almost as quickly as the flapper disappeared. A few songs about returning continued to appear through the 1930s even though getting home might mean riding the rails. For the most part, though, the optimism and anticipation of returning were as outdated as rouged knees. People were still dreaming of home, but they had no practical way to get there, not when they were broke or out of work. If life was often airy and awhirl in the twenties, then everything was weighed down and motionless in the thirties. Yet even here some love songs managed to make the link between place and person immediate. "Georgia on My Mind" is a reflective, melancholy song with no promise of imminent return (Hoagy Carmichael and Stuart Gorrell, "Georgia on My Mind," 1930). Although the young man in the lyric begins by remembering "the song of you" and he speaks to her directly, he can see her only in his dreams. At first, the lyric makes "Georgia" ambiguous. Is it the name of his home state or of the beloved who waits and for whom he longs? The tone is wistful as he resists the temptation of other arms that reach out and eyes that "smile tenderly" because "the road leads back to you." The elliptical lyric suggests, but never quite states, that the city is the source of temptation: he is another country boy who tires of the fast life. When he reaches the climactic line, "Just an old sweet song keeps Georgia on my mind," the place and the girl become one yet again, joined by the melody of a remembered sentimental ballad.

The appeal of these songs of returning was more complex for former southerners than for former midwesterners. A return to a place like Alabama was more laden with ambiguity than a return to, say, Michigan. Although Jewish songwriters in New York City wrote most of them, songs about Dixie reflected the burden of history that weighed so heavily on the South and its people. They touched a deep chord in a section of the country still struggling with the dislocations of the Civil War and still embracing a self-deceptively romantic view of itself that survived despite the years of devastation, Reconstruction, and—more recently—Jim Crow.

Songs set in the South sound like their midwestern cousins on the surface, but there are many more of them. The lyricist Gus Kahn explained why: "Our song boys are of the North. Paradise is never where we are. The South has become our never, never land, the symbol of the land where the lotus blossoms, and dreams come true."[13] Like songs about the Midwest, songs about the South miss the girl left behind and often associate her with specific places. Regardless of whether they are love songs, or whether they are content with a nostalgic view of what the traveler has lost, they evoke the land and limn its emotional geography. Whether or not the dream of return includes the girl left behind, the songs express a view of the South as pastoral perfection, a place to return to. But when many of the songs are "coon songs" and portray young black men eager to return, the emotions become suspect. Their unintentional function—to reflect and reconfirm white assumptions about blacks—dates back at least as far as the nineteenth-century minstrel songs that preceded them: in 1851, twelve years before the Emancipation Proclamation, one of the most famous of all American songs depicts a black man who wanders the land unable to return home but "still longing for the old plantation."

The songs of the early twentieth century were largely formulaic. To set a song in the South, all you had to do was wrap cotton blossoms and magnolias in a new bundle. Hundreds of songs portray a boy and girl who sneak away to kiss—in a front porch swing, down a deserted lane, or out in a canoe. Even when these youthful songs are about temptation and seduction, the final chorus usually looks ahead to marriage, because that was what the romantic formula required, and that was what Americans said they believed in:

> I'm gonna make a beeline straight for home,
> That's what I am,
> And I've a plan to buzz around with my honey lamb;
> Some Sunday afternoon,
> If I don't get stung, there'll be a honeymoon,
> When the bees make honey down in sunny,
> Oh! You Alabam'.
>
> (Walter Donaldson, Sam M. Lewis, and Joe Young, "When the Bees Make Honey Down in Sunny Alabam'," 1919)

Sam M. Lewis and Joe Young's lyric begins with bees to suggest the approaching summer when a young man intends to leave the city to return home to rural Alabama, but the image expands through the song. The buzzing identifies his plans for the future, as well as his successful attempt to kiss his girl. The song's treatment of what otherwise might have been tired is lively, amusing, and inventive, familiar and accessible without ever losing immediacy.

~ ~ ~

As Europe stumbled into war in the summer of 1914, bohemianism arrived in America, fervent but largely limited to Greenwich Village on Manhattan's Lower West Side. As it rejected middle-class propriety and restraint, bohemianism promoted modernism in the arts, socialism in politics, and free love in personal behavior. It advocated self-consciously revolutionary attitudes about politics, work, art, marriage, and sex. Its adherents set out to be irreverent and outrageous, to turn the world topsy-turvy and then remake it. As it influenced the rest of the country (though in diluted form), it accelerated the change from a culture of self-sacrifice and the work ethic to a new world of self-fulfillment and individualism. It embraced new ideas from socialism to psychiatry, and it saw marriage as a form of repression. It also believed in sexual pleasure for women.[14] Although bohemianism horrified most Americans at first, many of them—especially the young—eventually embraced its beliefs even though their motivations changed over time. For the bohemian woman in the teens, free love meant the pursuit of freedom; for the flapper in the 1920s, it meant the pursuit of pleasure.

In "Rose of Washington Square" from 1922, one of the few songs to treat bohemianism directly, the title character leaves the Bronx for the bohemian life in Greenwich Village. The working-class name of Rose, her "Roman nose," and the song's initial setting in the Bronx suggest that she's Jewish, as does the fact that Fanny Brice performed it with a comic Yiddish accent. She or her family left the Lower East Side because they were moving up in America. Rose is voluptuous but has little talent. She models for Harrison Fisher, an illustrator second in reputation only to Charles Dana Gibson, and poses in damp cellars for the covers of what used to be called "gent's magazines." Rose's choice—to forsake a culture where the body is shameful and to embrace one that approves of posing in scanty outfits—provides the basis for the song's ethnic joke. Rose feels no shame but, more important, lacks any sense of irony. She is a sensual innocent abroad in the city:

> The call me Rose of Washington Square,
> I'm withering there, in basement air I'm fading.
> Pose, with or without my clothes,
> They say my Roman nose,
> It seems to please artistic people.
>
> (James Hanley and Ballard MacDonald, "Rose of Washington Square," 1922)

After the turn of the century, the rigid social rules decreeing that proper young women must not venture out unaccompanied to theaters or restaurants or ride in autos began to relax. "The maiden of yore would feel rather sore / If she could see the girl of today," Sam M. Lewis wrote in "The Girl on the Automobile":

> This sweet little miss, once afraid of a kiss,
> In the dark, oh! How nervous she'd feel,
> Now has a strong grip, at a rather fast clip
> Really runs an automobile!
> (Jos. S. Nathan and Sam M. Lewis, "The Girl on the Automobile," 1905)

Love songs also depicted women aloft in airplanes, although a man was usually the pilot, as in Fred Fischer and Alfred Bryan's "Come, Josephine, in My Flying Machine." This hit song of 1910 combined the Wright Brothers' exciting invention with popular music's new conversational style: "Oh, say! Let us fly, dear. / Where, kid? To the sky, dear!" Soaring together above the clouds became a new metaphor for the thrill of romance and perhaps sexual bliss as well. Getting a girl into a car or up in a plane assumed that she would immediately cast off all inhibitions.

By the teens, the effect of technology interfered with Tin Pan Alley's ability to find old-fashioned girls to write about. Women challenged social restrictions in education and the professions, and in their leisure as well. Not content to sit in rural semi-seclusion dressed in a neat bonnet and shawl, the New Woman often held an office job and lived on her own in the city. Katy, an Irish working girl who waits on tables, loves the idea of being "an aviatress." Every time "the propeller starts to buzz," Katy drops her work and the restaurant has to close its doors. She is more interested in independence than the offer of a ring (Will Curtis and Irving Bibo, "Since Katy the Waitress," 1919).

"The girl of today" wanted to ride in—or even drive—an automobile, fly in an airplane, or go to the moving pictures and smoke a Fatima cigarette afterward. She wanted to escape from constant supervision, go out dressed in style, and dance the latest immodest dances, like the girls she saw in the pictures. A newspaper reported in 1911 that the boss of a Chicago piano company had been called out of town, leaving his staff of "seven lively girls" unsupervised. They finished their day's tasks in a couple of hours, pushed back the desks and wound up the gramophone, "and soon they were all two-stepping around the office," to the sound of "a tantalizing ragtime."[15]

Writers of songs met the challenge of these new images of womanhood, and plotted ways to woo and win women without discarding perfectly good rhymes like "spoon" and "honeymoon." Tin Pan Alley and the musical stage acknowledged the New Woman but often in a superficial or patronizing way. Florenz Ziegfeld's 1913 *Follies* (dedicated to "Glorifying the American Girl") included a comic song, "Ragtime Suffragette," which treated the women's suffrage movement pretty much as a fad on the level of the Cubanola Glide and the hobble skirt. The lyric concedes that the Suffragette was "no household pet," but deplores her "Raggin' with bombshells and raggin' with bricks, / Raggin' and naggin' with politics," while her long-suffering husband waits at home for his dinner. (Nat D. Ayer, Harry Williams, 1913)

Many of the humorous songs about independent women portrayed husbands as the victims of their wives' misadventures. In one song from the dance craze, a husband's complaint that his wife makes him get up at four in the morning to wax their floor for dancing leads to the title line: "My Wife Is Dancing Mad" (Arch Gottler, Howard Johnson, and E. Ray Goetz, 1914). "My Futurist Girl" written for the *Ziegfeld Follies of 1914*, exploits the notoriety of faddish movements in modern art. The printed score's cover illustration shows a girl preening before a mirror, dressed in the extremity of high fashion with an exaggerated hobble skirt and an eccentric hat. Despite this young "futurist's" ultra-modern trappings, the song depicts a conventional future for her:

> We'll have a Futuristic honeymoon
> In a Cubist house just built to spoon,
> If you'll only be my Futurist girl.
> (Dave Stamper, Gene Buck, "My Futurist Girl," *Ziegfeld Follies of 1914*, 1914)

Despite its Modernist references, the song offers the same future of domestic bliss depicted in mainstream lyrics like "I'd love to live in Loveland with a girl like you" (Will Rossiter, 1910) and "For Me and My Gal," (George Meyer, Edgar Leslie, E. Ray Goetz, 1917).

~ ~ ~

The mania for ragtime songs ushered in new styles of urbane dress and dance. The professional dance team of Vernon and Irene Castle introduced many of the new steps that fueled what came to be called the dance craze—the Castle walk, one-step, fox trot, and tango, among others.[16] The dance craze was exactly that—a craze so insistent and long lasting that it persisted through the teens and lingered in the early twenties. It was the popular American embodiment of modernity. Irving Berlin was right on the money when he wrote, "Come, come,

Figure 5.2. In the years leading up to World War I, Vernon and Irene Castle created the dance craze almost single-handedly. Library of Congress Prints and Photographs Division.

come, come let us start, / Ev'rybody's Doin' It Now" (Irving Berlin, "Everybody's Doin' It Now," 1911). The new dances were cosmopolitan, liberating, and up to the minute. People, especially women, couldn't get enough of them. They danced at tea dances in hotels on their way home from work; they danced outdoors in Central Park. Some factories even installed dance floors in cafeterias so workers could turkey trot during lunch. Dance studios sprang up everywhere, along with a new generation of instructors to teach the new steps. If you could walk, you could do the one-step.

The dance craze probably began when the San Francisco vaudevillian Blossom Seeley first danced to a song called "Toddlin' the Todalo" on Broadway in 1911 (A. Baldwin Sloane and E. Ray Goetz). Its popularity emerged from a confluence of the appeal of ragtime songs, the assertiveness of the New Woman, and a generation of new dance teachers eager to teach the new ragtime dances, but it achieved acceptance and respectability in the performances of the dancers Vernon and Irene Castle. When they met, he was getting by as a knockabout comic in vaudeville and on Broadway, and she was a stage-struck girl from New Rochelle, New York. After they married, they signed to appear in a French theatrical revue that never opened. Flat broke and stranded in Paris, they found a job dancing in a small restaurant called the Café de Paris. On the dot of midnight, a spotlight would pick them out at a ringside table. They would rise, bow to one another, and glide onto the floor to dance to "Alexander's Ragtime Band," a new song that had swept America and was now all the rage in Paris and London as well. Overnight, they became the toast of Paris, and America could hardly wait for them to come home.

Women began to copy Irene's look and style. She soon became the most influential female tastemaker of her time, an unintentional reformer in the guise of a chic ballroom dancer and fashion plate. Henrietta Rodman, a feminist and educator, had bobbed her hair as early as 1910, but she was dismissed as a bohemian and thus an eccentric. When Irene Castle did the same thing two years later, millions of women followed her lead. She discarded the whalebone corsets of the Victorian era to wear simple, flowing gowns. Because she was slim and svelte, the standard of beauty changed from buxom to slender. As a dancer, she preferred a new, more natural figure, and thus began the first fad for dieting. By 1917, Irving Berlin combined the craze for shedding pounds with the craze for ragtime dancing:

It's very simple if you care to try it
A million people are reducing by it
You needn't bother 'bout a silly diet
Try a One-Step or a Fox-Trot
Go right ahead and eat a great big luncheon
I guarantee that you will soon have one chin
Instead of two or three
Just take a tip from me
Dance and grow thin.

(George W. Meyer and Irving Berlin, "Dance and Grow Thin," *Dance and Grow Thin*, 1917)

Vernon was sleek and attentive, Irene charming and vivacious. Tall and elegant in flowing chiffon, whirling gracefully in the arms of her loving husband, she embodied modern femininity. Together, she and Vernon demonstrated that dancing was glamorous and healthy by bleaching the "blackness" out of their dances to make them safe and respectable. It was even reported that Mrs. Castle was giving private lessons to that pillar of rectitude, Mrs. John D. Rockefeller.

Before ragtime dancing there was ragtime itself. It began in the late nineteenth century as an improvised piano music performed by itinerant African American piano players in saloons and whorehouses along the Mississippi near St. Louis. When it became popular, Tin Pan Alley did what it always did: it stole. Songwriters added syncopation to their thirty-two-bar melodies and wrote about dancing in their lyrics. These "ragtime songs," with titles like "He's a Rag Picker," "I Love a Piano," and "They've Got Me Doing It Now"—all three written by Irving Berlin between 1913 and 1915—gave ragtime dancing the impetus it needed. The new hedonistic dances burst on the scene only a few years after respectable women began to take their pleasures outside the home. They forsook parlors for restaurants, theaters, and concert halls. When they had the opportunity to dance, they rebelled against Victorian restraint by dragging their male escorts onto the floor to do not the waltz, but the camel walk and the grizzly bear. The craze sounds frivolous, but it reflects the large social changes roiling the nation's family life. Typically, when faced with controversy over something too good to ignore, songwriters softened the potential conflict with humor. Numerous songs depict long-suffering husbands sympathetically because they have to live with wives who are constantly dancing and dieting. It may have been a joke in 1914, but in this comic complaint by a husband, the startling choice at the end of the final chorus suggests that more is wrong with the marriage than a disagreement over dancing. The wife knows that her husband doesn't want to have sex with her, so she finds a sexual outlet in dancing and threatens him with sex if he doesn't comply with her wishes. Even then he keeps his complaints to himself:

> I know my wife is dancing mad,
> She's got the dancing fever bad.
> She cries, "I've got to get thin
> And lose this double chin,"
> Then she skips and she dips.
> Ha, ha, ha, ha, I hope she slips
> 'Cause ev'ry night till break of day
> Upon a phonograph she'll play.
> She threatens, "If I cannot dance till three
> You will have to sleep with me."
> My wife is dancing mad.
> (Arch Gottler, Howard Johnson, and E. Ray Goetz, "My Wife Is Dancing Mad," 1914)

Comic songs about married couples often fell back on the stereotypes of an imperious wife and a henpecked husband. Women who wanted to learn to dance, used birth control, or marched for the vote soon became figures of mockery in songs. They were an easy source of humor, not because they were foolish, but because they wanted things to change. As with Mabel who did it "on twenty dollars a week," and Sadie, who did "that dance," the ultimate source of the humor is the obtuseness and rigidity of the men.

The Castles' influence spread widely across the country through their elegant nightclubs, their public appearances, their dancing schools, and, in 1914, their collaboration on a best-selling book they called *Modern Dance.* In each of his chapters, Vernon showed readers how to do the dances he and Irene performed and also taught in their schools, complete with line drawings of feet in the proper positions. In her chapters, Irene guided women on how to dress, conduct themselves publicly, and hold themselves when they walked and danced. As the Castles made what began as largely African American dances acceptable to white audiences, Irene was teaching them how to become New Women without surrendering their respectability or femininity. Yet during the years leading up to World War I, the Castles' refined style did not stop blue-nosed (and perhaps racist) attempts to suppress the tango and the ragtime dances as offenses against modesty and decorum.[17] People at the time were more likely to apply such language to European-based dances and behavior, rather than to the more athletic, more spontaneous, more clearly sexual dances of African Americans. But the Castles usually carried the day. Irving Berlin entitled a 1915 song "Everything in America Is Ragtime" (*Stop! Look! Listen!*). That was true for the socially prominent as well as young factory and shopgirls, to the consternation of the guardians of public morality. New York society women formed a Committee on Amusement and Vacation Resources for Working Girls, which kept "vigilant watch on the dance halls of New York." Along with similar groups in other cities, they campaigned against such "freakish and degrading dances as the Turkey Trot, the Grizzly Bear, and the Bunny Hug," as well as the fashion for shorter, skimpier skirts.

Tin Pan Alley also tut-tutted over girls' vampish behavior. A socially prominent settlement-house worker lamented in 1912, "Such fashions as obtain in New York now would have shocked almost to illness the girls I knew in youth and would have utterly disgusted old-time men. A man told me the other day that he could not now tell decent women from loose women on the streets here. Skimpy skirts and too few of them—well, I don't care even to talk about the costumes of today."[18] Four years later, in a song called "You're a Dangerous Girl," the lyricist Grant Clarke wrote:

> You're the kind that will charm
> And then do harm
> You've got a dangerous way. . . .
> Your lips have said, "Now don't be a stranger,"
> But they're both red, I know that means danger.
> (Jimmie V. Monaco and Grant Clarke, "You're a Dangerous Girl," 1916)

Immodest dress came in for censure as well. The song, "Eve Wasn't Modest Till She Ate that Apple," begins by praising modesty: "Everybody loves a girl who's modest / Everybody loves a girl who's shy," but is soon drooling over the current fashion:

> Once they only wore a leaf
> Clothes are getting just as brief,
> If ev'ry mother's daughter, wears dresses any shorter,
> We'll have to pass the apples again.
> (Albert Von Tilzer, and Charles R. McCarron, "Eve Wasn't Modest Till She Ate That Apple," 1917)

Tin Pan Alley lyricists, who generally had hazy notions of geography, history, and foreign cultures, always knew exactly what people were up to on the dance floor. They knew that the new face-to-face dances with animal names like the Bunny Hug and the Kangaroo Hop furnished couples with yet another way to embrace and spoon with impunity. A lyric by Joe McCarthy suggests that social dancing commonly led couples to try something more: "He'd trot her to a corner, then he'd steal a little squeeze, / While they were dancing around" (James V. Monaco and Joe McCarthy, "While They Were Dancing Around," 1913). Songwriters knew that "stepping out" unaccompanied to a tea dance in a hotel ballroom was considered risqué. In 1914, Al Jolson performed "Dancing the Blues Away" (Fred Fisher, Joe McCarthy, and Howard Johnson, 1914), a comic love song with a nod to the dance craze. A neglected wife goes out dancing by herself "in a nearby hall," something unheard of for a middle-class woman in 1900, but possible in the teens because of urban anonymity and changing standards. Her husband is stepping out at the same time, and encounters her dancing with another man. She assures her spouse that she is whiling away the time because of his neglect, and she swears she always pretends her partner is her husband. She adds, "You know this man with me / Is Uncle Billy, and he's ninety-three!"

Tin Pan Alley's image of ideal American womanhood was unsettled during these years. Old-fashioned modesty was "slow," but songs described these new "fast" women and girls as a little bit bohemian, a little bit dangerous, and at least implicitly city dwellers. If a man married one of these New Women, would she cook him his pot roast, or would he be forced to scour the cabarets to rescue her from the clutches of some "Tango pirate"?[19]

What sort of woman could a man call his ideal during this decade when women seemed to be acting in new and confusing ways? Serious, responsible women who demanded the vote were willfully disturbing the peace and going to jail. They made speeches and picketed the White House with signs comparing President Wilson to the kaiser. Things were getting out of hand. A famous doctor of divinity announced that he could no longer be sure which women were respectable and which were loose. In 1915, the theologian Dr. Walter Rauschenbusch remarked, "I used to be able to distinguish a woman of the streets, but now they cannot be told from other women."[20] Public fulminating about young women soon diminished, though, because the nation had other matters to worry about.

In the midst of these social upheavals, World War I broke out in Europe, eventually involving the United States. Ragtime songs and dances persisted, but civil liberties contracted and a martial spirit pervaded the nation. Typically, the songs of wartime are patriotic anthems, boastful assertions of fighting prowess, comic takes on military life, and love ballads about the predictable emotions that went with parting, separation, romantic longing, and the dream of return. As a body of songs, they were self-contained responses to a particularly demanding set of circumstances. It didn't matter where the soldiers were from, small town or great metropolis. They ended up in a camp together and eventually found themselves on a troopship to France. Where a lonely young woman waited for her doughboy's return was less important than her fidelity and his sustaining memory of their last embrace. People gathered on train platforms to bid young men farewell. An implied setting, either urban (Irving Berlin, "Smile and Show Your Dimple," 1917) or rural (Geoffrey O'Hara, "K-K-K-Katy," 1918), was suddenly less important than the romantic sentiments associated with the war:[21]

> Smile the while you kiss me sad adieu
> When the clouds roll by I'll come to you.
> (Richard A. Whiting and Raymond B. Egan, "Till We Meet Again," 1918)

Although people still danced to the urban rhythms of ragtime, for the next two years America would prefer the beat of a patriotic march.

6

THE FLAPPER AND THE JAZZ AGE

Millie Dillmount, fresh off the train from Nowheresville, has just arrived in Manhattan. In *Thoroughly Modern Millie,* the 1967 movie that bears her name, she dresses as if it's 1919 even though it's three years later: a straw hat ringed with make-believe flowers, a modest blouse buttoned to the neck, a skirt to midcalf, and high-laced shoes. But she's nobody's fool. In the opening sequence, she transforms herself into a flapper with a quick wit, an unerring eye, a lithe body, and a fetching eagerness. She bobs her hair, replaces her clothing, and flattens her bosom with a proper bra. As she says, it's her "chests" that keep her beads from lying right. Played by a youthful Julie Andrews, she looks absolutely smashing, and she is ready to take flapperdom by storm.

Millie was one of the throng that moved to New York City after World War I. At the end of the previous decade, a year or two after the Armistice, they joined the doughboys who refused to remain "down on the farm" after they had "seen Paree." Many of them had little interest in "a rake or plow / And who the deuce can parlez-vous a cow?" (Walter Donaldson, Sam M. Lewis, and Joe Young, "How Ya Gonna Keep 'Em Down on the Farm," 1919). In the song, ironically it takes an old farmer named Reuben to understand the migration to the city and anticipate the changes in sexual attitudes as well. He is smart enough to recognize that "wine and women play the mischief / With a boy who's loose with change." The song mirrored what the 1920 census would soon report: two years after the end of World War I, even though the United States' population was split down the middle, half rural and half urban, the country was already more industrial than agricultural.[1] In the aftermath of the war, the dramatic changes of the 1920s arrived pell-mell and helter-skelter. As New York City continued to grow, the new decade began with women casting their first ballots and ended with the onslaught of the Great Depression. But for the topsy-turvy twenties, the flapper was the decade-defining figure. Nearly a century later, millions of us can close our eyes and still see her—long of leg, angular of torso, frenzied of movement. Like a living mannequin designed by Erté (Romain de Tirtoff), she was an art deco dream come to life.

In 1890s England, *flapper* had been a slang term for a young girl or prostitute. The word soon dropped its second meaning and, newly respectable, started showing up in newspapers, magazines, and works of fiction. It first appeared in the United States in the 1920 movie *The Flapper*, starring Olive Thomas. Before long, Clara Bow, Joan Crawford, and other movie actresses would build their careers by turning themselves into flappers because a flapper had oomph. A figure of fantasy and desire, she was a potent female image—above all an image of youth. She was dazzlingly feminine even though she appeared to be constructed like a twelve-year-old boy. She rolled her stockings down and, if she was a little fast, rouged her knees. A dancing partner's eye might be drawn to a glimpse of bare inner thigh when she bent her knees and elbows and kicked up her legs for the Charleston. In the bright lights of Manhattan at night, nobody slept and nobody aged—or so you could kid yourself into believing. Zelda Fitzgerald, the quintessential flapper, said, "I don't want to be famous and feted—all I want is to be young always."[2] Out in Hollywood, Louise Brooks, who ran Zelda a close second, made much the same point with a lot less chic. "I like to drink and fuck," she said.[3]

The flapper affected a cynical veneer, loved to gossip, and was susceptible to fads and fashions, especially the modern look she loved—flat chest, square shoulders, narrow hips, and long legs.[4] She also lived a much more public life than her elders were used to. Stephen Gundle wrote that the flapper's "reengagement with all the novelties" of urban life "served as a codifier to modernity, a visual representation of everything that the modern age had to offer."[5] Seeking the freedom to define herself by her appearance and behavior, she was sexually active and dreaded boredom even though she knew she'd eventually marry and settle down. But first she would do whatever men did and whatever she wanted to do. She did it with such flair that her style and manner soon spread through the culture.

The popular novelist Barbara Cartland remembered fifty years later, "We didn't want to be ladylike in 1920. We wanted to be dashing, we wanted to be gay, and most of all we wanted to be romantic."[6] Nearly a century later, nothing says "Jazz Age" like the flapper and the jazzy songs that reveled in her pursuit of love, sex, and pleasure for its own sake. When she arrived, the bluenoses twitched and the Puritans

"It's all right, Santa—you can come in. My parents still believe in you."

Figure 6.1. A John Held drawing captures the exaggerated look of the flapper—long of leg, angular of torso. Courtesy of Photofest.

left town. She had dozens of names, from Susie to Lulu, but she was always the same irresistible female. The carefree songs she appears in repeated themselves for most of the decade until the Depression swept them away in a single swipe. The young men who pursued her tired of her by the end of the decade; she had little to show for it but her now-dated look. (Milton Ager and Jack Yellen, "Glad Rag Doll," 1928).

In 1928, a little over a year after Charles Lindbergh flew solo across the Atlantic and Babe Ruth hit sixty home runs, the American people elected the taciturn Calvin Coolidge, who had already become president on the death of the genially incompetent Warren G. Harding in 1923. Everything felt hunky-dory, partly because people weren't paying much attention. While the flapper caroused, immigration all but stopped, anti-Semitism flourished, the Ku Klux Klan expanded its power, and crime flourished with the onset of Prohibition. In cities, the young preferred to party their way through a time of newly intense self-awareness and absurd self-deception. Edward Lueders called the twenties "a unique combination of innocent, idealized sentiment with worldly, cynical, destructive dissipation."[7] Malcolm Cowley, who was there, wrote, "We thought of ourselves as being wise, disillusioned, cynical, but we were wide-eyed children with a child's capacity for enjoyment. Did other generations ever laugh so hard together, drink and dance so hard, or do crazier things just for the hell of it?"[8] The decade was irrepressibly iconoclastic, and its young people labored prodigiously in the service of fun.

Before the stock market crashed and the Roaring Twenties went mum, the number of divorces rose from one hundred thousand per year in 1914 to two hundred fifty thousand in 1929. Divorce became more common as the complexities of urban life replaced the stability of the small town. In a time of prosperity, Americans, especially urban Americans, came to believe that single people could be happy. Living in cities gave women in particular more opportunities to earn their own livings and get an education. The freer they believed themselves to be, the less reliant they were on marriage to provide them with security. The result was greater independence, matched only by a feeling of power from winning the vote.[9] At the same time, large numbers of men and women still "expected to gain their major life satisfactions from love and marriage. . . . But higher expectations of marriage created greater disappointments when marriage failed to deliver the satisfactions promised by popular culture."[10] No song underscored the point with a greater sense of irony than Walter Donaldson and Gus Kahn's "Makin' Whoopee" (*Whoopee*, 1928).

The number of automobiles also increased over the course of this decade, from just under 7 million to 23 million. You proved you had come of age by flashing your driver's license. An automobile freed mainly young men to drive on newly paved roads to bathing beaches and roadhouses just beyond the city limits. Meanwhile, lyrics were encouraging you to believe that without a car you'd never win a girl (Clarence Gaskill, "I'm Wild About Horns on Automobiles That Go Ta-Ta-Ta-Ta," 1928). Although the automobile made it easy for people to get around and gad about, the city stood at the center of American life and the American imagination through the twenties and thirties. In 1922, before the advent of talkies, the average weekly attendance at the movies was 40 million. ("Clara Bow, ain't she delish? / Season her with Lillian Gish," Ray Henderson, Lew Brown, and B. G. DeSylva, "Magnolia," 1927). In 1929, two years after the release of *The Jazz Singer*, the first full-length commercial talking picture, ticket sales rose to 95 million a week and, a year later, despite the crash, rose another 10 million. A decade after the first commercial radio stations began to broadcast in 1920, over six hundred stations were on the air and "Americans swam in music and information as never before."[11]

The ways in which these changes in technology affected attitudes and behavior was striking. By 1921, women had started going to the movies to fulfill fantasies they might have called romantic. The truth is, they were making forbidden vicarious love in the dark with a silent movie actor, former gigolo, and taxi dancer named Rodolfo Alfonso Raffaello Piero Filiberto Guglielmi di Valentina d'Antonguella, better known as Rudolph Valentino. Because familiar expressions fell so far short of defining him, his public discarded "matinee idol" and "romantic lead" for something that came much closer to what was actually going on. Projecting smoldering mystery and erotic danger, Valentino was the first great "screen lover." When he died of pleurisy in 1926 at only thirty-one, the eighty thousand people at his funeral—mostly women—nearly caused a riot. Soon after his death, his adoring fans snatched up copies of a bogus composite photo of him ascending to heaven.

Valentino's appeal was understandable. His features were sleek and almost feminine, but he also possessed daring, strength, and catlike grace. The women whose inner lives he touched were about to transform themselves publicly into flappers. In his most characteristic role in *The Sheik* (1921), he rode across the desert fearlessly on a great white stallion, sweeping up heroines who aroused lust and love in equal measure. The leading ladies who initially feared him soon melted in his arms. "The Sheik of Araby," written to capitalize on his popularity, became an overnight hit in the same year as the movie. Its lyric spoke to the hidden lives of his secret adorers all over America. It portrayed him as a man accustomed to having what used to be called his way with women, yet his seductive dominance would eventually lead to the happiest of marriages:

> I'm the Sheik of Araby,
> Your love belongs to me.
> At night, when you're asleep,
> Into your tent I'll creep.
> The stars that shine above,
> Will light our way to love.
> You'll rule this land with me.
> The sheik of Araby."
>
> (Ted Snyder, Harry B. Smith, and Francis Wheeler, "The Sheik of Araby," 1921)

Elizabeth Stevenson calls the 1920s "a blur, a kind of montage of gangsters terrorizing great cities and heedless flappers dancing the Charleston upon the tabletops of speakeasies about to be raided by lively but ineffective cops."[12] The origins of the flappers arose partly from the experience of women in World War I, when they found new freedom and something approaching equality with men. They drove ambulances, nursed soldiers, traveled on their own, and sometimes found themselves close to danger. They also endured the deaths of young men to whom they felt close. Once the war ended, they asserted themselves "with impudence and self-assurance" and "breezy independence."[13] Before long, energetic female characters wearing the latest fashions showed up in movies aimed at a youthful audience. The flapper was more like the girl next door than a heavy-lidded vamp, but she was still sexy. She was eager rather than voracious, more Clara Bow than Theda Bara, "ready to raise a little hell before she settled down to married life."[14] She was also more likely to appear in a suggestive song about tonight rather than a romantic song about forever: "I fixed the lights at half past ten, / They'll all blow out, oh boy, and then"[15] (Joseph Meyer, Bobby Buttenuth, and Irving Caesar, "Tonight's My Night with Baby," 1926).

Songwriters tailored most of their songs to both male and female singers. All anybody had to do was change a pronoun. Yet Tin Pan Alley remained largely a man's world. That's why so many songs were about sexy women and so few about the sexy (or maybe sex-starved) men who pursued them. Songwriters sold words set to music, but like the advertising agencies that would emerge in the twenties as an indispensable arm of modern business, they also sold people images of themselves. The flapper dominated all other images of women in popular love songs. The glorification (and sexualization) of the American Girl, or her image, had begun in the teens. By the early twenties a great many women had adopted this image of themselves as they also embraced the new freedom of shorter skirts and bobbed hair. Who wouldn't want to be devil-may-care, thronged by beaux, and the subject of "hot" novels, plays, and movies? The love songs addressed to her were a mirror image of what she set out to be: slangy, stylish, urban, and pleasure seeking. By describing her looks and behavior, songwriters helped to create her even if you sometimes came away with a sense that they were in on a huge collective joke: "When she struts her stuff around, / London Bridge is falling down!" (Ray Henderson, Lew Brown, and Billy Rose, "Don't Bring Lulu," 1925).

Nineteen twenty-five was the flapper's year and then some. The hits included a long list of "flapper songs" (Joseph Meyer and B. G. DeSylva's "If You Knew Susie"; Lew Pollack and Jack Yellen's "Cheatin' on Me"; Gene Austin's "When My Sugar Walks Down the Street"; and Walter Donaldson and Gus Kahn's "Yes Sir, That's My Baby"), but no song came closer to capturing the flapper than Ray Henderson, Sam Lewis, and Joe Young's "Five Foot Two, Eyes of Blue (Has Anybody seen My Girl?)."

In Lewis and Young's lyric, a young man who can't find his girl describes her to everyone he meets. She is a quintessential flapper. Best guess? She's in a back seat with some other guy. When her escort describes her, Lewis and Young pull a fast one: If you see a young woman dressed in furs and diamond rings, it almost certainly isn't her. The flapper was one of the most democratic images of the first half of the century. Being a flapper required only that you knew how to dress, knew the lingo and the dances, and eagerly pursued whatever was new and exciting. That usually meant necking and petting—newer, more suggestive words than *cuddling* and *spooning*—and drinking bootleg hooch. It had nothing to do with wealth or class except when it came to college (more on that in a moment).

Many of the flapper songs were interchangeable, especially from mid-decade on. Usually, a smitten beau describes her appearance, her behavior, how she walks and talks and dances, how irresistible she is to men and how enviable to women, but mainly he aches for her affection. That may mean anything from going on a date to having sex to accepting a proposal. In dozens of songs from the second half of the decade, bedazzled young men eagerly tell the world about the flappers they adore (Milton Ager and Jack Yellen, "Ain't She Sweet," 1927). True love may be what he seeks, but in song after song, he's most impressed by anything having to do with sex.

Whether or not the flapper returns her suitor's affection is something else again. Sometimes two points of view show up in a single song. In one case it's a batch of rhetorical questions from "Who is so hard to get" to "Who's got what satisfies" followed by the same satisfying answer that's also the title: "Who-oo! You-oo! That's Who!" (Milton Ager and Jack Yellen, "Who-oo! You-oo! That's Who!" 1927). Bud Green and Sam H. Stept's "Good-Little Bad-Little You" (1928) is direct but also contradictory as it dances back and forth between sin and safety.

These songs are so buoyant (and often so silly) that it's hard to think they might sustain anything like deep emotion. I suppose the young men are serious about being in love, but everything feels like an elaborate game the songwriters are in on. It's hard to imagine, for instance, that these airy songs could make room for longing, especially among the young men, but every now and then, there it is, even if they risk looking foolish:

> You sort of long to hug and kiss her close
> right in your arms;
> But if you try to tease her, goodness, see
> how it alarms. . . .
> My head's awhirl it's true,
> I've got those doggone Flapper Blues.
> (Bob Alterman and Claude Johnson, "Flapper Blues," 1922)

All this talk about sex cuts two ways. That's what makes these songs distinctive and innovative, what shows how much they depart from the standards of only five or ten years earlier. Free of chaperones and small-town restraints, the girls are as sexually assertive as the boys. Helen Kane sang "I Wanna Be Loved By You" in 1928 (Herbert Stothard, Harry Ruby, and Bert Kalmar, *Good Boy*), and it's more than likely that "loved" is a euphemism when she followed the title line by singing, "Boop boop a doop." More directly to the point, the next year she sang, "When you're learning what lips are for / And it's naughty to ask for more," before confessing that she wants to be "bad" (Ray Henderson, Lew Brown, and B. G. DeSylva, "I Want to Be Bad," *Follow Thru*, 1929).

Peppy tunes about jazz babies continued to pour from Tin Pan Alley through the decade. Yet songwriters also felt the need to warn the flapper that she was sure to burn herself out. "Big City Blues" (1929) by Con Conrad, Sidney D. Mitchell, and Archie Gottler tells a cautionary tale about a twenties girl in the city. It's no gay showcase for her madcap charm. She's alone in a heartless place. Lonely and burdened by sorrow and despair, she wails, "Before I know it, it's twelve o'clock, / I feel like jumping right off a dock." She hints that her anguish would disappear if only she could meet that special someone. In Tin Pan Alley, love was still the cure for troubles. It was always both the problem and its solution.

Some girls kept their innocence, although doing so was no longer all they'd been told it would mean. One rhyming joke from the twenties put it this way:

> She doesn't drink.
> She doesn't pet.
> She hasn't been to college yet.[16]

Two or three decades earlier, almost everybody on a college campus was male and came from an affluent family. That began to change in the 1890s. Young men and women from middle-class families enrolled because their parents had come to believe that college was the way to a successful life. Parents sent their children off to get an education, but by the twenties, the flappers and sheiks were leaving home to have fun. In the ten years between 1920 and 1930, college registration doubled—from six hundred thousand to 1.2 million. Even so, by 1928, the number of eighteen-to-twenty-one-year-olds in college had risen to only 12 percent of the college-age population; among young women, it was 10 percent. If you were one of the lucky ones, you suddenly discovered that you had "an enormous amount of freedom and leisure time."[17] Students went to class and the library during the day but devoted many of their evenings and weekends to football games, fraternity and sorority parties, dances, and—for flappers—the accumulation of beaus. Soon, whatever the college crowd was interested in became the latest fad. Kathleen Drowne and Patrick Huber conclude, "Even those Americans who had never been—and would never go—to college tended to agree that university students reigned as the chief arbiters of fashion and taste during the Roaring Twenties."[18] The most daring college boys were sitting atop flagpoles and swallowing goldfish, and coeds were smoking and drinking in public. It wouldn't take long for college students to make their appearance in popular songs.

Not all flappers were college girls, but to Tin Pan Alley all college girls were flappers, and all young men were smitten by them. Before the twenties, most songs about college life were about the men. Lyrics had them boasting about having a fraternity pin, playing football or rooting for the team, and chasing girls: "Tho' he sets a pace that kills, / Father has to pay the bills, / Because he's a college boy" (Theodore Morse and Jack Mohoney, "He's a College Boy," 1909). In the few early songs about college women, the girls are ready to be as busy as the boys, and the boys urge them on. "The Ragtime College Girl," a song from the dance craze, claims that the primary purpose of college is social:

> Don't you know it's wrong for you to waste your life for just an old diploma?
> You can find more fun in just one minute in that dance from Oklahoma.
> "Work makes Jack dull" is an old time saying,
> If you want to be a Ragtime College Girl.
> (Kerry Mills and S. M. Lewis, "The Ragtime College Girl," *The Fascinating Widow,* 1911)

In college during the teens, young women were supposed to have fun, learn the tango and the turkey trot, and meet their future mates. Although the women become more assertive and the songs more overtly sexual during the twenties, the young men continued to be the more outspoken characters. Things got progressively wilder in the twenties, when songs celebrated partying and made light of education.

By the middle of the decade, Tin Pan Alley's 1920s college girls had evolved into a version of the jazz baby, who mostly studied drinking, smoking, dancing, and playing around with boys. They emerge as knowing, shrewd, and aware of what it takes to be popular. As in other flapper songs, they hold out the promise of excitement and, more to the point, sex.

The change in only a decade was striking. The college boys in earlier songs at least tried to look respectable, but during the twenties they were hopelessly adolescent. A lyric about raccoon coats affirms that they wear them at Princeton, share them at Yale, and eat in them at Harvard, "But they sleep in them in jail" (J. Fred Coots, Raymond Klages, "Doin' the Raccoon," 1928). A young man who wears a raccoon coat, a porkpie hat, and baggy pants is a collegiate fashion plate. He also chases a girl who wears the flapper regalia and flirts in return. She finds it very hard to say no. (Martin Broones and Charlotte Greenwood, "Campus Capers," *So This Is College*, 1929).

Women had climbed down off their pedestals by now. High-minded propriety gave way to the temptations available on campuses populated by attractive young men. A lyric by Howard E. Johnson has a young man lay out the social life of an extremely busy young woman—Monday with Johnny, Tuesday with Jim, and on through the week until Sunday, when the unnamed beau complains in a typically wacky 1920s title, "She's the Sweetheart of Six Other Guys" (Robert King and Howard E. Johnson, 1928). In the most famous of the collegiate songs, she chooses fun over money (Moe Jaffe and Nat Bonx, "Collegiate," 1925). Even so, the boys still do most of the talking: "You have a way of campus petting that's perfection, / So in a moment I'll be going in your direction" (Al Sherman and Al Lewis, "Collegiate Fanny," 1929). Fortunately for them, Prohibition never got in the way of their partying.

~ ~ ~

The unflagging drive of a song like "Crazy Rhythm" was the sound of Manhattan during Prohibition, not because you couldn't drink, but because you could—with the excitement of lawbreaking in the bargain. The character in Irving Caesar's lyric, overwhelmed by the pace of life in New York City, longs to break away but feels helpless. The rhythm makes him as tipsy as Prohibition does and eventually drives him crazy. He blames the "Crazy Rhythm" that produces the same condition as Prohibition, and concludes, "Crazy rhythm, / I've gone crazy, too." Although the song resembles a break-up between two up-to-date lovers, common in the songs of the twenties, it makes no mention of love or even another person. As in the earlier "Fascinating Rhythm" (George and Ira Gershwin, *Lady Be Good,* 1924), the antagonist is rhythm itself.[19] Anyone drawn to Manhattan is sure to be spellbound by what lyricist Irving Caesar called "Crazy Rhythm" (Joseph Meyer, Roger Wolfe Kahn, and Irving Caesar, "Crazy Rhythm," *Here's Howe,* 1928).

All through the decade, Tin Pan Alley urged women and men to have as much fun as they could for as long as they could. For a woman, that meant playing the part of the flapper during Prohibition and then getting married and settling in the suburbs. Once she had her fill of bootleg hooch and bathtub gin, the red-hot jazz baby would eventually pair off with the right man—or so the song lyrics made her believe. After years of carousing, the good loving resulting from a happy marriage would domesticate her. In "Sleepy Time Gal," a suave little fox-trot, a former flapper will come to love cooking and sewing as long as she can become "a stay at home, play at home / Eight o'clock sleepy time gal" (Richard A. Whiting, Ange Lorenzo, Joseph R. Alden, and Raymond B. Egan, "Sleepy Time Gal," 1925).

But Prohibition came before settling down, even though song lyrics suggest that it wasn't what twenty-five thousand doughboys were anticipating when they marched up Fifth Avenue on September 10, 1919. That was almost a year after the armistice but just four months before Prohibition officially began on January 16, 1920. Although most songs about Prohibition sound lighthearted or mock-desperate, J. Keirn Brennan, Gus Edwards, and Paul Cunningham's lyric to "America Never Took Water and America Never Will" portrays the troops' reaction as a combination of surprise and defiance. As their "transport of joy" docks in New York, the returning veterans ask for the news. When "one fighting Yank" learns about Prohibition, he replies:

> Of water in the trenches,
> We surely had our fill,
> So we can't understand why you should hand it to us still,
> For America never took water,
> And America never will.
> (J. Keirn Brennan, Gus Edwards, and Paul Cunningham, "America Never Took Water and America Never Will," 1919)

Two years before, in 1917, with the troops still reeling from the carnage in the trenches and the mademoiselles on the rue de la Paix, the Senate back in Washington had passed the Eighteenth

Amendment to prohibit the manufacture, transport, and sale of alcohol for consumption, and turned it back to the states for ratification. Its goal, so the drys told the rest of the population, was to "morally uplift the people of the United States, ultimately creating a healthier citizenry, safer cities and workplaces, and a more efficient society."[20] Yet many Americans never bought the argument, and millions who supported it soon turned against it. By the time Congress repealed Prohibition in 1933, large numbers of citizens had broken the law with impunity.

Mark Thornton explains, "Prohibition may actually have increased drinking and intemperance by increasing the availability of alcohol. One New Jersey businessman claimed that there were 10 times more places one could get a drink during Prohibition than there had been before."[21] David J. Hanson put it more dramatically: "If the goal of Prohibition was to increase heavy episodic (binge) drinking, increase the consumption of dangerous illegal alcohol, reduce public health, foster violent and powerful organized crime, promote political corruption and encourage widespread disrespect for the law, then it was clearly a resounding success."[22]

Americans had long enjoyed the conviviality of taverns. Daniel Okrent writes that they had been "awash in drink" almost from the beginning—"wading hip-deep in it, swimming in it, at various times in its history nearly drowning in it."[23] Yet they had also tolerated a deep strain of advocacy for temperance, especially among Baptists, Methodists, and other Protestant groups. Even P. T. Barnum, the self-styled "Prince of Humbug,"[24] had enlisted in the cause of an early temperance movement as far back as the 1840s. Opposition to drinking in rural parts of the country only intensified as industrialization spread, immigration from central and southern Europe increased, and social reformers saw the effects of drinking on immigrant families packed into overcrowded tenements. The deepening concern for children found expression in opposition to both child labor and alcoholism in such sentimental ballads as "Father's a Drunkard and Mother Is Dead":

> Mother, why did you leave me all alone,
> With no one to love me, no friends and no home?
> Dark is the night, and the storm rages wild,
> God pity Bessie, the Drunkard's lone child.
>
> (Mrs. E. A. Parkhurst and "Stella," "Father's a Drunkard and Mother Is Dead," 1866)

The temperance movement found even greater traction in the "muscular Christianity" of the day and the tacit alliance between women who marched for the vote and those who marched against "King Alcohol." Okrent writes, "The rise of the suffrage movement was a direct consequence of the widespread prohibition sentiment."[25] Meanwhile, the popular Hutchinson Family Singers of New Hampshire toured the country to sing their songs of temperance.

Attitudes also changed dramatically in reaction against the large numbers of immigrants who arrived during the second half of the nineteenth century. In the view of many native-born Americans, the coming of the Irish, Italians, Germans, and Jews led to social upheaval and political unrest. Many of these newcomers were not Protestant and were thus immediately suspect. To make things worse, alcohol was an essential part of their cultures and played an important role in the forms of their alien, exotic worship.[26]

During World War I, native-born Americans discriminated against German immigrants on the mistaken assumption that their first loyalty was to Germany and Irish immigrants whose country had a long history of resistance against America's ally, Great Britain. President Woodrow Wilson warned his fellow citizens about these "hyphenated Americans" who had "poured the poison of disloyalty into the very arteries of our national life."[27] The Russian Revolution and the rise of Communism also led to the fear of prolabor agitators. After the War ended, the perceived violence and "otherness" of the immigrants gave rise to the Red Scare, a widespread fear of anything that smacked of radical left-wing beliefs. A broad public approved of the Palmer Raids of 1919–20, in which suspected left-wing radicals were arrested and deported.

The years after World War I also led to labor agitation. Recently formed unions (including the International Workers of the World, known as the IWW, or Wobblies) organized mainly among unskilled industrial workers. They were more radical and more confrontational than their predecessors and more willing to strike. When factory owners hired scabs protected by local police and when police tried to break strikes, workers fought back. These unionized workers were often recent immigrants whose political leanings had been shaped by the rise of Socialism and Communism in Europe. Among the immigrants were also Anarchists who soon became known to the public for bombings and armed robbery.

All this led, more broadly, to a rejection of almost everything "foreign," including tolerance for alcohol. Also in 1920, two Italian

Figure 6.2. New Yorkers hanged Old Man Prohibition in effigy to celebrate the repeal of Prohibition in 1933. Courtesy of Photofest.

anarchists named Nicola Sacco and Bartolomeo Vanzetti were convicted (in an extremely controversial court case) and eventually executed for murdering a guard and a paymaster during the armed robbery of a shoe store in Braintree, Massachusetts. In the end, support for Prohibition was fueled by xenophobia, a toxic mix of the moralistic and the jingoistic. Going dry looked like an answer. In January 1918, Mississippi became the first state to ratify the Eighteenth Amendment. Just one year later, on January 16, 1919, Nebraska became the thirty-sixth.[28]

Two weeks after Nebraska's vote, Congress ratified the Amendment. However, neither its original passage nor its ratification had much effect on America's drinking habits. Irving Lewis Allen observed, "The reputation of Times Square's bubbly nightlife and the gaiety of its visitors soon equaled the fame of its bright lights."[29] During the summer of 1919, Benjamin De Casseres called Broadway and Forty-Second Street "the corner of the Rue de Booze and the Great Wine Way."[30] Six months after that, the Amendment went into effect. Nobody who wanted a drink had to do without, then or throughout Prohibition's fourteen-year run. For a decade and a half, New York City, more than any other place, was "the foremost battleground in the war against demon rum."[31] New Yorkers responded with what Michael Lerner calls "creative determination . . . to buy, sell, and manufacture liquor."[32]

By 1925, there were more than thirty thousand speakeasies in New York City alone.[33] *Variety*, the show-business newspaper, reported that "there isn't a restaurant, cabaret or dance place of any description where a drink isn't obtainable."[34] At first, New Yorkers bought booze openly in taxicabs, and saloons sold it in soda bottles. In the lobbies of upscale Manhattan hotels, employees sold brews of "coffee" and "tea" without sugar or cream; almost immediately, restaurants initiated the ruse of drinking alcohol from teacups.[35] One New York restaurant owner bought some illegal hooch but, fearing a raid, drove immediately to his restaurant and parked out front at the height of the dinner hour. The restaurateur recalled, "Just to let you see what our average citizen thinks. . . . [W]hat happened was this. We handed the cases across the sidewalk, and every person supping inside helped pass them to the cellar by forming a chain. . . . We got every blessed one in without any interference, even with the traffic cop at the corner looking on."[36]

In "The Hollow Men," T. S. Eliot wrote, "Between the motion / And the act / Falls the Shadow." Less portentous than Eliot's poem, behavior in response to Prohibition reflected the sometimes contradictory ways that people understood the law and then mocked it by disobeying it. America's defiance was a combination of self-indulgence and self-satisfaction, but it was also an assertion of sorts. Such popular magazines as *Ladies Home Journal* and *Collier's* supported Prohibition on their editorial pages but also ran ads for home bars, mixers, and "Jazz Age fashions straight out of nightclubs."[37] Even though the Music Publishers Association urged its members not to market songs that slighted Prohibition, songwriters and their publishers could hardly wait to exploit a new subject for a ready market.[38] Songs that mocked Prohibition quickly became a Tin Pan Alley staple. Very few singing voices were raised in support of the drys, perhaps because Prohibition had become "a struggle over individual rights, personal liberty, and the limits of reform."[39] Popular songs were hardly political or philosophical, but as usual, they sided with the popular will and the "common man." Just as everybody got to fall in love, so everybody was entitled to take a drink. If people wanted to know what America thought of Prohibition, they had to look no farther than the borough of Manhattan, especially Broadway and Tin Pan Alley in Midtown and Harlem a few miles north.

Some of the first songs about Prohibition, appearing before the amendment took effect, regretted the approaching loss of alcohol because of what it contributed to a night out for dancing. In 1918 and 1919, as the country moved toward ratification, ragtime songs and the dance craze persisted as part of America's musical mix. Abner Silver and Alex Gerber's "At the Prohibition Ball" (1919) was one of many ragtime songs that invented a fancy-dress ball to promote the spirited, youthful dancing of the dance craze. Others were Robert Speroy and Jack Frost's "At the Funny Page Ball" (1918) and Joseph H. Santly and Howard Johnson's "At the Moving Picture Ball" (1920). Gerber's lyric describes men in white tie and women in ankle-length gowns who celebrate the coming of Prohibition, not because they're happy to bid drinking goodbye, but because the conventions of "ball" songs require an eagerness to go dancing. In another song, Irving Berlin's lyric protests that "You cannot make your shimmy shake on tea" because you need some "Scotch or rye to lubricate your knee" (Irving Berlin and Rennold Wolf, "You Cannot Make Your Shimmy Shake on Tea," *Ziegfeld Follies of 1919*, 1919). In the same edition of the *Follies*, the effects of Prohibition showed up "in a nightclub scene with showgirls parading around as Coca-Cola, sarsaparilla, grape juice, lemonade, and Bevo."[40]

As the start of Prohibition neared, New Yorkers began what the *New York Evening Post* called a "liquor stampede." Ads urged readers to "protect yourself against the dry days," and so they did. Then, after a final spasm of revelry, the town, like the rest of the country, went dry. People bemoaned the loss of tipsy conviviality. Even before Prohibition began officially, popular songs expressed mock sympathy for those whose favorite watering holes would soon disappear and purported to offer practical advice and even a satisfactory substitute for evenings previously spent leaning happily against a bar. Songs suggested that partakers hang on to whatever whiskey they had for as long as they could (James V. Monaco and Ballard McDonald, "Ten Little Bottles," 1920) or take a cruise ship to Havana, where the liquor still flowed freely (Irving Berlin, "I'll See You in C-U-B-A," 1919).

As usual, popular songwriters preferred a humorous approach when they took on a controversial subject. Months before the amendment took effect, songwriters and music publishers anticipated people's pining for a drink. Dozens of songs, virtually interchangeable, bemoaned the coming change with identical tongue-in-cheek sympathy, from William Jerome and Jack Mahoney's "Every Day Will Be Sunday When the Town Goes Dry" (1918) to Percy Wenrich, Francis Byrne, and Frank McIntyre's "How Are You Going to Wet Your Whistle When the Whole Darn World Is Dry?" (1919) to Harry Ruby's "What'll We Do on a Saturday Night? (When the Town Goes Dry)" (1919).

The lyrics vary in tone from irritation to disbelief, and from the mock patriotic ("We took this country from the Indians, / They can have it back again in July") to the mock romantic ("Imagine a fellow with a cute little queen, / Trying to win her on a plate of ice cream"), but the humorous approach was consistent throughout. A lot of mock bemoaning went on as song lyrics fell back on a series of familiar jokes and comic types, among them a woman who can't drive a man to drink so she'll have to drive him to the water faucet instead, the absence of hangovers on Monday mornings, and the inadequacy of tea as a substitute. "All the Boys Love Mary" was the most deceptive of these humorous songs. Its title makes it sound as if it's about a typically popular flapper like Margie or Lulu, but Mary's appeal doesn't lie in how cute or fast she is, but in what her father keeps hidden in the cellar (Gus Van and Joe Schenck, "All the Boys Love Mary," 1920).

One of the funniest lines in the numerous Prohibition anthems to hit the streets in 1919 and 1920 might have been adapted from Irving Berlin's World War I song "Oh, How I Hate to Get Up in the Morning," in which a recruit bemoans his inability to get a decent night's sleep. Where Berlin had written about the bugler, "I'll amputate his reveille / And step upon it heavily," two years later a frustrated drinker complains that "they amputated my booze" (Albert Von Tilzer and Edward Laska, "The Alcoholic Blues," 1919).

More than anything, at least in songs, Prohibition was a great big joke. Perhaps that's because murderous gangsters and crooked cops were too menacing for a song to handle. Rather than overtly discussing social or political themes, songwriters preferred to focus on ordinary individuals and their responses to what was going on around them. Instead of succumbing to any temptation to pontificate or sermonize, they preferred personal emotion. Songs of this sort also couldn't do justice to F. Scott's Fitzgerald's memorable line from "The Crack-Up," "In a real dark night of the soul, it is always three o'clock in the morning."[41] Yet the best songs did come tremblingly close, even though they were hindered by brevity and sentimentality. Besides, it was easier to kick up your heels than face the darker emotions of such torchy laments as "Don't Ever Leave Me" and "Just Like a Butterfly That's Caught in the Rain," both sung by Helen Morgan late in the decade in a voice that fluttered with melancholy.

When a song had the temerity to support Prohibition, it usually reaffirmed traditional domestic values. It could also flip the coin on expected behavior. One song tells the story of a husband who used to leave his wife alone while he frequented saloons, but when Prohibition began, he came to learn out of necessity that "I never knew I had a wonderful wife until the town went dry" (Albert Von Tilzer and Lew Brown, "I Never Knew I Had a Wonderful Wife Until the Town Went Dry," 1919). Other songs addressed the hypocrisy of those who fulminated against drinking but weren't above taking a drink when no one was looking. In a song about people who rowed out past the three-mile limit to buy smuggled whiskey from the Rum Row—a line of ships anchored beyond the reach of the law—Harry Ruby, Bert Kalmar, and George Jessel wrote, "Men who agreed Prohibition was right, / Hire a boat and then stay out all night" ("Where Do They Go When They Row-Row-Row?" 1920). As usual, the song observes what is happening with a sense of humor rather than righteous indignation.

Halsey K. Mohr and William Tracey's "It Will Never Be Dry Down in Havana" tells about a man whose friend encourages him to leave for "a happy land, far far away, / That Cuban Island, sweet Rock and Rye land," while the sheet music depicts a respectable man in a coat and tie, with his luggage packed, his steamship tickets in hand, and a broad grin on his face as he dreams of a tropical beauty dancing and beckoning on the beach. It's a common fantasy, but here it's rooted in an escape from Prohibition. Although he plans to go so he will be free to drink, he envisions a combination of the alcoholic and the erotic:

> This old town has gone all wrong,
> I want women, wine and song. . . .
> Down on Santiago Bay, where the Senoritas sway,
> "How dry I am" is a tune they never play.
> (Halsey K. Mohr and William Tracey, "It Will Never Be Dry Down in Havana," 1920)

As in Mohr and Tracey's song, sex and Prohibition often mixed. Eddie Cantor, who usually portrayed a lecherous innocent whose drinking was never anything more than fuel for his comic (and usually unsuccessful) seductions, made the point most explicitly when he sang Harry Akst and Howard E. Rogers's comic pro-dry number, "You Don't Need the Wine to Have a Wonderful Time (While You've Still Got Those Beautiful Girls)" in the *Ziegfeld Follies of 1919*:

> Lots of people like a cordial after dessert,
> But give me someone cordial wrapped in a skirt.
> (Harry Akst and Howard E. Rogers, "You Don't Need the Wine to Have a Wonderful Time (While You've Still Got Those Beautiful Girls)," 1919)

Some songs that regret the closing of saloons also wonder about the effect on romance—"I'm sorry for each spoony little pair. / It's raised the deuce with ev'ry love affair" and "It's seldom now that any girlie orders wedding clothes / There's nothing now that gives a man the courage to propose" (Harry Von Tilzer and William Jerome, "If I Meet the Guy Who Made This Country Dry," 1920). For the *Ziegfeld Follies of 1919*, Irving Berlin provided a number that finessed the problem by replacing drinking with frothy music "that goes right to your head." The lyric labels it a "syncopated cocktail," and advises listeners to set aside cocktail shakers in favor of shaking their lingerie (Irving Berlin, "A Syncopated Cocktail," *Ziegfeld Follies of 1919*, 1919). At the same time, Sophie Tucker, who built her career on a mix of saccharine ballads and bawdy vaudeville numbers, was singing a song devoted to self-discovery of a sort. Nothing can replace the effect of drinking like the effect of sex:

So if kisses are intoxicating like they say
I should worry 'bout the "bone dry" law,
I'll date up all the gals from Maine to 'Frisco Bay
I'll have the greatest time you ever saw,
I'll never draw a sober breath the live long day,
And I'll be happy as a king,
For if kisses are intoxicating like they say,
Prohibition you have lost your sting!
(J. Russel Robinson, Al Siegel, and Billy Curtis, "(For If Kisses Are Intoxicating as They Say) Prohibition You Have Lost Your Sting," 1919)

Songs about Prohibition were less common after 1920, but passing references to drinking showed up occasionally in Broadway musical comedies with their aura of slaphappy confidence and good will. One of the most appealing examples, "Button Up Your Overcoat," the show-stopping hit from Ray Henderson, Lew Brown, and Buddy DeSylva's score to *Follow Thru*, is a cautionary catalogue song devoted to mock good advice from one lover to another. From buttoning your coat to eating an apple daily, from looking both ways when you cross the street to wearing flannel underwear, the song ends with its most up-to-date advice, "Keep away from bootleg hooch when you're on a spree, / Take good care of yourself, you belong to me" ("Button Up Your Overcoat," 1929).

The contemporary critic Gilbert Gabriel wrote about Henderson, Brown, and DeSylva, whose collaborations were so much a part of the sound and style of the decade: "They seem dedicated to the task of making youth flame and love shout out, with crisp, crazy, lusty, ankle-loosing, hip-seizing songs, and lyrics that give this whole razzing, jazzing society circus its cue to get gay."[42] He might have added that the whole thing was fueled by illegal booze.

Beginning with Jerome Kern, P. G. Wodehouse, and Guy Bolton's Princess shows in 1915, American musical comedies had featured affluent, urbane young men and women who devote themselves to the pursuit of true love on college campuses and in big cities alike. Aside from revues, which featured sketches, punch lines, and the occasional song about Prohibition, surprisingly few book musicals had anything to say on the subject. According to John Bush Jones, "While the battle over Prohibition's pros and cons raged during the War years, the musical theater was silent on the subject."[43] By the midtwenties, though, there were a few notable exceptions. Probably the most important Broadway song about drinking had nothing to do with Prohibition. "Drink! Drink! Drink!" was part of Sigmund

Romberg and Dorothy Donnelly's 1924 score for *The Student Prince*, an operetta set at the university in the fictional German kingdom of Karlsberg. The singing and drinking of a group of boisterous students must have been especially pleasing to theater audiences during Prohibition. In 1926, the Gershwins' *Oh, Kay!* told the breezy story of a flat-broke duke who turns to bootlegging to make a few bucks. Four years later, the plot to Cole Porter's *The New Yorkers* lingered over the affair between a socialite and a bootlegger. In addition to "I Happen to Like New York," "Take Me Back to Manhattan," and "Love for Sale," Porter's score testifies to how hard people will struggle to find a drink in two long-forgotten numbers, "Drinking Song" and "Say It with Gin." The importance of bootlegging in both shows gives them a topical gloss, but what mattered in both cases was the high quality of their scores.[44]

Songs about Prohibition have less to say about romantic love than songs on any other subject from these years, but they're preoccupied with what will take the place of whiskey and gin. Reluctantly, a young man courting a "girlie" wonders about the need to rely on soft drinks, candy, and ice cream. According to Francis Byrne, Frank McIntyre, and Percy Wenrich, "ev'ryone will be a candy fiend" and they will "pack the soda fountains to the doors," even though they are poor substitutes for wine or whiskey ("How Are You Going to Wet Your Whistle? [When the Whole Darn World Goes Dry]," 1919). In fact, the Prohibition years included a substantial increase in ice cream consumption along with the invention of Popsicles, chocolate-covered ice-cream bars, and Dixie Cups.[45] Young men in song lyrics also worried about how they would be able to pop the question without a snort to fortify their courage.

"Coon songs," those degrading portrayals of blacks, written mainly by whites to be sung most often by white performers in blackface, were enormously popular in the late nineteenth and early twentieth centuries before they faded away in the early twenties. From 1917 through 1920, a number of Prohibition coon songs combined the ban on alcohol with a condescendingly racist view of African Americans who, according to the songs, were about to be separated from their best companion: alcohol.

In "Prohibition Blues," one of the earliest Prohibition tunes, an African American husband returns home from church to recite the parson's sermon to his wife:

De whole country am a goin' bone dry,
Prohibition am de battle cry,
'Scuse me while I shed a tear,
For good old whiskey, gin and beer.
(Al Sweet, "Prohibition Blues," 1917)

The lyric mocks the clergyman for his lack of morality and spirituality; he can talk about nothing but his despair at the coming of Prohibition. He suffers more than anyone from the "Prohibition Blues." Oddly, the sheet music cover, also racist, suggests a different story. Sitting in a restaurant, a grotesquely caricatured but obviously prosperous black man, dressed like a dandy in a striped wing-collar shirt, orange tie, and loud checked jacket, with rings on his fingers and a boutonniere in his lapel, points to an upside-down wine glass as winged bottles labeled "Private Stock" and "Ex Dry" fly out of the frame, and a waiter ignores his customer to sob into his napkin. The patron is a figure of ridicule for no other reasons than his blackness and his pretensions, a common point of view in coon songs.

In 1919, the short-story writer Ring Lardner and the great Broadway star Nora Bayes collaborated on another coon song, also entitled "Prohibition Blues." Like the clergyman in Sweet's lyric, the black man in this song suffers from the blues because he, too, will be unable to drink. Lardner and Bayes use a metaphor of friendship to portray his sense of loss:

I've had news that's bad news about my best pal
His name is old man Alcohol
But I call him Al.
(Ring Lardner and Nora Bayes, "Prohibition Blues," 1919)

In a third song, "The Alcoholic Blues," the complainer expresses his fear with typical coon song exaggeration in a parody of southern black speech that says he is "simply goin' to 'vaporate, / I'm just that dry" (Albert Von Tilzer and Edward Laska, "The Alcoholic Blues," 1919).

No one performed and recorded more Prohibition songs than the great African American star of the *Ziegfeld Follies*, Bert Williams. His initial appearance in the *Follies* marked the first time that a black performer had starred with whites in a major musical production. He was so popular with audiences that he went on to appear in every *Follies* but two between 1910 and 1919. This was also the decade when no other blacks worked on the Broadway stage. Only Ziegfeld had the clout and Williams the appeal to pull it off. When white members of the cast threatened to quit after Ziegfeld first hired Williams, the impresario stood by his new star: "Go if you want to. I can replace every one of you except the man you want me to fire."[46] Nobody left, but it would remain for the all-black *Shuffle Along* to reintegrate the Broadway stage in 1921.

Appearing for Ziegfeld, Williams performed all three of the most important Prohibition songs associated with blacks. Like many African American performers before the middle of the twentieth century, he used black stereotypes because white attitudes required him to do so, but he slyly turned them into commentary on whites. Over the course of his decade in the *Follies*, Williams had developed his onstage character of a "shiftless darkey" to become a "figure of human woe."[47] In a 1918 essay, "The Comic Side of Trouble," Williams explained that his 1906 signature song, "Nobody," is about "the human appeal of the friendless man."[48] He might be "shiftless" or woeful or both, but beneath the character's broad surface lay a subtext that combined a commentary on race with personal anger, both overlooked by the white audiences who cheered his comedy. By far the most popular song in his repertoire, "Nobody" is mournful, ironic, and wry. It is as much a commentary on the place of black men in America as it is a reflection on the character of an individual: "Williams' willingness to play a broken but sympathetic character provided him with something of a soapbox. The broad racial caricatures and coon songs of his early period became subtle social criticism in his middle to late years":[49]

> I ain't never done nothin' to Nobody.
> I ain't never got nothin' from Nobody, no time.
> And, until I get somethin' from somebody sometime,
> I don't intend to do nothin' for Nobody, no time.
> (Bert A. Williams and Alex Rogers, "Nobody," *Abyssinia*, 1905)

Dressed in a shabby top hat, tails, and pants that stopped well above his ankles, and always wearing blackface, Williams' character was the gent gone to seed, a luckless everyman. As a lone black man in a very white theater, Williams always knew what he was doing. Yet on the first night of the 1919 actors' strike that closed down thirty-seven plays including the *Follies*, he arrived at the theater ready to perform, only to find the house deserted and everyone else on strike. No one had bothered to tell him the performance was off. Later, he told friends the story and added, "Nobody really wants me."[50]

The *Follies of 1919*, one of Ziegfeld's best annual revues, was also Williams's last. Portraying the same familiar character, he half-sang, half-talked three Prohibition songs, the hits "Everybody Wants a Key to My Cellar," "The Moon Shines on the Moonshine," and "You Cannot Make Your Shimmy Shake on Tea." He also performed or recorded three more Prohibition songs and another five that either touched on Prohibition or drinking in a more general way, all between 1919 and 1921.

"Everybody Wants a Key to My Cellar" and "The Moon Shines on the Moonshine" attest to the appeal of illegal whiskey and the importance of the bootlegger in the city and beyond. In the comic tale of "Everybody," a bootlegger has told no one what he keeps in his cellar—except, he regrets to say, his talkative wife. Every night, he watches people he doesn't know party downstairs. What he won't do is tell anyone where he keeps the key. Even in a song attuned to the privations of Prohibition, Williams never departs from his classic character, a variation on the familiar image of a long-suffering husband:

> They can have my money,
> They can have my car,
> They can have my wife
> If they want to go that far,
> But they can't have the key that opens my cellar,
> If the whole darn world goes dry.
> (Ed Rose, Billy Baskette, and Lew Pollack, "Everybody Wants a Key to My Cellar," *Ziegfeld Follies of 1919*, 1919)

"The Moon Shines on the Moonshine" is largely an exercise in wordplay that leads to a country moonshiner "far from the eyes of cops." He outwits the police and the keepers of public morals by stashing his supply nowhere near the city's rusty "old distillery," but rather "in the mountain tops" where "the moon shines on the moonshine, so merrily!" (Robert Hood Bowers and Francis De Witt, 1920). His glee is palpable. Even in a song set in the country, the city is never far away and serves as an effective contrast for Williams' tale.

In addition to Bert Williams, the *Ziegfeld Follies of 1919* starred Eddie Cantor and Marilyn Miller. It had a diverse Irving Berlin score that included such songs as "You'd Be Surprised" and "A Pretty Girl Is Like a Melody." Berlin also contributed one of the most ambitious anti-Prohibition songs to the score—a production number that interwove song and dialogue to form a brief scene, the sort of thing that the librettist-lyricists Oscar Hammerstein II and Alan Jay Lerner perfected in the book musicals of the 1940s and 1950s. A waiter sings to a customer who remains unconvinced:

Have a little Coca-Cola
Really, it's a lovely drink
Percy, Clarence, Reginald, too,
They will recommend it to you.
Have a little Coca-Cola
It's the very best I think,
It isn't alcoholic but you can have a frolic
If you take enough to drink.

The number ends with an appearance by the Spirit of Alcohol, who promises to return "when you give Prohibition your shoe"[51] (Irving Berlin, "The Near Future," *Ziegfeld Follies of 1919*, 1919). In the same spirit of finding a soft or sweet substitute for drinking, "Candy Jag," a typically bouncy number in the musical-comedy style of the day, makes the best of a frustrating situation:

Fill me up, fill me up!
That's the only kind of stimulant to use.
With highball choc'late drops
And rye-ball lollipops
There isn't very much you lose, . . .
There's a lot of dissipation in a bag.
(Malvin M. Franklin and Robert B. Smith, 1919)

~ ~ ~

By the midtwenties, Tin Pan Alley's ethnic songs, mainly about the Irish and the Jews, had begun to feel dated. In a late fling between 1919 and 1923, Broadway paraded feisty Irish heroines in a series of successful musical comedies known as Cinderella shows. Because most of them followed a familiar boy-meets-girl, boy-loses-girl, boy-gets-girl formula, it took audiences only five years to tire of them. Of the 120 musicals that opened on Broadway between 1921 and 1924, nearly half were, to one degree or another, Cinderella shows.[52] Their heroines were almost always Irish. They usually lived in New York and worked as shopgirls or secretaries, but because they are characters in musical comedies, they win the men of their dreams—usually millionaires at the pinnacle of society. Just as any man could become president, so the American musical's myth went, any woman could marry a loving millionaire. These musicals affirmed the assimilation of ethnic arrivals—at the very least, the Irish—in America. John Bush Jones comments that Cinderella shows also reflected the increasing number of working women after World War 1. Before the war, musical heroines rejected aristocracy and wealth for a poor but honest American boy. Not in the twenties, though. "Our Cinderella heroines almost always go for the gold as well as the guy," and, in the process, suggest to more recently arrived immigrants that they, too, can make it in America.[53] If anything, the young women are a new breed of American Cinderellas—sweet and loving, but also self-made and assertive. No days spent cleaning the wicked stepmother's fireplace for them. They achieve happiness in the form of true love and great wealth, not through the wave of a fairy godmother's wand, but because America's class distinctions had become fuzzier and more elastic after the war (especially in cities) and because these young women have moxie. For every dowager ordering her servants to keep the doors barred, thousands of immigrant girls stood ready to push their way in without forsaking charm or humor in the process.

Irene, the first and most important of these shows, opened in 1919, a little more than a year after the Armistice. In act 1, the heroine sings Harry Tierney and Joseph McCarthy's "Alice Blue Gown" to demonstrate her charm and appeal. The song, like the show, straddles an orderly prewar world and the headlong twenties to follow. Its title alludes to the shade of blue that was the favorite of young Alice Roosevelt when her father, Theodore, was president. Despite Irene's admission in the song that she once had a gown—"it was almost new"—she emerges as self-aware and self-confident, a modern young woman who admits that "in every shop window I primped, passing by" (Harry Tierney, Joseph McCarthy, "Alice Blue Gown," *Irene,* 1919). She is urban rather than urbane, a down-to-earth and decent product of her working class background—not unlike the Pegs and Mollys of earlier Tin Pan Alley songs. She's hardworking, but she's no charwoman. By the end of the play, Irene has found her heart's desire in a world that, at least for her and her beloved, is more democratic than it was when the curtain first rose.

Irene's appeal came partly from its timing: a recession after the war had many Americans longing for the good old days. But it was also a swan song for an irretrievable past. Unlike those happy-go-lucky flappers who would soon inherit the earth for a few years, Irene O'Dare is a shop girl, but she's a lot smarter than her place in society suggests. She meets Donald Marshall, her husband-to-be, when she runs an errand to his family's Long Island mansion. Confronted by Donald's wealth and social position, she discovers a world beyond anything she has ever imagined. Although the heroines were almost always Irish, the heroes almost never were. They were not only rich; they were Protestant. Irene, who is proudly and sentimentally Irish, reflects the rising opportunities for the children of the immigrants in her song, "The World Must Be Bigger Than an Avenue," but nowhere in the original score is there anything resembling a stereotypical ethnic song. Before Irene and Donald can marry, though, both families must overcome their prejudices against the social mingling—but that is a matter of class rather than ethnicity.

Irene's mother's initial distrust of the rich reflected the fear and narrow-mindedness of many ethnic groups. The story sets this against the greater democratizing of American life after World War I, especially with the coming of the flapper, the spread of secondary education, and the rise of affluence until the Depression interceded. Higher taxation and the coming of Prohibition also contributed to America's sense that the nation and its values were in flux. Gerald Bordman writes, "World War I had . . . brought about perceptible cracks in society's former impregnability. . . . [Ethnic] minorities began to weave themselves into the national fabric."[54]

The happy endings that Cinderella shows provided for heroines who were ordinary people gave audiences an optimistic lift a year after the war ended. They brightened the world after the dangers of combat overseas and the high inflation, increased taxes, and shortages of food and coal at home. These had contributed to a repressive climate of contracted civil rights and free speech, and discrimination against citizens of German descent.[55]

After *Irene* came other hit Cinderella shows, usually with the heroines' names in the title: *Mary*, *Sally*, *Good Morning, Dearie* (with a score by Jerome Kern and P. G. Wodehouse), *Little Nellie Kelly*, and *Mary Jane McKane*, all of them with Irish heroines.[56] *Plain Jane*, in which a tenement waif marries a factory owner's son, was the last of them, only five years after *Irene*. The craze didn't last long, but the shows' admiration for spunky urban working girls who rise socially through love and marriage, their mixing of the classes with the arrival of boisterous Irish families in Park Avenue mansions, and their bouncy melodic scores made them an essential part of the spirit of the first part of the new decade.

~ ~ ~

It's always risky to conflate an actor with a role or a singer with a song, but with torch singers you have to take the chance. The great torch singers of the 1920s—Helen Morgan, Ruth Etting, Libby Holman, and Fanny Brice—seemed to feel unusually close to the songs they sang. The songs almost seem to border on personal history, as if the singers' unhappy love affairs deepened their understanding of what they were singing and gave their performances a combination of mournful self-pity and romantic cynicism that lent them the aura of conviction. Torch songs were laments for the hours after midnight, best heard in a smoky basement bistro or standing alone by a window looking out over the still-lit towers. By the 1920s, they were especially popular with white urban audiences.[57]

Torch singing is an intimate art, and no one practiced it more exquisitely than Helen Morgan. Small and sad-eyed, she perched atop a piano in a Broadway theater or a speakeasy over a garage on West Fifty-Fourth Street. Elegantly gowned but forlorn, she bent her fragile soprano to the wistful sorrow that characterized her best songs and poured out her heart about her unrequited love for a worthless man.

Morgan got her first big break a year before Jerome Kern and Oscar Hammerstein II's *Show Boat* made her a star. For her featured number in the Broadway revue *Americana* (1926), she would do what she always did: sit on a piano, this time in the orchestra pit, lit by a single spot, to warble the newest torch ballad of the day. A story (probably apocryphal) says that when Kern heard her sing Henry Souvaine and Morrie Ryskind's mournful "Nobody Wants Me," he knew that he wanted her to play Julie in *Show Boat.* He and Oscar Hammerstein II had begun to work on the show but hadn't found anyone to play the actress whose African American blood is revealed by a vengeful suitor and whose life collapses tragically in the years that follow. Kern was struck by how much she had changed since she had danced and sung in the chorus of *Sally,* his successful show from 1920.

Since then, Morgan had spent most of her time performing at Helen Morgan's Fifty-Fourth Street Club. She had ties to the mobsters who owned the place and had begun to drink heavily.[58] Even so, her most important and least predictable connection was to Kern, an austere, painfully shy man whose grounding lay in the rich melodies of Austria and Italy. He wrote snappy musical comedies and romantic operettas, but he disliked jazz and knew very little about the blues. He expected people to sing his songs exactly as he wrote them, and that was that. Regardless of how he discovered her, Kern saw in Morgan not only the loss of innocence but also the disillusion behind the outward dissipation. He had finally found someone to sing "Bill," the torch ballad he and the lyricist P. G. Wodehouse wrote in 1918 but had never used.[59] Kern and Hammerstein wrote an additional four torch songs that Morgan introduced: "Can't Help Lovin' Dat Man of Mine" for *Show Boat* and "Don't Ever Leave Me," "Here Am I," and "Why Was I Born?" for *Sweet Adeline* in 1929. These songs are poignant expressions of the love and despair that link Morgan and the characters in the songs, where you hear the struggle to keep love alive for as long as they can.

Early in *Show Boat,* before her exposure forces her to leave, Julie explains to her innocent young friend Magnolia that love is more powerful that any flirtation. Magnolia has just told Julie that she's met a very attractive man. When Julie cautions her to beware of people she meets along the river, Magnolia insists that she'll drop him if he's not honorable. "Oh, honey," Julie answers, "it's not that easy." She gives Magnolia a lesson in love's power that ironically anticipates Julie's loss of her loving husband later in the play. At this moment, Kern, Hammerstein, and Morgan raise torch singing from the expression of emotion to the revelation of character. (Jerome Kern and Oscar Hammerstein II, "Can't Help Lovin' Dat Man of Mine," *Show Boat,* 1927)

Morgan underplayed the bitterness in a song like, "Why Was I Born?" The lyric is largely a series of forlorn questions that begins with the title, while her quivering lips and the nervous twisting of the handkerchief she always clutched told you her heart was breaking. She drank too much and endured too many bad times. The uptown madam Polly Adler wrote that she once came across Morgan "helplessly drunk and crying her heart out in the ladies' room of a speak. When I tried to get her to pull herself together she wailed, 'I'm in love with that bastard at the bar, and he doesn't want me.'"[60] At about the same time,

Morgan was also singing Harry Woods and Mort Dixon's lines, "Here I am lonely, / Tired and lonely" (Harry Woods, Mort Dixon, "Just Like a Butterfly That's Caught in the Rain," 1927).

Whereas the flapper lingered as a figure of self-indulgent play, Morgan, Etting, Holman, and Brice sang the dark songs that became the counterpoint to their time. For every dozen songs that crowed about a flapper, another song keened over betrayal and desperation. Except for Brice, the daughter of a Brooklyn saloon owner, the other torch singers grew up in the Midwest and eventually made their way to Chicago or New York. Ruth Etting married Martin "Moe the Gimp" Snyder, a small-time hoodlum, early in her career. When she wanted to leave him for a piano player named Myrl Alderman, Snyder attempted to murder him. When Snyder went to prison, Etting divorced him, married Alderman, and left show business.

When Libby Holman told her husband, a Reynolds tobacco heir, that she was pregnant by another man, friends in the next room heard an argument and a gunshot, and discovered Reynolds dead on the floor. The police charged Holman and her lover with murder, but the Reynolds family had the charges dropped to avoid a scandal.

Fanny Brice had three husbands, including the professional gambler Nicky Arnstein, who served several prison terms, including one for stock fraud. On his release in 1927, he disappeared from Brice's life, and she reluctantly divorced him. The next year, Brice recorded a song that turned her loss into a Pollyanna song of sorts, but readers of the gossip columns would have seen through the deception: "Be a cheerful loser, / You have the world to gain" (Oscar Levant, Mort Dixon, and Billy Rose, "If You Want the Rainbow [You Must Have the Rain]," *My Man*, 1928). Brice and the others would have understood the kinds of songs they were singing. They were drawn to torch ballads and sang them so well because the emotions they found in them matched their own.

Torch songs were a white offshoot of the blues just when the blues had become an urban music. They feel bluesy, but they're also Tin Pan Alley songs that trace their roots back to such earlier city songs as "Heaven Will Protect the Working Girl" (A. Baldwin Stone and Edgar Smith, 1910) and "In the Heart of the City That Has No Heart" (Thomas S. Allen and Joseph M Daly, 1913). No other Tin Pan Alley songs from the twenties equal them except for a few romantic ballads, including Irving Berlin's great slow waltzes, "What'll I Do" (1923), "All Alone" (1924), "Remember" (1925), and "How About Me" (1928).

The torch singers emerged just as Bessie Smith and the great classic blues singers reached the height of their power and, thanks to recordings, found a wider, whiter audience. The blues had always included laments about longing, unrequited love, and, occasionally, revenge. When African Americans left the Mississippi Delta, they carried the blues with them. In cities such as New Orleans, Chicago, and New York, they created a new voice for the blues. Mainly performed by women, the blues were about defiance and sexual pleasure in such songs as "Wild Women Don't Get the Blues." Torch-song singers learned from the urban blues to affirm their sexuality, their broken hearts, and the good-for-nothing men they couldn't help loving. They suffered for love and from love, with little hope for tomorrow. A few characteristic titles express their points of view as clearly as any explanation: "I Must Have That Man" about loneliness and longing, "Mean to Me" about unrequited love, and "I Cried for You" about revenge.

Flappers may have been sleeping around helter-skelter, but they were as innocent as they were morally obtuse. They jabbered about love all the time, but you have to wonder if they understood anything about it. The characters in torch songs were alone, but they knew all there was to know. Believers to the end, they refused to deny their own faith in love's worth. Bruised romantics, they would surely fall again if only they had the chance. And they would probably pick another two-timing man unworthy of their loyalty. Their emotional antennae were incredibly keen, but not until it was too late. Love blinded them; only betrayal rewarded them with clarity. When it came to love, they had no luck and no judgment—only their honesty with themselves and their ability to survive.

None of the early torch singers had the lusty trumpet of a Bessie Smith or the husky velvet of a young Peggy Lee in the forties. All of them had an unsurpassed ability to clarify and enlarge the intense emotionalism of an unhappy love ballad, but Morgan's high, tremulous soprano projected vulnerability, sorrow, and loss. When she sang the pleading "Don't Ever Leave Me," you understood how her wounded heart had reduced her to dependence, even helplessness. (Jerome Kern and Oscar Hammerstein II, "Don't Ever Leave Me," *Sweet Adeline*, 1929)

The flapper was a type, an image. The torch singer was a woman—alive to her surroundings, emotionally responsive to experience, sexually knowing. She revealed the darker passions that lurk beneath the flapper's frenzied joy. The gossip columnist Walter Winchell wrote about Libby Holman, his favorite torch singer, "She is the torch singer *par excellence*—the best of those female troubadours with voices of smoke and tears, who moan and keen love's labors lost to the rhythm and boom of the Roaring Twenties."[61]

Despite the decade's manic frivolity, torch ballads were there almost from the start. In 1921, four years before flappers began to dance the Charleston, one of the first songs to carry a torch appeared in that year's *Ziegfeld Follies.* In the first act, the comedian Fanny Brice introduced one of her most important comic songs, "Second Hand Rose." In the second act, wearing a simple black dress, standing by a lamppost, she changed from a comic to a torch singer with "My Man," an English version of a French song that Ziegfeld had been wise enough to choose for her. For the song's first rehearsal, Brice had arrived in "a red wig, black velvet dress, sparkling earrings, and ballroom shoes. Ziegfeld said she looked like a female impersonator. He made her tousle her hair and had someone cut the skirt in half, tear it down the side, rip her stockings, and smear her costume with ashes. 'Now,' he said, 'sing it.'"[62] In Channing Pollock's English lyric, the woman claims possession of a man who cheats with two or three other women and beats her in the bargain, but "When he takes me in his arms / The world is bright, all right" (Maurice Yvain, Jacques Charles, Albert Willemetz, and Channing Pollock, 1921).

Like many of the best torch ballads, "My Man" comes perilously close to self-pity but saves itself through a combination of self-knowledge and honesty. The character confronts her own despair. None of the torch singers ever fools herself within a song. They know what they need, because it's the one thing they don't have. There's nothing girlish about them; they are women in every way even though they lack the rambunctiousness of the flapper and the independence of the women of the thirties.

Torch singers cut against the grain of the twenties but found the dark years of the Depression more conducive to their message. During the twenties, the torch song was an antidote to the decade's mindless whirl, but in the thirties, says Timothy Scheuer, it expressed "the cynicism of confronting the hangover" of the previous decade.[63] Yet even in the thirties, a decade characterized by personal hardship and social upheaval, men out of work and broken families, the torch singer stood alone, isolated by her misery and integrity. She revealed not only her lost love and deep sadness but also her blighted emotional life. Speaking from a woman's aching heart, the songs uttered a cry of discontent and terrible necessity: "Torch singers expressed the torment that many women felt in the early 1930s: they were emotionally involved with men who could not provide or who did not see marriage in their future."[64] A woman like the taxi dancer in "Ten Cents A Dance" dances away the night, not because she expects to find true love but to earn a few bucks to pay the rent. As she dances with a gay customer, what might have been romantic becomes self-mockery instead (Richard Rodgers and Lorenz Hart, "Ten Cents A Dance," *Simple Simon*, 1930).

The torch songs of the thirties often have an element of irony. It wasn't the Roaring Twenties anymore. How did you look back from the Depression's vantage point without a teary plaint or cynical smirk—or both? Most popular songs celebrated romance, but torch singers, "'sexually experienced and wised-up,' . . . sang [about] 'America's preoccupation with love and romance.'"[65] Beneath the melancholy lay grit. The movie characters played by such female stars as Katharine Hepburn, Barbara Stanwyck, Carole Lombard, Ginger Rogers, and Jean Arthur were strong, confident, and smart. Irreverent and loving, they lived pretty much on their own terms. Under the weight of the prudish Motion Picture Production Code, their sexuality appeared in their intelligence, in the clever, patient way they outsmarted their male prey, and in their language. It was repartee as foreplay. Yet in nearly every one of their films, they ended up trading their independence for a wedding ring. These tough career women became dependent on men, but at least they were choosing freely. Ian M. Post writes that on the other hand, torch singers "yearned for the love of a man, who was seen as the solution to their insecurity." Unlike the movie stars, "torch singers perceived their lives as glum and unstable without a man, which led them to sing for their return. . . . These singers rejected the autonomous lifestyle and instead pined for a man they could depend on once again."[66]

The women suffer because women in torch ballads always do. Helplessness, need, and longing are constant no matter when the torch songs were written, but Ian Post overlooks the irony that shapes many of these songs in the thirties. During the twenties, women bemoaned "their ill treatment at the hands of abusive, unfaithful men."[67] No matter what, they're unable to stop loving the men who make their lives hell, but a decade later the songs are often about the women's need not to be alone—to endure the emotional pain of a man's staying or the deeper pain of his going . It's a nuanced distinction but a real one. The emotions are no less intense, but a number of songs come with a layer of wit to provide not detachment but fearless honesty. Irony is everywhere—in the mockery of supposed friends, in a woman's view of herself, and in the circumstances she can't escape. A woman uses streetwise wit (and brilliantly playful rhyming) to ward off the anguish in Ira Gershwin's lyric to "But Not for Me" (George Gershwin and Ira Gershwin, *Girl Crazy*, 1930).

The use of irony during the Depression was also very much an urban ploy. You get through the long nights by denying there's a problem in the first place or by defanging it with understatement or wit. "I get along without you very well," the woman says—convincingly, perhaps. But then she adds the line that gives the game away: "Of course I do" (Hoagy Carmichael, "I Get Along Without You Very Well," 1939). In another song, this time from 1936, the woman harks back to the twenties by expressing a willingness to slave for her man, but then adds with a combination of honesty and self-mockery: "If that isn't love / It will have to do" (Alberta Nichols, Saul Chaplin, and Mann Holiner, "Until the Real Thing Comes Along," *Rhapsody in Black*, 1936).

The loneliness these women feel—their need for a man—puts them out of fashion nearly a century later. You can say no man is worth it, but that's too easy a way out to satisfy the complex promptings of the heart. Torch singers bore witness in songs whose emotions weren't unique to a city but whose isolation and need make them feel as if that's where they belong. What gives these songs their bite is the absence of illusion and the courage to face the truth without self-deception. There was something stirring and unsettling about them. These women may not have survived gracefully, but survive they did, to sing the songs of shattered love and broken hearts, women of spirit offering their tribute to the fragility of all that's precious.

~ ~ ~

Suburbs first became an important part of urban planning and real estate development—and songs—more than half a century before the first Levittown. Yet the American idea of something resembling a suburb is as old as William Penn's original plan for Philadelphia. After surviving the great London fire of 1666, Penn designed "a greene countrie towne, which will . . . always be wholesome."[68] It was an

American vision of an Eden that eventually took recognizable form in the late nineteenth and early twentieth centuries.

Through the 1920s, large numbers of people continued to pour into city neighborhoods as the middle class first began to move out. They left for the suburbs in ever larger numbers as soon as train and trolley lines made the move feasible. Streetcars—the beginnings of rapid transit—had appeared in the 1870s. By the midtwenties, the number of trolley riders declined dramatically, because the automobile had joined the commuter train to take on the task of carrying men to their jobs each morning and back home again each night.[69] During the twenties, more than nine hundred thousand new houses sprang up in areas near but not in cities.[70]

Of course, a few people still preferred to leave the city for a place where farmers still plowed. For a while, some of the songs about them came with an arched eyebrow and a comic point of view. In 1917, P. G. Wodehouse's lyric for "A Bungalow in Quogue" gave us a married city couple, both affluent and out of their element. They settle down in the Long Island village of Quogue (pronounced "Kwahg"), where they expect to find a satisfying bucolic encounter with Bill the bull and Hildebrand the hog, and opportunities to "sniff the scented breeze, / And pluck tomatoes from the trees." Instead, they spend their time "sitting up at nights, / Comparing our mosquito bites" (Jerome Kern and P. G. Wodehouse, "A Bungalow in Quogue," *Riviera Girl*, 1917).

Hart wrote an equally inventive lyric for "Mountain Greenery" (1926), the only hit to emerge from his and Rodgers's second edition of *Garrick Gaieties.* A sequel of sorts to "Manhattan," their one hit from the first edition of *Garrick Gaieties,* it celebrates the joys of country living, even though its frame of reference is the city. Like "Manhattan," it portrays a couple of smart, youthful newlyweds from New York, but instead of exploring the five boroughs with a kind of dazzling jauntiness, they decide to move to what the title calls their "Mountain Greenery." Hart's inventive rhymes make the song less a paean to rural life than a look at what happens when urban sophistication collides with the country. They give up their jobs for the simple life laid out in witty, complicated rhymes. No rube could have written them.

The city offered opportunity and excitement, but the suburb provided natural beauty and the allure of emotional fulfillment just beyond the skyscraper's shadow. Dolores Hayden writes that "suburbia is the site of promises, dreams, and fantasies. It is a landscape of the imagination where Americans situate ambitions for upward mobility and economic security, ideals about freedom and private property, and longings for social harmony and spiritual uplift."[71] In popular songs, it was also the final destination. Flappers could dance until dawn as long as they understood, at least tacitly, that the trappings of domesticity awaited them when the band stopped playing.

When songwriters turned their attention to the move to suburbia, they focused on what Hayden called "promises, dreams, and fantasies" rather than "economic security" and "private property." When they wrote about a tiny house for two, they were interested in what one song calls "a dream castle" (Willard Robison and Larry Conley, "A Cottage for Sale," 1929), not a real estate investment. In many songs from the late teens and twenties, the desire of young men and women to find and sustain true love extended past the anticipated wedding to married life itself. Songs idealized, elevated, and romanticized love after marriage. Love lost none of its premarital ardor as it expressed "spiritual uplift" in the ability of a loving couple—on their own and alone at last—to live out their dream of love deepened yet solidified by marriage. In an Irving Berlin lyric from 1925, newlyweds live contentedly in a bungalow that gives them both seclusion and privacy ("Little Bungalow").

In the suburbs, Americans could have the best of both worlds, so the myth ran—one place to live in and another to dream about, both under the same roof. Songs from the turn of the century had portrayed young city dwellers dreaming about the satisfactions of country life while remaining where the action and opportunity were. Songs about the suburbs provided a response to the tension between rural and urban America and the widening gap between the rich and the rest of us. These were the years when the few Americans who had amassed great wealth built enormous cottages on Long Island's Gold Coast (the North Shore) and elsewhere, each one a small city in itself, with dozens of rooms (and just as many servants), defined by grandeur (or grandiosity) of design and furnishing, and by the use of every modern contraption from indoor plumbing to electric lights. Then their owners surrounded the houses with lavish gardens, and the gardens with acres of pasture and wooded groves. The pastures had their own cows and sheep for picturesque grazing. They were complete and self-sufficient, a merging of the natural and the built that aimed to be grand, civilized, and comforting. It was America's own little squirearchy an hour out from Wall Street.

When the middle class began to build suburban houses a decade or two later, it imitated on a smaller scale what the wealthy had already built—block after block of residences set back from the road and surrounded by lawns to suggest the feel of country living and confirm its value as well as to assert a tacit right to privacy. Wealthy New Yorkers, moving between Fifth Avenue and Long Island's North Shore, had taken immediate advantage of the arrival of the automobile. Because these people were rich and powerful, governments soon built roads and provided amenities for them to use. Where roads went, real estate developers followed. Wealthy families such as the Morgans, Vanderbilts, and Fricks wanted to live like European royalty—surrounded by tapestries, Old Master paintings, and suits of armor—but the public roads they needed for their automobiles also opened Long Island to the middle class.[72] And where the middle class went, the songwriters followed. When you were single, you rented an apartment in the city and you courted. When you married, you bought a car and a cottage, and you moved to the suburbs. As Frederick Law Olmstead wrote as early as 1868, "The essential qualification of a suburb is domesticity."[73]

In 1920, the citizens of the United States had registered over 9 million automobiles. By 1925, that number had reached nearly 20 million.[74] But their effect was becoming clear as early as 1905 in Jean Schwartz and William Jerome's "On an Automobile Honeymoon." A young man, properly proud of his new motorcar, takes his girl for a Sunday spin up Riverside Drive in Manhattan. He's single and living in the city but is affluent enough to own his own car. As he drives, he envisions driving to church on his wedding day, and then driving away with his new wife on their "automobile honeymoon" (Jean Schwartz and William Jerome, "On an Automobile Honeymoon," 1905).

Addressing the suburban theme from a different angle, "Wedding Bells Are Breaking Up That Old Gang of Mine," a hit from 1923, portrays an unattached young man who realizes that his life has changed dramatically. The song's chorus begins on an urban street corner at night, deserted because his friends are leaving to be with their sweethearts. Instead of barbershop harmonies, the young man is more likely to hear the wedding bells that, the title announces, are "Breaking Up That Old Gang of Mine" (Sammy Fain, Irving Kahal, and William Raskin, "Wedding Bells Are Breaking Up That Old Gang of Mine," 1929). Other songs that make the same point about urban friends who fall in love and move away include “That Old Gang of Mine” (Ray Henderson, Mort Dixon, and Billy Rose, 1923) and “The Gang That Sang ‘Heart of My Heart’” (Ben Ryan, 1926).

By the 1920s, marriage increasingly led to a move to a suburban cottage. Like the Gold Coast mansion, it occupied imaginatively what earlier had been a clearing in the wilderness, but America’s Eden has always been settled and cultivated rather than wild. From the start, gently curving suburban streets took their names from trees and flowers, but those streets were soon paved and automobiles sat at the curbs.

Like the wealthy who preceded them to the suburbs, the middle-class arrivals “idealized the house and yard rather than the model neighborhood or the ideal town.”[75] No song makes this attitude more explicit than “Back in Your Own Backyard” from 1928. The lyric combines a Pollyanna song with one about returning. It urges someone whose heart is weary to head for home. Most songs of returning lead to a beloved and the promise of marriage. Here, though, the wanderer finds satisfaction in nature’s beauty, embodied in an image of serene happiness, the bluebird, along with stimulation for his imagination. Without a trace of envy or loss, he will dream contentedly of exotic locales without ever leaving home again (Dave Dreyer, Billy Rose, and Al Jolson, “Back in Your Own Backyard,” 1928).

We have very few songs about “Commodore” Vanderbilt’s mansion or J. P. Morgan’s private railroad car because popular songwriters viewed millionaires through a populist lens when they viewed them at all. Wealth was something we could all aspire to, especially if it did not change us, good democrats all. As George M. Cohan has one of his characters sing in *Forty-Five Minutes from Broadway*, “I want to be a popular millionaire” (“I Want to Be a Popular Millionaire,” *Forty-Five Minutes from Broadway*, 1906). Despite the degradations of the sweatshop and child labor, wealth spread more widely than ever before in the first decades of the new century, and working people ended up with a few dollars in their pockets. They could escape the tenements on a Sunday afternoon to stroll on the boardwalk at Coney Island, the cooling Atlantic on one side and the spectacular Cyclone on the other, their own less exclusive merging of the natural and the man-made. For a young working-class couple in love, their day off was the high point of their week as they sought a way to spend some time alone together:

On a Sunday afternoon
In the merry month of June,
Take a trip up the Hudson
Or down the Bay,
Take a trolley to Coney
Or Rockaway.
(Harry Von Tilzer and Andrew Sterling, "On a Sunday Afternoon," 1902)

The country was changing rapidly, but allowing young men and women to be alone together was still new and daring. The place a couple went in the first days of their married lives—their own place—became the fulfillment of their dreams. It was also a particularly American place, available to anyone, no matter how modest. A cottage or bungalow said little about class but a great deal about self-sufficiency and independence. Although the style may suggest otherwise, it was the Jeffersonian dream wrapped in a love song, a home elevated through love to a personal paradise. (James F. Hanley and Eddie Dowling, "The Little White House [At the End of Honeymoon Lane]," 1926).

Songs of married love, usually set in the suburbs, ranged from a description of a spouse's typical day to the quality of the couple's life as newlyweds to a loving description of their cottage or bungalow. Even the songs of the twenties, with their new freedom for women and their interest in sex, dwelt on marriage as much as the songs of the teens, thirties, or forties. Many of the sheiks who pursued flappers in Jazz Age song lyrics also looked ahead to marriage. Despite the irreverence and sexiness of these songs, the romantic ideal remained intact. In "My Troubles Are Over," from 1928, a young man with a keen interest in lovemaking is even more interested in domesticity. He intends to marry and settle down in the suburbs surrounded by cars, kids, and clover. (James Monaco and Edgar Leslie, "My Troubles Are Over," 1928). Monaco and Leslie's view of America is every bit as idyllic as the return to the farm and the small town in earlier songs.

Bungalows and cottages are common in love songs from the twenties, among them "You're Just the Type for a Bungalow" and "Our Bungalow of Dreams." In "While Others Are Building Castles in the Air," a young man asserts his practicality and, implicitly, his sense of responsibility as a new husband: "While others are building castles in the air, / I'll build a cottage for two" (Fred Fisher and Jack Mahoney, "While Others Are Building Castles in the Air," 1919). Even earlier, in 1917, a husband shows his wife plans for "a dear little bungalow," including "a dear little room to dream in," where they will set up housekeeping while they bill and coo. (Anonymous, "Our Bungalow," unpublished, ca. 1917). These songs give mundane household tasks a gloss of romantic independence, privacy, and playful eroticism as they depict a dream world for married lovers.

Three years later, a successful musical comedy named *Mary* told the story of Jack Keene, who dreams of going west to build inexpensive houses that young couples can afford. He gives them the provocative name of "love nests." The score's hit song describes them as "cozy and warm" and announces its moral with the directness of a fable:

> Better than a palace with a gilded dome,
> Is the love nest you can call home.
> (Louis A. Hirsch and Otto Harbach, "Love Nest," *Mary*, 1920)

Songs expressed similar sentiments throughout the twenties. In a song from 1928, a suburban cottage surrounded by roses was "a nest for Mary" built by her husband, complete with a nursery and a front porch, where "someday, we'll rock away our cares / In our rocking chairs," (Jesse Greer and Billy Rose, "Building a Nest for Mary," 1928).

In other words, what Amos St. Germain wrote about the movies of the 1920s was also true of the decade's songs: they affirmed the traditional values of American life at the same time that they made transgressions appear very attractive.[76] Similarly, songs about married lovers who want to buy a house and move to the suburbs were surprisingly popular when everybody was also singing about flappers. These songs, with their new interest in domesticity, were more common in the twenties than in any other decade, and range from the everyday to the idealized, both images of happiness. A young man thinks about washing the dishes with his sweetheart: "Oh gosh, I get so excited / I can hardly think" (Peter Dixon, Tom Neely, and Dave Ringle, "Washing Dishes [with My Sweetie]," 1930). Or, more important, he defines the idyllic life for married lovers as raising a family together: "We will raise a family / A girl for you, a boy for me" (Vincent Youmans and Irving Caesar, "Tea for Two," *No, No, Nanette*, 1925).

The songs are also likely to emphasize specific times—from the end of the honeymoon until the raising of small children—and choose specific places—an apartment in the city or a cottage or bungalow in the suburbs. These people are relative newlyweds. In a surprising twist, the man usually tells the story—just as he does in flapper songs—and enjoys what has changed in the couple's lives. If they plan to stay in the city after tying the knot, the new hubby can hardly wait to move in:

> We will start to bill and coo,
> When it's nesting time in Flatbush, in Flatbush Avenue.
> (Jerome Kern and P. G. Wodehouse, "Nesting Time [in Flatbush],"
> *Oh, Boy!*, 1917)

The more likely choice in these songs, though, is the suburban cottage. Decades earlier, references to a cottage or bungalow almost always meant someplace rural, but that quickly changed to include suburbia. By the 1920s, it had become desirable for young couples to live "halfway" between the city and the small town. In an early lyric by Al Dubin, a recently married couple settles into a suburban cottage or bungalow. It's small, but it's theirs, with enough room for escape from the world, for lovemaking, and for the child who is bound to come along. Each night, a husband returns from work, whistling with happy anticipation until his wife meets him "Halfway up the pathway, / Halfway to heaven and home" (J. Russel Robinson and Al Dubin, "Halfway to Heaven," 1928).

Maybe the least likely example of these sentiments showed up in 1927, in Rodgers and Hart's score to *A Connecticut Yankee*, adapted from Mark Twain's 1889 satiric novel *A Connecticut Yankee in King Arthur's Court.* "Thou Swell" is a courting duet notable for its wittily anachronistic mix of medieval diction and contemporary slang. The contemporary character Martin, transported back to King Arthur's court courtesy of a knock on the head with a Champagne bottle, is put in charge of industrializing the country. He also finds himself falling for Demoiselle Alisande. When he asks for a kiss, he begins to think about settling down contentedly in nothing more than a couple of rooms and a kitchen.

Two years later, the African American songwriter Clarence Williams portrayed a young married woman who divides up the responsibilities between husband and wife in a conventional way: he earns the money and she saves it; when he goes to work, she works in the garden and is "itchin' to be in the kitchen." Williams usually wrote much less domesticated fare, with such titles as "Take Your Black Bottom Outside" and "I Need a Little Sugar in My Bowl." "In Our Cottage of Love" gets its edge from its suggestion of eroticism upstairs where "there's only gonna be one blue room / In our cottage of love"

(Clarence Williams, "In Our Cottage of Love," 1929). Likewise, even in the Gershwins' torch song "The Man I Love," a woman's need for a soul mate culminates in her assertion that they'll build a home big enough only for two (George Gershwin and Ira Gershwin, "The Man I Love," 1927).

In a world populated by *flappers*, it's suitable to have a couple interested in having a *nest* of their own, especially if it requires *feathering* in anticipation of the move to the suburbs (Milt Ager and Jack Yellen, "I'm Feathering a Nest [for a Little Blue Bird]," 1929). Songs about an impending marriage might still have some of the zip of a flapper tune (Walter Donaldson, "Because My Baby Don't Mean Maybe Now," 1928), but songs about married lovers resulted in some of the most idyllic, most romantic ballads of the decade, and some of the most important. Marriage in these songs often affirmed that the youthful pleasures of being single didn't fade away at the altar. They could bring the rhythm of the Charleston to lovemaking, along with its happy-go-lucky approach to life, no matter what problems arise: "Not much money, Oh, but honey, /Ain't we got fun" (Richard A. Whiting, Gus Kahn, and Raymond B. Egan, "Ain't We Got Fun," 1920). It had become acceptable by the twenties for newlyweds to sing about their bedroom, the most important room in the house. Although Lorenz Hart's lyric has a husband-to-be planning a house with rooms for his in-laws and the children, he is mainly interested in the marital bedroom, which he says in a charming oxymoron is just upstairs but also far away (Richard Rodgers and Lorenz Hart, "Blue Room," *The Girl Friend*, 1926).

The next year, in a similar song, Walter Donaldson spoke for a young husband who returns home "where a loving smile" greets him. The song expresses his view of a life he finds idyllic. Each day, as love calls him home to "a cottage cozy," he sighs, "I'm in heaven" (Walter Donaldson, "At Sundown," 1927). Similarly, the lyricist George Whiting has a husband describe his small house in one of the biggest hits of 1927. In "My Blue Heaven," the young man returns each evening to his "cozy . . . little nest," but what's most important to him is "Mollie . . . and Baby makes three." It is the formula for happiness in what he calls "My Blue Heaven" (Walter Donaldson and George Whiting, "My Blue Heaven," 1927). After fifty years of *blue* representing melancholy and betrayal, it reverted in the hands of white songwriters to its meaning of happiness just when the blues became a national music through the recordings of such performers as Ma Rainey and Bessie Smith.

As for songs where the suburban dream of blissful marriage goes wrong, one of Cole Porter's earliest Broadway songs tells the sad story of a commuter who falls for a city girl. They marry and move to "one of those bungalows God grows" in Flushing. All is well until he returns home one night to find her gone; she has run off with the man of her choice, "and he's got a Rolls-Royce" (Cole Porter, "Bring Me Back My Butterfly," *Hitchy-Koo of 1919*, 1919). Just over a decade later, in 1930, after nearly three decades of cottages and bungalows in popular songs, the mention of "a cottage for sale" was enough to suggest the end of a marriage. Near the beginning of the song, lyricist Larry Conley portrays the character's heaviness of heart "as I gaze upon a cottage for sale" (Willard Robison and Larry Conley, "A Cottage for Sale," 1930). The rest is elaboration, even though references to bungalows and cottages nearly disappear from songs during the more difficult decades of the Great Depression and World War II. In the thirties and forties, life was not so serene and the world not so easy to escape.

If you're looking for a more skeptical view of married bliss, the best of the few examples is Walter Donaldson and Gus Kahn's "Makin' Whoopee," in which a husband, sick of washing dishes and baby clothes, seeks consolation elsewhere. When his wife threatens divorce and a trip to the cleaners, an unsympathetic judge offers the best advice: keeping her is a lot cheaper than fooling around and getting caught (Walter Donaldson and Gus Kahn, "Makin' Whoopee," *Whoopee!* 1928). Love songs have little to say about the realities of everyday life, including parenthood. What makes "Whoopee" unusual is its undermining of romantic expectations.

∽∽∽

By the time the great migrations north and east slowed in the 1920s, city dwellers had begun taking vacations. A wide variety of songs emerged to reflect their attitudes and behavior. As affluence increased, people fled the city's summer heat. These weren't songs of returning, though; the city folks they describe have no immediate connection to small towns or farms. Those who might ordinarily mock the rubes were setting up temporary housekeeping just down the road from them. The long tradition of making fun of country people found new impetus in lyrics by George M. Cohan, every inch a New Yorker. He was the perfect wise guy for ragging the yokels. In 1906, the man who wrote, "Give my regards to Broadway, / Remember me to Herald Square," had to go no farther afield than New Rochelle to find the source of his amusement—the rubes who lived only forty-five minutes away (George M. Cohan, "Forty-Five Minutes from Broadway," *Forty-Five Minutes from Broadway*, 1905). Unlike Florenz Ziegfeld, whose *Follies* aimed at the carriage trade, Cohan wrote for working people. They were less likely to repair to fashionable resorts each July and more likely to enjoy his twitting of the hicks who were the victims of slick urban wisecracks. Cohan's best songs mirrored the attitudes of his audience.

Although the increases in affluence and leisure time in the 1920s meant that more people could afford to take vacations, the urge to escape had begun before World War I. Those who took vacations usually went to the mountains, the seaside, or the lakeshore. If you were New Yorkers, that usually meant the Catskills to the north or the Jersey shore to the south. You rented a bungalow and tried not to do anything for a week or two except indulge themselves. Ocean swimming became popular during these years, as "bathing costumes" gave way to skimpier swimsuits for women to wear on public beaches.

Swimming was especially important to Robert Moses, the powerful bureaucrat who, during the Great Depression, changed shorelines, built the parkway system in New York City and its surrounding counties, and disrupted and destroyed neighborhoods for the sake of his grand plan. By favoring the automobile over public transportation, he helped to create suburban development—along with its accompanying traffic jams. The recreational facilities he championed were the end points of the parkways he built. Yet his underlying assumptions were sometimes less sanguine. Moses saw a need to rescue people from what Burton W. Peretti called "the decadent, multiethnic, walled-in artifice of urban leisure in the 1920s."[77] Moses's former colleague Frances Perkins said that he considered the public "a great amorphous mass. . . . [I]t needs to be bathed, it needs to be aired, it needs recreation, but not for personal reasons—just to make it a better public."[78]

Yet to the people whose vacations turned up in songs, being on a beach in a bathing suit was sexy and playful. The childlike behavior that often came with a vacation's respite from responsibility soon made its appearance in song lyrics. From the teens into the early thirties, songs depicted ordinary people sitting on a beach and playing in the sea, among them Harry Carroll and Harold R. Atteridge's comic tongue twister "By the Beautiful Sea" (1914); J. Fred Coots and Nick and Charles Kenny's mournful ballad of love that departs like the tide, "Love Letters in the Sand" (1931); and Sigmund Romberg and Ballard MacDonald's naughty vaudeville number "I Love to Go Swimmin' with Women" (1921):

> I get that navy notion when I see floating queens,
> I dive right in the ocean and I play submarine.
> I love to go swimmin' with women,
> And women love swimmin' with me.
> (Sigmund Romberg and Ballard MacDonald, "I Love to Go Swimmin' with Women," *Love Birds*, 1921)

The most interesting of these songs dwelt on the vacation itself, a sign that during these years enough New Yorkers could afford to spend a week in the country reading or strolling or making mischief at their own expense. Not surprisingly, vacation songs decreased substantially during the hard times of the 1930s and the restrictions of the war years. But before the crash, New Yorkers heard songs about leaving the city in a serious way for a break in routine, or in a comic way as a joke on city dwellers like themselves who turned into blissful incompetents the minute they left the city behind.

The city dweller in Irving Berlin's "Lazy" is nostalgic, not for the ways of country life, but for his own youth. Longing to be lazy and sleep like a child, he has brought along on his vacation a suitcase full of books to read where the setting is serene (Berlin, "Lazy," *The Music Box Revue*, 1924). "Lazy" is devoted to the restorative qualities of killing time but takes the opposite view from Berlin's first hit song, "My Wife's Gone to the Country," about the advantages of remaining behind in the city. One of Berlin's few collaborations, the earlier song portrays Mr. Brown, whose wife and children leave for the country to get away from the city's heat. As we saw in the introduction, in the suggestive lyric, Brown is soon on the phone telling everyone he knows. He puts an ad in the paper, calls on a pretty girl to tell her about his newfound freedom, and buys a parrot to squawk the news: "My wife's gone to the country, / Hurrah! Hurrah!" (Ted Snyder, George Whiting, and Irving Berlin, "My Wife's Gone to the Country [Hurrah! Hurrah!]," 1909).

Things always change, so the country was different in the following decades—and so were its songs. Few lovers in the songs of the thirties and forties were goofy. People out of work or at war had trouble keeping their spirits up. The urban songs of the Great Depression preferred to describe either a gritty New York struggling to hold on to its heart or an art deco dream of a city, where everybody knew exactly what to say and what to wear and nobody ever needed to worry about money. Made in Hollywood but set mainly in New York, the movie musicals of the 1930s gave us love songs of both confrontation and escape. They played an essential role in the Great Depression's evolving urban sensibility.

7

THE GREAT DEPRESSION

The stock market crashed on October 29, 1929, and the flapper vanished faster than her sheik could swallow a goldfish. In 1925, Ray Henderson, Sam M. Lewis, and Joe Young had written "Five Foot Two, Eyes of Blue." Three years later Cole Porter replaced "Let's Misbehave" with the equally naughty "Let's Do It."[1] By 1930, however, Ira Gershwin had spun out a plaintive lyric to "But Not for Me," (George Gershwin and Ira Gershwin, *Girl Crazy*, 1930), Al Dubin wrote the lachrymose "Dancing with Tears in My Eyes" (Joe Burke and Al Dubin, 1930), and Leo Robin wrote the self-pitying "Prisoner of Love" (Russ Columbo, Clarence Gaskill, and Leo Robin, 1931). The characteristic ballads of the Depression tell a much different story than do the lighter-than-air love songs of the twenties, but despite what Peter Flynn calls their "forlorn escapism,"[2] they ensured the survival of an urban sensibility for at least another decade. Woody Guthrie and the Almanac Singers were out on the road, singing labor songs and helping factory workers organize, but most Americans in big cities and small towns alike continued to embrace Tin Pan Alley and Broadway songs that rose, at least figuratively, from the hard pavements of New York City. It was a different kind of urbanity. In 1928, Milton Ager and Jack Yellen wrote the happy-go-lucky "Happy Days Are Here Again," for a scene in an early talkie that depicted soldiers celebrating the end of World War I. But no one performed it until Black Thursday, when jeering listeners at New York's Hotel Pennsylvania belted it out along with George Olsen's Orchestra to transform it into an ironic Depression anthem,[3] the other side of the same coin as a song such as Jay Gorney and E. Y. Harburg's "Brother, Can You Spare a Dime?"

Broadway mounted 233 productions, musical and otherwise, during the 1929–30 season. The next year, the number dropped to 187. The Broadway historian Robert Rusie observes that "the talent that Hollywood absorbed from Broadway was in the vicinity of 75%. By 1939, there were only 98 new openings. Things were even tougher for vaudeville. In 1925, vaudeville circuits controlled 1500 theaters. By 1930, only 300 remained and most of them were sharing performance time with movies."[4]

Many of the best Depression love songs, often set in dystopian cities, survived an ominous decade. Harold Arlen and Ted Koehler's "Stormy Weather" (1933) depicts a life that was as gloomy and bleak as the stormy night. The wind brings only heartache in their "Ill Wind" (1934). Blue skies turn cloudy and gray, and the starless night looks forbidding in Johnny Green and Edward Heyman's "I Cover the Waterfront" (1933). In Heyman's lyric, a woman prowls the docks through a silent, bone-chilling night in a hostile city. Desperate, she seeks the return of the lover who has sailed away. The striking word in the title is "Cover." She covers the waterfront in the same way a reporter covers a beat, exploring every cranny, trying desperately to find what she needs. It feels constricting. She never encounters another person; only the questions matter: will the lover remember and will he ever return. The listener comes away with a sense that this has gone on for a very long time. She seems more obsessive than patient, as obsession gives expression to her yearning but offers no respite.

Tin Pan Alley had little to say about the Dust Bowl or the migration of the Okies to California. It looked at life in America's cities instead. Many of its songs portray a heartless, unforgiving place, but, through all the Depression's urban woes, Tin Pan Alley also confirmed whatever optimism America could muster, laced with a dose of reality. Through their mix of sentiment and wit, these songs depicted a kind of tough-minded emotionalism. Whether the songwriters remained in New York or gave Hollywood a try, they wove versions of the city's emotional state, often set in the theaters and nightclubs of Broadway and Harlem. Even in the talkies, chorus girls wanted to be stars, not on the screen, but on the Great White Way. Songwriters found a perfect place to set their songs, even though most Americans couldn't have afforded the ticket price.

Out in Hollywood, songwriters did the same thing as their Broadway counterparts. As the Depression swirled around them, they wrote songs that polished the allure of New York City. Some of the very first movie musicals resembled stage revues with a famous star as emcee; a dozen or so performers, all under contract to the studio making the movie; and individual numbers that ranged from comedy sketches to a line of dancing girls in slickers as Cliff Edwards strummed his ukulele and sang "Singin' in the Rain" (Nacio Herb Brown and Arthur Freed,

1929). Edwards's performance was in *The Hollywood Revue of 1929*, produced by Metro-Goldwyn-Mayer and featuring a large curtain that opened and closed at the start and finish of each act. It gave the audience the sensation of being in a Broadway theater, because Hollywood hadn't yet figured out how to make a musical that didn't look like a stage show.[5]

In all those backstagers between the late twenties and midforties, everybody wanted to be a star on Broadway. From Ruby Keeler and Dick Powell to Betty Grable and John Payne, movie stars played characters who dreamed of making it big on the stage. These showbiz wannabes longed to play the Palace or, if they dared, make the leap from vaudeville to Broadway. At the very least, they itched to sing in those gleaming, oversized art deco nightclubs where the men wore crisp, double-breasted tuxedos, the women poured themselves into shimmering satin gowns, and the maître d' led only the right people past the velvet rope to a ringside table.

In *The Broadway Melody*—the first sound picture to boast that it was "All Talking! All Singing! All Dancing!"—the title song reaffirmed the myth of Broadway, where flickering neon lights and pulsating hearts were inseparable (Nacio Herb Brown and Arthur Freed, "Broadway Melody, *The Broadway Melody*, 1929). During the Great Depression, the image of a particular street in a single city could hold out hope, and nobody wove more persuasive momentary dreams than the tunesmiths of Tin Pan Alley, regardless of which coast they worked on. They crafted lyrics that refused to surrender as long as love survived. Everybody gets to fall in love, regardless of wealth, education, or profession—what better angle for a songwriter who aimed to sell his wares to as many people as possible? Al Sherman and Al Lewis had it just right for Depression audiences. When "potatoes are cheaper" and "tomatoes are cheaper / Now's the time to fall in love" ("Now's the Time to Fall in Love," 1931).

If America had had multiplexes in the thirties, moviegoers could have watched Fred Astaire and Ginger Rogers glide across the floor of a Manhattan nightspot, while on the screen across the hall, the gold diggers would have been tapping as if their lives depended on it. The two poles of the decade's movie musicals stood firm at RKO and Warner Bros. Astaire and Rogers sang and danced at RKO to songs by Berlin, the Gershwins, Porter, and Jerome Kern and Dorothy Fields. Meanwhile, Ruby Keeler, Dick Powell, and the rest of the contract players at Warner relied almost exclusively on the overworked songwriting team of the composer Harry Warren and the lyricist Al Dubin. Somewhere between Warner and RKO, 20th Century Fox turned out a batch of musicals that starred Alice Faye and eventually Betty Grable. These musicals began in the years leading up to World War II, mostly with music by Harry Revel and lyrics by Mack Gordon. In movies set in New York, including such titles as *Wake Up and Live* (1937), *You Can't Have Everything,* (1937), and *Tin Pan Alley* (1940), Faye typically plays a brassy, ambitious (but lovable) singer who works in rowdy joints or second-rate vaudeville houses. Her character has left the farm far behind.

The Astaire–Rogers movies were urban, too, but urban fairy tales set in Venice and London and Manhattan supper clubs. Even when they performed in dance studios (*Swing Time*) or seedy clubs (*Follow the Fleet*), Rogers always had a sparkling gown hanging in her closet, and Astaire always owned a set of perfectly pressed tails. Rarely did anybody in these Depression-era movies worry about money. During these early days of commercial aviation, somebody was always flying off to Rio or Venice for a weekend. The stories added songs to old-fashioned romantic comedies—plays in which members of the smart set with plenty of free time pursue true love foolishly but find it anyway. Listen more closely to the songs, though, and it becomes clear that these are modern Depression songs acted out by a fortunate few, their often "sunny romanticism overlying fear."[6]

The elegant, insouciant Fred Astaire sang and danced his way through the thirties, not by ignoring the times, but by singing and dancing with Ginger Rogers to transform them. Even in movies where the bad times affect him—especially *Swing Time,* where he plays an unemployed gambler on a temporary lucky streak—his dances with Rogers lift them (and us) beyond the workaday. Although he sang the occasional melancholy ballad, he was more likely to sing something hopeful or upbeat like "I'm Putting All My Eggs in One Basket" (Irving Berlin, *Follow the Fleet,* 1936). The slang expression in the title, common in the thirties, often referred to money, a familiar image in a lot of Depression-era love songs. The accumulation of newly laid eggs was ironic city slang, even though it sounded like something from the farm, and the next line—in the argot of a gambler—combines romantic commitment with a city guy's unequivocal confidence. He places a bet on the woman he's falling in love with. Other songs introduced by Astaire also had a Depression sensibility, although neither he, his performance style, nor the movies' plots put a great deal of emphasis on bad times: such songs as "No Strings," in which a star dancer celebrates

Figure 7.1. Elegant Fred Astaire, accompanied here by Irving Berlin, gave moviegoers a break from Depression troubles. Courtesy of Photofest.

his freedom when his long-running show closes; the Pollyanna song "Pick Yourself Up"; the therapeutic "Change Partners" and "Let Yourself Go"; and even "A Fine Romance," an ironic celebration of unrequited love. His two darkest songs from the 1930s were Berlin's "Let's Face the Music and Dance" from *Follow the Fleet*, and Kern and Fields' "Never Gonna Dance" from *Swing Time*, both from 1936. Both were set in large cities, the first in San Francisco and the second in New York.

In *Follow the Fleet*, Rogers plays a small-time dancer and Astaire a sailor and her former partner. When they reunite to put on a benefit, they perform "Let's Face the Music and Dance" as two ruined socialites tempted by suicide. The dark ambiguity in the song's title reflects the sensibility apparent in the lyric and the dance as Astaire successfully lures Rogers back from the brink. He convinces her that although trouble may come, as long as they have the moon to light their love, at the very least, they can dance. (Irving Berlin, "Let's Face the Music and Dance," *Follow the Fleet*, 1936) For Astaire, Rogers, and their audiences, that was more than enough.

"Never Gonna Dance" is every bit as bleak and even more moving because its circumstance, however artificial, has emotional resonance beyond the dance. It is not a performance number but rather an extension of the plot. Astaire's and Rogers's characters have fallen in love, but she has to marry someone else because of a bet gone wrong. She comes to say goodbye, but he whirls her into a dance that she keeps trying to break off. They dance in a gleaming black and white urban setting until he releases her at last and she walks away dejectedly, leaving him motionless and brokenhearted. Without her, truly, he will never dance again; he gives away his necktie and his top hat, part of his regalia when he dances (Jerome Kern and Dorothy Fields, "Never Gonna Dance," *Swing Time*, 1936). This is the last number in the movie; the happy ending is about ten minutes away.

Despite the darkness of these songs, the movies they're part of insist on offering hope—and hope also was the stock-in-trade of the backstage musicals cranked out at Warner Bros. These were working-class movies about gold diggers determined to find stardom or a sugar daddy, whichever came first. Astaire and Rogers were in the market for true love, and so were Ruby Keeler and Dick Powell, who starred in seven of the Warner Bros. musicals, but the gold diggers link love and sex to a desperate need to survive. They're also very good at deflecting what they're doing with a cynical wisecrack. The Astaire–Rogers romantic comedies play out their temporary confusions and conundrums in shimmering cabarets and boudoirs, but the gold diggers spend their lives in drafty dressing rooms and cramped apartments. Warren and Dubin gave lilting, rhythmic love songs to Keeler and Powell, but they gave the gold diggers their pounding, pulsating anthems, including "Forty-Second Street" and "Lullaby of Broadway." Love had nothing to do with it unless it came with a diamond brooch. The rotund Guy Kibbee often played the silly sugar daddy who bankrolled the show in exchange for a gold digger's marketable affections.

Learning from its tough-guy crime movies—for example, *Little Caesar* and *Angels with Dirty Faces*—with such hardboiled stars as Edward G. Robinson and James Cagney, Warner Bros. applied the same street-smart spirit to its musicals. The characters in most of these movies seem to be talking out of the sides of their mouths in a kind of wise-acre slang, suggesting that these ambitious, nearly desperate youngsters have taken some hard knocks but are still fighting back.[7] You can discern the street-corner strut in Warren and Dubin's catchphrases—"Pettin' in the Park," "Young and Healthy," "She's a Latin from Manhattan." A frenetic song like "Forty-Second Street," inhabited by "little nifties from the fifties" and "sexy ladies from the eighties" is all New York even without the giveaway title (Harry Warren and Al Dubin, *42nd Street*, 1932). The people in this love song for the Depression-era city don't have a lot of time for romance; they're too busy keeping the hustle going.

Like the movies they appeared in, Warren and Dubin's songs are eager and edgy because the plots are usually backstagers about tough but vulnerable gold diggers trying to make it on Broadway. The songs, like the city, come with attitude. They have the hard rhythms and smart-alecky manner that let you know they're New York born and bred—even in Hollywood. No songwriters for the movies wrote about Broadway more often or more convincingly than Warren and Dubin. In snappy, confident songs like "Dames," "About a Quarter to Nine," and "Lulu's Back in Town," something—someone—is always on the move and on the make. The songs are active, alert, pushing ahead, up there on the screen larger than life in black and white, but feeling as if they had sprung full blown from Broadway or Times Square. Concrete is their natural habitat.

Warren and Dubin created the sound of the decade, just as Henderson, Brown, and DeSylva; Ager and Yellen; and Donaldson and Kahn had created the musical sound of the twenties. For Warren and Dubin, it combined brass and percussion, taxi horns and tap shoes.

They wrote in Hollywood, but their songs emulated the clatter and racket of New York's streets. Dubin's smart-guy romanticism fitted perfectly with Warren's percussive lyricism. Dubin wrote his share of romantic lyrics—"I Only Have Eyes for You," "September in the Rain"—but he was at his best in the brief musical sketches that caught the after-hours dames you never failed to find near Broadway. Damon Runyon, a writer known for his stylized, romantic view of Broadway, could have been his patron saint. Rather than write about Broadway itself, Dubin preferred to populate it with people drawn there in search of fame and fortune. Even in movies, the characters fill Times Square to sing and dance "a rhapsody of laughter and tears" ("Forty Second Street"). Dubin's lyric creates several quick vignettes of the dames who are so much a part of Broadway's passing scene. From the "sexy ladies . . . who are indiscreet" to the "daffydills who entertain," they are all-night "Broadway babies" who never get to bed before dawn (Harry Warren and Al Dubin, "Lullaby of Broadway," *Gold Diggers of 1935*, 1935). Dubin's wisecracking words merged with the staccato but melodic dance of Warren's music to create the hard-boiled romanticism of the 1930s Warner Bros. musicals.

Then Warren and Dubin turned some of their songs over to Busby Berkeley for his phantasmagoric production numbers. Whether or not the lyrics mention the city didn't matter; Berkeley turned songs into fantasies that evoke the city. "Lullaby of Broadway" (*Gold Diggers of 1935*, 1935) features row after row of furiously tapping dancers in semimilitary garb on a set of monumental abstract forms. In an earlier number from *Gold Diggers of 1933*, dozens of violin-playing chorus girls clad in tight silver bodices and tiered white skirts resemble living skyscrapers in motion, with their violins and bows framed in neon as they whirl to Warren and Dubin's melodic "The Shadow Waltz."

Harry Warren spent nearly his entire career in Hollywood, but his partner knew that Warren, born Salvatore Guaragna in Brooklyn, always longed to return to New York. Warren once admitted, "I never liked Hollywood but I got used to it."[8] Dubin wrote "Lullaby of Broadway" for Warren because he knew how much his partner missed the city. It was their only Oscar winner together.[9] Yet the lyric's view of an impersonal, harshly lit Broadway late at night offers nothing affectionate or nostalgic; it's thrilling but ominous.

These tough, available young women appear often in Warren and Dubin's songs because they're related to the backstage dames who usually perform the songs. They include the soon-to-be-unemployed gold

Figure 7.2. With their tight silver bodices and tiered white skirts, the chorus girls in *Gold Diggers of 1933* resemble living skyscrapers. Courtesy of Warner Bros. and Photofest.

diggers and chorines who affirm with sassy conviction what they know to be untrue, that they're "in the money," and, when it comes to the landlord, "they can look that guy right in the eye" (Harry Warren, Al Dubin, "We're in the Money," *Gold Diggers of 1933*, 1933) In "Keep Young and Beautiful," from the same year, one girl listens to a man urging her to "take care of all those charms . . . / if you want to be loved" (Harry Warren and Al Dubin, "Keep Young and Beautiful," *Roman Scandals*, 1933). In "Shuffle Off to Buffalo," she finally gets to play a bride—the one who runs home from her new husband's apartment to get her "scanties" before the two of them leave for Niagara Falls because "there's no honeymoon that's cheaper" (Harry Warren, Al Dubin, "Shuffle Off to Buffalo," *42nd Street*, 1932). She wears a lot of different faces, but in the showbiz stories that unfold in the Warner musicals, she's always the chorus girl so memorably defined by Ginger Rogers: "She makes twenty a week and sends thirty of it home to her mother."

Irving Berlin explained to an interviewer in 1942, "You see, a war song doesn't have to be about wars."[10] Being written during wartime was sufficient. Berlin may not have been right about every song, but he was on to something that went beyond World War II. Not every song written between the stock market crash of 1929 and the attack on Pearl Harbor is about the Great Depression, but most of them have a Depression sensibility—ways of perceiving within a song, as well as feeling, reacting, and speaking that express their time. It came from the choices songwriters made for setting, situation, imagery, and tone. It's what gave the city songs of the thirties their distinctive quality. It includes, among other things, a persistent melancholy ("I Don't Stand a Ghost of a Chance with You," 1933), a deepening sense of need ("Say It Isn't So," 1932), a recognition of loneliness ("But Not for Me," 1930), a breathy sensuality ("I'm in the Mood for Love," 1935), and a surprising, insistently upbeat stance in Pollyanna song after Pollyanna song ("New Sun in the Sky," 1930) (see below). This sensibility sounded like a description of what a lot of people assumed city living was like.

Even so, after nearly forty years of defining popular music, the urban sensibility showed signs of diminishing during the Great Depression. It didn't disappear by any means, but during the dark times that began in the thirties and intensified during the forties, songs turned more reflective and introspective, less about the outside world, more about the state of a lover's feelings. Many of them tempered melancholy with wit and unflinching honesty. The speakers[11] in "Glad to Be Unhappy" sort out emotions and memories in an attempt to accept the paradox they live with (Richard Rodgers and Lorenz Hart, "Glad to Be Unhappy," *On Your Toes*, 1936). The more inward looking songs became, the less the setting and the outside world mattered. First came a depression and then a war, and that was sufficient. The city and its vitality persisted, but another change had begun.

After a decade of songs devoted to the sexy, feather-light irreverence of the flapper, romantic ardor returned in the thirties. Women were less playful than the flappers had been—certainly less carefree—but smarter and shrewder because they had to be. They bore their experiences with deeper joy and equally deep sorrow. Whereas flappers came of age in a city, these women belonged to it. Love songs of the 1920s promised a secure future of sexual bliss followed by cozy domesticity, but American women found that sort of thing a lot less likely after 1929. A dystopia of lost jobs and broken nest eggs underlay the portrayal of women in many love songs of the new decade. More women than before worked outside the home during the thirties. The Depression, which threw a quarter of the nation's men out of work, turned many women back on their own resources to support their families. Women still hoped for true love despite the grim economic outlook, or perhaps because of it. The characteristic love songs stressed women's support for men hit hard by the Depression but also offered love as a panacea.

Depression songs confronted hard times by insisting that love still mattered despite ennui among the rich—"I get no kick from champagne, / Mere alcohol doesn't thrill me at all" (Cole Porter, "I Get a Kick Out of You," *Anything Goes*, 1934)—and poverty troubling nearly everybody else. Nothing is guaranteed, although Lee Wiley's throaty rendering of one of the decade's most characteristic songs brings you as close as you're likely to get. The promise is so confident that it's easy to overlook the unsettling hesitation of "Long as": "Poor, no one is poor / Long as love is sure" (Harry Warren and Al Dubin, "Boulevard of Broken Dreams," 1933).

Despite the gloom of so many Depression ballads, from "When Your Lover Has Gone" at one end of the decade to the ironic "I Get Along without You Very Well" at the other, the 1930s also produced love songs with happy endings. Although love works out in some of them, they still fall short of the boundless optimism so common in the 1920s. They offer a sense of relief, a momentary stay against misery. Hoping against hope pays off because there's something in their melodies' wry lyricism that lifts them above—but not too far above—the complexities of daily life and the insistent claims of romance, at least temporarily. Their lyrics trade in surprise and spontaneity, as the people in the songs go looking for something, hope to find it, and then celebrate when they do. Many of them describe anticipation without fulfillment, but others delight in the moment when love arrives. The characters in these songs find a way out of the rut the Depression has landed them in. Somebody in one of the decade's most celebratory love songs feels stuck. Time stands still until someone unexpected knocks on the door. As soon as the right person walks in, everything changes. It may be a fairy tale but it offers hope to counter a world without purpose. Love at first sight means that life seems to start anew

(George Gershwin and Ira Gershwin, "Love Walked In," *The Goldwyn Follies*, 1937).

Although the lyrics use images of weather and climate—imagery that Pollyanna songs and torch songs, strangely, have in common—these rhythm ballads sport a city sensibility and often rely on urban images. No matter how happy they are, they always leave room for the tentative and the temporary. Even when they're unhappy, emotion brightens the tempo as they search for love and hope to find it around the very next corner. In "Looking around Corners for You," a song of anticipation, the lyric isn't about finding love, but about getting back with the loved one who left (Harry Revel and Mack Gordon, "Looking around Corners for You," *Head Over Heels*, 1937).

These songs also sound a note of defiance, especially when they portray women. The urban blues of the 1920s had contributed to the new ways women spoke and behaved in songs. The singers and the characters they portrayed weren't girlish flappers; they were tough, outspoken women. In the 1920s, when Ma Rainey, Bessie Smith, and Mamie Smith first performed and recorded the blues, they transformed it into a national music. They also broadened its subject matter and deepened its outlook. Betrayal and loss have always been part of the blues, mainly because of a cheating lover, but these women did more than moan and cry. In urban blues-like songs that followed the 32-bar pattern of popular songs rather than the repetitive three-line stanzas of traditional blues, they pursued other men on their own. Defiant and sexually knowing, they wanted to sing about how much they enjoyed themselves when a good man provided "a little hot dog on my roll" (Clarence Williams, J. Tim Brymn, and Dally Small, "I Need a Little Sugar in My Bowl," 1931). Ida Cox sang about the wild women who never get the blues (Ida Cox, "Wild Women Don't Have the Blues," 1924). Bessie Smith warned her "Aggravatin' Papa" that he'd "better not two-time me" (J. Russel Robinson and Roy Turk, "Aggravatin' Papa," 1923). Even Al Jolson, in no way a blues singer, told the story of Jenny Lee, who warns her man that "if he ever does two-time one time, / Then he's never gonna two-time no more" (Walter Donaldson, "My Papa Doesn't Two-Time No Time," 1924).

The characters in songs who may have learned from the blues songs of the twenties are usually more sophisticated but no less independent, outspoken, or sexually knowing. At one end of the social scale, Maude and Mabel remember Eadie, "a sucker for a bottle and a glass" right out of a grade B film noir. She was a tough broad with "a shady past," but her friends agree that she "had class, with a capital K" (Nacio Herb Brown, Richard A. Whiting, and B. G. DeSylva, "Eadie Was a Lady," *Take a Chance*, 1932).

At the other end, in Lorenz Hart's satiric view of the habits of the urbane upper class, a lady insists on getting to the theater on time, won't wear furs to Harlem, and refuses to gossip. She's probably on the outs with most of the people she knows because she's not afraid to show how much she detests them; yet her elegance comes as naturally as her vivacity. She loves to live that way—and to tell you she lives that way. She's a scintillatingly independent show-off, but you also wonder if being a tramp doesn't imply a trace of melancholy beneath her iconoclasm. No apologies and no regrets, but she understands the price she pays: she is all alone when she turns out the light (Richard Rodgers and Lorenz Hart, "The Lady Is a Tramp," *Babes in Arms*, 1937). Dorothy Parker could have had her in mind when she wrote about the time of day when the light fades: "There is no such hour on the present clock as 6:30, New York time. Yet, as only New Yorkers know, if you can get through the twilight, you'll live through the night."[12] Somewhere else, partway between Eadie and the Lady, Rodgers and Hart created a sexually eager middle-aged woman who wittily defines her day in terms of her busy sex life. She is both sardonic and self-aware, and she has no illusions about the younger man who is something of a lout but is great in bed (Richard Rodgers and Lorenz Hart, "Bewitched, Bothered and Bewildered," *Pal Joey*, 1940).

These songs are world weary and wise, not the most common stance for a romantic love song. Perhaps it's because we know they come from the Great Depression, but they feel more honest than the ardent ballads of the crooners that surround them. Love is as precious as ever, but skepticism shapes the responses, and the songs often speak in a clear, unadorned way, made more appealing by touches of wordplay that begin in their titles, as in Richard Whiting and George Marion, Jr.'s "My Future Just Past" (1930) and John Green and Edward Heyman's "Hello, My Lover, Goodbye" (1931). But the more the mockers dismiss love in a song like "This Can't Be Love," a humorous self-examination of love sickness, the more love exposes the mockery as false, even self-deceptive. If it's love, you're supposed to feel miserable, but this speaker feels just fine. (Richard Rodgers and Lorenz Hart, "This Can't Be Love," *The Boys from Syracuse*, 1938).

Although some thirties songs end happily, anxiety and insecurity persist in such songs as "I've Got a Feeling You're Fooling" (Nacio

Herb Brown and Arthur Freed, *Broadway Melody of 1936*, 1935); "My Fine-Feathered Friend" (Jimmy McHugh and Cliff Friend, *You're a Sweetheart*, 1937); and "I'm All Dressed Up with a Broken Heart" (Fred Fisher, Stella Unger, and Harold Stern, 1931). Even when things are going well and you keep your fingers crossed, you never know how long it will be until trouble pays you a visit (Jimmy McHugh and Ted Koehler, "I've Got My Fingers Crossed," *King of Burlesque*, 1934).

Some rhythm ballads are so tentative they can go no farther than giving pessimism an optimistic spin. A love affair ends as the two lovers prepare to start their lives over again, but despite their intentions, "We just couldn't say goodbye" (Harry Woods, "We Just Couldn't Say Goodbye," 1932). In a final example, a lover expresses emotion not through the use of typical imagery, but by comparing how he feels with the way the world looks during the Depression. It starts conventionally enough with rain and thunder but soon moves on to businesses going bankrupt. With great spirit, he defies the Depression in the name of love. He then starts again with shrewd comic hyperbole, as if he knows this is the sort of cliché a love song counts on: the sky may fall and banks may fail, but what matters is your kiss. (George Gershwin and Ira Gershwin, "Who Cares?" *Of Thee I Sing*, 1931). It's hard to imagine a more enthusiastic merging of sentiment and wit.

Songs are almost always about love but often something more as well. Just as earlier love songs combined with telephone songs and automobile songs, a lot of thirties love songs talked about work, money, and dreams. The first two subjects seemed to be more interesting when they were harder to come by. Dreams, on the other hand, have always played an important role in love songs, but what do they have to do with anything urban?

When daily life threatened to get tougher than people could bear, songwriters turned not only to Pollyanna songs that urged people to "give the blues a chase" (George W. Meyer, Arch Gottler, and Sidney Mitchell, "Little Sunshine," 1930) but also to ballads that encouraged dreaming. The Pollyanna songs were downright simple-minded. They insisted on optimism because gloom and misery will dissipate as surely as storms, both meteorological and emotional. People scraped together the few cents to buy 78-rpm recordings to play on wind-up phonographs and listened for free to the same songs on that other modern contraption, the radio. No image was more important than the blue skies that replaced the clouds, especially in a setting that's implicitly urban, where a rainbow appears around the very next corner (Irving Berlin, "Let's Have Another Cup of Coffee," *Face the Music*, 1932).

From the day she arrived as the title character of a 1913 novel by Eleanor Porter, Pollyanna Whittier was an irrepressible optimist who found only the good in everything. Within a decade, she had given her name to a body of popular songs with the same sunny outlook. Pollyanna songs require that you ask nothing of them. Ask a sensible question and they melt away. Raise an objection and they pop. Everybody knows better, but if you suspend your disbelief, they float and glimmer, dispensing pleasurable nonsense for a couple of minutes. In the 1930s, though, when Americans hung on to them for dear life, they offered a curious and sometimes surreal mix of realism and fantasy: "You'll find your fortune falling all over town, / Make sure that your umbrella is upside down" (Arthur Johnston and Joe Burke, "Pennies from Heaven," *Pennies from Heaven*, 1936).

Some Pollyanna songs rely on fulfillment, others on anticipation. Those from the 1920s are more likely to find the good news on their doorsteps; those from the Depression are still expecting it to arrive. In 1928, people sang, "My Blackbirds are Bluebirds Now," but by 1932, they preferred "The Clouds Will Soon Roll By." The Depression's Pollyanna songs lacked the effortless confidence of the 1920s versions. During the earlier decade, they felt spontaneous and easy, part of the way things were: "And love can come to everyone, / The best things in life are free" (Ray Henderson, Lew Brown, and B. G. DeSylva, "The Best Things in Life Are Free," *Good News*, 1927). An equally rosy song from the 1930s feels driven, even though Henderson, Brown, and DeSylva wrote it as well. The later song follows a reminder with an admonition, potentially cold-eyed but given a sense of delight that clearly makes it a Pollyanna song: "You can't take your dough when you go, go, go. / So keep repeating it's the berries" ("Life Is Just a Bowl of Cherries," *George White's Scandals of 1931*, 1931).

Pollyanna songs from the 1930s were insistent and imperative, as if saying something strongly enough would help to make it so. Titles like "There's a New Day Coming," "When My Ship Comes In," and "(We've Got to) Put That Sun Back in the Sky," were common, but some songs hedged their bets, including "I'd Rather Be a Beggar with

You," "Stringin' Along on a Shoe String," "It's a Good Life (If You Don't Weaken)," and "Cheer Up! Smile! Nertz!" The most characteristic Pollyanna songs of the time require action and maybe even struggle before the storm clouds finally pass. You have to be able to take a punch to survive (Sam Coslow, "Sweepin' the Clouds Away," 1930). That attitude holds true in the most unusual Pollyanna song and least likely hit of the decade, but it also adds mockery to the mix:

> Who's afraid of the big bad wolf,
> Ha, ha, ha, ha, ha.
> (Frank Churchill and Anne Ronell, "Who's Afraid of the Big Bad Wolf," *Three Little Pigs*, 1933)

That said, none of these songs had more of an awareness of its time than "Smile, Darn Ya', Smile." It encourages optimism and believes in happy endings, but it also understands the struggle to get there. It precedes every bit of good news with a caution. It insists that because things are never as bleak as they seem, you need a combination of defiance and endurance. You have to be able to show that you can grin and bear it (Charles O'Flynn, Jack Meskill, and Fred Rich, "Smile, Darn Ya', Smile," 1931).

Songwriters couldn't do much to solve the nation's economic woes, but they could bring some grit to romantic love, especially in the form of irreverence with such provocative titles as "Nasty Man" (Ray Henderson, Jack Yellen, and Irving Caesar, *George White's Scandals*, 1934); "Danger, Love at Work" (Harry Revel and Mack Gordon, *You Can't Have Everything*, 1937); and "Are You in the Mood for Mischief?" (Harry Revel and Mack Gordon, *Tailspin*, 1939). These songs trade in irritations and insults about sex, infidelity, and true love. They hope you'll eventually land the one you want despite the contrariness that often comes along for the ride. In tone, at least, they're the bright side of torch ballads. The people who sing in most of them feel younger and more resilient than the women in torch songs, even though their situations are similar—a feeling of confusion or betrayal, followed by an affirmation of love's necessity. But rather than bemoaning their fate, these women fight back. The melodies have bounce and the lyrics are direct, but with an accusatory and sometimes cynical undertone. In songs that sound like dramatic monologues, they look their opposite numbers squarely in the eye. They don't always win out, but they always let you know where they stand. They've been burned and they know what they've learned.

When you do something stupid, love is the teacher who shows up (Harry Revel and Mack Gordon, "Danger, Love at Work," *You Can't Have Everything*, 1937).

The man may be a louse, but the woman doesn't plan to sit by quietly and take it. Unfortunately, the worse the man is, the more appealing he is. As in torch songs, he cheats, but she can't break it off. She endures his infidelity because she understands, without ever quite saying it, that she'd never find anyone who can be "as bad or better than / You, you nasty man!" (Ray Henderson, Jack Yellen, and Irving Caesar, "Nasty Man," *George White's Scandals*, 1931).

Very few of these irreverent songs refer to living in a city, but the individuals who speak in them take a consistently urban stance. They combine outspoken skepticism and tough-mindedness with a readiness to give love another try. No lyricist caught that suspension of personal history—suspended but not forgotten—better than Lorenz Hart. This character remembers everything that ever happened in a love affair, including, most notably, the self-delusion and the arguments, but the song's title demonstrates that somebody's ready to give love a second chance or maybe even a third: "I Wish I Were in Love Again" (Richard Rodgers and Lorenz Hart, *Babes in Arms*, 1937).

The characters in these songs weave a series of responses to the people they fall for, and from whom they learn hard lessons about love and sex. Even when the song isn't explicitly about sex, it's bound to have the kind of charge that comes from the feistiness of the lovers and a view of sex that's as youthful as a flapper's but much more knowing. That outlook is especially strong when the characters appear to be women. You hear their sharp tongues in most of these songs, including "Danger, Love at Work" and "Nasty Man." These songs are grounded in the here and now. Only one of them—"You're a Sweet Little Headache"—mentions dreaming. Maybe that's why it's also less cynical than the others and appears to be sung by a male. Boy tells girl how he feels about her in the song's oxymoronic title and then spends the rest of the lyric explaining. A more romantic song might affirm that he dreams about her every night and longs for his dream to come true, but here he complains that she troubles his dreams. Typically, he holds onto the hope that what began as a headache will soon turn into a similarly oxymoronic heartache (Ralph Rainger and Leo Robin, "You're a Sweet Little Headache," *Paris Honeymoon*, 1939).

Harold Arlen, Ira Gershwin, and E. Y. Harburg collaborated in that same spirit when they wrote, "You're a Builder-Upper," their musical tribute to masochism. Originally performed as a duet in the 1934 revue *Life Begins at 8:40*, it's an infectious comic tribute to lovers' discontent. For every good thing the lover says or does, he balances it with something lousy. The woman knows what he's doing but she's hooked. And then the shoe skips to the other foot as he complains about her. They take turns berating one another, but they never stop loving one another. Arlen's melodic drive never falters and Gershwin and Harburg's lyric matches it in wit and self-awareness (Harold Arlen, Ira Gershwin, and E. Y. Harburg, "You're a Builder-Upper, *Life Begins at 8:40*, 1934).

~ ~ ~

If nothing else, Depression songwriters knew how to write about dreaming. A Pollyanna song is one kind of dream, a love ballad another. In fact, thirties songs about dreams had an unusually wide range. Some offered the respite that comes from hanging on to a dream even though a song's tone might vary from happy-go-lucky to sympathetic, from bubbly satisfaction in the present to hope for the future, from

> I'm no millionaire but I'm not the type to care,
> 'Cause I've got a pocketful of dreams.
> (Jimmy Monaco and Johnny Burke, "I've Got a Pocketful of Dreams," 1938)

to

> I'm waltzing in a dream with you, love,
> Won't you make the dream come true, love?
> (Victor Young, Ned Washington, and Bing Crosby, "Waltzing in a Dream with You," 1932)

Aside from these songs, which have a touch of the Pollyanna to them, other thirties ballads about dreaming are straightforward in their emotional intent but also surreal in the way they link the loved one to everyday reality. That's how they hold on to hope. The beloved takes form in dreams that, one way or another, become inseparable from reality. Depression songwriters became especially adept at turning this surreal trick as the beloved becomes the embodiment of a dream who walks (Harry Warren and Mack Gordon, "Did You Ever See a Dream Walking?" *Sitting Pretty*, 1932) and then, stepping from the dream, becomes real (Nacio Herb Brown and Gus Kahn, "You Stepped Out of a Dream, *Ziegfeld Girl*, 1940). In still other songs, escapism crumbles as the dream of love becomes a confrontation with reality. When a song gives up on hope, it turns instead to an image of urban despair. In the aftermath of broken dreams, the melody takes on weight and weariness. This song is a cry of sorrow:

> I walk along the street of sorrow,
> The boulevard of broken dreams.
> (Harry Warren and Al Dubin, "Boulevard of Broken Dreams," *Paris*, 1933)

Images of dreams and dreaming are everywhere in Depression songs. They flourish in slow romantic ballads where dreams come true—less likely during the thirties than earlier. They may sing about anticipation, but unlike Pollyanna songs where the good news is never very far away, even dreams don't necessarily keep their promises. On one hand, a catalogue song like "When My Ship Comes In" is so optimistic it borders on the Pollyanna-ish, but it's also playful and direct. The absence of love turns it into a child's song, and Eddie Cantor actually sings it to a gang of kids. He promises to buy them a circus because they've never seen a show before (Walter Donaldson and Gus Kahn, *Kid Millions*, 1934). Compare that with the decade's impassioned dream ballads where the emotional stance sounds more ambiguous, less certain. The most important word in a lot of these songs is "if." The title of this song is reassuring—"I'll Never Have to Dream Again"—but then the lyric steps back from certainty (Isham Jones, Charles Newman, 1932). Elsewhere, the key lies in the title line's repeated question. The song offers no answers to someone who aches with sadness and disillusion (Sammy Fain, Irving Kahal, "I Can Dream, Can't I?" *Right This Way*, 1938).

Dozens, perhaps hundreds, of other Depression songs describe dreaming without mentioning the word. These are not Pollyanna songs, but rather love songs that imagine a happy, even prosperous, future or that try, in another surreal twist, to rearrange the world. The more difficult the lovers' daily lives, the more extreme the escape or transformation needs to be. In a ballad like "June in January," love causes universal disruption for the lover who calls the result a miracle. Amid winter's cold and wind, he sees warm blue skies because someone loves him. Familiar images of seasons and weather shape the song as they do many ballads. Perhaps that means they're set in the country, but as sometimes happens in 1930s songs, common imagery feels detached, afloat in the world of the song and its single-minded devotion to romance, whether won or thwarted. Whatever attachment the imagery has is not to a place but to lovers and the depth of their feeling (Ralph Rainger and Leo Robin, "June in January," *Here Is My Heart*, 1934).

Similarly, the ardent lyric of "Stairway to the Stars" offers nothing more than the conviction of the lovers and their attachment to one another. The outside world doesn't exist except as an unstated motivation for their need to escape to a place where love fills the night with imagined music. No more than that but, within the song, it's everything (Matty Malneck, Frank Signorelli, and Mitchel Parrish, "Stairway to the Stars," 1939). The lovers dream as a sailboat carries them not to a place but to a state of the heart. The image of sailing and then settling changes something specific—a hill—into nothing more than abstract ardor.

The most extreme escape occurs in the most beloved of the Depression's songs about dreaming, Harold Arlen and E. Y. Harburg's "Over the Rainbow," written as an afterthought to give Judy Garland a song in *The Wizard of Oz*. Others have told the familiar story of the song's composition and survival.[13] Certainly no one doubts its persistent appeal. It is probably the most universally known American song, suited to both twelve-year-old Dorothy and eighteen-year-old Judy, who played a lonely child but had the voice of a grown woman. Poor orphaned Dorothy lives on a Kansas farm far from town. Her only playmates are three adult farm hands, Hunk, Zeke, and Hickory, but everyone is busy with farm work and she is underfoot. Banished to the yard and feeling alone, she sings to her dog, Toto, but Harburg's lyric transforms her plaint into a song of hope. It suits its time as that oddity of oddities, a melancholy Pollyanna song. During the Depression, audiences could use all the rainbows songwriters could give them. At the same time, nearly every song that survives beyond its own time eventually loses its connection to that time. More than three generations later, Americans still grow up singing "Over the Rainbow." It has become part of our common musical memory. It's hard to think of it now as a quintessential Depression anthem, but that's exactly what it was when it was new (Harold Arlen and E. Y. Harburg, "Over the Rainbow," *The Wizard of Oz*, 1939).

That said, how does the song fit the urban perspective I'm writing about? Arlen's sweeping melody mixes the lyrical with the bravura, and

Harburg's lyric merges sadness that stops just short of self-pity with a make-believe world of wishing on stars, troubles that melt like candy, and bluebirds that fly beyond rainbows. With supple ease, he applies the well-worn imagery of Pollyanna songs to hone a familiar dream, but it feels fantastical rather than rural, the conventional matter of a young imagination, no matter where the child lives. Dorothy is a farm girl, but the allusions are not to a barnyard. There are no chickens, cows, or cornfields. Like the star and the bluebirds, the one possibly urban reference to troubles that melt above the rooftops belongs not in the country or in town, but in a realm of the imagination.

So it's less that songs ceased to be urban in the thirties and more that the sense of place became less solid, less essential. Over the course of the decade, songs relied less on the kind of image that grounds a character or narrative in time and place and more on imagery that floats on the air of romantic emotionalism. Imagery is often a song's only defense against sliding off into abstraction. Irving Berlin's "Say It Isn't So" from 1932 is illustrative because it lands between the alternatives of imagery and abstraction. The brief lyric carries the unhappy lover (and the listener) from gossip to heartbreak. The song relies on none of the common images that appear and reappear in songs. Instead, it grounds the lover's melancholy in what people whisper among themselves. The speaker refuses to believe that her lover has found someone new. In response, the title line tolls like a pleading chorus, hoping against hope. The lover repeats it seven times, counting two variations, in a seventy-six-word lyric. The blasé gossips and the fickle beloved play against the lover's impassioned refusal to give up.

To make the point through contrast, consider a song that does rely on city streets. Its imagery is concrete and defining. Without its imagery, "Over the Rainbow" is little more than air. Without its imagery, Irving Berlin's "Easter Parade" still has two characters in love who have something important to do. Imagery enlivens the story of the excited young couple, who join the Easter Parade for the first time. In a lyric typical of love ballads from any period, a man praises the beauty and behavior of his beloved. Then, more distinctively, he imagines the other paraders' envy as she poses for a photographer so her picture can appear in the rotogravure section of the next day's newspaper. More than anything, her bonnet—the image at the heart of Berlin's lyric—reveals her lover's pride in her but also suggests that they are not the swells in their finery who usually stroll along Fifth Avenue on

Easter morning. The tone is affectionate, even sweet, but also ironic (Irving Berlin, "Easter Parade," *As Thousands Cheer*, 1933). On a different Sunday, the two of them might find themselves in the working-class gang that decides to go "Slumming on Park Avenue," in yet another Berlin lyric. Rather than throwing bricks at passing swells, they prefer to thumb their noses (Irving Berlin, "Slumming on Park Avenue," *On the Avenue*, 1937).

Although Judy Garland sang the greatest of the Depression dream songs, nobody sang more of them than Bing Crosby—from Ray Henderson, Lew Brown, and B. G. DeSylva's "I'm a Dreamer, Aren't We All" in 1929 to Sammy Fain and Irving Kahal's "I Can Dream, Can't I?" in 1938. Although most of them are the ardent, often melancholy ballads characteristic of the time, they don't include the upbeat love songs that Crosby sang so jauntily, with the appealingly jazzy looseness he turned away from in the forties. Unlike the melancholy ballads in which dreams die and lovers despair, these songs approach dreaming with optimism. They can even be playful. One in particular harks back to the "cuddling songs" of the century's first two decades, as the lovers dance the night away. (Carmen Lombardo and Joe Young, "Snuggled on Your Shoulder," 1932).

Although this typical ballad is distinctive enough to be a hit, it lacks a sense of place. The outside world disappears in the presence of dreaming and snuggling, but also because of the dominance of language about temptation, longing, betrayal, desperation, pleading, and—only occasionally—happiness ranging from pleasure to ecstasy. Most of the time, crooners love to suffer, so Crosby would sigh something like, "I'm through with love, / I'll never fall again" (Matty Malnick, Jay Livingston, and Gus Kahn, "I'm Through with Love," 1931). The romantic crooning of Crosby and his contemporaries found its footing in the deepening emotionalism in songs and how singers performed them. Microphones and radio broadcasts made possible a new intimacy of style, especially an elevated but unhappy tone that never quite lost touch with the conversational lyric that had begun decades earlier. References to sunsets and flowers are images rather than place markers. Rather than setting the relationship between the lovers in a recognizable location, they articulate and enhance the singer's feelings. In one of Bing Crosby's biggest hits, each of them becomes a question for which the answer is the song's title, "Love in Bloom" (Ralph Rainger and Leo Robin, "Love In Bloom," *She Loves Me Not*, 1934).

Only during the Depression and World War II did sensual escape through dreaming become the stock-in-trade that replaced allusions to the urban outlook and experience. During these dark and dangerous times, Crosby in particular developed an affinity for songs that promoted the saving power of love. These songs lifted his most intent listeners—mainly women—out of their workaday worlds into a realm of romantic imagining. Yet crooning didn't start out that way. The early crooners—Gene Austin, Nick Lukas, and "Whispering" Jack Smith among them—usually had high tenors rather than deep baritones. They skimmed along the surface of such urban songs as "When My Sugar Walks Down the Street" (Jimmy McHugh, Gene Austin, and Irving Mills, 1925) and "Me and My Shadow" (Dave Dreyer, Billy Rose, and Al Jolson, 1927). At first, the songs told at least part of a story. In "When My Sugar," a young man watches the reactions as his girl walks down the street. Even the birds twitter and tweet. The young man in "Me and My Shadow" walks along the avenue without finding anyone who will listen to his troubles. He wanders the streets until he finally returns home at bedtime.

The rise of crooning in the late twenties and early thirties led to songs that were more sophisticated and urbane than the giddy gobbledygook of "Barney Google, with the Goo-Goo-Googly Eyes" (Con Conrad and Billy Rose, "Barney Google," 1923) and "Goodness gracious, I'm no chump / I just bit off a camel's hump" (Sam Lewis, Harry Link, Fred Rich, "I'm Just Wild About Animal Crackers," 1926). It was no time to kick up your heels or behave childishly. Nothing would have looked more callow or callous than being frivolous during the deadly serious new decade. This new romanticism was also seductive. Such singers as Crosby and Russ Columbo learned to use the microphone to make their singing captivating but also deeply felt. Their restrained styles (compared to, for example, Al Jolson's bravura belting), combined with their insinuatingly warm masculine voices and overheated, sometimes emotionally masochistic lyrics, gave their ballads a new immediacy: "I'm just a slave, only a slave to you" (Nacio Herb Brown and Arthur Freed, "Temptation," *Going Hollywood*, 1933).

~~~

The coming of distinctively American musical comedies just before World War I; the emergence in the twenties of a generation of lyricists
~~~

who prided themselves on their ability to merge sentiment and wit to create more complicated characters within individual songs; and crooning beginning in the late twenties: only with these precedents did popular music in the 1930s break out of Tin Pan Alley's long-standing interest in telling stories about love. New songs relied less on narrative and were less engaged by the distractions of the everyday world, despite many songs' insistent allusions to the Depression. As the lovers in songs concentrated more intently on their own emotions, the outer world of action and behavior became less compelling for them and their listeners. It was a matter of emphasis and tone. The songs felt overheated but still personal. The radio brought a new level of intimacy and seductiveness to singing, and of emotional engagement to listening. As Bing Crosby sang in 1933 to someone far away: "For the torch I bear Is burning there / Right in my heart" (Harry Warren, Al Dubin, "I've Got to Sing a Torch Song," *Gold Diggers of 1933*, 1933).

At the same time, some interest persisted in how love makes people feel, as did an impulse to make a moment of intense feeling fit an implied narrative. But only in a 1930s song could a character wander the city streets alone sometime after midnight, "covered by the starless sky above," wondering where love had gone (John L. Green and Edward Heyman, "I Cover the Waterfront," 1933), or sit alone in her hotel room, puzzled by a lover's departure as she orders a single glass of orange juice (Richard Rodgers and Lorenz Hart, "It Never Entered My Mind," *Higher and Higher*, 1940). Despite the isolation and unhappiness in these songs, they manage to keep their connection to a real world. Rather than merely naming emotions, the lyric evokes them from the details of behavior and experience expressed in the rhythms of American speech and then lifted through imagery and wit to song: the discarded lover sits alone in her hotel room playing solitaire.

Popular music's merging of sentiment and wit continued as an essential part of the urban sensibility. In "It Never Entered My Mind," it lies in Hart's successful weaving of mundane allusions presented with understated irony and played off against the unadorned directness of the title line. In each chorus, though, emotion extended by wit precedes the catchphrase that is the title. In one example, the play is on drinking orange juice alone, in another, the clever word shift from uneasy to easy.

During this same period, ballads also became more erotic than before. No songwriter of the time more consistently combined the urbane and erotic than Cole Porter, who wrote many standards through the 1930s after writing his first successful musicals in the late twenties. "Night and Day" (*Gay Divorce*, 1932) and "Begin the Beguine (*Jubilee*, 1935) throb seductively, but the lyrics to such ballads as "All Through the Night" and "I've Got You Under My Skin" are more directly erotic. A lover delights in his beloved because "All through the night you're so close to me" and "You and your love brings me ecstasy" (*Anything Goes*, 1934). Virginia Bruce's original performance of the insinuating "I've Got You Under My Skin" in the movie *Born to Dance* has an understated Latin rhythm as well as a trace of wit, both typical of Porter's songs. The lover affirms that the beloved is "under my skin. . . . So deep in my heart, you're really a part of me" (*Born to Dance*, 1936). This was the kind of ardent ballad well suited to crooning.

Because most of the important crooners were male, crooning gave greater importance to young women as popular music's primary subject and audience. "I Surrender, Dear" was a routine ballad about a lover's suffering until Crosby transformed it into a combination of seductive tenderness, masochism, and sexual heat (Harry Barris, Gordon Clifford, and Bing Crosby, "I Surrender, Dear," 1931). This song has no substance beyond its emotions; they are its true subject. It is a lover's self-pitying moan that floats abstractly in the ether of Crosby's crooning. His arresting baritone is the only thing about the song that is real.

~ ~ ~

Love songs about having money and a job weren't unique to the thirties, but they were more typical and more common than at any other time. In these lyrics, love may not depend on landing a job and having some money, but marriage does. Some of the tunes sound as upbeat as a Pollyanna song, but then you stop to listen to the lyric. In the movie *Gold Diggers of 1937*, Dick Powell's character sings Warren and Dubin's "With Plenty of Money and You" (1937) when he's broke. He plays a young songwriter who writes the music and lyrics for a Broadway show that's in danger of folding unless more financing arrives, but he's also telling Joan Blondell he loves her. Although he knows that money is "the root of all evil, of strife and upheaval," he also knows—and everybody watching the movie would have agreed—that he could find happiness "with plenty of money and you."

In other words, during the 1930s, references to jobs and money were inseparable from love. They kept hope alive, made happy endings possible, and were at the very least conscious of social class. Two major songs from the late twenties, "I Can't Give You Anything But Love, Baby" (Jimmy McHugh and Dorothy Fields, *Blackbirds of 1928,* 1928) and "She's Funny That Way," (Neil Moret and Richard A. Whiting, 1928) had also implied a sense of poverty that makes them harbingers of the Great Depression. The first is a confession that feels upbeat even though the speaker's so broke that he can offer only his love; the second is an affirmation of the importance of being loved, even though the speaker admits that he's worthless. Yet the songs' catchy talk and hopeful endings also suggest that anybody with the right outlook who has someone to love will end up okay.

Bing Crosby's dramatic rendering of Jay Gorney and E. Y Harburg's "Brother, Can You Spare a Dime?" stands out as one of the least likely and most successful songs (and recordings) of the Depression years. Everything about the song is unusual. It has nothing to do with love, perhaps because it was part of a politically oriented Broadway revue, *Americana* (1932). The show flopped, but the song survived. Although Gorney based his melody on a Yiddish lullaby and originally thought it would lend itself to torchy words, Harburg asked the composer if he would object to a different approach to the lyric. A left-leaning idealist, Harburg wanted to address the plight of a down-on-his-luck working stiff who had fought in World War I, toiled to build the nation, and now found himself on the streets. Crosby's experience as a crooner prepared him to sing about the emotions of loss, confusion, even bitterness, but he also brought a stentorian quality to his performance. The style is conversational, but Crosby's strong baritone hardens his normal warmth to create a lost soul, begging for a dime.

Harburg's lyric in "Brother" is a dramatic monologue that portrays a solitary individual named Al. As he begs on a city street corner, Al encounters someone he used to know but who fails to recognize him—or chooses not to. Al's plight is as specific and detailed as his memories of wartime service and the hard labor of plowing a field and building both a railroad and a high tower. Now forgotten, broke, and reduced to begging, he speaks out of bitterness and confusion: "Say, don't you remember? / I'm your pal." Its powerful portrayal of a man on the edge, its social commentary, and its lack of interest in love make "Brother, Can You Spare a Dime?" unique in popular song.

Like "Brother, Can You Spare a Dime?" Warren and Dubin's "Remember My Forgotten Man" (*Gold Diggers of 1933*, 1933) paints a compelling picture of Depression woes. Each song is a portrait of an individual, yet each is less a love song than an anthem whose emotional circumstances encapsulate its time. Dubin's lyric portrays a woman pleading on behalf of the man she loves, now forsaken by the land he served despite the work he did. She appears fearful, trying her best to protect her man. Although she speaks, it's really his story.

Another song much like "Brother, Can You Spare a Dime?" is just as dark, although this time the tone is bitingly ironic and the character is a woman. The speaker in Rodgers and Hart's "Ten Cents a Dance" is a New York taxi dancer. Desperately weary rather than bitter, she's too exhausted to protest against the hardened men who push her around the floor. The most she can muster is an occasional spasm of sarcasm to get her through the night (*Simple Simon*, 1930).

She has kindred spirits in the singers of at least three other songs in which brutally cynical women speak about their lives. In the first, probably a direct follow-up to "Ten Cents," a woman leaves the sticks to find fame on Broadway. Now, hired to sell cigars and cigarettes in a speakeasy, she spends most of her time "smoking coke and snow" and making her money from "the guys who've never learned what 'no' means" (Harry Revel and Mack Gordon, "Cigarettes, Cigars," *Ziegfeld Follies of 1931*, 1931). Two other songs from about the same time also portray prostitutes. "Try to be sweet," one of them says, but the men "make it plain / I'm good for nothing but love" (Bernard Maltin and Pat Ballard, "I'm Good for Nothing but Love," *Ziegfeld Follies of 1931*, 1931). A year earlier, a Cole Porter ballad portrayed a prostitute who offered "appetizing young love for sale . . . / Ev'ry love but true love" (Cole Porter, "Love for Sale," *The New Yorkers*, 1930).

During the 1920s, everybody partied; during the 1940s, they left to serve or kept a solitary vigil at home. But during the 1930s, they pounded the pavements looking for work. Finding a job, working, and making some money are everywhere in Depression love songs. They're part of a story or they're metaphors. The characters in these songs need more than they have. Not surprisingly, they dream—about something as small as landing a job and as large as finding a million bucks. One man dreams of yachts, limousines, and meetings with Rockefeller before he meets "a girl divine." As they head for Niagara Falls, the dream ends abruptly when the alarm rings, and "I gotta get up and go to work again." But at least he has a job (Milton Pascal and Edgar Fairchild, "Gotta Go to Work Again," 1936).

Those who don't have a job dream about finding one and what that will mean. These also are "if" songs, but even when they're amusing, they have an undertone of desperation. "If" can mean everything from finding a small apartment to hobnobbing with old friends. Mainly, though, it means something more typical of a song: "We'll be rehearsing lullabyes, / If I ever get a job again" (Abel Baer and Sam M. Lewis, "If I Ever Get a Job Again," 1933). A more romantic song asks what someone would do with a million dollars. Its insistence on describing each dream in terms of its value makes it a Depression song. The money makes everything possible, as does the dream of having the money (Matty Malneck and Johnny Mercer, "If I Had a Million Dollars," 1934).

Popular music has always traced the progress of a love affair one song at a time, from first meeting to proposal to wedding day. If love is a very long line, then each song is a single tick along that line. In Depression songs, though, the treatment had a different feel, dictated by the times. This number-one hit starts with the couple's first meeting. A man, probably out of work, gets caught in a rainstorm. He ducks inside a store, where he finds the woman of his dreams. The song skips over their courtship to emphasize what happened eventually: the singer invites the listener into his cottage to meet his wife, that same "Million Dollar Baby" he first identified in the song's title (Harry Warren, Billy Rose, and Mort Dixon, "I Found a Million Dollar Baby [In a Five and Ten Cent Store]," *Billy Rose's Crazy Quilt*, 1931). Just because it's the Depression doesn't mean that dreams don't sometimes come true—at least in songs.

With people likely to postpone marriage until they have a job, some of the focus in these songs shifts to lovers who anticipate, but can't quite manage, a wedding. One young man admits that he has unbearable debts but refuses to let them get him down. After all, he boasts with a combination of irony and affection, he has five bucks in his pocket and he'll gladly give everything he has to the one he loves (Richard Rodgers and Lorenz Hart, "I've Got Five Dollars," *America's Sweetheart*, 1931). Another song, also brimming with confidence and good humor, edges up to a proposal of sorts. A fellow who insists that he's "not a doubting Thomas" keeps raising the same question. It's the title line in Herman Hupfeld's "Are You Makin' Any Money?" (*Moonlight and Pretzels*, 1933). In the same vein, a man insists on going shopping with the woman he loves because he will see to it that on her finger "a ring's gonna linger." He also imagines a cottage where they'll live together and a baby sometime in the future, but for now he's content to say that "I'm going shopping with you" (Harry Warren and Al Dubin, "I'm Going Shopping with You," *Gold Diggers of 1935*, 1935). In this new kind of Depression romanticism, a married man, devoted to his wife and mindful of his responsibilities, recommits himself as he puts on his socks and eats his breakfast. He'll do his best to earn some money so he can announce when he comes home: "We're out of debt, and it's really so, / You'll never regret our wedding day" (Herman Hupfeld, "I've Gotta Get Up and Go to Work," *Moonlight and Pretzels*, 1933).

Ultimately, money and work were two of the major images in Depression songs. Most famously, in Ira Gershwin's lyric, wit replaces need, and delight takes the place of desperation. The "if" of Depression songs remains but leads immediately to anticipation and expectation. Work becomes a metaphor for pursuing a girl, falling in love, and imagining that cottage door through which so many young married couples in songs choose to step. Include the song's verse and it becomes something more: a clever, warm-hearted lesson in life beyond a list of pleasing possibilities. The verse advises against living only to earn money or fame, and the moral suggested in the title offers a clever musical guide to happiness and romance (George Gershwin and Ira Gershwin, "Nice Work If You Can Get It," *Damsel in Distress*, 1937).

Other songs play similar word games without Ira Gershwin's wit and precision. They were part of a Tin Pan Alley gambit of writing about the Depression with comic irony and perhaps a touch of mordant flippancy, as in James Monaco, Edgar Leslie, and Ned Washington's "I'm an Unemployed Sweetheart (Looking for Somebody to Love)," 1931) or James F. Hanley and Joe McCarthy's "I'm in the Market for You" (1930), which mocked the recent stock market crash by being bullish on romance. As for the worst things in life, popular songs gave pride of place to the loss of love over every catastrophe the turbulent thirties could whip up. The recurring message in the decade's love songs is that lovers can survive being broke as long as they have each other.

The reality of Depression songs is that nobody had any money. The characters singing the lyrics dream of it and pretend to spend it, or else they let you know they think they're better off without it. No dreaming necessary because, they say, they like the life they've chosen. The movie, *Hallelujah, I'm a Bum* takes a two-sided view of a tramp's life—both romantic and satiric. The direct opposite of "Brother, Can You Spare a Dime?" the movie's defining song celebrates the virtues of living on the road. The rhetorical question in the title makes the point: "What Do You Want with Money?" Later in the movie, though, Lorenz Hart's lyric (sung by Al Jolson as the lead hobo) makes gentle fun of the life of poverty Jolson and his pals choose: Rockefeller keeps busy giving away money but a hobo keeps just as busy picking up Rockefeller's discarded cigars (Richard Rodgers and Lorenz Hart, "Hallelujah, I'm a Bum," *Hallelujah, I'm a Bum,* 1933).

Songs about looking for a job are similar to those that create a sense of class. (They disappear during World War II, when most people floated in the same emotional boat.) Love songs are generally classless; perhaps *populist* is a better word. Everybody gets to fall in love, and the great diversity among the people in a city underscores the point. Rather few love songs are explicitly about poor people or millionaires. The romantically inclined people who sing in ballads may be cleverer with words and more eloquent with emotion than the rest of us, but listeners recognize themselves in what they hear. Only in the 1930s did popular songs assert a sharp sense of class tension—at the very least, a sense of class difference. This title sounds as if it comes from the twenties but it's a Depression song, pure and simple—"When I Take My Sugar to Tea." It might suggest a young man who is getting serious about the young woman he's dating, but like the fellow in "Easter Parade," he's trying to move in different circles. If things work out between them, he'll be marrying up. He doesn't take her where his friends congregate; instead, they go for tea where the millionaires hang out (Sammy Fain, Irving Kahal, and Pierre Thomas, "When I Take My Sugar to Tea," 1931).

Even in the Broadway musical, usually that most politically neutral terrain, an awareness of class showed up, especially in revues. In 1937, Harold Rome wrote most of the songs for what became his first Broadway show, a revue called *Pins and Needles.* Produced by the International Ladies Garment Workers Union, it consisted mainly of satiric songs and sketches performed by ILGWU members for ILGWU members. But it succeeded so well that it moved to Broadway, where it became the longest-running musical of the decade.[14] The show celebrated working people and affirmed their need for a union, but it also traded in hope and optimism despite their struggles. Broadway audiences were relatively well heeled, but when these working people begin to sing, they become recognizable.

In addition to some witty writing about organizing, unemployment, and the looming war in Europe, Rome portrayed workers at their leisure, with enough time to stroll in the park and fall in love. The score is upbeat and happy, and true love conquers, but it never loses its connection to the cause of working people who live and toil in the city. The score includes a love song, "It's Better with a Union Man," and a reflection on marriage, "One Big Union for Two," but a third number rejects "moon songs" and "June songs" for what the title calls "A Song with Social Significance." Although "Sing Me a Song with Social Significance" is unusual for something as mainstream as a Broadway musical, Rome relied on popular music's typical way of framing a provocative subject: he made sure to include allusions to love. Social activism becomes the test as the lover calls for songs about strikes, breadlines, and "courts that aren't impartial" or "I won't love you" (Harold Rome, "Sing Me a Song with Social Significance," *Pins and Needles*, 1937).

Another of *Pins and Needles*' most appealing songs has working people leaving a hot, stuffy apartment to ride the subway to the park, an oasis in the city, with "lots of room to spare" where they "can play and spark" until the end of the day (Rome, "Sunday in the Park," *Pins and Needles*, 1937). Whether or not it mentions a city, a song set in a park is implicitly urban, including "Bench in the Park" (Milton Ager and Jack Yellen, 1930), and "Got the Bench, Got the Park" (Al Sherman, Al Lewis, and Fred Phillips, 1931). A different kind of song, "By a Waterfall" from *Footlight Parade* is a Busby Berkeley extravaganza set in a lush, grassy area. It begins simply enough, with a young man in a suit and a young woman in a stylishly long dress who meet in a park for a moment of privacy (Sammy Fain and Irving Kahal, *Footlight Parade*, 1933). Berkeley takes it from there with dozens of swimmers in form-fitting bathing suits, cavorting to the music in an obviously artificial pastoral pool that eventually turns into an art deco spectacular, complete with towers, walls, and underwater floodlights, as the girls dive, swim, smile, bounce, and form kaleidoscopic figures before evolving into an elaborate six-tier rotating fountain. Berkeley's erotic urban fantasy leaves Mother Nature far behind.

In addition to songs set in parks mainly on Sunday afternoons, Depression songs often listen in on people who are taking walks, either because strolling is a way for them to get to know one another or because it lets lovers steal a few moments alone. In the courting song "Would You Like to Take a Walk?" a young fellow spots a nice-looking girl. His attempts at a pickup quickly turn into a series of conversational gambits about the weather, the latest songs, and going to the movies. An eternal optimist, he sees opportunity in everything she says. He invites her to take a walk, she fends him off, but he refuses to be discouraged and draws his own optimistic conclusion: something good will come from taking a walk together (Harry Warren, Mort Dixon, and Billy Rose, "Would You Like to Take a Walk," *Sweet and Low,* 1930).

At the turn of the twentieth century, finding a way to be alone together tested the limits of propriety and ingenuity; thirty years later, it was a matter of what a couple could afford. In a song reminiscent of "I Can't Give You Anything But Love, Baby" (1928), a working-class boy explains that he could never afford to go anywhere. He's never even made it to Jersey City across the Hudson, but he's determined to hold on to his girl and keep their hopes up. Now that they're saving their money, he's confident that someday they'll travel the world. For now, though, the best he can offer is the loving invitation that appears first in the title and repeats at the end of each chorus (Harold Arlen, Ira Gershwin, and E. Y. Harburg, "Let's Talk a Walk Around the Block," *Life Begins at 8:40,* 1934).

City songs may offer a temporary respite in an escape to a park or a walk around the block, but a rooftop can serve just as well. The Depression produced a number of songs about penthouses, all of them affectionately tongue in cheek, more about hope and aspiration than wealth. They include Irving Berlin's "On a Roof in Manhattan (Castles in Spain)" (*Face the Music,* 1932), and Sammy Fain and Irving Kahal's "Our Penthouse on Third Avenue" (*New Faces of 1937,* 1937). In the most important of these songs, "Penthouse Serenade," a young man and woman, in love but living with their families somewhere in New York, have no money and no way to be alone except on the roof of an apartment building. They can't afford to marry; the best they can do is meet each night to dream about the future. The song is romantic rather than sexual as they cheer one another by imagining what life will be like when they're rich, married, and blissfully alone. It's so far off, so improbable, that their imagining is both amusing and fantastical:

Just picture a penthouse way up in the sky
With hinges on chimneys for stars to go by.
(Val Burton and Will Jason, "Penthouse Serenade," 1931)

In the populist world of popular songs, these kinds of dreams are for everyone, especially during tough times.

Although typical Depression songs anticipate rather than providing the payoff, the relatively few songs about married love underscore the differences between the 1920s and 1930s, between songs such as "Blue Room" (1926) and "My Blue Heaven" (1927), and deeper, more serious, but also funnier songs such as "Two Sleepy People" (Hoagy Carmichael and Frank Loesser, *Thanks for the Memory*, 1938) and "Thanks for the Memory" (Ralph Rainger and Leo Robin, *The Big Broadcast of 1938*, 1938). Shirley Ross and Bob Hope sang both of them. Ross's warm alto and Hope's half-talking style embodied their shared intimacy and emotionalism, one a happy celebration of marriage and sex by two people at ease with themselves and one another, the other an encounter between a former husband and wife who can't let go of their memories. They reminisce over a drink in a dimly lit bar.

Although they describe opposite emotional poles of a marriage, both songs are conversational duets in which Loesser in one and Robin in the other demonstrate their mastery of the lyricist's craft. Both songs combine a deft handling of the rhythms of ordinary talk, an awareness of the music inherent in language, and the ability to use wit to enhance serious emotions. At the same time, they seamlessly blend the words with Carmichael's and Rainger's music, respectively. "Two Sleepy People" is a sweet, sexy conversation that begins in the hours after lovemaking and continues until dawn because the lovers are much too much in love to let the night end. Although they're sitting there, doing nothing but picking over leftovers, you sense the sexual charge between them. Husband and wife are far from being newlyweds, but romance, passion, and a sense of humor have survived nicely in their marriage.

When Paramount assigned Rainger and Robin to *The Big Broadcast of 1938*, the movie's producer told them they had to write a serious song, but Hope would sing it and "a guy like that has got to get laughs."[15] With no confidence that they would be able to pull it off, Rainger wrote a gentle melody to which Robin set sad but witty lyrics that go back over a couple's marriage: still in love but unable to recognize it for what it is—a mix of fun and folly. The result is a duet in the form of a catalogue song that describes the lives of young urban sophisticates who still retain some of the innocent desire of young love. Robin sets up clever contrasts that reveal the manners and morals of the two people, and illuminate the lingering affection between them. The two songs are intimate, heartfelt, and clever—the embodiment of the urban sensibility, 1930s edition.

Because everything America cherished was at risk during the Depression and again during World War II, it seems reasonable to assume that the love songs of these two decades would be similar. Not so: the widespread unemployment and poverty, the class conflicts, and the internal dissensions of the thirties nearly tore the nation apart because the conflict boiled over at home; it came from within. During World War II, the conflict came from without. In retrospect, it's no surprise that the war united the American people, at least emotionally. The defining love songs of the Depression were often bleakly urban, somewhere at the edge of despair, but the ballads of the war years were rooted in parting and separation and the dream of returning home. In 1933, a woman urged the world to "Remember my forgotten man," but men in the forties were in peril rather than forgotten.

8

WORLD WAR II

In 1938, the bandleader Harry James's recording of a new ballad called "I'll Be Seeing You," with a vocal by a little-known crooner named Frank Sinatra, made barely a ripple. It was just another song that failed to survive the Depression, its imagery of a carousel and a wishing well too precious by half. Six years later, though, its conjuring up of memory and anticipation transformed it into a persuasively simple expression of how America felt in a different kind of troubled time. This Depression flop became one of the biggest hits of World War II. Its mournfully sweet melody and its imagery of childhood and first love had felt mawkish during the 1930s but now struck a responsive chord; its references, while specific, could be located anywhere. Like so many wartime hits, it sang about parting, separation, longing, loneliness, and the dream of return. After failing six years earlier, it now reminded lovers of what they remembered and desired. The title line, initially a casual conversational farewell, became an affirmation of lasting devotion in a war-torn world. (Sammy Fain and Irving Kahal, "I'll Be Seeing You," *Right This Way,* 1938).

The places the lover remembers were gone, not because they had suddenly turned to rubble, but because the young man who had wooed in their shadow was gone. Neither recollection nor desire had the power to bring him home again. In the United States at the height of World War II, more than 12 million men left home to serve in the armed forces.[1] More than 6 million women took jobs; 3 million "went to work who would not have worked if there hadn't been a war."[2] Many of these working women chose to leave home to find a job in a defense plant or on a farm and were away for the duration of the war. Even for those who stayed put, the sense of upheaval was profound.[3] The popular music of World War II gave them an anchor; it understood how they felt. In his oral history of the war years, Archie Satterfield wrote that "the absence of an entire generation of men between the ages of seventeen and thirty leaves a lonely void in a nation, and a common refrain among the young women was that they got sick and tired of talking only to other women, kids, and old men."[4] As a humorous lyric from 1943 complained about the remaining males, "They're either too young or too old, / They're either too gray or too grassy green" (Arthur Schwartz and Frank Loesser, "They're Either Too Young or Too Old," *Thank Your Lucky Stars*, 1943). The other men, those who were neither too young nor too old, were not merely absent; they were in peril.

The antics of Frank Loesser's lyric have that kind of ironic stance that puts a song squarely on a street corner. That makes it one of the relatively few songs of World War II to feel like a city song. Most of the love ballads from those years feel suspended outside place and even time, in a kind of limbo where only emotion provides gravity and motion, where everything stops except the day-in, day-out waiting for the war to end. There is an arc of history here: the defining urban outlook, now four decades old, gives way before the insistent feelings and musical tastes of the people who are living through the war at home. The songs take place within the hearts of those who wait. Regardless of what they do to earn a living or pass the time, and regardless of where they do it, only their emotions feel real—and nothing is more real than dread. And yet, the exceptions matter. "I'll Walk Alone" could be set anywhere; where the woman goes when she takes her lonely walks doesn't matter. On the other hand, "Don't Get Around Much Anymore," gives us a familiar Saturday-night dance and a neighborhood club, a woman's cryptic refusal to explain herself, the busyness of people around her, and her isolation even though she is surrounded by friends. It feels much like "The City That Has No Heart" from forty years earlier. She can find no one to turn to; the feeling of being alone in a dark apartment overwhelms her.

Although the urban sensibility is less obvious during the war years than in any other decade of the first half of the twentieth century, it does persist in individual songs and in Broadway and Hollywood musicals—sometimes as a matter of tone or outlook, sometimes indirectly as an alternative to unfocused emotion or as an element of temptation in an idealized setting. One of the best examples lies in the dark side of Richard Rodgers and Oscar Hammerstein II's *Oklahoma!*, which I write about later in this chapter.

Although love remained the essential subject and the urban sensibility had survived for four decades, the differences in American songs between the early twentieth century and the start of World War II are striking. The earlier songs were less introspective and reflective; they were more often about behavior than feeling. When the older songs confronted emotion directly, it was more likely to be emotion translated into action rather than emotion evoked and articulated. By the 1940s, a generation had outlasted the Great Depression and perceived the world with a new degree of psychological awareness. People had endured social dislocation and personal struggle. It had been a time of anxiety and fear amounting to a deeper emotional knowledge of what the nation would face next—another world war.

Beginning in 1942, lushly romantic songs affirmed loyalty and fidelity, admired sacrifice, and embraced hope, despite the subtext of dread in lyric after lyric. At the same time, they possessed little sense of place. The departure of men for war could have occurred anywhere; the feeling of isolation for the women who remained behind was unaffected by the difference between getting through the night in a city or in a small town. It was hard to tell from most of the lyrics if the women who speak in them were employed or not, married or single, innocent or worldly. Yet the songs felt intensely personal in a country that had gotten used to the ardent buh-buh-buh-booing of radio baritones, who seemed to assume that their listeners were women alone in their living rooms, curled up by the radio after dark. A wartime poll asked women whether they would rather give up the movies or the radio. As important as going to the movies was, their preference was clear: 79.3 percent would give up the movies; only 13.9 percent were willing to get by without the entertainment and music that were broadcast every night.[5]

Unlike love songs from previous decades that emphasized familiar behavior as well as common emotions, the love songs of the forties usually focused single-mindedly on the feelings that the song's primary audience of women grasped so deeply. The war required women to stand on their own without men to "protect" them. Those who were married had households to manage and children to raise, but large numbers of them also held down jobs. They were on their own except for the company and guidance of other women in the same boat. The songs of the war years that meant the most to these women seemed designed for the late hours when they could give their emotions full play. These songs were also more abstract and introspective than anything that preceded them. They were more likely than earlier songs to speak emotional truths simply and directly in such lines as "I can't begin to tell you / How much you mean to me" (James V. Monaco and Mack Gordon, "I Can't Begin to Tell You," *The Dolly Sisters*, 1945).

~ ~ ~

To listen to the love songs of the home front is to trace an emotional history of World War II, to limn the geography of the heart between December 1941 and the months after August 1945. Although popular music has always been attuned to the attitudes of the American people, this populist awareness was never keener than during the war. Many of the love songs could have been written at any time during those four years. Songs about dreaming, so common in 1942 and 1943, persisted into 1945—from "I've Heard That Song Before" (1942) to "My Dreams Are Getting Better All the Time" (1945) and "I'll Buy That Dream" (1946)—even though the dread of separation eventually shifted to the anticipation of return. Similarly, songs whose speakers ached for lovers to come home safely, most common in 1944 and 1945, had begun to appear as early as 1942 with such titles as "Wonder When My Baby's Coming Home," "After It's Over," and "When My Dreamboat Comes Home."

Even so, other songs conveyed an immediate sense of the ways in which the progress of the war affected not only public opinion but also the women who listened and hummed along. The lyricists for these songs could not have written in 1945 what they wrote in 1942, and vice versa. Perhaps because gasoline was rationed and tires were unavailable, perhaps because a few moments of solitude gave a woman an opportunity for uninterrupted emotion, a number of important songs from the war were about walking. (The same was true in Depression songs but that's because everybody was broke.) In the aftermath of Pearl Harbor, American forces suffered defeat after defeat while the nation mobilized. Casualty figures were high, and no one could foresee victory. In the face of a growing sense that this war would last a very long time and that many young men would die, songs translated national concerns into individual experience and personal emotion. It was a time to wonder if the one you loved would return and what you would have to endure if he did not.

In 1942, Jule Styne and Frank Loesser's "I Don't Want to Walk without You," portrayed a woman who had said goodbye to her beloved only recently. Peter Townsend suggests that the song takes on "a special resonance" from "a yearningly emotional performance by Helen Forrest" and because it was recorded only four days after Pearl Harbor.[6] A woman realizes how little she understood her depth of feeling. The weight of unfamiliar despair drives her away from the friends who most care for her. She prefers to sit alone in the gloom so she can talk to her beloved as if he's there. She also realizes that she can't go walking again until he returns and that her heart—even, perhaps, her capacity for love—is in danger of breaking (Jule Styne and Frank Loesser, "I Don't Want to Walk without You," *Sweater Girl,* 1941). It is a song about a retreat from the world; its sentiments reflect the bleakest year of the war.

Two years later, "I'll Walk Alone," another song about taking a walk, portrayed another woman who is alone, but the world is different by then and so is she. This was the year of D-Day and the liberation of Paris. In the Pacific, islands closer to Japan fell to the US Marines. War-weary Americans began to realize that victory was only a matter of time, even though a lot of fighting and dying was yet to come. In that context, the woman in the later song has come to terms with her loneliness and isolation. Yet like the woman in "I Don't Want to Walk without You," she also rejects companionship in favor of solitude. As she remembers their closeness, the lyric suggests a night of lovemaking before they parted. The emotions are no less deeply felt than in songs of despair, but a sense that her lover is as lonely as she is makes a different outlook possible. That is the bond between them, played out against the nation's growing optimism; she will hold true until he returns and asks only that he send his love and kisses back to her—the ethereal and the physical, the romantic and the sexual—as she walks alone, praying but also remembering the last time they made love. Shaped by a loving determination that eases the dread, "I'll Walk Alone" became one of the most successful and most important ballads of World War II (Jule Styne and Sammy Cahn, "I'll Walk Alone, *Follow the Boys,* 1944).

Unlike in many earlier songs from the war years, Herb Magidson's 1945 lyric to "I'll Buy That Dream" focuses on the future. The title transforms dreaming into something practical and graspable; its title uses "buy" in the sense of "accept" or "believe in." The woman dreams of being reunited with her beloved, but she is also confident enough to have a sense of humor. Man and woman kiss—the implication of lovemaking—and in the next chorus they marry as the rest of the song quickly lays out their idyllic life to come, including settling down in a tiny postwar house. It culminates with her at eighty-three and him at ninety-two and a final understated affirmation (Allie Wrubel and Herb Magidson, "I'll Buy That Dream," 1945).

The Academy Award for Best Picture of 1946 (and six other Oscars) went to *The Best Years of Our Lives,* about three returning servicemen who learn that adapting to civilian life is more complex than they had anticipated. In one of the film's most memorable scenes, the oldest of the three men, a staff sergeant and former bank executive, rings the bell to his large apartment. When his teenage children answer the door, the movie audience sees what he sees: down the hall into the kitchen where his wife, her back to the camera, is preparing dinner. She calls out to ask who it is. When no one answers, she realizes that her husband has returned. The homecoming is sweet and passionate, as they stand in the entry, covering one other with kisses.

Just a year earlier, a month after the war actually ended, Bing Crosby released the last Jule Styne–Sammy Cahn wartime hit to romanticize the moment of homecoming. The returning lover asks for a kiss, another kiss, and then another kiss, as if to compensate for the years spent apart. To replace the dreams he relied on, he wants the physical reality. Who can blame him? Still unsatisfied, he asks, "kiss me once again, / It's been a long, long time" (Jule Styne and Sammy Cahn, "It's Been a Long, Long Time," 1945). It is one of those songs that could have been written at no other time during the war, just as no studio could have released *The Best Years of Our Lives* before the war's end in August 1945. Each seems to be a rough emotional equivalent of the other. Ballads like these touched the private emotions of millions of sweethearts and wives who were limited largely to the company of other women. Though that was often satisfying for them, as was the independence they found in doing jobs previously reserved for men, the songs articulated their loneliness at a time when people were used to keeping such emotions to themselves.[7] Love ballads between 1942 and 1945 took the point of view of those left behind to wait, fear, and hope. The emotional strain was intense, and the best songs of the war captured it implicitly with honesty and economy. Despite social lives that often revolved around work, many women were deeply lonely. Again and again, the songs of the time spoke not only to them but also for them, few with greater insight than Duke Ellington and Bob Russell's elliptical "Don't Get Around Much Anymore." Russell added his lyric to Ellington's 1938 instrumental "Never No More" in 1942, the year when war news was at its worst. So was the emotional state of growing numbers of young women who were listening to both the news and popular songs on the radio. For the withdrawn young woman in the song, the outside world is less bearable than her own emotions. She can bear the loneliness more easily than the solicitude of friends. She writes to her beloved that she missed a dance but heard it was crowded;

she also tried going to a familiar club but stopped at the door. Because she cannot endure the kindness of friends, what remains is the emotion, so raw she can express only the understated fact of it; the key to the song's emotionalism lies in its title (Duke Ellington and Bob Russell, "Don't Get Around Much Anymore," 1942).

Writing in 1946, the anthropologist Margaret Mead asserted that tens of millions of people had become anonymous during the war. It was a striking observation: "Each became merely a soldier standing in formation or wandering around a small town on leave."[8] She describes a young woman working in a factory, sleeping in a rented room with three other young women, none of whom she knows very well; a young wife follows her soldier husband from base to base until he ships out and she remains, alone and isolated, in a place where she has no family, no memory, and no emotional attachment.[9] Between 1942 and 1945, these were the women, single and married, who bought the popular recordings and listened to the radio.

The song lyrics of the day both personalized and universalized the emotions of the women who remained behind. A heightened, idealized mirror image of their lives set to the slow rhythms of a foxtrot, a love song lyric also suggested that what they felt was not unique to any one of them. Songs gave public voice to their emotions as they embraced the content of the lyrics with a dreamy yet profound fervor that confirmed the longing and loneliness they felt. In the vast majority of cases, the emotions expressed in lyrics were those of the women who waited. In love songs written before World War II, references to urbanization, technological innovation, the arrival of immigrants, and even the search for a job were woven into songs about finding or losing love. During World War II, though, women's common emotions *became* the songs. The songs felt motionless; nothing moved because the lover was gone and nothing was as real as emotion itself. People still went to work and listened to the radio; they still read a magazine and cooked supper; they took in a movie and struggled with shortages and rationing—but not in love songs. There were always exceptions, mainly in such novelties as "There Won't Be a Shortage of Love" and "Fighting on the Home Front Wins" with its appeal to lonely homemakers: "We're the dustpan crew / Standing back of you" (Kay Swift, "Fighting on the Home Front Wins, 1943). But none of these songs about daily life became a hit. The songs of the war years that mattered reflected not what Americans were doing but what they were feeling.

Among the ballads of World War II are some of Tin Pan Alley's most deeply felt songs. Yet it took a while for songwriters to find their way. In the aftermath of Pearl Harbor, composers and lyricists were urged to provide the American people with war songs to stir the public mood. Congressman J. Parnell Thomas implored Tin Pan Alley, "What America needs today is a good five-cent war song . . . a good, peppy marching song, something with plenty of zip, ginger, and fire."[10] Gene Buck, the president of ASCAP, urged his fellow songwriters to contribute to the war effort by writing "fighting songs."[11]

Occasionally, during the first few years of the war, songs also gave Americans an emotional portrait of soldiers, sailors, and airmen in combat, where they fought heroically and victoriously and sometimes died. A young friend of the composer Jimmy McHugh had written to him about a close call on a bombing mission. McHugh and the lyricist Harold Adamson idealized the story in "Comin' In on a Wing and a Prayer" so that it included not only the pilot's skill but also his faith in God (Jimmy McHugh and Harold Adamson, "Comin' In on a Wing and a Prayer," 1943). In that same year, in "Praise the Lord and Pass the Ammunition," Frank Loesser portrayed a navy chaplain who replaces a wounded sailor during an attack at sea and helps to fire back at Japanese planes (Frank Loesser, "Praise the Lord and Pass the Ammunition," 1942), and, in 1944, he told the story of a courageous private, Rodger Young, who sacrifices his life to save his comrades (Frank Loesser, "The Ballad of Rodger Young," 1945). These songs met a patriotic need, confirmed the heavy price the nation was paying, and implicitly promised victory, but they were among the very few combat songs to become hits.

Some songs portrayed the drudgery of military life, though nowhere near as many as during World War I. The songs of World War II weren't very long on humor either. Most of the attempts at comedy took on such predictable gripes as reveille, KP, and long marches, but in 1941, J. Fred Coots and Clarence Kulseth borrowed a title from Jimmy McHugh, Dorothy Fields, and George Oppenheimer's "I Feel a Song Coming On" to tell the amusing story of a bashful fellow who proposes to his girl with a marriage license in hand because "I feel a draft coming on" (J. Fred Coots, Clarence Kulseth, "I Feel a Draft Coming On," 1941). Among the few comic songs that succeeded were Irving Berlin's "This Is the Army"; a revival of his World War I song, "Oh, How

I Hate to Get Up in the Morning"; and Johnny Mercer's "G. I. Jive," which cleverly merges military "alphabet soup" with jive talk.

The early years of the war were overloaded with patriotic songs, partly because any war would probably have created a market for them, but also because the new Office of War Information encouraged songwriters to produce them. As the nation went to war, the federal government, through the OWI, began extensive efforts to control the message about the war in newspapers, on the radio, and in the movies. The OWI produced its own radio shows and made films, but it also encouraged Hollywood to make theatrical releases that would support the war effort and build morale. Such movies as *Air Force*, *A Walk in the Sun*, and *Destination Tokyo* humanized the brave men fighting the Germans and Japanese. *Since You Went Away* and *The Human Comedy* celebrated the travails—the courage and decency—of those who remained at home. Even though the submission of scripts to the OWI was voluntary, it soon became clear to the Hollywood studios "that without the OWI stamp of approval, movie projects would not be allowed to proceed."[12] As Allen L. Wohl explains, the studios went along without much protest because "it was no secret that the leaders of the film industry feared the imposition of government censorship."[13] What the OWI wanted was propaganda, pure and simple: "In the OWI/Hollywood vision, the war produced unity; labor and capital buried their differences for a greater cause; class, ethnic, and racial divisions evaporated in the foxholes and on the assembly line; even estranged family members were reconciled through the agency of war."[14]

In a misguided effort to urge songwriters to produce many more martial songs and many fewer romantic ballads, the OWI also asked Tin Pan Alley to write what soon came to be known as the "Great American War Song." Abel Green, the longtime editor of *Variety*, reported that he had attended a meeting in which an OWI representative dismissed what he called "slush songs."[15] By July 1942, writes Katherine E. L. Smith, a secret gathering "described as 'a group of disinterested publishers' began sifting through hundreds of compositions looking for the 'right kind' of war songs." The OWI said that keeping "boy-and-girl roseate stuff" in the closet until the end of the war was "a matter of patriotism."[16] It spent the entire war pressing for fighting songs, but no one ever came close to George M. Cohan's World War I classic "Over There," the song the agency held up as its model.

That doesn't mean the songwriters didn't try. They cranked out such jingoistic pap as "Remember Pearl Harbor" and "We Did It

Before and We Can Do It Again," as well as racist novelty songs like "The Jap and the Wop and the Hun" and "When Those Little Yellow Bellies Meet the Cohens and the Kellys." Even highly regarded songwriters tried to do their bit but fell well short of OWI's goal in such songs as Cohan's tribute to the American family, written shortly before his death in 1942, "For the Flag, For the Home, For the Family"; Harry Warren and Mack Gordon's "Let's Bring New Glory to Old Glory"; and Rodgers and Hart's "Bombardier Song (Dedicated to the Bomber Crews of the US Army Air Forces)."

Even though people were ready to embrace the war effort, the OWI's attempt flopped. The first batch of war songs was written on the run right after Pearl Harbor and showed it. Many of them were militaristic rather than patriotic, and dwelt more on bashing the Japanese and punishing the Germans than affirming love of country.[17] Most of them disappeared unnoticed, though not before some critics had scalded them. *DownBeat* magazine's critic wrote about "Let's Put the Axe to the Axis" (Corday, Mann, and Weiss, 1941): "This department agrees with the sentiments expressed . . . but music as foul as this is far more likely to impair the morale of the nation. Like most of the new so-called 'patriotic' tunes—composed overnight by Broadway writers who figure they can grab a quick bag of loot for their efforts—'Axis' is a feeble piece of music."[18]

If any song from World War II surpassed "Over There" in its lasting effect on the American people during wartime, it was Irving Berlin's "God Bless America." Although Berlin wrote a routine martial song, "This Time," during the early months of the war, he wrote "God Bless America" long before the OWI came into being. Berlin had originally intended it to be it an anthem for doughboys departing for France in his World War I all-soldier show *Yip, Yip, Yaphank!* He chose to cut it before opening night, but when he revised it two decades later, he transformed it into what he called a "peace song." Soon after, the popular radio singer Kate Smith approached him about writing a new patriotic song that she could introduce over the air. She told him that she believed her audiences would be responsive during troubled times. He offered her the song, which she first sang on Armistice Day in 1938.[19]

Smith's performance of "God Bless America" in the 1942 movie version of *This Is the Army* underscores the perfect match between singer and song. The scene recreates the initial performance. The nation is not yet at war, but as Smith sings, the film cuts away from the studio audience to show ordinary people, both civilian and military, in their living rooms and on air corps bases, taking stock as they listen to the radio. Smith's clarion performance became a stirring image of America's unity during a terrible time. The sheet music sold out almost immediately. For the duration of the war, Smith sang "God Bless America" on the radio and for men in uniform all over the country.

At a time when most female big band singers were youthful and perky, Kate Smith was an anomaly. Whereas most "canaries" projected the image of a kid sister or the girl next door as they bounced their way through a song, she was a large woman with a trumpet for a voice. Already in her midthirties when America entered the war, she had been in show business professionally for a decade and a half. She had begun her career in vaudeville and moved up to Broadway in the midtwenties, when she first played a character named Tiny Little. It was the first of many humiliations she suffered in the theater because of her size. In 1931, soon after record producer Ted Collins became her manager, she moved to radio, where she became one of America's best-loved (and highest-paid) entertainers.

In 1939, only two months before Germany invaded Poland, Franklin Roosevelt invited the king and queen of England to visit the United States as part of his mission to prepare the American people for the war he was convinced the nation would have to fight. He brought the royal couple up to the rambling Roosevelt family estate along the Hudson for a typical American picnic of hot dogs and strawberry shortcake. He also invited Kate Smith to sing after dinner. He introduced her by saying, "Your majesties, this is Kate Smith. This is America." Some years later, the jazz critic George Simon observed, "Kate Smith did indeed seem to personify the country—idealistic, generous, homespun, sentimental, emotional, proud."[20]

When Smith sang the war songs of the forties, she somehow epitomized America's sense of itself. She was never a great interpreter of lyrics, but she sang in a hearty, straightforward way as if she believed what she was singing. She recorded and performed a wide range of songs during these years but no romantic ballads of any significance. She generally kept away from anything ardent or implicitly sexual. After "God Bless America," she sang patriotic numbers that had little effect on a public largely unreceptive to martial music. Because her radio audiences were always predominantly female, during the war she often chose songs that those back home would find reassuring. The most important love song she introduced was Irving Berlin's pedestrian "I

Threw a Kiss in the Ocean" in 1942. For the most part, though, the songs that Smith performed during the war emphasized patriotism and familial devotion rather than erotic heat or the agonies of lovers apart.

Among the love songs that were explicitly about the war, the most appealing were ballads about a girl back home and a boy in the service. The necessities of wartime shaped these songs about ordinary people during extraordinary times. Because of the war, they have little control over their lives, and their emotions bend to the dangers of service, separation, and combat. In "He Wears a Pair of Silver Wings," originally a hit in England, a woman describes her feelings of love in conventional terms before the lyric focuses on her lover's service in the war; she describes him as an ordinary person who's doing a very hard job (Eric Maschwitz and Michael Carr, "He Wears a Pair of Silver Wings," 1942). In "He's 1-A in the Army and He's A-1 in My Heart," slightly less romantic in tone but equally connected to the war, a women's love and fidelity combine to form a kind of romantic patriotism. She praises him for enlisting and then passing his physical because her feelings for him are inseparable from his eagerness to serve (Redd Evans, "He's 1-A in the Army and He's A-1 in My Heart," 1941). In yet another example, a young woman admits that her absent lover is an average-looking fellow, but "he was the first one to answer the call" (Matt Dennis and Paul Herrick, "That Soldier of Mine," 1942).

The most emotional of these songs reunite women with their soldier lovers who have come home on leave. Not surprisingly, in Ted Shapiro and Kermit Goell's "He's Home for a Little While," the woman who speaks in the lyric is thrilled to have him near her once again, but she is also honest with herself. More deeply felt than even her sexual excitement, she knows that she will have to let him go again to do his duty when his leave comes to an end (Ted Shapiro and Kermit Goell, "He's Home for a Little While," 1945). Her outlook mingles sadness with pride. No matter how touching these songs were, their immediate connection to the war limited their popularity to the time of their first appearance. Despite the many similarities between these and the more generalized ballads of the time, the vast majority of love songs from these years—and certainly those that became standards—never explicitly mention the war; the *emotions* of wartime were what mattered. Irving Berlin once observed that, regardless of its content, a song's "popularity during wartime was enough to make it a war song."[21] It was as if the OWI's insistent pressure had a lingering reverse effect; the more it wanted songwriters to write patriotically about the war and set love aside, the less likely it was to happen. Love songs set during wartime suggested everything their audience wanted to hear.

The OWI's stab at reshaping Tin Pan Alley also failed because the "mood of the United States in this war differed perceptively from that in previous conflicts. . . . In previous conflicts Americans filled the streets with flags, staged wild recruiting rallies, cheered departing fighters madly, and roared patriotic songs. . . . In this war there was happily no such . . . frothy enthusiasm. . . . [People] were too anxious, busy, and determined to waste time cheering."[22] That may have been so because they "were simply too burned out on ideology after the Great War, the ensuing Great Depression, and the great failure of the League of Nations."[23] Even men in the service had no desire to hear military songs during the early months of the war. John Bush Jones quotes a local bandleader in Omaha who observed that both officers and enlisted men "recoiled from the playing" of songs "with a martial or war flavor."[24] The OWI effort also failed because it misread America's most personal emotions and the forms they took. Pearl Harbor roused the people's deep core of patriotism, so sorely tested during the previous decade, but its full range, from bumptious jingoism to deep love of country, could not compete in songs with the more intense and intimate emotions cultivated over half a century by Tin Pan Alley. Even in the darkest times, Americans turned to songs for lessons in love and expected to find them there.

Women have always bought more sheet music and recordings than men have. During the war, there was no way around it. Huge numbers of men on military posts in the States or in combat overseas had few opportunities to buy and store recordings, partly because 78-rpm discs shattered so easily.[25] Beginning in 1943, V-discs and Armed Forces Radio eased the isolation of sailors and soldiers, but even then, the audience for popular music remained mainly female. Women listened to the radio, played the pianos, fed the jukeboxes, bought the recordings, and even danced together when there weren't enough men to go around.

Instead of buying recordings of brass bands and rousing glee clubs, the audience for popular music chose to listen to crooners whispering love songs against a background of breathy reeds and muted trumpets. One music publisher observed that he knew "for a fact that the public doesn't want fighting songs. . . . Until such time as the government is ready to foot the bill, I'm not going to lose money printing fighting songs."[26] The OWI continued to press for patriotic songs, but the effort was futile. Within a few months, the public had opened its wallets to let Tin Pan Alley, Broadway, and Hollywood know what it wanted. Among the number-one songs of 1942 were "Moonlight Cocktail," "Chattanooga Choo-Choo," and "Sleepy Lagoon"—not exactly what the OWI had in mind. What could the bureaucrats have been thinking? Tin Pan Alley wanted to do its part, but did anybody really think that people would give up their appetite for love songs, especially when a large part of the audience consisted of lonely women who missed both romance and sex? Frank Loesser observed that to become popular, a song would have to appeal to a woman, to "give her hope without facts; glory without blood. You give her a legend neatly trimmed."[27]

The love songs did their part by exploring wartime life and emotion on the home front. They expressed the common thoughts and feelings of diverse women who remained behind to work on the assembly line, raise children and tend house, volunteer for the Red Cross and the USO (United Service Organizations), and then write letters at night before going to sleep. As one young woman who lived through it explained, "The greatest hardship . . . for those who were left at home, was the secret and constant anxiety for those we loved. It was seldom spoken but always there as we read and listened to the news, following the course of the war."[28] Almira Bondelid, another young woman, said, "While he was gone, there was just that kind of hurt, an ache inside that must be there. . . . I always had the hope he would be back, and I could be laughing and talking to friends, and the ache would be right there."[29] At work one morning, Constance Stirrup Lackey heard soldiers marching and stepped outside to watch: "There went my boyfriend marching past. They never told them they were being shipped out or anything, and there went the boy I was in love with, heading overseas. . . . Tears were running down my cheeks and not a soul teased me. Nobody thought it was funny at all."[30]

No single song or movie came closer to capturing the feel of family life lived in a state of constant anxiety than *Since You Went Away*, from 1944. Its popularity reflected the sympathetic intelligence of performances by Hattie McDaniel, Joseph Cotten, Monty Woolley, and especially Claudette Colbert as Anne Hilton, a wife and mother who struggles to hold her family together in the face of separation and even death. Despite its sentimentality and its reliance on stereotypes, the movie paints a vivid portrait of life on the home front for the Hiltons, ordinary Americans, though a good bit more affluent and attractive than most. They find everyday satisfactions but they also never escape the looming heartache and fear, something everyone in the audience, and especially the women, would have grasped. To underline the movie's central theme, its score included repeated renditions of "Together," a song from 1928. The loved one may be far away and the return is in jeopardy: "But in my memory / We always will be together" (Ray Henderson, Lew Brown and B. G. DeSylva, "Together," cut from *Follow Thru*, 1928).

The movie historian Thomas Doherty writes, "With the ham-handedness typical of OWI-stamped melodrama, *Since You Went Away* taught a dozen lessons in proper homefront behavior." Ham-handed or not, the movie carefully positions the husband's absence in the center of the narrative by showing his empty leather chair, his pipe, his dog, and a service banner in the window, ensuring that "the absent patriarch leaves an aching emotional gulf in the lives of his wives and daughters."[31] Late in the movie, Anne Hilton berates herself for not doing enough for the war effort. She takes a job in a defense plant where she learns to weld, makes a new female friend who had escaped the Nazis, and finds a new level of commitment and fulfillment.

In both the iconic *Saturday Evening Post* cover by Norman Rockwell and the song by Redd Evans and John Jacob Loeb, Rosie the Riveter came to symbolize women all over the country who, like Anne, took jobs in factories and gave legitimacy to the essential work they did. Describing Rockwell's portrait, the World War II historian Ronald H. Bailey writes, "The traditional picture of the all-American girl with the toothy smile was supplanted with the image of a dirt-streaked face beneath hair bound up in a bandana."[32] As she works to help win the war, Rosie is also aware that she is making history as a woman and, at the same time, helping her marine boyfriend. She is never prouder than when her efforts earn her company an E-for-Excellence award from the War Department. The lyric combines commitment, patriotism, and true love in a casually direct way; the personal and patriotic interweave. (Redd Evans and John Jacob Loeb, "Rosie the Riveter," 1942).

What Bondelid and Lackey reveal about themselves in their memoirs, songwriters said for millions of others. Even for those who had no loved ones in the military, the songs were part of the nation's emotional bond. Lyrics stopped short of exploring emotional collapses at home or carnage overseas. What joined Americans to one another was

Figure 8.1. Rosie the Riveter, more glamorous than usual, stands ready to begin her shift. Courtesy of Photofest.

not only a mix of patriotism and determination but also the longing for return and peace expressed in the song lyrics of the time. Some songs made it to *Your Hit Parade*, many more slid almost immediately into obscurity, but whoever turned on the radio heard the songs' recurring emotional messages. They gave women a way to deflect for a moment the common despair expressed by a young wife named Genevieve Eppens: "How could we have known that the next three and a half years would seem like a nightmare?"[33] Even though the heartache and isolation felt by Eppens and others were genuine and widespread, a few songs eventually confronted these emotions with something approaching a comic outlook—not because they were funny, but because they had the kind of honesty and resilience that we associate with a sense of humor. "Saturday Night (Is the Loneliest Night of the Week)" became a hit in 1945, perhaps because it came so late in the war or because it tied familiar emotions to common experience. There is nothing surprising in its lyric: a young woman confesses to loneliness every Saturday because that's the night when she and her sweetie would go dancing. The other days of the week go quickly enough, but Saturday night is always melancholy, the time when memories return and she imagines hearing him at the door and holding him in her arms. But then she manages to get through the next week as well (Jule Styne and Sammy Cahn, "Saturday Night [Is the Loneliest Night in the Week]," 1944).

Among the songs played and replayed on phonographs, at dances, and on the air were several revivals that found new popularity. Like "I'll Be Seeing You," they seemed to be more relevant than when they had first appeared in the twenties or thirties. "I'll Get By," from 1928, resonated with new poignancy during the war. What had been a generic torch song now portrayed a woman who spoke about endurance in the face of troubles that ranged from the natural—"rain / and darkness, too"—to the economic—"Poverty / May come to me." The title line echoes through the lyric, lifting it from a statement of determination to one of conviction and belief in the one she loves (Fred E. Ahlert and Roy Turk, "I'll Get By," 1927). Although a woman is speaking in the song, Dick Haymes had the hit recording. It didn't matter. Women speak implicitly in these songs even when the singer is a man; the content of the lyric is what counted.

The most important of the revivals was Herman Hupfeld's only major ballad, "As Time Goes By." Although Rudy Vallee's recording had had some limited success in 1932, the song had largely been forgotten by the time it reappeared in *Casablanca* a decade later. When the playwrights Murray Burnett and Joan Allison needed a love song for the lovers in their unproduced play, *Everybody Comes to Rick's*, Burnett remembered "As Time Goes By," a song he had liked as a Cornell undergraduate during the early thirties. It survived the play's adaptation into *Casablanca* even though Max Steiner, the composer of the movie's score, wanted to replace it. However, once the producer Hal Wallis realized that he would have to reshoot scenes with Ingrid Bergman and would have to have a wig made for her because she had cropped her hair for her part in her next movie, *For Whom the Bell Tolls*, he withdrew the offer. "As Time Goes By" survived because Bergman got a haircut.[34]

The song itself teaches a reassuring lesson on the abiding power of love. Remembering that a kiss and a sigh can outlast almost anything was a powerful message in the dark years of the war, especially when movie audiences could view it, first in terms of Rick and Ilsa's love affair and the wartime sacrifices it required, and then as a romantic idealization of their own circumstances (Herman Hupfeld, "As Time Goes By," 1931). Within the movie and for its audiences, "As Time Goes By" became another example of the merging of the patriotic and the personal.

This sense that Americans were all in it together was deeper than living with rationing or planting a victory garden. The women who took jobs in factories and on farms and, in the process, changed America's sense of what women could accomplish, sat home alone at night, listening to love songs that reaffirmed the emotions of traditional womanhood. Wartime song lyrics spoke for wives, lovers, and sweethearts in language that was personal and intimate. They possessed an impassioned confessional streak that gave them the feeling of conviction, something to be whispered only to a beloved, but they also gave public expression to women's most private longings. Yet despite their broad appeal, each song was different. The women who spoke in "I Don't Want to Walk Without You" and "I'll Walk Alone" felt the same loneliness, but they were not the same people; each saw the world through her own eyes, as an extension of her own personality and character. But the lyrics also spoke for many others who responded to what was true in these songs by buying recordings in large numbers and listening to the songs over and over again. In recorded performances, they heard themselves portrayed hyperbolically yet still truly in the heightened lyric of a love song.

During World War II, song lyrics were usually devoted to the preciousness of the speaker's emotions and were much less interested in the fads and fancies of the passing scene. Although they were only infrequently about the war, the war was everywhere within them. Loneliness and longing were their defining emotions. Again and again, they expressed what everyone felt as they endured parting and separation, and held onto the promise of return though with an underlying sense of dread. Although Ted Koehler's lyric to "Sweet Dreams, Sweetheart" begins reassuringly with a reference to tomorrow, it treats parting as if it will last much longer than a single night. Dread rises despite the attempts at comfort and reassurance. Intensifying these emotions was the song's initial appearance in the movie *Hollywood Canteen*, in which servicemen find a respite, and perhaps true love, before they leave for combat. When Kitty Carlisle sings it in a suddenly hushed canteen, the movie takes on a tone of sadness and an implied recognition of what is most precious (M. K. Jerome and Ted Koehler, "Sweet Dreams, Sweetheart," *Hollywood Canteen*, 1944).

The song's lyric is also representative in its mingling of dreams and prayers, or in this case dreams and angels. In such a world, where lives change mainly from drudgery to loneliness and back, songs about dreaming struck a responsive chord in their audience and often evolved into prayers. They are among the defining references in the ballads of the time. Dreaming is the imagination at work, an image of hope. Prayer is a reassuring acknowledgment of the reality of danger and fear. Together they help the women who speak in these lyrics get through another night, and then another night after that, as they find temporary respite from the anxieties of the present. These songs began to appear as early as 1940, as if to anticipate what Americans would face, among them "(There'll Be Blue Birds Over) The White Cliffs of Dover" (Walter Kent and Nat Burton, 1941) and "The Last Time I Saw Paris" (Jerome Kern and Oscar Hammerstein II, 1940). Both songs look back nostalgically to prepare the way to the future; both also prefer to dream of a better tomorrow.[35] Yet praying in a lyric is the most a woman could do to ensure the safety of the man she loves, although sometimes songs about prayers focus more broadly than on one woman and the one man she fears for. The prayers become communal, something everyone can do to bring all "our loved ones safely through." One particular song calls on everyone to "say a prayer for the boys over there" (Jimmy McHugh and Herb Magidson, "Say a Prayer for the Boys Over There," 1943), its final words a reminder that the troops are away to fight in a great but perilous cause.

Lyrics portrayed both women and men who dream, women at home and men in the barracks. Despite its abstraction, the allusion is charged and immediate. Soldiers who dream in these songs never pray for their own safety; that was something one expected women to do. After a day of hard duty, one soldier looks forward to sleeping so he can dream, and, through dreaming, be with his beloved. When he puts her picture beneath his pillow, the sexual implication is clear: she will be with him all night long. He will dream until reveille wakes him for another wearying day, but first he hopes that she, too, will dream of him (Irving Berlin, "I'm Getting Tired So I Can Sleep," *This Is the Army*, 1942). No matter how far apart they are, lovers in songs have dreams in common. They believe that when one of them dreams, the other does as well; parallel experience binds them together.

"I'll Walk Alone" is a much more important example of a song that links dreams and angels than "Sweet Dreams, Sweetheart" or "I'm Getting Tired So I Can Sleep." A woman who chooses to walk alone explains that she dreams as a way to remember their lovemaking on the night they parted. The dream brings him close to her, but she also affirms her closeness to him in her prayers for his safety. Now joined through dreaming, prayer, and the remembrance of lovemaking, they walk alone together (Jule Styne and Sammy Cahn, "I'll Walk Alone," 1944).

Actually, dreaming occurs much more frequently in lyrics than prayer does, perhaps because songs generally avoided religious references and because dreams turned out to be more varied in their implications; they were about anticipation as often as memory. They were also less immediately sentimental. References occurred throughout the war, from Johnny Mercer's 1942 lyric to "Hit the Road to Dreamland" in which "Dreamland" becomes a jive-talking celebration of sex (Harold Arlen and Johnny Mercer, "Hit the Road to Dreamland," 1942) to Mercer's mellow uplift in "Dream," in which the lyric takes the listener from memory to the possibility that the dream might come true because "things never are as bad as they seem" (Johnny Mercer, "Dream," *Star-Spangled Rhythm*, 1943). In 1944, some listeners might have found reassurance in its admonition to accept the fear that comes with memory but also the hopeful insistence that dreaming must continue.

In many songs, the line between dreaming and memory blurs. The woman who speaks in "I've Heard That Song Before" remembers a time when she and her lover were together, but often the memory rises only in dreams, away from the everyday world in which he is absent and she is busy. Accidentally hearing an old song recalls a frequent dream that brings the speaker's absent lover close, especially because the lyric sings about being together forever. Hearing it brings back the memory of the last time she heard it, when they were still together (Jule Styne and Sammy Cahn, "I've Heard That Song Before," *Youth on Parade*, 1942). In "I'm Making Believe," a dream provides relief for the moment. It becomes a helpful pretense of talking, dancing, and "making believe that you're in my arms / Though I know you're so far away" (James V. Monaco and Mack Gordon, "I'm Making Believe," 1944). "My Devotion" goes even farther. The woman dreams of a future that will come true only when her lover returns (Roc Hillman and Johnny Napton, "My Devotion," 1943). The easing of romance and sexual hunger mixes with an awareness that it is all make-believe. It helps even though the lonely woman never escapes her recognition of what is real.

The feelings of the women on the home front and those expressed in the love ballads of the time were virtually identical, even though it was usually impossible to tell if the women in the songs were sweethearts or wives. Lyrics rarely distinguished between them. To be in love and alone was sufficient. Lovers of all ages, married or not, were in the same boat. Lyrics for lovers separated for long periods of time over vast distances possess intensity close to tears and an aura of sexuality that suggests the women are young. At the same time, the great social pressure on single women to marry soldiers before they shipped out reflected the ways in which wartime experience changed women: "People, especially young people, have come to . . . marry now even though the day is inauspicious, to pour whatever they have into one hour or one evening, taking no thought for the morrow except that the morrow may not be there. This [also] means that there has been more illicit love . . . as moments were grasped without benefit of clergy or divorce courts."[36]

These attitudes were reflected in numerous movies and songs, beginning as early as 1942. That year, in the plot-driven movie version of Irving Berlin's all-soldier revue, *This Is the Army*, Sergeant Johnny Jones and his fiancé Eileen Dibble (played by Ronald Reagan and Joan Leslie) quarrel over whether to marry before he ships out or wait until after the war.[37] Johnny is the more sensible, Eileen the more romantic. His attitude reflects the widely held views of parents, clergy, and newspapers and magazines that young lovers ought to be "wary of wartime romance . . . There will be plenty of time for emotion after the War. Real love can wait."[38] Eileen and Johnny are equally adamant, so it appears that they are washed up until, just before the finale, she arrives at the Stage Door with a minister in hand. Johnny's determination dissolves and the clergyman performs the ceremony. Like many young women who actually did marry during those uncertain times, Eileen sought what Ronald Bailey has called "an emotional anchor among the new uncertainties of war."[39]

Even when songs aimed mainly at an audience of young people, some lyrics approved of waiting until the War ended, most notably "When the Lights Go on Again (All Over the World)," which links marriage to the coming of peace and joy: "Then we'll have time for things like wedding rings / And free hearts will sing" (Bennie Benjamin, Eddie Seiler, Sol Marcus, "When the Lights Go on Again [All Over the World]," 1943). Once the tide of war had shifted, the Andrews Sisters revived "I'll Be with You in Apple Blossom Time," a 1920 song by Albert Von Tilzer and Neville Fleeson. Unlike many other songs about returning, this one was not afraid to dream of a happy future, especially since the absent man makes the promise. He tells her that's when they will marry: "I'll be with you in apple blossom time, / I'll be with you to change your name to mine" (Albert Von Tilzer, Neville Fleeson, "I'll Be with You in Apple Blossom Time," 1920). The song is more than a simple promise of return, though; it offers a restoration of their familiar lives made richer by the promise of marriage but only in a world at peace.

For the women remaining behind, popular songs provided that anchor, even in a song that portrayed a soldier's departure. In a number from *This Is the Army*, a soldier, returning to base and perhaps about to sail into combat, leaves a letter behind for his girl. Although Irving Berlin's "I Left My Heart at the Stage Door Canteen" never mentions marriage, the young soldier confirms that he has left his heart with her even though he knows that the emotional attachment puts him at greater risk (Berlin, "I Left My Heart at the Stage Door Canteen," *This Is the Army*, 1942). During that same year, the Mills Brothers introduced the more upbeat, "I Met Her on Monday" by Allie Wrubel and Jack Newman, a song that tossed aside long-held conventions about courting. The exigencies of warfare changed the rules. Boy and girl meet for a casual date on Monday. By Wednesday he has met her parents and by Thursday he has kissed her. Finally, the boy and girl conclude the week by meeting the preacher (Allie Wrubel and Jack Newman, "I Met Her on Monday," 1942). The playing out of the lyric at the end adds an amusing touch of sexuality to the love story. It begins with a question and replies with a hum of pleasure to delay the real answer. Only then does the preacher arrive. Despite the song's light touch, the underlying sense of urgency is obvious. In 1942, it was reasonable to assume that after a weekend of honeymooning, the young man would leave his bride to report for duty on Monday morning.

On Broadway in 1944, tough, sexy Gertrude Niessen sang a comic number that gives all the reasons for getting married without delay (Phil Charig, Dan Shapiro, and Milt Pascal, "I Wanna Get Married," *Follow the Girls*, 1944). It's not about the man; it's about her. The lyricists Dan Shapiro and Milt Pascal had latched onto an idea that began early in the War and never changed. Marriage rates had exploded: "In the first five months after Pearl Harbor, an estimated 1,000 women a day married servicemen"[40] and 1.8 million couples married during 1942, a huge increase over 1941. As one bride put it, "He may come back a cripple. . . . The separation will break you up. . . . You can't tell how you'll change or how he'll change . . . but I married my soldier anyway."[41] Anyone who was single "yearned for someone who was waiting for them or for whom they were waiting."[42] If young men were going to fight and perhaps die, the argument went, they ought to leave home having experienced something precious before they did. One young woman said, "That women married soldiers and sent them overseas happy was hammered at us."[43] The difficulties faced by these young wives and mothers, and the loneliness they felt found expression in popular songs and provided them with some relief. The public nature of a song, the implicit sense of having something in common, suggested on one level or another that they were not entirely alone in their circumstances or their emotions.

Americans were fighting and dying to protect and preserve what they said they believed in. Yet these same soldiers were also perfectly normal young men who were almost certainly going to have sex while they were away from home. The same was true of women on the Home Front, who suddenly found themselves on their own for the duration. Regardless of what Americans told themselves in movies, magazine articles, and songs, it is hard to believe that tens of millions of them remained celibate for four long years. Women in the work place met men, men in the military met women, and America's assumptions about monogamy changed, in practice if not belief.[44] As one young woman who came of age soon after Pearl Harbor observed, "There wasn't anything foolproof except abstinence, and who needed that?"[45] The sexual underpinnings of the drive to marry appeared in a number of songs. A young woman asks her fiancé's indulgence for a final night of freedom so she can give the boys goodbye kisses. Elsewhere in the song, she urges him to keep an open mind as she sets out to give the departing soldiers more than they might have hoped for. Lyricist Frank Loesser handles the suggestive one-sided conversation with comedy because the couple is about to begin their life of wedded bliss the following day. It's a sexual joke that, in its own backhanded way, encourages people to marry (Victor Schertzinger and Frank Loesser, "Kiss the Boys Goodbye," *Kiss the Boys Goodbye*, 1941). It's not surprising that Cole Porter also joined in the sexual merrymaking. In the title song from the Broadway musical *Something for the Boys*, the sexually experienced Blossom Hart, played by Ethel Merman, explains her contribution to the war effort in a barely disguised reference to sex. Explaining why she stays out each night until three, she sings:

> 'Cause I'm always doing something for the boys
> Or they're doing something for me.
> (Cole Porter, "Something for the Boys," *Something for the Boys*, 1942)

What comes through in the letters of the time is the intermingling of loneliness and sexual desire. In a nation devoted, at least publicly, to premarital chastity and marital fidelity, most of the love songs appear at first glance to be largely sexless. They speak of dreams and prayers and long nights of waiting. A good deal of sublimation is going on, especially since songs with a sexual subtext rarely go beyond a kiss or an embrace. "I Had the Craziest Dream" is one of the many songs in which separated lovers resort to dreaming. The woman dreams that she finds "your lips close to mine / So I kissed you and you didn't mind it at all." Although that never actually happened before they separated, the woman, alone, dreams of her fondest desires. The sexual longing is intense even though it is limited by the conventions of the time to nothing more than a kiss—and an imagined kiss at that (Harry Warren and Mack Gordon, "I Had the Craziest Dream," *Springtime in the Rockies*, 1942).

Most of the love songs that touched on sex disguise it, but women wrote about it with surprising frankness in their letters and journals. One young wife's letter to her husband strikingly links sexual release with the end of the war: "I want to hear your voice, see your eyes looking deeply into mine, feel your hands searching my body, and be at peace."[46] Another wrote, "Oh God, I think I'll go nuts. I see you everywhere. . . . Every place I go you are always with me in the back of my mind."[47] Romance and sex interweave privately in the letters just as they do publicly in song lyrics.

The most important of these sexual ballads was also one of the most assertive and, in its original performance, one of the most poignant. For forty years, lyricists had alluded to sex in songs that were ostensibly about romantic love. By now, they had mastered the language, the point of view, the tone, and even the use of irony and wit in such a lyric—as Alice Faye's original movie performance of Harry Warren and Leo Robin's "No Love, No Nothin'" makes clear. Faye had signed her first movie contract with Fox Studios in 1934, when Jean Harlow was all the rage. Everybody wanted the trashy Harlow look, and Faye soon had the platinum hair and plucked eyebrows, the satin negligee and the sex-tiger stare. When Twentieth Century Pictures bought the Fox Film Corporation in 1935, Darryl F. Zanuck became vice president of the new 20th Century Fox studio. He softened Faye's appearance by returning her hair to its original color and dressing her less provocatively. *Mirabile dictu,* she went from vamp back to virgin in a blink of Zanuck's eye. He must have been prescient; war was coming, and social values in wartime often turn conservative.

In the 1943 movie *The Gang's All Here,* Faye played a nightclub singer who, at one point, rehearses a new number dressed in a long housecoat and an apron. You can't get much farther from Jean Harlow than that. As she irons a blouse in the small apartment she has taken for herself, she looks frequently at a photograph of a man in uniform. This imagery of domesticity tells the audience all it needs to know: she has married and her husband has gone to war. When she finishes ironing, she removes the apron and begins to ruminate in song. She has been busy, but now, in close-up, she leans back to daydream. At a time when most ballads were unabashedly ardent about love yet never more than indirect about sex, the character's erotic desires and her ability to face them honestly and with humor are striking. The lyric opens with the title line—"No love, no nothin'"—which winks at the audience knowingly, but the second line ("Until my baby comes home") balances the light tone with a sacred promise. It balances her sexual hunger with her pledge. As the lyric unfolds, loneliness becomes desire, fidelity becomes celibacy, and longing returns as sexual longing expressed with deft irony: "I'm getting plenty of sleep" (Harry Warren and Leo Robin, "No Love, No Nothing," *The Gang's All Here,* 1943). The lyric's light touch lets the sexual innuendo go about as far as a forties movie could allow, but its intentions are unmistakable.

Even a ballad as romantic as "You'll Never Know," the Oscar winner for Best Song in 1943, describes a long-lasting love that one of the lovers affirms hyperbolically. This ardent ballad becomes more pointed in the second chorus, when the lover remaining behind acknowledges their separation and adds, "If there is some other way to prove / That I love you, I swear I don't know how" (Harry Warren and Mack Gordon, "You'll Never Know," *Hello, Frisco, Hello,* 1943). There is nothing salacious here, nothing even erotic, only a discreet but heartfelt expression of lovemaking as a sign of love's completeness and a demonstration of faith in its permanence.

Despite the nation's affirmation of fidelity and thus abstinence by men in the service and women on the home front, "the truth was that long separations, the burgeoning independence of women who entered the workforce or traveled as service wives, and the reality of postadolescent men thrown together and segregated from the rest of society created a pent-up sexual desire that was acted on much more often than not."[48] Although love songs specialized in elevated romanticism, their lyrics also found ways to express the reality of sex, as seduction and as something inseparable from true love. Many wartime movies portrayed American GIs on leave as lovable wise guys and wolves who spend their waking hours on furlough trying to get what movies had to portray as the pursuit of a kiss but which then evolved into true love. Songs were actually more open-minded and realistic than movies despite their patina of romance. To be blunt, many of the soldiers on furlough were out to get laid. The boy was less interested in true love than in a one-night stand, but the songs approached women's reactions in several different ways. Because soldiers saw themselves as irresistible sexual pursuers, and because the women were usually smart enough to see through them, love songs that portrayed soldiers often used humor. In one 1942 song, a soldier's attempts at flirtation and seduction lead inevitably to the title line, "I Said No," except eventually her refusal evolves from refusal to perhaps to a resounding yes. In the final line of this double-entendre song, what she gets is a magazine subscription, but nobody is foolish enough to believe the weak punch line (Jule Styne and Frank Loesser, "I Said No," *Sweater Girl*, 1942). In that same year, "You Can't Say No to a Soldier" made the point much more bluntly; it tells a girl to make herself beautiful because she has to submit if she wants him to win the war (Harry Warren and Mack Gordon, "You Can't Say No to a Soldier," *Iceland*, 1942). This song blatantly mixes patriotism and sex, sex and victory. The *Yank Magazine* writer Steve Kluger called it "a training manual for the companion arts of promiscuity and infidelity."[49] Two years later, in 1944, these sentiments had not changed: a soldier who has been away for a long time looks forward to seeing his family and eating Mom's home cooking, but mainly he anticipates "ten days with baby" for "ten days of lovin'" (James V. Monaco and Mack Gordon, "Ten Days with Baby," *Sweet and Low-Down*, 1944).

Implicitly sexual but far more discreet, "In My Arms" is a "gripe song" that describes a young soldier about to sail off to combat. Most wartime songs that complained were about the absurdities of life in the service; this one is more heartfelt than usual. All around him, his buddies are romancing their sweethearts, but he remains an innocent. Even though his cousin knits him a sweater and his sister writes him a letter, they're not what he wants. On his last night in the USA, his comic frustration and desire boil over: "In my arms, in my arms, / Ain't I never gonna have a girl in my arms?" (Ted Grouya and Frank Loesser, "In My Arms," *See Here, Private Hargrove*, 1943). Comic songs were much less common in World War II than in World War I, but the tone of the country had changed enough by 1943 to make room for a few musical jokes about parting and remaining behind, including Arthur Schwartz and Frank Loesser's "They're Either Too Young or Too Old," Rodgers and Hart's "The Girl I Love to Leave Behind," and Allie Wrubel's "Cleanin' My Rifle (And Dreamin' of You)." Perhaps the most pointed of these comic songs, "He's Got a Wave in His Hair (And a WAAC on His Hands)," describes a young fellow pursued by an overly eager young woman. He joins up to escape overseas (Hughie Prince and Sonny Burke, "He's Got a Wave in His Hair [and a WAAC on His Hands]," 1943).

At the same time, soldiers on leave were also capable of finding true love. Despite the comic songs about enlisted men on the loose, more songs were about men's emotional state than about men in combat. They included references to military life—the barracks and the marching—but for the most part, love songs from a soldier's point of view expressed the same emotions as home front ballads. In "I Left My Heart at the Stage Door Canteen," Irving Berlin portrays a soldier who has fallen in love with one of the volunteers he meets at Manhattan's Stage Door Canteen. The song begins with the man's need to leave before he can say goodbye. He feels the distress of parting and understands all too well what it might mean (Irving Berlin, "I Left My Heart at the Stage Door Canteen," *This Is the Army*, 1942). Unresolved endings were important in many wartime love songs because resolution was impossible. Even home front ballads, such as "Don't Get Around Much Anymore" and "I Don't Want to Walk Without You," offered little respite from melancholy. Despite their romantic sentimentality and their frequent insistence on hope, there was something genuine in their refusal to lie to themselves.

Songs presenting the soldier's point of view had the same emotions but different assumptions and experiences. When a woman in a song looks to the future, she plans to welcome her beloved home by throwing her arms around him. Toward the end of the war, those songs began to anticipate marriage. But a soldier and his buddy, talking about their future, anticipate familiarity rather than excitement. One of them recalls in detail such places as the drug store and the schoolhouse before listing such common memories as baseball games, kids gathered around a jukebox, reading a Dick Tracy comic strip, and finally, "the smiling face of someone I'm forever dreaming of" (Bernie Wayne and Ben Raleigh, "The Things That Mean So Much to Me," 1943). The song conjures up an idealized town similar to those in earlier songs about returning. The effect is more sentimental, though, because the wartime songs were composed in the same slow style as love ballads.

The servicemen faced the reality that military service might lead to danger. Like songs that describe women left behind, songs from a serviceman's perspective are also about returning home. They all make the same promise, but the diversity of tone is striking. The first of them to become a hit, "Don't Sit Under the Apple Tree," envisions the moment when an absent soldier returns. For now, he asserts his need for his lover's fidelity in a series of imperatives that include sitting under the apple tree and holding someone else on your knee. Unfortunately, he has reason to be suspicious, but he insists on her propriety as he promises his own in return. The lyric's only allusion to the war is to marching, but it is enough to remind her of what he is doing and to suggest that he will return with a sense of purpose. The lyric never goes beyond the moment of return; in 1942, that was about as far ahead as a lot of songs were willing to look (Sam H. Stept, Lew Brown, and Charles Tobias, "Don't Sit Under the Apple Tree," *Private Buckeroo,* 1942).

The song's good-natured insistence on fidelity was popular music's implicit response to the growing number of "Dear John" letters from women telling absent servicemen that their affair or marriage was over. Although all these songs required loyalty for the duration, each song had its own tone, often recognizable in the title. Many of them spoke from the soldier's point of view, reflecting his emotional needs and linking his state of mind and his safety. "A Soldier Dreams (of You Tonight)" portrays a soldier who dreams about walking with his beloved in a world at peace. It sets out to reassure the women left behind by urging loyalty without ever saying so explicitly (Cliff Friend and Al Dubin, "A Soldier Dreams [Of You Tonight]," 1941). On the other hand, Charlie Tobias, Nat Simon, and Harry Tobias's "Wait for Me, Mary" (1942) is insistent and anxious. It has none of the easy confidence of "Don't Sit Under the Apple Tree" or Al Goodhart and Kay Twomey's amusingly conversational "Better Not Roll Those Blue, Blue Eyes (At Somebody Else)" (1942). At least one other song, "Don't Steal the Sweetheart of a Soldier" (J. Fred Coots and Lew Brown, 1942) addresses itself not to the women, but to the men still in civvies. A cautionary tale of sorts, it calls on these men not to cajole women into breaking their promises. Ironically, it manages to put the burden of responsibility on the women who are willing to be untrue because they are lonesome. The man needs to exercise restraint and responsibility; the implication is that the woman, guided only by her emotions, will not. Other songs prove that outlook wrong as the women speak out to demonstrate their fidelity. The lyric to "I Was Here When You Left Me (I'll Be Here When You Get Back)" is the direct opposite of a "Dear John" letter in its promise of commitment (Sam H. Stept, Sam Coslow, Edie Cherkose, Felix Bernard, and Phyllis Lynne, "I Was Here When You Left Me [I'll Be Here When You Get Back]," 1945). The woman in Vick Knight's "Savin' Myself for Bill" (1942) speaks in a dramatic monologue to someone who has asked her out. She loves to go dancing but she refuses, as the title echoes through the lyric. The alternatives to the "Dear John" letters were those that affirmed a woman's love and loyalty. As in so many songs of separation, lovers put a letter beneath their pillow as an imaginative way of creating intimacy and easing the longing. In "I Dreamt the War Was Over," a woman dreams that her lover's troopship lands at the pier and they race to hold one another (Al Jacobs, 1943). In song after song, letters keep love alive. They become acts of projection and antidotes to loneliness as the lovers imagine talking to one another from afar. They imagine everything from conversation to sex (Nat Simon and Charles Tobias, "I Wish That I Could Hide Inside This Letter," 1943).

~ ~ ~

During the war's first months, "daily recountings of battlefront agonies turned theatergoers away from more serious, innovative efforts. Light, escapist material was not merely acceptable, it was encouraged. . . . The public wanted conventional musicals, and . . . it got them"—at least for a while.[50] *Banjo Eyes*, the first musical to reach New York after the attack on Pearl Harbor, inserted the jingoistic "We Did It Before (And We Can Do It Again)" into a silly show about a salesman who talks to horses in his dreams. The first musical to acknowledge the war in any sustained way was the all-soldier revue *This Is the Army*, Irving Berlin's World War II version of his World War I revue *Yip, Yip, Yaphank.* With an all-soldier cast featuring professional singers, dancers, and comedians who had enlisted or been drafted, it was the first Broadway musical whose score included the kinds of love songs that mattered most during the war: "I Left My Heart at the Stage Door Canteen," "I'm Getting Tired So I Can Sleep," and "With My Head in the Clouds." They were notable for expressing the emotional outlook of the men in the service rather than the women at home. It was no surprise that the points of view were identical; loneliness, longing, and the desire to return dominated at home and in camp.

Like so many Broadway book shows and revues since the Princess shows during and just after World War I, *This Is the Army* had an essentially urban feel even though its setting changed from scene to scene. It was a quick-paced Broadway revue with jitterbugging, rapid-fire wisecracks, and soldiers smart enough to outwit the system but true enough to fight for their country before returning home to their girls. Until *Oklahoma!* opened in March 1943, Broadway musicals, those that had long runs and those that closed in a week, relied on that same kind of jivey citified style—from the limp revue *Let Freedom Ring* in late 1942 to Cole Porter's *Something for the Boys* in early 1943. The Porter show ran for a year and a half, its upbeat mood the result of mixing

Figure 8.2. Bing Crosby, stage, screen, and radio star, sings to Allied troops at the opening of the London stage door canteen in Piccadilly, London, England. August, 1944. National Archives at College Park.

rifle drill with romance and soldiering with sex. Its thin plot took place on a rundown ranch in Texas, but with Ethel Merman playing the lead, it might as well have set down in Times Square. Porter's songs were bright and suggestive ("I'm always doing something for the boys / Or they're doing something for me"), but none was the sort of wartime ballad that was likely to become popular on the radio.[51]

Oklahoma!, the next successful musical after *Something for the Boys*, was Rodgers and Hammerstein's first collaboration. At least two thirds of Rodgers' two dozen earlier musicals with Lorenz Hart took place in and around New York City, but he and Hammerstein set their first show together in the Oklahoma Territory in 1907. *Oklahoma!* also marked the beginning of the decline of the urban sensibility in musical theater. Dating back to the Princess musicals of the mid-1910s and continuing through such shows as the Gershwins' *Oh, Kay!* (1926), Cole Porter's

Figure 8.3. GIs jitterbugging, perhaps at one of the many USO canteens in cities around the country during World War II. Courtesy of Photofest.

The New Yorkers (1930), Irving Berlin's *Face the Music* (1932), Rodgers and Hart's *Pal Joey* (1940), and Kurt Weill and Ira Gershwin's *Lady in the Dark* (1941), Broadway musicals usually spotlighted characters who were urban (and sometimes urbane) and who sang, danced, and fell in love somewhere in or near Manhattan. Berlin's score to *Face the Music* typifies the ways these shows firmly established themselves as city dwellers in such songs as "Lunching at the Automat," "Let's Have Another Cup of Coffee," and "(Castles in Spain) On a Roof in Manhattan." If the characters left the city, as in Porter's *Anything Goes* (1934), they took their sensibility with them. On an ocean liner in the middle of the Atlantic, they sang Porter's sophisticated lyrics to "I Get a Kick Out of You," "Anything Goes," and "You're the Top."

From the beginning of his career, Rodgers drew on a rich inner strain of melody, but his shows with Hart in the twenties and thirties were usually fast-paced and city-centered. They told romantic stories, but their characters represented what musical comedy had to offer—young, vivacious men and women who lived and loved in the big city.

When he wrote with Hammerstein, their first shows were fictionalized idyllic visions of rural America. Both men had been born in New York, attended Columbia University, and spent most of their careers working on Broadway musicals. Without hindsight, it's hard to imagine their tackling an adaptation of Lynn Riggs's regionalist play *Green Grow the Lilacs* as their source for *Oklahoma!* In addition to running for nearly twenty-three hundred performances, it was a different kind of musical, a fully integrated show in which every aspect of the writing and performing contributed to the story and the inner lives of the characters.

Steve Swayne argues that "the serious turn toward rural America" was significantly "a result of the Great Depression and the Dust Bowl" and extended far beyond Broadway musicals.[52] It includes the regionalist art of Thomas Hart Benton and Grant Wood, as well as modern dance and American classical music, including such works as "Rodeo," a ballet scored by Aaron Copland and choreographed by Agnes de Mille (1942), and "Appalachian Spring," an orchestral suite also by Copland that premiered in 1944. But this change also reflected Hammerstein's sense of what sort of material best suited his talents, what his biographer Hugh Fordin described as something that expressed "his own feelings and thoughts about the things in life that mattered most to him." Hammerstein had never thought a great deal of "of the critics and the smart New York theater crowd."[53] He said to his wife a few hours before *Oklahoma!* opened, with a mix of anxiety and self-awareness, "I don't know what to do if they don't like this. I don't know what to do because this is the only kind of show I can write."[54]

The rediscovery of rural America both influenced and reflected changes in how Americans viewed themselves and their nation. At a time when the country was in danger, audiences turned to a mythic escapist view of the American West for reassurance. The historian Frederick Jackson Turner had written that "to the frontier the American intellect owes its striking characteristics . . . that restless, nervous energy; that dominant individualism, working for good and for evil, and withal that buoyancy and exuberance which comes with freedom."[55] In the midst of the war, an idealized, often sunny view of a bucolic past returned Americans to an elemental belief in the future as individual farmers and ranchers worked to transform the West from wilderness to civilization. The cultural critic David Lehman adds that Turner's comment is about domesticity.[56] Sometime in the future, some of these towns would become cities, but for now audiences rediscovered a kind of everyman heroism in an innocent cowboy who defeats evil and marries the girl of his dreams. In a sweet, boisterous, but sometimes dark coming-of-age story, an epic tale that conjures up the settling of the West was itching to emerge. It offered its original audiences nostalgia not for cowboys and outlaws but for building towns.

Oklahoma!'s characters ride the range and farm the open prairie. The dangers for these good people come from an engaging but amoral peddler and a hardened drifter. They are the loners and outsiders, the troublemakers with nothing solid under their feet. They arrive without conscience or purpose beyond bedding the nearest young woman. We never learn where they come from but they put *Oklahoma!*'s Eden-like rural innocence at risk. They represent the glamour and allure of the city, where behavior seems to have no goal beyond gratification. Ali Hakim is an ingratiating seducer, Jud Fry a potential rapist. But despite his likable comic flamboyance, Hakim's smile is as false as Fry's glowering resentment and suppressed rage are real. It's no surprise that the peddler sells Jud the secret blade he intends to use to maim the hero, Curly.

By focusing on a few young men and women who come of age just as the Oklahoma Territory becomes a state, *Oklahoma!* embodies the values of the myth of the garden and the frontier, the struggles to settle a continent, and, in the midst of these great undertakings, the roles of individual men and women sustained by love for one another, who bend their lives to the shaping of a new nation. In the middle of the first act, Curly and Laurey, a cowboy and a farm girl, sing the romantic duet "People Will Say We're in Love." They are too innocent to understand their feelings for one another but intuitively caution one another against acting too hastily. The song lacks the ardor of many World War II ballads, but Curley and Laurey's eventual profession of their love culminates in marriage and suggests what young Americans are capable of in a world at peace.

At the same time, the city lurks in the background, symbolically in the presence of Ali Hakim and Judd, but also in the return of Will Parker. He and Ado Annie—the comic lovers—introduce a note of good-spirited but sanitized sex in act 1. Will tells the story of his recent adventures in Kansas City, where he encountered a voluptuous woman who becomes a source of boisterous humor among Will and his cowboy friends. Eventually, he and Ado Annie have a few minutes alone together. She admits that when she sits on a velveteen settee with a young man she remembers the Golden Rule and gives back the kisses that he's just given her. She is as naive a sexually predatory female as one could imagine. Sex played for comedy eventually draws her and Will together.

Once Curly wins Laurey and disposes of the dangerous Jud Fry, *Oklahoma!* closes on an image of a serene America to which men at war were yearning to return. The score's final song—the title song—celebrates Oklahoma's change from territory to state as the nation moves inexorably west. It is also an essential part of Curly and Laurey's wedding day as they begin new lives together, a harmonious joining of the cowman and the farmer. Ultimately, though, the song is the show's affirming anthem to America (Richard Rodgers and Oscar Hammerstein II, "Oklahoma!" *Oklahoma!*, 1943). Despite the fearfulness of everyday life on the home front, Rodgers and Hammerstein discerned a new expansive optimism in the American people. Curly and Laurey may have lived forty years earlier than their audiences, but ultimately they were us. Americans were acquiring historical memory even though a nostalgic gauze softened its harshest colors.

After the dark suspicions about American democracy during the 1930s, *Oklahoma!* affirmed the nation's belief in its own elemental optimism in the midst of its most trying war. The show recognized the violence just beneath the surface of American life, but in the end it affirmed the value of true love triumphant in a settled town where decent people could build their lives. At the very least, it expressed a new and deepening sense of what America was supposed to mean. Its melodious score and buoyant dancing thrilled audiences, and its characters' affirmation of their lives in an idealized American West opened those same audiences to a deeper kind of delight. During a war for survival, *Oklahoma!* contributed to America's recognition that it possessed a history and culture worth examining, preserving, and passing on. The nation embraced its own art and literature and began to view them with a new seriousness and depth.

The diversity of musicals in the years after World War II included shows derived in spirit from the rural escapism of *Oklahoma!*—Rodgers and Hammerstein's *Carousel* (1945) as well as Irving Berlin's *Annie Get Your Gun* (1946), Burton Lane and E. Y. Harburg's *Finian's Rainbow* (1947), and Frederick Loewe and Alan Jay Lerner's *Paint Your Wagon* (1953). Despite these successful shows, the Broadway musical's natural urbanity also reasserted itself over the next decade or so in a strikingly varied group of musicals, among them *Kiss Me Kate* (1948), *Guys and Dolls* (1950), *The Pajama Game* (1954), and *West Side Story* (1957).

I want to write about Rodgers and Hammerstein's shows just enough to show that—as in *Oklahoma!*—the conflicts between outsiders and insiders are central to each of them, and that, regardless of location and situation, the outsiders express attitudes and behave in ways we often associate with cities. In these rural musicals, hero and heroine alike prefer the homey virtues of the small town to the more sophisticated delights (and dangers) of the city.

A number of the shows mix unlikely elements together, including urban and rural perspectives. The plot of *Allegro* (1947) combines small-town and big-city life in its tale of a young man from a country town who practices medicine in an urban hospital before disillusionment drives him back home.

Soon Rodgers and Hammerstein's shows adopted more exotic elements as alternatives to familiar city or country life. The first of them was *South Pacific* (1949), adapted from two short stories by James Michener. The plot contrasts the navy nurse Nellie Forbush, a small-town girl from Kansas, and Emile de Becque, the urbane planter she falls in love with. It also contrasts life on a navy base during World War II with de Becque's plantation, and forces Nellie to face her own (and America's) attitudes toward race when she meets de Becque's mixed-race children. Similarly, Lieutenant Cable, a navy officer, falls in love with Liat, a native girl, but realizes he cannot have a wife of a different race in the United States. Romantic exoticism comes with a high price. The irony in *South Pacific* lies in the imposition of American attitudes on an island that the navy will occupy only until the war ends. The Americans correspond to arrivals from a city who disrupt the patterns of pristine rural life. The navy officers have their own rules and regulations, as do the sexually restless and irreverent sailors who bring a different kind of urban element to the island.

Two years later, in 1951, Rodgers and Hammerstein adapted *The King and I* from Margaret Landon's novel about Anna Leonowens, a respectable but determined British widow and the governess to the children of King Mongkut of Siam during the 1860s. The story is essentially true (if not always accurate) because Landon adapted her novel from Leonowens's memoirs. As with the presence of the Americans in *South Pacific*, Anna and the British diplomats who attend the king late in the play are the outsiders. Much of the play's comedy and dramatic intensity lie in the struggles of the king and Anna to understand

and accommodate one another as Mongkut tries to balance traditional monarchy with the coming of modernity.

After these two shows, Rodgers and Hammerstein took a step back in *Flower Drum Song* (1958). The place and time are San Francisco in the present. Its young people are Chinese, but they are also recognizable Americans. The heart of their conflict appears in the young Chinese man who feels torn between his father's traditional values and the appeal of modern American city life.

The Sound of Music (1959), Rodgers and Hammerstein's final musical, is set in Salzburg, Austria. Nobody American or even British ever appears. The plot combines a conventional domestic drama about a widower (Captain Georg von Trapp), his seven children, and their youthful governess (Maria) with an equally conventional Cinderella romance between Georg and Maria. One song, dropped from the movie, cuts into the theater version's sentimentality. Faced with the imminent arrival of the Nazis, von Trapp and his friends discuss their best course of action. They counsel him to set aside his political convictions and adjust to the new reality. In "No Way to Stop It," they argue that von Trapp should make the invaders think he is on their side. However, von Trapp is determined to flee with his family. Once again, the coming of outsiders disrupts the idyllic lives of those who call this place their home.

Unlike such wartime Christmas songs as "White Christmas" and "Have Yourself a Merry Little Christmas," which set out to express the same attitudes as the love ballads of the time, many of the songs in movie musicals were interpolations that had been popular a half century earlier. The stories were set in the late nineteenth and early twentieth centuries, and the revived songs helped to cast a golden glow over a portrait of a less troubled America. A few of these escapist "period musicals" look back to an earlier war, among them *Yankee Doodle Dandy*, with a performance of "You're a Grand Old Flag" by James Cagney in a Civil War uniform, and sequences set during World War I in *This Is the Army* and *For Me and My Gal.* More often, though, they were backstagers set in a period whose songs, styles, and standards were still familiar to many Americans. The first of them actually preceded the war and then continued for several years after it ended, from *Alexander's*

Ragtime Band (1938) to *Mother Wore Tights* (1947) and *In the Good Old Summertime* (1949). 20th Century Fox made more of them than any other studio by reapplying a few familiar formulas for its three leading ladies, Alice Faye, Betty Grable, and June Haver. Many of them were set in show business and in cities: everything from turn-of-the-century dance halls and vaudeville houses to elegant nightclubs and Broadway theaters. Their scores typically combined familiar old songs like "Cuddle Up a Little Closer" (1908), "On Moonlight Bay" (1912), and "When You Wore a Tulip" (1914) with new ballads by songwriters under contract to the studio. Among the songs written for these movies were Harry Warren and Mack Gordon's "You'll Never Know" and "My Heart Tells Me," and James Monaco and Gordon's "I Can't Begin to Tell You," the kind of ardent ballads that provided reassurance for those on the home front.

That reassurance took a somewhat different form in one of the most important of the period musicals, MGM's *Meet Me in St. Louis*, based on a series of stories by Sally Benson in the *New Yorker*. The adaptation revived only two songs, the title number from 1904 and "Under the Bamboo Tree," a 1902 cakewalk by the African American songwriters Bob Cole, James Weldon Johnson, and J. Rosamond Johnson. The rest of the score, by Hugh Martin and Ralph Blane, successfully evokes both character and situation. The movie is a classic example of a sentimental domestic drama, but its setting is a city rather than a small town. One of its most successful numbers features a ride on a newfangled contraption, a trolley car. "The Trolley Song" became a number-one hit on *Your Hit Parade* and was nominated for an Academy Award for best song.[57] The Smith family—father and mother, grandfather, four daughters and a son, and the longtime live-in cook and maid played with irresistible grumpiness by Marjorie Main—faces a crisis. Because Father's promotion requires him to move the family to New York City, everyone will miss the opening of the St. Louis World's Fair. Thanks to Mother's sympathetic good sense, Father's essential decency, and Grandfather's good-natured meddling, the crisis dissolves and the family remains in St. Louis. In the end, they visit the fair together. The heroine, Esther, continues to live at 5135 Kensington Avenue, next door to the young man she has fallen in love with. The movie and its songs have nothing to do specifically with wartime, but the deepest emotions arise from the sense of warm family life, the impending separation of Esther and her beau ("The Boy Next Door"), and the heartbreak of Tootie, the youngest sister, at the thought of leaving the only home she has ever known. The evocation of emotions associated with the home front is strong and convincing.

The success of *Meet Me in St. Louis* led to a series of movie musicals that emphasized family life in earlier times—the Rogers family of Philadelphia in *Centennial Summer* (1946), with songs by Jerome Kern and Oscar Hammerstein II; the Millers of Danville, Connecticut, in *Summer Holiday* (1948), with songs by Harry Warren and Ralph Blane; and the Winfields of Indiana in both *On Moonlight Bay* (1951) and *By the Light of the Silvery Moon* (1953), with revived songs from the early twentieth century. Even though these domestic period musicals extended beyond the war, they and the Americana musicals that followed *Oklahoma!* on Broadway during these same years gave the public an idealized image of what America had fought for—a view of families that combined comic spats with deep affection and affirmed conventional morality spiked with harmless idiosyncrasy. The songs emphasized the decency of these people and the importance of the love story that allowed the young members of the family to come of age.

In 1945, two years after *Oklahoma!* opened on Broadway, Richard Rodgers and Oscar Hammerstein II wrote their only Hollywood score together for *State Fair.* Set in the present day, it extends the point of view of the domestic period musicals of the midforties and early fifties. Even though 20th Century Fox released it just two weeks after V-J Day, the movie makes no mention of the war. There's not a uniform in sight. Instead, the movie tells the story of Melissa and Abel Frake, a middle-aged farm couple, and their two grown children, Margy and Wayne, all of whom spend three nights at the Iowa State Fair. Both parents compete for blue ribbons, she for her mincemeat and pickles and he for his prize boar, Blue Boy. The naive but restless Margy falls for a slick newspaperman who's covering the fair, and Wayne is smitten by a beautiful but married band singer before returning to the hometown girl he's been in love with since they were kids.

For this rural family from the heartland, the fair plays the role of the city and its temptations. Although the reporter and the singer are decent enough despite his love-'em-and-leave-'em attitude and her deceptiveness, the fair seduces the Frake offspring with its dazzling lights, late nights, and sexually tinged romance. The story (and its happy ending) plays out mainly at the fairgrounds, but the camera also dwells lovingly on the Frakes's farm, an image of American peace and plenty. The movie's vision of an idealized rural America follows in the footsteps of *Oklahoma!*, where worldly but unreliable outsiders embody transience and temptation, but young men and women find lasting happiness on farms and ranches. Although Wayne falls for a woman from the city, he identifies himself throughout the movie as a farmer, and, although Margy will move to Chicago to marry the formerly jaded reporter, her essential goodness has changed his heart.

Other World War II movie musicals focused on men in uniform and recognized that the country was at war despite their lighthearted tone—*The Fleet's In*, *Thank Your Lucky Stars*, and *The Gang's All Here*, among others. The titles of their most important songs reflect their awareness—Victor Schertzinger and Johnny Mercer's "I Remember You," Arthur Schwartz and Frank Loesser's "They're Either Too Young or Too Old," and Harry Warren and Leo Robin's "No Love, No Nothin.'" Other musicals set in the present—including *Moon over Miami*, *Sun Valley Serenade*, *Springtime in the Rockies*, *Billy Rose's Diamond Horseshoe*, and *Cover Girl*—could have been shot just as easily in the 1930s or 1950s; they act as if the war didn't exist. Such important composers and lyricists as Jerome Kern, Harold Arlen, Harry Warren, Johnny Mercer, Ira Gershwin, Mack Gordon, and Leo Robin wrote the songs for these movies, but most were conventional romantic ballads or swing tunes. The movies existed in the kind of willfully irrelevant bubble that musicals have always known how to create. Nevertheless, the occasional song was an exception, especially Warren and Gordon's "I Had the Craziest Dream" and "I Wish I Knew."

Several of these movies had a very odd premise. In 1940–42, a handful of Hollywood musicals sent its heroes and heroines to Latin America on brightly lit ocean liners as if the world were not at war and no German U-boats prowled the South Atlantic. Once they arrived, they toured such cities as Rio de Janeiro and Buenos Aires during the day, dressed up and went dancing in nightclubs at night, and eventually fell in love. Alice Faye, Betty Grable, John Payne, Don Ameche, and even a post–Rogers Fred Astaire were among those who took the improbable cruises in such movies as *Down Argentine Way*, *That Night in Rio*, *Weekend in Havana*, and *You Were Never Lovelier*. Many of their songs used the Latin rhythms so popular at the time, and whenever 20th Century Fox produced the movie, it included elaborate production numbers conjured up by Busby Berkeley for Carmen Miranda. The irrelevance of the plots extended to the songs. Jerome Kern and Dorothy Fields's "Remind Me" and Kern and Johnny Mercer's "Dearly Beloved" and "I'm Old Fashioned" are fine songs but lack the intense emotionalism of typical World War II ballads.

~ ~ ~

The idea of coming home recurs throughout this chapter; even when a song only implies it, it provides the emotional subtext for many of the love ballads. During the early years of the century, songs about returning expressed the outlook of those who had gone away, but thirty-five years later, they spoke for those left behind. No matter what else a song might be about, the idea of returning was its musical endgame—a sign of peace for the nation and love and safety for the men who fought and the women who waited. One song unintentionally became a kind of emotional fulcrum, partly because it was such a good song and partly because Frank Loesser wrote it in 1943, late enough in the war for people to begin to accept the possibility of good news—not yet, but coming before too long. "Spring Will Be a Little Late This Year" is a melancholy ballad that anticipates change; emotionally, it is of two minds. Despite the striking image of delaying the arrival of spring, Loesser quickly returns it to human scale: spring will be only "a little late" even though the world is lonely and "winter continues cold." In the interim, there will be time for fear to ease and, implicitly, a heart to begin to heal. The unidentified woman in the song no longer needs to "cling to this fear" because spring will come as will the implied peace and return (Frank Loesser, "Spring Will Be a Little Late This Year," 1943).

Although by late 1944, everyone understood that the war would be coming to an end before too much longer, the emotions of loneliness, longing, and isolation persisted in songs until the Germans and Japanese finally surrendered; then, when Americans no longer needed them, they disappeared almost immediately. Yet months before V-E Day and V-J Day, hopeful songs that imagined the return increased in frequency. Mann Curtis and Vic Mizzy's "My Dreams Are Getting Better All the Time" from 1945 feels as if a young woman can finally let herself be happy; the song has no sense of dread. A man and woman meet in her dreams and, in the space of a few nights and a few more dreams, go from strangers to lovers. Its confident, almost carefree quality helped to make Doris Day's recording the country's number-one hit for six weeks. In songs like these, mundane tasks take on a new urgency as the moment of return approaches—counting the days and watching the clock in "Counting the Days" and listening for the locomotive in the wistful "Waitin' for the Train to Come In," set to the rhythm of a moving train (Hy Zaret and Alex Kramer, "Counting the

Days," 1945; Sunny Skylar and Martin Block, "Waitin' for the Train to Come In," 1945).

Following "My Dreams Are Getting Better All the Time," another recording by Doris Day and the Les Brown Orchestra occupied the number-one position for the next nine weeks. It was "Sentimental Journey," the most important and successful of the songs that focused on imminent return—another song set to the rhythm of a railroad train, but this time from a man's perspective. Even though the fighting is over, a soldier still has a long journey home. His comments are eager and heartfelt: "Like a child in wild anticipation, / Long to hear that 'All aboard'" (Bud Green, Les Brown, and Ben Homer, "Sentimental Journey," 1945). Of all these hopeful songs from the last years of the war, none was more intense or more beautiful than Jerome Kern and Ira Gershwin's hushed moment of recognition, "Long Ago and Far Away." The song expresses a rare sense of wonder in the return of a lover. (Jerome Kern and Ira Gershwin, "Long Ago [And Far Away]," *Cover Girl*, 1944).

In his 1920 run for the presidency, Warren G. Harding had used the slogan "Return to Normalcy," but for the next ten years, the country was anything but normal by the standards of the previous decades. Personal and social values changed dramatically, especially how women dressed and behaved in public, and how everybody cavorted in private. It would have made much more sense to apply Harding's slogan to the years after World War II. Nobody wrote a song like "How Ya' Gonna Keep 'Em Down on the Farm" in 1945. People wanted to get back home and settle down. In 1943, Bing Crosby crooned a song that seems in retrospect as if it should have written two years later. Without ever mentioning the war, the character in the song looks forward to the day when he can stay put and never leave home again (Gordon Jenkins, "San Fernando Valley," 1943).

As difficult as the adjustment to peacetime was, men and women alike wanted to get settled as quickly as they could, not by flouting convention and shocking their elders as their parents had done in the 1920s, but by getting a job or a college education thanks to the new GI Bill, and getting married, starting a family, and buying a car and a first house. Now that the war was over, a song lyric could reclaim the everyday pleasures that a boy and girl could count on in this new world. Rather than dining on pheasant, "just serve me tomatoes / And mashed potatoes" as typical of the simple life (Harry Ruby and Bert Kalmar, "Give Me the Simple Life," 1947). In 1941, American workers built 185,000 houses, but in 1946, the number more than tripled.[58] Because automobile manufacturers produced no new cars during the war, they needed time to adapt to full peacetime production. Their factories produced fewer cars in 1945 than they had in 1909, before the advent of the production line, and dealers sold fewer than seventy thousand, but in 1946, the number reached an incredible 2.1 million and by 1949 rose to 5.1 million.[59] There were few songs about going driving right after the war, but songwriters and music publishers adapted to peacetime even more rapidly than industry did. No song expressed America's new attitudes more winningly than "Oh, What It Seemed to Be," a song about promises kept and dreams come true, the joy of the familiar taken for granted once more. The lyric provides a list of things that young people would remember and then experience anew but with keener delight. Its conclusion with the wedding the lovers have waited for is the perfect final step for new and better times (Bennie Benjamin, George Davis Weiss, and Frankie Carle, "Oh, What It Seemed to Be," 1945).

Postwar songs were different because they had to express the nation's changed emotional outlook. Women found the reassurance they were seeking in a ballad introduced by Dick Haymes: "The more I see you, / The more I want you" (Harry Warren and Mack Gordon, "The More I See You," *Billy Rose's Diamond Horseshoe*, 1945).

For nine weeks, from mid-September until mid-November of 1945, almost immediately after the war's end, the most popular song in the country embraced the idea of an endless future for love. It was a return to the breathless hyperbole and syrupy ardor that had long been one of the staples of ballad writing, to the kind of claim that is possible only when lovers have time to imagine what life might be like, and when dreams come and go without fear to darken them. The title's catchphrase—"Till the End of Time"—recurs in one form or another throughout the lyric to confirm the speaker's ever-deepening love and commitment (Buddy Kaye and Ted Mossman, "Till the End of Time," 1945). It was exactly what the women had been waiting to hear, but it wasn't the whole story. Songs that welcomed the men home also saved a little room for sex. Although "You Can't Say No to a Soldier" from 1942 had instructed women to help out by providing sexual favors, by now the women had figured it out for themselves, especially in a happy, lively song like "I'm Gonna Love That Guy (Like He's Never Been Loved Before)" (Frances Ash, 1945). Awaiting her lover's return, a woman reviews the promises she's made in her imagination. At the top of the list is her determination to demonstrate that she adores him. Even more than the pleasures of sex, it means to her that they'll be able to start their lives over and will never part again. An underlying theme of domesticity runs through a number of these songs. Occasionally the lyric portrays a woman who is neither a fiancé nor a newlywed, but implicitly a wife looking forward to the romance and sex that come with settling down. Beginning with the song's title, she muses with almost kittenish contentment because "It's So Nice to Have a Man Around the House" (Harold Spina and Jack Elliott, "It's So Nice to Have a Man Around the House," 1950).

It is hard to overstate the importance of home in the songs of the midforties. Initially a place for an absent soldier or sailor to return to, it soon became something for a newly married couple to aspire to. Once the boys started returning, songs found a new interest in love that led immediately to marriage. If you had agreed to wait until the war's end, the time had finally come. In a state of elation, a young woman plans to start driving again because gas rationing will be coming to an end. More important, she plans to call the preacher because, as the title puts it, "My Guy's Come Back" (Mel Powell and Ray McKinley, "My Guy's Come Back," 1945). At the same time, women on their own for three years had developed a healthy independence that they were often reluctant to surrender. Just as the country was of two minds, so were the songs. They mixed the romantic and the practical: marriage was a dream of desire fulfilled, so let's get to it. But for the men who had been away, ironically, marriage was pure romance, a dream of the familiar and the safe. The person who dreams of being together in "Till the End of Time" is probably a man; the one who can't wait to have sex in "I'm Gonna Love That Guy" is definitely a woman.

The difference between practicality and romance also shows up in several songs from Broadway musicals. In *On the Town* (1944), a secondary comic plot concerns a shy sailor and his pursuit by an assertive woman who is spending the duration working as a taxi driver. Because so few men are around and she takes a shine to him, she lets the sailor know that she's the best cab driver in town, a great cook, and an even greater lover. Every time he wants to see the sights, she counters, "Come up to my place." The point of the song, especially in conjunction with another number from Leonard Bernstein, Betty Comden, and Adolph Green's score, "I Can Cook, Too," is that the woman is competent, strong, independent—and feminine.

Another woman's song, "Legalize My Name," from Harold Arlen and Johnny Mercer's score to *St. Louis Woman*, tempers romance with earthy good humor and surprising assertiveness. Even though the lyric never talks about the years of waiting, anyone hearing it in the spring of 1946 would have understood the larger context. With no fuss or nonsense, she lets him know that billing and cooing will not do: "If you prize me" she insists, "notarize me" (Harold Arlen and Johnny Mercer, "Legalize My Name," *St. Louis Woman,* 1946).

Two and a half months later, Irving Berlin's *Annie Get Your Gun* also opened on Broadway. Both shows had superb scores, although only Berlin's show was a hit. *St. Louis Woman* was one of the dozens, perhaps hundreds, of Broadway flops with great scores undermined by weak books and backstage tensions. It ran for 113 performances, whereas *Annie Get Your Gun*'s original production lasted for 1,147. The main characters, Annie Oakley and Frank Butler, both crack shots in Buffalo Bill's Wild West Show, squabble while they are falling in love. Frank explains to the rough-and-tumble Annie that he wants a different kind of girl. Butler's charmingly old-fashioned song of explanation touched audiences all over the country and was recorded successfully by Frank Sinatra. Butler wants to marry not a woman, but a "girl" whose dominant characteristic is her innocence. He is a nineteenth-century man selecting a woman from his own time, but the purity of his desire resonated with listeners who were content with a postwar image of simplicity and serenity. In the lyric to Berlin's pretty waltz, he promises fidelity as they sit together—an image of domestic bliss but perhaps also of implied sexuality that will lead eventually to the need for a nursery (Irving Berlin, "The Girl That I Marry," *Annie Get Your Gun,* 1946). Young men and women had had enough adventure for a while. They wanted lives without upheaval. It didn't turn out that way, but it was what they wanted as the boys came home.

AFTERWORD

The docking of HMS *Queen Mary* in New York Harbor on June 20, 1945, was a cause for celebration. The fabled ocean liner was bringing home over fourteen thousand American soldiers from the war in Europe.[1] Before long, Times Square, where Broadway and Forty-Second Street crossed, would once again blaze with light. It was a sign of yet another transformation of the city and the nation that would require massive adjustments to peacetime life for both the returning veterans and the women they had left behind. Over the next decade, they would confront the coming of the nuclear age and the Cold War and their effects on politics and individual liberty; the rise of affluence along with the spread of higher education and the emergence of consumerism; and on a much different level of concern, the slow decline and eventual end of the Great American Songbook.

Figure A.1. HMS Queen Mary returning GIs to New York at the end of World War II. Courtesy of Photofest.

The songwriters who had given new voice to the "varied carols" of American life, were beginning to age. Lorenz Hart, consumed by alcohol and his own inner demons, died in 1943; Jerome Kern would be gone before the end of 1945. Within a decade, those who remained would eventually begin to lose, however slowly, their dominance over the music business and the nation's tastes. What they represented continued for a while, though, in music as well as in the patterns of daily life. The best Broadway and Hollywood musicals were blessed with extraordinary scores during the 1950s and into the early 1960s.[2] At the same time, rock and roll swept away the increasingly banal writing, bloated arrangements, and second-rate crooning that characterized too much postwar popular music. Many of the people who went to see such hits as *South Pacific, The King and* I, and *My Fair Lady* on Broadway in the late forties and the fifties also bought recordings on the new long-playing discs by the likes of Joni James and Guy Mitchell, even though their children preferred Frankie Avalon and Pat Boone. Many of the new songwriters and singers were young and unsophisticated, barely past adolescence themselves. How else to explain such titles as "Dungaree Doll," "Blue Suede Shoes," and "Teen Age Prayer"? And then, in the aftershock of their successful recording of "I Want to Hold Your Hand," The Beatles flew to New York to appear on Ed Sullivan's TV show on February 9, 1964. Seventy-three million viewers watched them, according to the Nielsen rating service, "the largest audience that had ever been recorded for an American television program."[3]

As for the larger demands of life at home as the war came to a close, "an immigrant ship occasionally docked on the West Side, and passersby might glimpse its passengers from Europe, wide-eyed, shabby-clothed and emaciated from Europe, stumbling through the customs formalities in the echoing arrivals shed: out of the sea like so many before them, bewildered and tongue-tied, but ready to accept, as they stepped with their bags and blankets into the street outside, the island's limitless chance and bounty."[4] And didn't the songwriters of the American Songbook, mostly men in their fifties and sixties now, know about that. They were the musical chameleons from an earlier generation of "rags." They had mastered black syncopation—hot, sexy, loose, and low-down—and made it America's. Just as they had learned it from ragtime, the blues, and jazz, so these new Americans would learn it in turn, except it would soon be a different music.

No matter. The Songbook wasn't about to exit without raising a rumpus. The "platinum folderol" that made Broadway gleam during the postwar years shone especially brightly in the scores of new Broadway musicals. Irving Berlin, along with Richard Rodgers and Oscar Hammerstein II, continued to write hit shows. New composers and lyricists also came into their own: Frederick Loewe and Alan Jay Lerner with *Brigadoon* (1947); Frank Loesser with *Where's Charley?* (1948) and then *Guys and Dolls* (1950); and Leonard Bernstein, Betty Comden, and Adolph Green with *On the Town* (1944) and then *Wonderful Town* (1953). *Brigadoon* was a fantasy set in a mythical town in Scotland, and *Where's Charley?* was set at Oxford University in 1892, but the rest of these shows, like so many of their predecessors, called New York City home.

"Yiddish had become the unofficial language of Broadway," as early as the 1920s, according to the social critic Jerome Charyn. As Jewish songwriters dominated Tin Pan Alley and Broadway, its expressions and idioms sprinkled the conversations of songwriters and gangsters alike, especially in a place like Lindy's after midnight. To his *landsmen,* Irving Berlin was Izzy, but there was no trace of Yiddish in his love songs. Only after World War II did Jewish songwriters—a new generation who had missed the struggles on the Lower East Side—feel settled and secure enough to write shows such as *Fiorello!* and *Fiddler on the Roof.* Frank Loesser was born a generation after Irving Berlin. He grew up in a cultivated family, the son of a piano teacher who fled Prussia to escape military service. Yet at the age of forty, he wrote "Sue Me," a musical plaint for the small time gambler Nathan Detroit in *Guys and Dolls.* It was, writes Charyn, "nothing but New York Yiddish patois rendered in perfect conversational English."[5] "Give a holler and sue me" is not the sort of thing an unreliable lover, vintage 1950, was likely to say (or sing) in Peoria. Even the bagel had not yet become ubiquitous.

In that decade after the war, Hollywood musicals turned to original stories built around the songbooks of such important songwriters as Irving Berlin (*Easter Parade,* 1948), Nacio Herb Brown and Arthur Freed (*Singin' in the Rain,* 1952), and Arthur Schwartz and Howard Dietz (*The Band Wagon,* 1953), as well as what *Time* magazine called "biopix" of Richard Rodgers and Lorenz Hart (*Words and Music,* 1948), Harry Ruby and Bert Kalmar (*Three Little Words,* 1950), and George Gershwin (*Rhapsody in Blue,* 1945).

Although no one could hold back the onslaught of rock and roll, the songs of the previous fifty years had served Americans so well and with such warmth and wit that America would continue to sing them for many years to come. The best of them have become part of our collective musical memory. What is remarkable is that so much of what we believed, celebrated, embraced, and endured took form as the irresistible urban hubbub of our popular songs. Regardless of the latest style or the most insistent craze, we could not imagine ourselves or our nation without remembering and singing the city songs that gave voice to America and its people for half a century.

NOTES

Notes to the Reader

1. Twain, *The Tragedy of Pudd'nhead Wilson*, 85.

Introduction

1. "Fascinatin' Rhythm (WXXI)," 1994, *Peabody: Stories that Matter*, accessed February 6, 2019, http://www.peabodyawards.com/award-profile/fascinatin-rhythm.
2. Author's conversation with Ezra Jack Keats, spring 1981.
3. Noel Coward, *Private Lives: An Intimate Comedy* (New York: Samuel French, Inc., 1930), 18.

Chapter 1

1. E. B. White, "Here Is New York," in *Essays*, 122.
2. Stephen Holden, "Pop View: Irving Berlin's American Landscape," *New York Times*, May 10, 1987, accessed February 6, 2019, http://topics.nytimes.com/top/reference/timestopics/people/b/irving_berlin/index.html.
3. Holden, "Irving Berlin's American Landscape."
4. "Letter from Jerome Kern to Alexander Woollcott," from *The Story of Irving Berlin*, in Sears, *The Irving Berlin Reader*, 83.
5. Rybczynski, *City Life*, 33.
6. Furia and Lasser, *America's Songs*, 17.
7. Doctorow, *Ragtime*, 3–4.
8. "The Lower East Side of New York: Jewish Life in America," Museum of Family History website, accessed February 6, 2019, http://www.museumoffamilyhistory.com/mfh-les.htm.
9. Rybczynski, *City Life*, 155.
10. George Gershwin, "Jazz Is the Voice of the American People," *Theatre Magazine* (June 1926), 528, in *The George Gershwin Reader*, ed. Robert

Wyatt and John Andrew Johnson (New York: Oxford University Press, 2004), 91–94.

11. S. N. Behrman, *People in a Diary*, 256.

12. John Updike, quoted in Jen Carlson, "John Updike on Leaving New York City," *Gothamist*, December 18, 2013. http://gothamist.com/2013/12/18/john_updike_on_leaving_new_york_cit.php.

13. During the 1920s, the "Forty-Second Street Moon" meant the lights of the Theater District.

14. Lasser, "The True Collaborator" in Furia, ed., "The Ira Gershwin Centenary," *Dictionary of Literary Biography*, Yearbook: 1996, 156–58.

15. Benjamin Sears and Bradford Conner, "'Alexander's Ragtime Band' at One Hundred," *Ben & Brad—In the Media*, accessed February 6, 2019, http://www.benandbrad.com/alexander.html.

16. Furia and Patterson, *The Songs of Hollywood*, 18.

17. Rachel Rubin, "Way Down Upon the Hudson River: Tin Pan Alley's New York Triumph," *America's Music*, available on the Lawrence University website, accessed February 6, 2019, http://www2.lawrence.edu/library/americasmusic/broadwayessay-short.pdf.

18. Pierpont, "George Gershwin," in *American Rhapsody*, 103.

19. Fitzgerald, "The Crack-Up," in *The Crack-Up*, 69.

20. Whitman, "Song of Myself," *Leaves of Grass*, 78.

21. Furia and Lasser, *America's Songs*, 44.

22. Lankevich, *American Metropolis*, 138–50.

23. Paul Slade, "Black Swan Blues: America's First Motown," PlanetSlade.com, 2009, updated October 2014, http://www.planetslade.com/black-swan-blues.html.

24. See Douglass, *Terrible Honesty*, 3–31.

25. Pierpont, "The Chrysler Building," in *American Rhapsody*, 115.

26. Irving Berlin, "Irving Berlin Remembers Lorenz Hart," ThePeaches.com, accessed February 6, 2019, http://www.thepeaches.com/music/composers/rodgershart/BerlinOnHart.htm.

27. Irving Berlin with Justin Dickinson, "Love-Interest as a Commodity," *Green Book Magazine* (February 1915), cited in Bergreen, *As Thousands Cheer*, 55–56.

28. Bowers, *American Musical Theater*, 109.

29. Sheed, *The House That George Built*, 11–39.

Chapter 2

1. Cullen, Hackman, and McNeilly, *Vaudeville, Old and New*, 84.

2. Hicks, *John Reed*, 301.

3. John Kenrick, "Theatre in NYC: History—Part IV," *Musicals 101*, 2003 http://www.musicals101.com/bwaythhist4.htm.

4. Allen, *The City in Slang*, 60. The novel is Albert Bigelow Paine and Chauncey Gale, *The Great White Way* (New York: J. F. Taylor & Co., 1901).

5. Stephen Crane, "New York Sketches," in *Last Words*, 179.

6. Allen, *The City in Slang*, 60.

7. Groce, *New York: Songs of the City*, 73.

8. Traub, *The Devil's Playground*, 8–11.

9. Kenrick, "Theatre in NYC: History—Part IV."

10. Charyn, *Gangsters and Gold Diggers*, 16.

11. Cited in Lewis Erenberg, "Impresarios of Broadway Nightlife," in Taylor, *Inventing Times Square*, 158.

12. Quoted in Taylor, *Inventing Times Square*, xvii.

13. Taylor, *Inventing Times Square*, xvii.

14. Dreiser, *Sister Carrie*, 2.

15. Charyn, *Gangsters and Gold Diggers*, 200.

16. Groce, *New York: Songs of the City*, 73.

17. Tawa, *The Way to Tin Pan* Alley, 138–43.

18. Traub, *The Devil's Playground*, 25.

19. Jones, *Our Musicals Ourselves*, 22.

20. See Green, *Encyclopedia of the Musical Theatre*, 78.

21. Hischak, *Boy Loses Girl*, 1.

22. See McCabe, *George M. Cohan, passim.*

23. Michael Lasser, "The Glorifier: Florenz Ziegfeld and the Creation of the American Showgirl," *American Scholar*, 63, no. 3 (Summer 1994), 441–48, at 444.

24. Lasser, "The Glorifier," 441.

25. Lasser, "The Glorifier," 443.

26. Lasser, "The Glorifier," 443.

27. Lasser, "The Glorifier," 447.

28. Furia and Lasser, *America's Songs*, 25–26.

29. Lasser, "The Glorifier," 441–42.

30. Lasser, "The True Collaborator," in Furia, *Dictionary of Literary Biography Yearbook: 1996*, 156–58.

Chapter 3

1. Sarah Delany and A. Elizabeth Delany, with Amy Hill Hearth, "Harlem Town," from *Having Our Say: The Delany Sisters' First 100 Years*, in Boyd, ed., *The Harlem Reader*, 12.

2. Lerner, *Dry Manhattan*, 199.

3. Dumenil, *The Modern Temper*, 161–62.

4. Locke, "The New Negro," in *The New Negro*, 4.

5. Loos, *A Girl Like I*, 202.

6. In his review of Natalia Naish and Jeremy Scott's *Coke: The Biography*, Michael Prodger notes that the use of cocaine spiked in the 1920s, "when it was the drug of choice of the jazz age." Michael Prodger, "Reading between the Lines: The History of Cocaine," *Mail Online*, July 4, 2013, http://www.dailymail.co.uk/home/event/article-2356212/Cocaine-Reading-lines-The-history-drug.html.

7. David Grafton, quoted in McBrien, *Porter*, 129.

8. Lewis, *When Harlem Was in Vogue*, 5.

9. Lewis, *When Harlem Was in Vogue*, xx.

10. Furia and Lasser, *America's Songs*, 30–31.

11. Kimball and Bolcom, *Reminiscing with Sissle and Blake*, 101.

12. James Weldon Johnson, "The Dilemma of the Negro Author," in *Essential Writings of James Weldon Johnson*, x.

13. Vance, *Fats Waller*, 1.

14. Groce, *New York: Songs of the City*, 83.

15. "The New Negro Movement," *NAACP: A Century in the Fight for Freedom, 1909–2009*, Library of Congress, accessed February 6, 2019, https://www.loc.gov/exhibits/naacp/the-new-negro-movement.html.

16. Matthew Small, "Harlem's Hidden History: The Real Little Italy Was Uptown," *Harlem Focus*, July 17, 2016, https://medium.com/harlem-focus/harlems-hidden-history-the-real-little-italy-was-uptown-ac613b023c6b.

17. Gill, *Harlem*, 171.

18. Groce, *New York: Songs of the* City, 84.

19. Locke, "The New Negro," 6–7.

20. Gill, *Harlem*, 227.

21. Ironically, a similar character—an aged black man named Uncle Joe—appears in Henry Clay Work's "Uncle Joe's Hail Columbia," sixteen years before Foster's song. One of the most moving songs of its time, it is one of the few abolitionist songs in which a slave speaks directly for himself: "Blessed days, I lib to see them, / Hail Columby! / I hab drawn a breff of freedom, / Now let me die."

22. Jasen and Jones, *Spreadin' Rhythm Around*, 25.

23. Forbes, *Introducing Bert Williams: Burnt Cook, Broadway, and the Story of America's First Black Star* (New York: Basic Books, 2008), 238.

24. Marianne Moore, "Black Earth," Poetry Foundation, accessed February 6, 2019, https://www.poetryfoundation.org/poems/51565/black-earth.

25. Forbes, *Introducing Bert Williams*, 239.

26. Forbes, *Introducing Bert Williams*, 239.

27. Forbes, *Introducing Bert Williams*, 112.

28. Lasser, *America's Songs II*, 35.

29. Lasser, *America's Songs II*, 35.

30. Leadbelly, *Complete Recorded Works, 1939–1947 in Chronological Order*, vol. 1, 1 April 1939 to 15 June 1940, track 18, Document Records DOCD-5226, 1995, 33 1/3 rpm.

31. See Murray, *Stomping the Blues,* 128.
32. Handy, *Father of the Blues,* 14.
33. Handy, *Father of the Blues,* 76.
34. Handy, *Father of the Blues,* 77.
35. James Weldon Johnson, *Black Manhattan,* 160–61.
36. Another important spot where the races mingled freely was the Savoy Ballroom, where blacks and whites could gather to hear the great bands of the day, dance, and watch the flamboyant Savoy Lindy Hoppers. Located on Lenox Avenue between 140th and 141st Streets, it opened in 1926 and could hold up to five thousand people. In 1934, Andy Razaf added a lyric to Edgar Sampson's tune "Stompin' at the Savoy": "Savoy, where we can glide and sway, / Savoy, let me stomp away with you."
37. Locke, *The New Negro,* 6.
38. Charyn, *Gangsters and Gold Diggers,* 57.
39. Lerner, *Dry Manhattan,* 218; Fox, *Showtime at the Apollo,* 44.
40. Haskins, *The Cotton Club,* 33.
41. Lena Horne, quoted in Fox, *Showtime at the Apollo,* 44.
42. Cited in Jablonski, *Harold Arlen,* 44.
43. Hughes, "Harlem Sweeties," in *Collected Poems,* 245.
44. Nathaniel Sloan, cited in Tanu Wakefield, "Stanford Music Scholar Redefines Jazz and Cabaret Culture of 1920s Harlem," *Stanford News,* May 15, 2015, https://news.stanford.edu/2015/05/15/jazz-culture-harlem-051515/.
45. Beckman, *Harlem Renaissance Artists and Writers,* 57–59.
46. Cited in Tracy Owens Patton, "Hey, Girl, Am I More Than My Hair? African American Women and Their Struggles with Beauty, Body Image, and Hair," in Garcia, ed., *Contested Images,* 113.
47. Van Deburg, *Slavery and Race,* 149; Carolyn West, "Mammy, Jezebel, Sapphire, and Their Homegirls: Developing an 'Oppositional Gaze' Toward the Images of Black Women," in Chrisler, Golden, and Rosee, eds., *Psychology of Women,* 286–99.
48. Kirkeby, with Schmidt and Traill, *Ain't Misbehavin',* 78.
49. Mary Lou Williams, quoted in Furia and Lasser, *America's Songs,* 67.
50. Kirkeby, *Ain't Misbehavin',* 92.
51. The songwriter Harry Brooks also collaborated with Waller and Razaf on the writing of "Ain't Misbehavin' and (What Did I Do to Be So) Black and Blue." His other songs include "Can't We Get Together," "My Man Is Good for Nothin' But Love," and "Sweet Savannah Sue."
52. Furia and Lasser, *America's Songs,* 67–68.
53. Kirkeby, *Ain't Misbehavin',* 122–23.
54. Winer, *Sunny Side of the Street,* 27.
55. Fox, *Showtime at the Apollo,* 43.
56. The one major exception was Smalls Paradise, integrated by its owner, Ed Smalls, himself an African American.
57. Durante and Kofoed, *Night Clubs,* 114.

58. Fox, *Showtime at the Apollo*, 44.

59. Horne and Schickel, *Lena*, 50–51.

60. Roy Ottley, "Springtime in Harlem," in Boyd, *The Harlem Reader*, 35.

61. William Safire, "On Language: Off the Dime," *New York Times Magazine*, October 6, 2002, http://www.nytimes.com/2002/10/06/magazine/the-way-we-live-now-10-6-02-on-language-off-the-dime.html.

62. Hughes, *The Big Sea*, 176.

63. Graham, *New York Nights*, 252–54.

64. "The Jim Cullum Riverwalk Jazz Collection," Stanford University Libraries, March 13, 2015, http://riverwalkjazz.stanford.edu/program/night-cotton-club-music-duke-ellington-harold-arlen-cab-calloway.

65. Ellington, "Nights at the Cotton Club," in Boyd, *The Harlem Reader*, 74–79.

66. Smith, *Duke Ellington*, 53.

67. John Fordham, "50 Great Moments in Jazz: Duke Ellington Develops the 'Jungle Sound,'" *The Guardian*, March 15, 2017, http://www.theguardian.com/music/musicblog/2009/apr/20/jazz-duke-ellington-jungle-sound.

68. Jablonski, *Harold Arlen*, 43–44.

69. Jablonski, *Harold Arlen*, 44.

70. Paul Woodbury, "Ted Koehler," in Furia, ed., *Dictionary of Literary Biography: American Song Lyricists, 1920–1960*, v. 265, 307–8.

71. Quoted in Fox, *Showtime at the Apollo*, 47.

72. Gill, *Harlem*, 232–33.

73. Manning and Millman, *Frankie Manning*, 23.

74. Gill, *Harlem*, 233.

75. Haskins, *The Cotton Club*, 77.

76. Minh, "A Dirty Song Called All That Meat and No Potatoes? (and Lyrics)," *Digital Citizen*, October 29, 2010, https://digitalcitizen.ca/2010/10/29/a-dirty-song-called-all-that-meat-and-no-potatoes-and-lyrics/.

77. McBrien, *Cole Porter*, 130.

78. Waters, *His Eye Is on the Sparrow: An Autobiography*, 174–75.

79. Taylor and Austen, *Darkest America*, 213–14.

80. Jones, *Reinventing Dixie*, 143.

81. Jones, *Reinventing Dixie*, 143.

82. Jones, *Reinventing Dixie*, 143.

Chapter 4

1. Gene Lees, quoted in Maltin, *The Great American Broadcast*, 259.

2. Millard, *America on Record*, 106.

3. Ruhlmann, *Breaking Records*, 46; Adam Gussow, "'Shoot Myself a Cop": Mamie Smith's 'Crazy Blues' as Social Text," *Callaloo* 25, no. 1 (2002), 8–44, https://muse.jhu.edu/article/6714.

4. Jas Obrecht, "Mamie Smith: The First Lady of the Blues," Jas Obrecht Music Archive, 2010, http://jasobrecht.com/mamie-smith-the-first-lady-of-the-blues/.

5. "History of the Record Industry, 1920–1950s. Part Two: Independent Labels, Radio, and the Battle of the Speeds," *Vinylmint*, June 8, 2014, https://medium.com/@Vinylmint/history-of-the-record-industry-1920-1950s-6d491d7cb606.

6. Ewen, *All the Years of American Popular Music*, 278.

7. Millard, *America on Record*, 100.

8. Millard, *America on Record*, 6.

9. Ewen, *All the Years of American Popular Music*, 278.

10. Ruhlmann, *Breaking Records*, 21–22.

11. Ruhlmann, *Breaking Records*, 30.

12. Millard, *America on Record*, 100.

13. Ruhlmann, *Breaking Records*, 40.

14. Ruhlmann, *Breaking Records*, 41.

15. Ewen, *All the Years of American Popular Music*, 280–81.

16. Irving Berlin, quoted in Maltin, *The Great American Broadcast*, 261.

17. Jones, *Blues People*, 100.

18. Ewen, *All the Years of American Popular Music*, 285.

19. Ruhlmann, *Breaking Records*, 56–57.

20. Ewen, *All the Years of American Popular Music*, 281–82.

21. Ruhlmann, *Breaking Records*, 40.

22. Ruhlmann, *Breaking Records*, 40.

23. Ruhlmann, *Breaking Records*, 57.

24. Maltin, *The Great American Broadcast*, 259.

25. Maltin, *The Great American Broadcast*, 260.

26. Robert S. Gallagher, "Heigh-ho, Everybody!" *American Heritage* 23, no. 4 (1972), accessed February 6, 2019, https://www.americanheritage.com/content/%E2%80%9Cheigh-ho-everybody%E2%80%9D.

27. "Mere Man Wins First Prize in Rudy Vallee Contest," *Radio Revue*, January 1930.

28. George Burns, quoted in Timothy D. Taylor, "Music and the Rise of Radio in 1920s America: Technological Imperialism, Socialization, and the Transformation of Intimacy," *Historical Journal of Film, Radio and Television*, 22, no. 4 (2002): 425–43, published online August 2, 2010, https://www.tandfonline.com/doi/abs/10.1080/01439680220000121388?journalCode=chjf20.

29. Ruhlmann, *Breaking Records*, 48.

30. Maltin, *The Great American* Broadcast, 264.

31. "Pioneer Disc Jockeys: Al Jarvis, Martin Block and the 'Make Believe Ballroom," *Gino's Place: A Place to Rock 'n' Roll*, http://www.geocities.ws/doo_wop_gino/Block.htm, last updated July 8, 2003; Ewen, *All the Years of American Popular Music*, 287–88.

32. Timothy D. Taylor, "The Rise of Radio in 1920s America: Technological Imperialism, Socialization, and the Transformation of Intimacy," *Historical Journal of Film, Radio and Television* 22, no. 4 (2002), 425–43, https://www.tandfonline.com/doi/abs/10.1080/0143968022000012138?journalCode=chjf20.

33. Taylor, "The Rise of Radio in 1920s America.

34. Taylor, "The Rise of Radio in 1920s America."

35. Yagoda, *The B-Side*, 41–43.

36. Eyman, *The Speed of Sound*, 160.

37. Robinson, *From Peepshow to Palace*, 23.

38. Robinson, *From Peepshow to Palace*, 168.

39. Lasky, *RKO*, 20.

40. Gomery, *The Coming of Sound*, 29.

41. Crafton, *The Talkies*, 71–72.

42. Gomery, *The Coming of Sound*, 51.

43. John Kenrick, "History of Musical Film, 1927–30: Part II"; Kenrick, "1930s: Parts 1 and II," 2004, Musicals101.com.

44. Jon Ponder, "Schwab's Drug Store: Where Lana Turner Was Not Discovered," *Playground to the Stars*, April 25, 2018, http://www.playgroundtothestars.com/2013/06/schwabs-drug-store-where-lana-turner-was-not-discovered/.

Chapter 5

1. Harris, *After the Ball*, 62.

2. For a discussion of the importance of trains to the Great Migration, see Isabel Wilkerson, *The Warmth of Other Suns: The Epic Story of America's Great Migration* (New York: Random House, 2010).

3. Sarah Grand, "The New Aspect of the Woman Question," *North American Review* 158, no. 448 (March, 1894), 270–76.

4. Wikipedia, s.v. "Gibson Girl," last modified December 21, 2018, https://en.wikipedia.org/wiki/Gibson_Girl; Patterson, *Beyond the Gibson Girl*.

5. Wetzsteon, *Republic of Dreams*, 166.

6. Snyder, *The Voice of the* City, xx.

7. Sanders, "The Loosening," in Botton, ed., *Goodbye to All That*, 225.

8. See Smith, *Virgin Land*, 123–24.

9. Groce, *New York: Songs of the City*, 79.

10. See Tawa, *The Way to Tin Pan Alley*, 18, 138–43.

11. Lewis, *The American Adam*, 5.

12. Townsend, *Pearl Harbor Jazz*, 47.

13. Goldberg, *Tin Pan Alley*, 131.

14. American bohemianism was limited largely to new York City's Greenwich Village. For a history of Greenwich Village that emphasizes the importance of bohemianism, see Wetzsteon, *Republic of Dreams*.

15. "When Boss Is Away from Office," *Chicago Daily Tribune*, February 12, 1911, E5.

16. Ehrenberg, *Steppin' Out*, 158–71.

17. "Society Bars 'Tango' Dance; Governors of Assembly Rouse Anger of Younger Set. Forbid 'Turkey Trot,' Too. Youths Practicing New Steps, Despite Various Hostesses," *Chicago Daily Tribune*, December 9, 1912, 3.

18. "Polite Dances Are Shown to Society," *New York Times*, March 26, 1912, 13; "New York's Biggest Problem, Not Police, but Girls; Immodesty, Extravagance, and Ignorance Are Among their Characteristics, Says Miss Trenholm, Head Worker of the East Side Settlement," *New York Times*, August 4, 1912, SM7.

19. Newspapers alerted Americans to the danger of the "Tango pirate," a type of man also known as a "lounge lizard." These suave male dancing partners lay in wait for well-heeled girls at fashionable cafés and *thés-dansants* in order to help them dissipate their fortunes. Some were said to introduce girls to such drugs as cocaine. Richard Barry, "Tango Pirates Infest Broadway; Afternoon Dances Develop a New Kind of Parasite Whose Victims Are the Unguarded Daughters of the Rich," *New York Times*, May 30, 1915, SM16.

20. "Women Warned to Curb Styles Which Surpass the Modesty Limit," *Washington Post*, July 18, 1915, E7.

21. For a fuller treatment of wartime songs, see the discussion of the songs of World War II in chapter 9.

Chapter 6

1. United States Census Bureau, "Urban and Rural Areas," accessed February 6, 2019, https://www.census.gov/history/www/programs/geography/urban_and_rural_areas.html.

2. Quoted in Charyn, *Gangsters and Gold Diggers*, 54.

3. Zeitz, *Flapper*, 245.

4. Lehman, *Fashion*, 32.

5. Gundle, *Glamour*, 69.

6. Cartland, *We Danced All Night*, 54.

7. Edward Lueders, "Revisiting Babylon: Fitzgerald and the 1920s," in Broer and Walter, eds., *Dancing Fools and Weary Blues*, 106.

8. Broer and Walter, eds., *Dancing Fools and Weary Blues*, 3.

9. Haley Carmichael, "Marriage and Divorce (1920s)" (slide presentation), December 4, 2013, https://prezi.com/thjihln2vsaq/marriage-and-divorce-1920s/.

10. Stephanie Coontz, "Origins of Modern Divorce," Family Process 46, no. 1 (2006), 7–16, https://firstsearch.oclc.org/ECOPDFS/BLACKWLL/A0147370/FAMP_188.PDF.

11. Amos St. Germain, "The Flowering of Mass Society: An Historical Overview of the 1920s," in Broer and Walter, eds., *Dancing Fools and Weary Blues*, 20–40.

12. Elizabeth Stevenson, "Flappers and Some Who Were Not Flappers," in Broer and Walter, eds., *Dancing Fools and Weary Blues*, 121–29, at 121.

13. Stevenson, in Broer and Walter, eds., *Dancing Fools and Weary Blues*, 123–25.

14. Patricia Erins, "The Flapper: Hollywood's First Liberated Woman," in Broer and Walter, eds., *Dancing Fools and Weary Blues*, 131–39, at 134.

15. John W. Parker, "Lemon, Jelly, and All That Jazz," in Broer and Walter, eds., *Dancing Fools and Weary Blues*, 141–59, at 141.

16. "Mrs. Parker" (Michele Gouveia), "Running Wild: College Students in the 1920s," *Flapper Jane*, September 2004, http://www.sarahbaker.org/flapperjane/September%2004/running_wild.htm.

17. Drowne and Huber, *The 1920s*, 32.

18. Drowne and Huber, *The 1920s*, 32–35.

19. Furia and Lasser, *America's Songs*, 203.

20. Lerner, *Dry Manhattan*, 2.

21. Mark Thornton, "Alcohol Prohibition Was a Failure," Cato Institute Policy Analysis no. 157, July 7, 1991, Cato Institute, accessed February 6, 2019, http://www.cato.org/pub_display.php?pub_id=1017&full=1.

22. David J. Hanson, "Was Prohibition Really a Success?" *Alcohol Problems and Solutions*, accessed February 6, 2019, https://www.alcoholproblemsandsolutions.org/Controversies/20070322134427.html.

23. Okrent, *Last Call*, 7.

24. Jim Dale, vocalist, "Prince of Humbug," by Cy Coleman and Michael Stewart, track 18 on *Barnum*, Sony Classical/Columbia/Legacy, SK 89999, 2002. Compact disc.

25. Okrent, *Last Call*, 14.

26. Okrent, *Last Call*, 12.

27. Wilson, *Woodrow Wilson: Essential Writings*, 412.

28. Shepley, *The Palmer Raids and the Red Scare*, 219–20.

29. Allen, *The City in Slang*, 60.

30. Benjamin De Casseres, "That Last Night of King Alcohol; Hilarity and Gloom Vied with Each Other as New York Said a Hesitant Farewell to J. Barleycorn—Broadway's Queerest Celebration," *New York Times Sunday Magazine*, July 6, 1919, 8.

31. Lerner, *Dry Manhattan*, 3.

32. Lerner, *Dry Manhattan*, 58.

33. Kerry C. Kelly, "The Volstead Act," Educator Resources, National Archives, February 24, 2017, https://www.archives.gov/education/lessons/volstead-act/.

34. Lerner, *Dry Manhattan*, 48.

35. Lerner, *Dry Manhattan*, 58.

36. Jackson Kuhl, "Eight Million Sots in the Naked City: How Prohibition Was Imposed on, and Rejected by, New York," *Reason* 8, no. 10, November 1, 2007.

37. Lerner, *Dry Manhattan*, 49.

38. Lerner, *Dry Manhattan*, 150.

39. Lerner, *Dry Manhattan*, 6.

40. Green, *Broadway Musicals*, 31.

41. Fitzgerald, "The Crack-Up," in *The Crack-Up*, 75.

42. Green, *The World of Musical Comedy*, 137.

43. Jones, *Our Musicals Ourselves*, 44.

44. Bordman, *American Musical Theatre*, 397–98, 418–19, 465–66.

45. Arnold, *Everybody Loves Ice Cream*, 22.

46. Allen G. Debus, "Bert Williams on Stage: Ziegfeld and Beyond," in booklet for *The Complete Bert Williams*, vol. 2, *The Middle Years, 1910–1918*, 5, Archeophone Records 5003, 2002, compact disc.

47. Richard Martin and Meagan Hennessey, "Epilogue: Representations of Race and War" in booklet for *The Complete Bert Williams*, vol. 2, 20.

48. Bert Williams, "The Comic Side of Trouble," *American Magazine*, cited in Debus, 10.

49. Martin and Hennessey, "Epilogue," 20.

50. Martin and Hennessey, booklet for *The Complete Bert Williams*, vol. 3, *His Final Releases, 1919–1922*, 5, Archeophone Records, 5002, compact disc.

51. The lyric includes Berlin's borrowing of a similar but much older plaint, "How Dry I Am." Although the song was a production number in the *Ziegfeld Follies of 1919*, and is included in the listing of the score on the Internet Broadway Database (IBDB), it receives no mention in Kimball and Emmet, eds., *The Complete Lyrics of Irving Berlin*, or in Lawrence Bergreen's biography of Berlin, *As Thousands Cheer*. "Ziegfeld Follies of 1919," IBDB, accessed February 6, 2019, http://www.ibdb.com/ProductionSongs.aspx?ShowNo=394720&ProdNo=394721.

52. Bordman, *American Musical Comedy*, 107.

53. Jones, *Our Musicals Ourselves*, 58.

54. Bordman, *American Musical Theatre*, 116.

55. In an unlikely move, Tin Pan Alley had addressed some of the most troubling aspects of the war both at home and abroad in such songs as "The Devil Has Bought Up All the Coal" and "The Voice of Belgium," both by Irving Berlin.

56. Taking full advantage of the fad, there was even a 1922 musical titled, *Sally, Irene and Mary*. It was a hit, too.

57. Stratton, *Jews, Race and Popular Music*, 59.

58. Decker, *Show Boat*, 58–59.

59. Decker, *Show Boat*, 58–63, *passim*.

60. Adler, *A House Is Not a Home*, 73–74.

61. Bradshaw, *Dreams That Money Can Buy*, 92.

62. Furia and Lasser, *America's Songs*, 34.

63. Timothy Scheuer, "Goddesses and Gold Diggers: Images of Women in Popular Music of the 1930s," *Journal of Popular Culture* 24, no. 1 (Summer 1990), 30–31.

64. Ehrenberg, *Steppin' Out*, 24.

65. Scheuer, "Goddesses and Gold Diggers," 31, cited in Ehrenberg, *Steppin' Out*, 23.

66. Ian M. Post, "Popular Culture's Ambivalence toward Female Autonomy: The Great Depression," *Grand Valley Journal of History* 2, no. 1 (December 2012), article 4, https://scholarworks.gvsu.edu/cgi/viewcontent.cgi?article=1034&context=gvjh.

67. Furia and Lasser, *America's Songs*, 91.

68. Conn, *Metropolitan Philadelphia*, 31.

69. Wikipedia, s.v. "Streetcar Suburb," last modified December 7, 2018, http://en.wikipedia.org/wiki/Streetcar_suburb.

70. Kushner, *Levittown*, 7.

71. Hayden, *Building Suburbia*, 3.

72. Baxandall and Ewen, *Picture Windows*, 8–9.

73. Quoted in Rybczyski, *A Clearing in the Distance*, 292.

74. "Streetcar Suburb."

75. Hayden, *Building Suburbia*, 5–6.

76. Amos St. Germain, "The Flowering of Mass Society: An Historical Overview of the 1920s," in Broer and Walter, eds., *Dancing Fools and Weary Blues*, 37–38.

77. Peretti, *Nightclub City*, 146–47.

78. Peretti, *Nightclub City*, 147.

Chapter 7

1. The show was *Paris*, Porter's first successful Broadway score. It opened on October 8, 1928, and ran for 195 performances, a respectable run for a 1920s show.

2. Peter Flynn, "Gus Kahn—Writer," *Film Reference*, accessed February 6, 2019*e*, http://www.filmreference.com/Writers-and-Production-Artists-Ja-Kr/Kahn-Gus.html#b.

3. Furia and Lasser, *America's Songs*, 72–73.

4. Robert Rusie, "The Great White Way," *Talkin' Broadway Presents Broadway 101: The History of the Great White Way*, accessed February 6, 2019, http://www.talkinbroadway.com/bway101/1.html.

5. Furia and Lasser, *America's Songs*, 237.

6. Sullivan, *Great Popular Song Recordings*, 5.

7. Lasser, "Al Dubin," in Furia, *DLB: American Song Lyricists*, 116–17.

8. "Lullaby of Broadway," *Sold on Song*, accessed February 6, 2019, https://www.bbc.co.uk/radio2/soldonsong/songlibrary/indepth/lullabyofbroadway.shtml.

9. Lasser, "Al Dubin," in Furia, *DLB: American Song Lyricists,* 120.

10. Berlin, *Complete Lyrics,* 351.

11. This song was initially performed in *On Your Toes* as a duet by Doris Carson and David Morris.

12. Dorothy Parker, "New York at 6:30 P.M.," *Esquire,* November 1964, quoted in Meade, *Dorothy Parker,* 401.

13. See, among numerous sources, Jablonski, *Harold Arlen,* 130–38; and Meyerson and Harburg, *Who Put the Rainbow in The Wizard of Oz?,* 155–56.

14. Henry Merton Goldman, "'Pins and Needles': A White House Command Performance," *Educational Theatre Journal* 30, no. 1 (March 1978), 90.

15. Furia and Lasser, *America's Songs,* 145–46.

Chapter 8

1. Satterfield, *The Home Front,* 51.

2. Margaret Mead, "The Women in the War," in Goodman, ed., *While You Were Gone,* 280.

3. Mead, in Goodman, *While You Were Gone,* 280.

4. Satterfield, *The Home Front,* 51.

5. Yellin, *Our Mothers' War,* 78.

6. Townsend, *Pearl Harbor Jazz,* 19.

7. Collins, *America's Women,* 388.

8. Mead, in Goodman, *While You Were Gone,* 276.

9. Mead, in Goodman, *While You Were Gone,* 276.

10. Bloomfield and Shain, with Davidson, *Duty, Honor, Applause,* 73.

11. Jones, *The Songs That Fought the War,* 8–9.

12. Bloomfield and Shain, *Duty, Honor, Applause,* 279.

13. Wohl, *The Hollywood Musical Goes to War,* 13.

14. Koppes and Black, *Hollywood Goes to War,* 325.

15. Quoted in Jones, *The Songs That Fought the War,* 10.

16. Smith, *God Bless America,* 105. A year later, Oscar Hammerstein II led a group of songwriters to form the Music War Committee. Its goal was to find a song "to do for this war what George M. Cohan's 'Over There' did for the last one." After a year of futility, the committee gave up.

17. Matthew (Hattie) Hein, "So Strike Up the Band! A Review of God Bless America," *Reconstruction: Studies in Contemporary Culture* 3, no. 4 (Fall 2003), https://reconstruction.eserver.org/smiths-god-bless-america.

18. Cited in Townsend, *Pearl Harbor Jazz,* 37.

19. Furia and Lasser, *America's Songs,* 150–51.

20. Quoted in Hemming and Hadju, *Discovering Great Singers of Classic Pop,* 65.

21. Hein, "So Strike Up the Band!"

22. Alan Nevins, "How We Felt About the War" in Goodman, *While You Were Gone*, 8–9.

23. Hein, "So Strike Up the Band!"

24. Jones, *The Songs That Fought the War*, 10.

25. See Bloomfield and Shain, *Duty, Honor, Applause*, 436–44. Once the military solved the problem of durability by using vinyl rather than shellac, it had to persuade James C. Petrillo of the American Federation of Musicians to allow his striking musicians to record for the troops. He agreed on the condition that the recordings would never be used for commercial purposes and would be destroyed at the end of the war. The first shipment of V-discs featured recordings by Glenn Miller's Orchestra—2,000 boxes of 30 discs each, along with extra phonograph needles, sheets of song lyrics, questionnaires for the troops, and 125,000 wind-up phonographs. By the time the program ended six years later, it had shipped more than 8 million discs—3,000 recordings of 2,700 songs. None of the musicians or singers received any pay for their services.

26. Smith, *God Bless America*, 105.

27. Frank Loesser, quoted in Hein, "So Strike Up the Band!"

28. Yellin, *Our Mothers' War*, 30–31.

29. Quoted in Satterfield, *The Home Front*, 113.

30. Quoted in Satterfield, *The Home Front*, 64–65.

31. Doherty, *Projection of War*, 170.

32. Bailey, *The Home Front*, 86.

33. Eppens, *Waiting for My Sailor*, 9.

34. Furia and Lasser, *America's Songs*, 172–74.

35. Bailey, *The Home Front*, 39.

36. Mead, in Goodman, *While You Were Gone*, 287.

37. Warner Bros. also stacked the cast with contract players well known to audiences at the time. Among the best-known were the song-and-dance man George Murphy, the comic foils George Tobias and Alan Hale, Charles Butterworth, and the maternal Rosemary DeCamp.

38. Yellin, *Our Mothers' War*, 5.

39. Bailey, *The Home Front*, 52.

40. Bailey, *The Home Front*, 52.

41. Yellin, *Our Mothers' War*, 5.

42. Collins, *America's Women*, 387–88.

43. Collins, *America's Women*, 388–89.

44. Leder, *Thanks for the Memories*, ix–x.

45. Quoted in Satterfield, *The Home Front*, 57.

46. Yellin, *Our Mothers' War*, 11.

47. Yellin, *Our Mothers' War*, 30.

48. Leder, *Thanks for the Memories*, xi.

49. Cited in Bloomfield and Shain, *Duty, Honor, Applause*, 74.

50. Bordman, *American Musical Theatre*, 525.

51. Bordman, *American Musical Theatre*, 531–36.

52. E-mails between Steve Swayne and the author, November 2017.

53. Fordin, *Getting to Know Him*, 200.

54. Quoted in Fordin, *Getting to Know Him*, 201.

55. Frederick Jackson Turner, "The Significance of the Frontier in American History," 1893, 6, available via the National Humanities Center, accessed February 6, 2019, http://nationalhumanitiescenter.org/pds/gilded/empire/text1/turner.pdf.

56. Lehman, *A Fine Romance*, 21.

57. Tyler, *Hit Songs, 1900–1955*, 278.

58. Mary F. Carney, *Nonfarm Housing Starts, 1889–1958: Bulletin of the United States Bureau of Labor Statistics, No, 1260* (Washington, DC: GPO, 1959), 19, accessed February 6, 2019, https://fraser.stlouisfed.org/title/4543.

59. Kaledin, *Daily Life in the United States, 1940–1949*, 55.

Afterword

1. Morris, *Manhattan '45*, 3–4.

2. The Tony Award winners for best musical during the 1950s included *Guys and Dolls, The King and I, Wonderful Town, My Fair Lady*, and *The Music Man*. In the same decade, the Freed Unit at MGM, led by the producer and former lyricist Arthur Freed, produced such movie musicals as *An American in Paris, Singin' in the Rain, The Band Wagon*, and *Gigi*. Except for those in *Gigi*, nearly all the songs in these movies had been written during the 1920s and 1930s.

3. Gould, *Can't Buy Me Love*, 3.

4. Morris, *Manhattan '45*, 238.

5. Charyn, *Gangsters and Gold Diggers*, 11.

BIBLIOGRAPHY

Adler, Polly. *A House Is Not a Home.* New York: Rinehart, 1953.

Allen, Irving Lewis. *The City in Slang.* New York: Oxford University Press, 1991.

Arnold, Shannon Jackson. *Everybody Loves Ice Cream: The Whole Scoop on America's Favorite Treat.* Cincinnati: Emmis Books, 2004.

Bailey, Ronald H. *The Home Front: U.S.A.* Alexandria, VA: Time-Life Books, 1977.

Baxandall, Rosalyn, and Elizabeth Ewen. *Picture Windows: How the Suburbs Happened.* New York: Basic Books, 2000.

Beckman, Wendy Hart. *Harlem Renaissance Artists and Writers.* Berkeley Heights, NJ: Enslow, 2013.

Behrman, S. N. *People in a Diary: A Memoir.* Boston: Little, Brown, 1972.

Bergreen, Laurence. *As Thousands Cheer: The Life of Irving Berlin.* New York: Viking, 1990.

Berlin, Irving. *The Complete Lyrics of Irving Berlin.* Edited by Robert Kimball and Linda Emmet. New York: Knopf, 2001.

Bloomfield, Gary L., and Stacie L. Shain, with Arlen C. Davidson. *Duty, Honor, Applause; America's Entertainers in World War II.* Guilford, CT: Lyons Press, 2004.

Bordman, Gerald. *American Musical Comedy.* New York: Oxford University Press, 2003.

———. *American Musical Theatre: A Chronicle.* New York: Oxford University Press, 1978.

Botton, Sari, ed. *Goodbye to All That: Writers on Loving and Leaving New York.* Berkeley, CA: Seal Press, 2013.

Bowers, Dwight Blocker, annotator and producer. *American Musical Theater: Shows, Songs, and Stars.* Washington, DC: Smithsonian Collection of Recordings/CBS RD 036 A4 20483, 1989, 4 compact discs.

Boyd, Herb, ed. *The Harlem Reader: A Celebration of New York's Most Famous Neighborhood, from the Renaissance Years to the Twenty-First Century.* New York: Three Rivers Press, 2003.

Bradshaw, Jon. *Dreams That Money Can Buy: The Tragic Life of Libby Holman.* New York: William Morrow, 1985.

Broer, Lawrence R., and John D. Walter, eds., *Dancing Fools and Weary Blues: The Great Escape of the Twenties.* Bowling Green, OH: Bowling Green State University Popular Press, 1990.

Cartland, Barbara. *We Danced All Night: A Dazzling Memoir of the Glittering Twenties.* London: Robson, 1970.

Charyn, Jerome. *Gangsters and Gold Diggers: Old New York, the Jazz Age, and the Birth of Broadway.* New York: Thunder's Mouth Press, 2003.

Chrisler, Joan C., Carla Golden, and Patricia D. Rozee, eds. *Lectures on the Psychology of Women,* 4th ed. (Long Grove, IL: Waveland Press, 2012).

Collins, Gail. *America's Women: Four Hundred Years of Dolls, Drudges, Helpmates, and Heroines.* New York: William Morrow, 2003.

Conn, Steven. *Metropolitan Philadelphia: Living with the Presence of the Past.* Philadelphia: Pen Press, 2006.

Coward, Noel. *Private Lives: An Intimate Comedy.* New York: Samuel French, Inc., 1930.

Crafton, Donald. *The Talkies: American Cinema's Transition to Sound.* New York: Scribner, 1997.

Crane, Stephen. *Last Words.* London: Digby, Long & Co., 1902.

Cullen, Frank, Florence Hackman, and Daniel McNeilly. *Vaudeville, Old and New: An Encyclopedia of Variety Performers in America.* Vol. 1. New York: Routledge, 2007.

Decker, Todd. *Show Boat: Performing Race in an American Musical.* New York: Oxford University Press, 2015.

Doherty, Thomas. *Projection of War: Hollywood, American Culture, and World War II.* New York: Columbia University Press, 1993.

Doctorow, E. L. *Ragtime.* New York: Random House, 1975.

Douglass, Ann. *Terrible Honesty: Mongrel Manhattan in the 1920s.* New York: Farrar, Straus and Giroux, 1995.

Dreiser, Theodore. *Sister Carrie.* New York: Signet Classics, 1961.

Drowne, Kathleen, and Patrick Huber. *The 1920s.* Santa Barbara, CA: Greenwood Publishing Group, 2004.

Dumenil, Lynn. *The Modern Temper: American Culture and Society in the 1920s.* New York: Hill & Wang, 1995.

Durante, Jimmy, and Jack Kofoed. *Night Clubs.* New York: Knopf, 1931.

Ehrenberg, Lewis A. *Steppin' Out: New York Nightlife and the Transformation of American Culture, 1890–1930.* Chicago: University of Chicago Press, 1981.

Eppens, Genevieve. *Waiting for My Sailor.* Lincoln, NE: Infusion Media Publishing, 2000.

Ewen, David. *All the Years of American Popular Music.* Englewood Cliffs, NJ: Prentice-Hall, 1977.

Eyman, Scott. *The Speed of Sound: Hollywood and the Talkie Revolution.* New York: Simon & Schuster, 1997.

Fitzgerald, F. Scott. *The Crack-Up and Other Essays.* Edited by Edmund Wilson. New York: New Directions, 1931.

Forbes, Camille F. *Introducing Bert Williams: Burnt Cork, Broadway, and the Story of America's First Black Star.* New York: Basic Books, 2008.

Fordin, Hugh. *Getting to Know Him: A Biography of Oscar Hammerstein II.* New York: Random House, 1977.

Fox, Ted. *Showtime at the Apollo.* New York: Holt, Rinehart and Winston, 1983.

Furia, Philip, ed. *Dictionary of Literary Biography: American Song Lyricists, 1920–1960.* Detroit: Gale, 2002.

———. *Dictionary of Literary Biography,* Yearbook: 1996. Detroit: Gale Research, 1997.

Furia, Philip, and Michael Lasser. *America's Songs: The Stories Behind the Songs of Broadway, Hollywood, and Tin Pan Alley.* New York: Routledge, 2006.

Furia, Philip, and Laurie Patterson. *The Songs of Hollywood.* New York: Oxford University Press, 2010.

Garcia, Alma M., ed. *Contested Images: Women of Color in Popular Culture.* Lanham, MD: AltaMira Press, 2012.

Gill, Jonathan. *Harlem: The Four Hundred Year History from Dutch Village to Capital of Black America.* New York: Grove Press, 2011.

Goldberg, Isaac. *Tin Pan Alley.* New York: John Day, 1930.

Gomery, Douglas. *The Coming of Sound: A History.* New York: Routledge, 2005.

Goodman, Jack, ed., *While You Were Gone: A Report on Wartime Life in the United States.* New York: Simon & Schuster, 1946.

Gottlieb, Robert, and Robert Kimball. *Reading Lyrics.* New York: Pantheon, 2000.

Gould, Jonathan, *Can't Buy Me Love: The Beatles, Britain and America.* New York: Three Rivers Press, 2007.

Graham, Stephen, *New York Nights.* New York: George H. Duran Company, 1927.

Green, Stanley. *Broadway Musicals, Show by Show.* Revised and updated by Kay Green. New York: Applause Theater & Cinema Books, 2008.

———. *Encyclopedia of the Musical Theatre.* New York: Da Capo Press, 1976.

———. *The World of Musical Comedy.* 4th ed. New York: Da Capo Press, 1984.

Groce, Nancy. *New York: Songs of the City.* New York: Watson-Guptill, 1999.

Gundle, Stephen. *Glamour: A History.* New York: Oxford University Press, 2008.

Handy, W. C. *Father of the Blues: An Autobiography.* New York: Da Capo Press, 1941.

Harris, Charles K. *After the Ball: Forty Years of Melody: An Autobiography.* New York: Frank Maurice, 1926.

Haskins, Jim. *The Cotton Club.* New York: Random House, 1977.

Hayden, Dolores. *Building Suburbia: Green Fields and Urban Growth, 1820–1900.* New York: Pantheon, 2003.

Hemming, Roy, and David Hadju. *Discovering Great Singers of Classic Pop: A New Listener's Guide to the Sounds and Lives of the Top Performers.* New York: Newmarket Press, 1991.

Hicks, Granville, with John Stuart. *John Reed: The Making of a Revolutionary.* New York: Macmillan, 1936.

Hischak, Thomas S. *Boy Loses Girl: Broadway's Librettists.* Lanham, MD: Scarecrow Press, 2002.

Horne, Lena, and Richard Schickel. *Lena.* Garden City, NY: Doubleday, 1965.

Hughes, Langston. *The Big Sea: An Autobiography.* New York: Hill & Wang, 1940.

———. *The Collected Poems of Langston Hughes.* Edited by Arnold Rampersad and David Roessel. New York: Vintage Books, 1994.

Jablonski, Edward. *Harold Arlen: Rhythm, Rainbows, and Blues.* Boston: Northeastern University Press, 1996.

Jasen, David A., and Gene Jones. *Spreadin' Rhythm Around: Black Popular Songwriters, 1880–1930.* New York: Schirmer Books, 1998.

Johnson, James Weldon. *Black Manhattan.* New York: Athenaeum, 1968.

———. *The Essential Writings of James Weldon Johnson.* Edited by Rudolph P. Byrd. New York: Random House, 1990.

Jones, James Bush. *Our Musicals Ourselves: A Social History of the American Musical Theatre.* Lebanon, NH: Brandeis University Press, 2003.

———. *Reinventing Dixie: Tin Pan Alley's Songs and the Creation of the Mythic South.* Baton Rouge: LSU Press, 2015.

———. *The Songs That Fought the War: Popular Music and the Home Front.* Hanover, NH: University Press of New England, 2006.

Jones, LeRoi. *Blues People: Negro Music in White America.* New York: Harper Perennial, 1999.

Kaledin, Eugenia. *Daily Life in the United States, 1940–1949: Shifting Worlds.* Westport, CT: Greenwood Press, 2000.

Kimball, Robert, and William Bolcom. *Reminiscing with Sissle and Blake.* New York: Viking, 1973.

Kirkeby, Ed, with Duncan P. Schmidt and Sinclair Traill. *Ain't Misbehavin': The Story of Fats Waller.* New York: Da Capo Press, 1966.

Koppes, Clayton R., and Gregory D. Black. *Hollywood Goes to War: How Politics, Profits, and Propaganda Shaped World War II Movies.* New York: Free Press, 1987.

Kushner, David. *Levittown: Two Families, One Tycoon, and the Fight for Civil Rights in America's Legendary Suburb.* New York: Walker, 2009.

Lankevich, George. *American Metropolis: A History of New York City*. New York: New York University Press, 1998.

Lasky, Betty. *RKO: The Biggest Little Major of Them All.* Santa Monica, CA: Roundtable, 1989.

Lasser, Michael, *America's Songs II: From the 1890s to the Post-War Years*. New York: Routledge, 2013.

Leder, Jane Mersky. *Thanks for the Memories: Love, Sex, and World War II.* Washington, DC: Potomac Books, 2009.

Lehman, David. *A Fine Romance: Jewish Songwriters, American Songs*. New York: Schocken, 2009.

Lehman, LaLonnie. *Fashion in the Time of* The Great Gatsby. Oxford: Shire Publications, 2013.

Lerner, Michael A. *Dry Manhattan: Prohibition in New York City*. Cambridge, MA: Harvard University Press, 2007.

Lewis, Daniel Levering. *When Harlem Was in Vogue.* New York: Knopf, 1981.

Lewis, R. W. B. *The American Adam: Innocence, Tragedy and Tradition in the Nineteenth Century*. Chicago: University of Chicago Press, 1955.

Locke, Alain, ed. *The New Negro: Voices of the Harlem Renaissance.* New York: Boni and Liveright, 1925.

Loos, Anita. *A Girl Like I.* New York: Viking, 1966.

Maltin, Leonard. *The Great American Broadcast: A Celebration of Radio's Golden Age.* New York: Dutton, 1997.

Manning, Frank, and Cynthia Millman. *Frankie Manning: Ambassador of Lindy Hop*. Philadelphia: Temple University Press, 2008.

McBrien, William. *Cole Porter: A Biography*. New York: Knopf, 1998.

McCabe, John. *George M. Cohan: The Man Who Owned Broadway*. New York: Da Capo Press, 1973.

Meade, Marion. *Dorothy Parker: What Fresh Hell Is This?* New York: Penguin Books, 2006.

Meyerson, Harold, and Ernie Harburg. *Who Put the Rainbow in the Wizard of Oz? Yip Harburg, Lyricist.* Ann Arbor: University of Michigan Press, 1993.

Millard, Andre. *America on Record: A History of Recorded Sound.* 2nd. ed. Cambridge: Cambridge University Press, 2005.

Morris, Jan. *Manhattan '45*. Baltimore: Johns Hopkins University Press, 1998.

Murray, Albert. *Stompin' the Blues*. New York: McGraw-Hill, 1976.

Okrent, Daniel. *Last Call: The Rise and Fall of Prohibition*. New York: Scribner's, 2010.

Ottley, Roi. *New World A-Coming: Inside Black America.* New York: Arno Press, 1969.

Patterson, Martha H. *Beyond the Gibson Girl: Reimagining the American New Woman, 1895–1915.* Champaign: University of Illinois Press, 2005.

Peretti, Burton W. *Nightclub City: Politics and Amusement in Manhattan.* Philadelphia: University of Pennsylvania Press, 2007.

Pierpont, Claudia Roth. *American Rhapsody: Writers, Musicians, and One Great Building.* New York: Farrar, Straus and Giroux, 2016.

Robinson, David. *From Peepshow to Palace: The Birth of American Film.* New York: Columbia University Press, 1997.

Ruhlmann, William. *Breaking Records: 100 Years of Hits.* New York and London: Routledge, 2004.

Rybczynski, Witold. *City Life: Urban Expectations in a New World.* New York: Scribner's, 1995.

———. *A Clearing in the Distance: Frederick Law Olmstead and America in the Nineteenth Century.* New York: Scribner's, 1999.

Satterfield, Archie. *The Home Front: An Oral History of the War Years in America, 1941–1945.* New York: Playboy Press, 1981.

Sears, Benjamin, ed. *The Irving Berlin Reader.* New York: Oxford University Press, 2012.

Sheed, Wilfrid. *The House That George Built (with a Little Help from Irving, Cole, and a Crew of About Fifty).* New York: Random House, 2007.

Shepley, Nick, *The Palmer Raids and the Red Scare 1918–1920: Justice and Liberty for All.* Luton, Beds., UK: Andrews UK, 2011.

Smith, Henry Nash. *Virgin Land: The American West as Symbol and Myth.* Cambridge, MA: Harvard University Press, 1950.

Smith, Kathleen E. R. *God Bless America: Tin Pan Alley Goes to War.* Lexington: University Press of Kentucky, 2003.

Smith, Kent. *Duke Ellington: Composer and Band Leader.* Los Angeles: Holloway House, 1992.

Snyder, Robert W. *The Voice of the City: Vaudeville and Popular Culture in New York.* Oxford: Oxford University Press, 1985.

Stratton, Jon. *Jews, Race and Popular Music.* Farnham, UK: Ashgate, 2009.

Sullivan, Steve. *Encyclopedia of Great Popular Song Recordings.* Lanham, MD: Scarecrow, 2013.

Tawa, Nicholas. *The Way to Tin Pan Alley: American Popular Song, 1866–1910.* New York: Schirmer Books, 1990.

Taylor, William R., ed. *Inventing Times Square: Commerce and Culture at the Crossroads of the World.* Baltimore: Johns Hopkins University Press, 1991.

Taylor, Yuval, and Jake Austen. *Darkest America: Black Minstrelsy from Slavery to Hip-Hop.* New York: Norton, 2012.

Townsend, Peter. *Pearl Harbor Jazz: Change in Popular Music in the Early 1940s.* Jackson: University Press of Mississippi, 2007.

Traub, James. *The Devil's Playground: A Century of Pleasure and Profit in Times Square.* New York: Random House, 2004.

Twain, Mark. *The Tragedy of Pudd'nhead Wilson and the Comedy of Those Extraordinary Twins.* Edited by Hsuan L. Hsu. Peterborough, ON: Broadway Editions, 2016.

Tyler, Don. *Hit Songs, 1900–1955: American Popular Music of the Pre-Rock Era.* Jefferson, NC: McFarland & Company, 2006.

Van Deburg, William L. *Slavery and Race in American Popular Culture.* Madison: University of Wisconsin Press, 1984.

Vance, Joel. *Fats Waller: His Life and Times.* Chicago: Contemporary Books, 1977.

Waters, Ethel, with Charles Samuels. *His Eye Is on the Sparrow: An Autobiography.* New York: DaCapo, 1992.

Wetzsteon, Ross. *Republic of Dreams: Greenwich Village; The American Bohemia, 1910–1960.* New York: Simon & Schuster, 2007.

White, E. B. *The Essays of E. B. White.* New York; Harper & Row, 1977.

Whitman, Walt. *Leaves of Grass.* Boston: Small, Maynard & Company, 1904.

Wilson, Woodrow. *Woodrow Wilson: Essential Writings and Speeches of the Scholar-President.* Edited by Mario R. Di Nunzio. New York: New York University Press, 2006.

Winer, Deborah Grace. *On the Sunny Side of the Street: The Life and Lyrics of Dorothy Fields.* New York: Schirmer Books, 1997.

Wohl, Allen L. *The Hollywood Musical Goes to War.* Chicago: Nelson-Hall Publications, 1983.

Yagoda, Ben. *The B-Side: The Death of Tin Pan Alley and the Rebirth of the Great American Song.* New York: Riverhead Books, 2015.

Yellin, Emily. *Our Mothers' War: American Women at Home and at the Front During World War II.* New York: Free Press, 2004.

Ziegfeld, Richard E., and Paulette Ziegfeld. *The Ziegfeld Touch: The Life and Times of Florenz Ziegfeld, Jr.*. New York: Abrams, 1993.

Zeitz, Joshua. *Flapper: A Madcap Story of Sex, Style, Celebrity, and the Women Who Made Modern America.* New York: Three Rivers Press, 2006.

Nothing defines the songs of the Great American Songbook more centrally than their urban sensibility. During the first half of the twentieth century, songwriters such as Harold Arlen, Irving Berlin, Dorothy Fields, George and Ira Gershwin, and Thomas "Fats" Waller flourished in New York City, the home of Tin Pan Alley, Broadway, and Harlem. Through their songs, these artists described America—not its geography or politics, but its heart—to Americans and to the world at large.

In *City Songs and American Life, 1900–1950,* renowned author and broadcaster Michael Lasser offers an evocative and probing account of the popular songs—including some written originally for the stage or screen—that America heard, sang, and danced to during the turbulent first half of the twentieth century. Many songs portrayed the glamor of Broadway or the energy and Jazz Age culture of Harlem. But a city-bred spirit—or even a specifically New York City way of feeling and talking—also infused other widely known and loved songs, stretching from the early decades of the century to the Twenties (the age of the flapper, bathtub gin, and women's right to vote), the Great Depression, and, finally, World War II.

Lasser's deftly written book demonstrates how the soul of city life—as echoed in the nation's—developed and changed in tandem with economic, social, and political currents in America as a whole.

Michael Lasser, a former teacher and theater critic, is host of the syndicated public-radio show *Fascinatin' Rhythm* (winner of the Peabody Award) and the author of two previous books.

"*City Songs and American Life, 1900–1950* draws on Michael Lasser's lifetime of close and thoughtful listening to some of the most sparkling and enduring works of American creativity. His insights throughout make this a fresh and valuable work, thoroughly researched and well-documented, yet entirely accessible to a wide swath of curious readers and listeners. Literate, authoritative, and engaging. Bravo!"

—John Edward Hasse, Smithsonian Institution

"Michael Lasser's *City Songs* is the most engaging, comprehensive, and provocative examination of the Great American Songbook that I've encountered. No surprise to anyone familiar with his award-winning weekly radio series *Fascinatin' Rhythm,* Lasser writes with the 'dazzling economy' of the best lyrics and lyricists that he elucidates. His book convinced me that the songs of the first half of the twentieth century were indeed 'urban creatures' that 'sang the city electric' by merging sentiment and wit into a unique amalgam, mingling the 'jingle of jazz and the jangle of slang' with 'the clang and clamor' of the American metropolis, as Lasser so unforgettably characterizes it!"

—Kim Kowalke, Eastman School of Music, University of Rochester

"Reading Michael Lasser's *City Songs and American Life, 1900–1950* is a surprisingly moving experience. Progressing through the twentieth century, as music and lyrics evolve to reflect our changing national life, Lasser locates the yearning heart in us and in those who came before us—in times of war, prosperity, giddy peace, or economic depression—in all who stir to the syncopated rhythms and conversational syntax, the fine sentiment and matchless wit, of the Great American Songbook."

—Jimmy Roberts, composer of the hit musical *I Love You, You're Perfect, Now Change*